NURTURING UNIQUE KIDS:

A Practical Guide for

Intuitive Children, Families & Adults

Carolyn,
Thanks for being such
a good friend & intuitive
Fellow traveler!
Linda Dunning

by

Linda Dunning

PROSPERITY · IN · PRINT ·
SALT LAKE CITY

This book is dedicated to all the many children and colleagues who taught me or told me what they needed by taking me on a life-long quest to find ways to assist others on their own paths in life. But I especially want to thank all those others who inspired me in teaching, writing, and as an intuitive traveler. Thank you all for helping me to learn to teach with my heart.

I also want to acknowledge Brett Jensen for doing the graphic designs and cover, Taylor Jensen for his Tree of Life drawing, as well as Lennan Jensen for helping me to draw some of the charts for the book.

Nurturing Unique Kids is an educational book. Names, characters, places, and incidents are products of the author's research or personal experiences. Any resemblance to actual persons, living or dead, events or locales is entirely coincidental.

Published in the United States by First Road Press, LLC
A division of the Thinx Group Publishing Coalition
Salt Lake City, Utah

ISBN 978-0-9845882-4-4
Registered with Library of Congress

NURTURING UNIQUE KIDS:

A Practical Guide for Intuitive Children, Families & Adults

TABLE OF CONTENTS:

INTRODUCTION

My Story or Why I Wrote This Book

"Lost energy, lost love, lost power, lost anything is the result of denial, of holding it away from you by not accepting it. What was lost returns when you forgive yourself for denying it and accept it

--Right Use of Will, spiritual text, received by Ceanne DeRohan

"Most adults have lost the child mind and have forgotten how imaginative they once were, how real the images that danced in their heads seemed. In fact, some adults who have retained a powerful imagination are considered crazy by those who haven't."

--Ibid, Spiritual Parenting, p.170

Why I Wrote This Book

I was born into an intellectual, agnostic and questioning family. I knew I was a square peg in a round hole as soon as I was aware of how other people functioned in my family. I had no generational supportive family of psychics and intuitives to fall back on, but I made the best of it under the circumstances and took my place as the entertainment committee for my siblings and parents in both positive and negative ways. On the other hand I did not have anyone trying to convince me that I was going to the devil or that organized religion would have all the answers for me. I do know that I came in with a feeling about God and the universe, that later became a belief, and that my parents were kind enough to let me have this illusion or delusion as they considered it. I also came in with the ability to celebrate for others and seemed to be blind to the usual prejudices that people develop over time and through their experiences. I just had compassion for others and could inhabit their souls as easily as my own. One friend told another friend she ran into in Colorado, where I had lived for several years, when the friend asked how I was, that I was still doing the same things only now it had a name.

My sister says that she remembers just how irritating I was, with telling all of those made up stories and that I couldn't be trusted to keep a secret and rarely did my share of the weekly chores. Instead I would sneak out and hide in my favorite apple tree in the backyard to escape those chores and really my family's judgments of me and my parent's disapprovals. They loved me and worried for me that I would not have a good successful life because of all of my daydreaming and fantasizing in that vivid imagination world that I seemed to live in. I can remember many a night sitting in a field or laying on my back in our backyard and gazing at the night sky, wondering what planet I had come from because I didn't seem to be from this one or from the particular family that I was living in. My mother, a brilliant person, but also an amazing intuitive herself, never knew it, and bought into the physical world wholeheartedly. She spent much of her life blaming my father for her unhappiness and never really found her spiritual purpose nor believed she had to have one to be happy. Instead, she lived in my father's shadow, and never realized that she had, right at her fingertips, the means to an incredible life that would have made her the famous, well-known person that she yearned to be.

My father who died on Christmas Eve at the age of 96, was also a balanced intuitive. He used his left brained skills to achieve his many accomplishments, and he used his right-brained intuitive skills to become a real people pleaser. He was a real "whole brainer" who probably gave me some of his intuition with people too. As many people said of our dad, he was an outgoing, gregarious giant, and as my older brother added: "While he did not suffer fools well, he charmed virtually everyone he met and was loved by many students, colleagues, friends and family alike." My father, years after my mother died, told me one day that they just didn't know what to do with me because I was so very different from the rest of their children. And my mother did her best to force me into that round hole in order to save me from the life she feared that I would live if I didn't learn how to live in the physical world. And typical of the fifties, my dad was a good provider but was an absentee father whom everyone loved but was emotionally absent from his own children. I, in particular was a "groupie" for his academic "rock band," but even so, I loved and worshipped him like everyone else, always hoping for that one glance or touch.

They say that we choose the parents and the family that we need before we come here, and I believe that. Because had I not had the parents I had, I would have never learned those down to earth skills that got me through life, all those left brained, logical and analytical or common sense skills that one needs to not only have a good life, but also to counsel others. Born in small towns they chose on their own to be curious rather than prejudice. And once choosing this, they then went further and began studying and experiencing what they did not understand. This led them both to understanding difference of all kinds and developing the ability to see things from various perspectives. We grew up with our mother's desire to travel and have a world view, and our father's career bringing into our home people from different countries, perspectives, ethnic groups and cultural heritages. Going "against the grain" and quiet leadership, were two qualities that we were all shown by example, through our parent's eyes and the role modeling that they did.

And although it was emotionally painful to learn them for me specifically, they came in handy many times in my life, especially as a teacher. Like many empathic, intuitive and visual-spatial learners with a learning disability, I had to find my way on this journey alone. And it was not until I was teaching resource children that I discovered I did have a learning disability as well. There was no gifted classification in those days and so this was unexplored territory, and it was not until I got an IQ score one time as an adult that I realized this was one of my problems too. Besides, it certainly was unpopular to announce that you might be very smart and intuitive, especially if you were a girl, and a tall one at that! In the end, I came to love my family very much, and my parents too, for trying their best to make me into what they thought would serve me best in life.

Ironically, my critical mother never saw herself clearly at all, so I had to flounder in the dark on my own in trying to reawaken what I had had so effortlessly done as a little girl. Yet she taught me my greatest lesson as I mirrored her soul against mine and realized that being true to one's self was the most important thing you could do to be happy in life, regardless of how difficult this might become. Mom never did know just why she was so unhappy, hid her gorgeous Technicolor and prophetic dreams for fear of being accused of being crazy, and remained oblivious to something right at her fingertips. It was not until the very end of her life that she suddenly realized that perhaps she had missed something about herself, something important, when other people recognized her talents as an intuitive and asked her why she had never done anything with them. I would pick her up as she grew more and more ill and drive her to our study group once a month where people who did not know each other, and for the first time in her life, were telling her about her "gifts." What convinced her was that "educated" people were coming to these things and felt they were important. People with actual degrees and a lot of them, began to gather around my sad, unhappy and very quietly intimidating mother, to ask her opinions on things. She had been to too many University functions with my father, where she quietly smoldered, as he got all of the attention, yet suddenly, here she was getting attention for something she had been oblivious too.

In high school when I got a "1" on my ACT scores in math, which dragged my other scores down – the ACT test went from 1-36 and even though I got pretty good scores in science and history and excellent ones in English – I was deemed not college material and was advised by my counselor to become a hairstylist. Coming from this education prone family, this made me really angry and I was determined to go to college anyway. I had already had a life time's worth of humiliation and anxiety from my math teachers in school. Both math and languages were taught at that time in the step-by-step fashion that auditory processors are accustom too and not even in a whole brain approach, and by the time the teacher had gotten to step "C" or "D" in learning a new concept, I was already lost. Then I was called on in class and humiliated in front of my peers as a dumb bell. So like most people with a silent and hidden disability, I just found ways of fooling teachers and used my other skills to survive. But college was a different ballgame altogether. Where in public school I could manipulate myself around math, and even as an elementary teacher later, I just studied and worked twice as hard as anyone else to keep up with my third grade students. I could never teach at a higher grade than this unless we had rotations and some other teacher taught the math.

But in college, I just threw myself into my other classes pushing those basic algebra, geometry, physics and chemistry classes and teacher math, at the time, further and further away in hopes that they would just go away. The biggest disappointment came when after two solid years of art classes I realized after flunking Spanish, German and French, that I could never graduate in art and would not be "allowed" to be an "artist" because all college art schools required five quarters of a foreign language. I tried psychology and then English, and finally it began to get late and I had to find something easy so I chose elementary education just to get out of college. And in my case something did come along to help me out, a miracle happened, and for about five years you could take six science courses in place of basic geometry and algebra and six more to get out of taking chemistry and physics. So it took me a whole extra year to get out because I had to take all those science courses in which I got either "C"s or "B"s but passed them all. But there was still that one teacher math course and there I was a senior with one class standing in my way of graduation, "teacher math." My grade point on graduating was 2.7.

I still remember to this day the process of getting through that one large obstacle that I would never understand. My goal therefore, was to get around it or through it, anyway I could. I was told that the math department might be better than the education department and so I signed up. I had a wonderful math teacher who took me on as a private tutor at no extra expense. I think he saw it as a challenge and really put his heart into it as far as a math professor can do this. After a few sessions after class, he yelled at me, "I don't know how someone so brilliant can be so dumb in math!" He then stood up, turned his back to me, threw up his hands as he walked away and slammed the door behind him. After this experience, which I have remembered all my life and really taught me to be a better teacher especially when I taught resource, I signed up in the education department. I had a much kinder, concerned teacher, but on the other hand he was not going to privately tutor me either. When I realized I was flunking out of the class I dropped it and went to one of my roommates, who happened to be a math major.

She tried to tutor me, but rather than wounding me more, when she figured out I could not really do anything, she had an idea. She said, "What you need is a tutor who is just a little ahead of you and can understand where you are." She found a friend of hers who really knew the art of teaching – most people think anyone can teach but what a myth that is! This friend was just a little ahead of me in math. She worked with me, basically to prep me for the teacher math test. She found out what concepts were to be taught in the curriculum and taught them to me, just enough to squeeze by. I found out that unlike the regular classes if you took the course by correspondence through Continuing

Education and then went up to that department and took a math test on the material, you could then pass the course. Realizing that this would be a great deal less stressful and the least amount of stress that I could find, I went up and took the test. I got a "C-"and passed the course and got to graduate but at an odd time and so I could not go through graduation with my peers.

Like any learning difference, it is often the way a subject is taught that is the problem and not how one receives the information. But over time and in a system rife with step-by-step learning and one-of-a-kind teaching that turns new ways of teaching right back into what is familiar, the emotional and psychological damage mounds up on the learner. Many years later a friend of mine who struggled in math but at a much higher level than I, suggested that the two of us take a college math class and improve our skills. I was absolutely horrified at the idea! Not only did I not want to go near the subject, but even this good friend did not know my secret, that the math I did know was so little we would never be able to take the same level class together. Researchers in China, who in the eighties did an amazing thing by schooling all of their children in psychic abilities as part of the school curriculum, soon discovered that if put under pressure to perform for foreigners from America and Canada, the children failed miserably. And that was because, Americans and Canadians still ran by the methods of scientific research, and were there not to encourage but to disprove what they were seeing the children do. Researchers from other countries showed up to be awed and inspired by what they saw, and the children performed especially well. Even other antagonistic Asian countries changed their minds to some degree and went home to start their own research programs.

It is surprising that all these experts didn't realize that those of us with hidden difficulties in learning had the same challenges and pressures to perform. And everyone knows that if put under stress and pressure to do anything, people are likely not to do as well, especially if you are trying to do something you are not very good at. In Bulgaria in their psychic research, they discovered that you can teach anything through a form of hypnotic suggestion or in a relaxed and meditative state and there will be an extraordinary retention rate for anyone. They decided to call it Suggestology and since this time, some of this type of teaching has become main stream, at least commercially. However, it is kind of scary because this also means that there is some kind of mind control going on as well and in the wrong hands – I think you get the picture.

Anyway, in graduate school they let me in on probation because of my low grade point average and a great deal of begging on my part. They warned me that I would have to maintain a "B" or above average to continue because my math scores had been so low on the placement test. I said, "No, problem," because I knew by this time I could complete all the classes. I graduated with a 3.8 average in Special Education and even got through the data class with a lot of extra hard work. But most of all I remembered all this and when I taught all those many children, I knew irrevocably, that self-worth, intention, belief, being inspired, using your intuition, introducing many interests, having a sense of humor – a great stress reliever – and really knowing my individual students' learning style, gaining not only their respect but their caring, would get everyone of them somewhere better than where they were.

When I was in my twenties, teaching the multi-handicapped and headed down the same path as my mother, growing sadder and sadder by the minute, I had become embattled with her own intensities and mine. I was very intense, had stopped laughing and hugging, which was my natural nature and began carrying the world on my shoulders, quite literally then, but of course I still did not know this either. I had found writing and art as my solaces for my vivid imagination and had realized that it was okay to "tell stories" and that many people even liked them. But it had still not occurred to me that what I was writing, drawing and feeling were real experiences and intuited events that made the world much more expansive and internally deeper than I could ever have conceived of. But I did have an incredible amount of "heart" experiences with both grieving parents and little multi-handicapped children in my first years of teaching. I learned both about death and dying, as well as guilt and pathos from these children's parents. It was an amazing training ground, which led me to a second evening job of in-home parent training which I did on and off throughout my years with the multi-handicapped. I soon discovered that I would have to work with the whole family, siblings and parents, to help out my little severely handicapped client.

In my thirties I taught, I wrote, and I got all sorts of chronic ailments. I already had had several food allergies as a child, with more environmental ones on the way. My sensitivities, it seems, carried over into the physical realm in many ways as an adult. I used all sorts of my intuitive skills and "gifts" every day, but never quite recognized this, although others did. My first years with the severely multi-handicapped became profoundly spiritual learning experiences, while at the same time I had intense back pain from several minor injuries I had from several falls. Lots of ear infections as a child had affected my balance, so rather than being a klutz, I was just stuck with what I thought were "sea shell" sounds in my ears. My balance, falls, and weaving walk, would just increase as I aged. My later years with the low income multi-ethnic resource kids were enlightening in many ways, and during this time I had a series of spiritual awakenings that became a crisis. Through a series of unfortunate events that led to sterility and permanent nerve damage in my legs, starting at 29 years of age, the sensitivities of an unaware empathic intuitive, began to mound up on me.

By 32, the Copper Seven IUD had given me toxic shock, PID, endometriosis, and sterility, but I never joined the other women who sued the pharmaceutical companies when I found out I could not have children, a few years later. I had a miscarriage shortly before this, later having the rather profound realization that this would become my one and only chance at having a child. By the time I was 39, I was a mass of chronic ailments, leapfrogging from one to the next in ever increasing ripple effects. All this finally culminated in being given birth control to shrink a cyst, that may not have been there in the first place, because this was considered less invasive than surgery. Later I had surgery for the endometriosis, which was the more likely culprit. But it was years before I put together my own theory on what had happened. I was told over and over by the experts that a month and a half of birth control pills could not possibly have given me lifelong peripheral neuropathy. Diagnosed as phlebitis, which it probably was at the time, I ended up afterwards with permanent and quite painful nerve damage in my legs. When I had learned more, I came to believe that the metal inserted into my body had wreaked havoc on my internal workings, especially when I read that neuropathy can be caused by chemotherapy and that chemical toxic poisoning can also cause the disease. The abnormal hormonal changes had simply been a catalyst, I believed.

I began my journey into the holistic world at this point and it really was the two years of Spinal Touch massage that got me walking again after 5 weeks of not moving around at all. I had less pain then, although it seemed horrific at the time. Now, over twenty years later and having made peace with the pain, the very thought of someone touching my lower legs terrifies me. I can remember my younger brother once asking me what it felt like. I explained quite seriously to him that it was like hundreds of miniature men running up and down my legs and poking them with pins and needles, with an occasional big sharp knife thrust through the bottom of my feet. He said, "Why are they men?" I had to really think about this one! I finally reached the conclusion that most health professionals, both medical and holistic, that I had seen, had been men. But I really don't think that the few women I had seen would have been any different. They all had good intentions and great advise of all kinds, but they weren't me. I did the herbs, saw many holistic experts of all kinds and finally made peace with it. So it was hard when all those healers, thinking they were the one with an answer for me, began blaming me for not getting well. Either seeking co-dependency from me, or egocentric in their barrage of techniques which overwhelmed me, I began to see both the medical world and the holistic world in the same way. People who would unintentionally hurt me in one way or another, and for the most part this rang true. I was then told by my esoteric friends that I had brought this on myself through my non-belief in self healing. Or that I had to have "more" pain before I could have less. This often rang true with many physical ailments, but not neuropathy, and apparently not with me in particular. I was flabbergasted!

It was not until I read an article about a man who had a severe ailment that only allowed him to sit upright for an hour a day where he could see nature in all its glory outside his bedroom window, that I found my answer. He wrote about the fact that there are some of us who have a message for the world in not healing, something that was necessary as an example for others. That people who went out and threw their bodies over fractures in the earth to help heal our planet, were not so crazy after all, and that in taking this particular journey, we were the ones who would lead others to understand these particular spiritual travels. Rather like one of the six Buddhist precepts that states that: "In short, I will learn to offer to everyone without exception, all help and happiness directly and indirectly, and respectfully take upon myself all harm and suffering of others." It only hurt, when others did not understand what an immense journey this had been to get there.

In 1985, my mother took me to the Women's UN Peace Conference in Kenya. The changes in my awareness were profound in terms of feeling and seeing the world grow smaller and much more of a community, as well as seeing and meeting women from all over the world in a rainbow of native costumes, lifestyles, and beliefs. I came home sick, got better and then got sick just a few years later. At 39, I was extremely ill, both physically and soul wise. I had already been through one spiritual emergency when I left teaching the multi-handicapped, another upon seeing the world for the first time, and now a third was on its way, a profound illness that would lead to a breakthrough of massive proportions for me. I had reached the end of the medical profession and started into the holistic world to get better. We began our Spiral Path study group, and I slowly got better physically, emotionally and spiritually. At the same time as my mother began to awaken to her own powerful intuitive gifts, but then passed away at 79, the study group ended. But I had come out the other end doing spiritual counseling sessions for others, a clairvoyant and sometime medium, whose confirmations came pouring in as did my life review upon rediscovering myself. The illness had been my near-death experience, as well as my most profound awakening. In my forties and fifties, I came into my stride, spiritually awake, intuitively growing, and beginning to publish many of my books that lay about my house like leaves of a very private library.

In my last years of teaching, the gifted children often introduced adversities that taught me how to be tough and tender at the same time. I had to question everything I had been or was doing now, but in the end I came back to knowing that I had been on the right track all the time. I made peace with all of my ailments. I made peace with the life that I was to lead both physically and emotionally. And I eventually healed my heart, as far as having children was concerned. Of course this was easy, because of having over a thousand "children" in my life as a teacher, it was only when I retired and other women had grandchildren that I missed something that I had really wanted. However, when I visited the last school I had worked at, about a year after I retired early, partly because of my physical ailments, a bunch of little former students came up to me with their hands on their hips, stomped their feet, and asked, "Where have you been?" I can remember thinking, they were right and I had to ask myself, "Just where have I been?" I had been thinking, resting, recuperating, and finally, going back to the children in a new way.

Over the years since, at least two other spiritual emergences have taken place for me. One was to understand the multi-verse and to experience it as a reality of huge proportions. The other, was to go through a series of healings in order to be a better healer myself. I had to understand that there were all sorts of healings in the world and I had

had a few in my physical and etheric bodies. That these healings were both emotional and physical, and were just as much memory driven as they were physically driven. I began to realize that my gifts entailed intuitive counseling, remote viewing illness, and doing physical healing with my hands to make people more comfortable. I also realized that gifts of any kind took a lot of hard work to make them usable as well. But all this had to be done on myself first, or at least be on-going until the day I dropped, and there would be required layer after layer of personal "healings" going on. I now speak my truth, I try every day to live a spiritual life for myself and for others, I am very aware of the ripple effect that each life can have on many other lives, and I have discovered the power of my many avenues for helping others heal, quietly and humbly thanking God and his angels or light beings for letting me be a channel for others.

I have also realized that the early years of teaching, the years that I thought at the time, were wasted, actually flowed on by themselves, it was just my own consciousness that was asleep. The children did receive all that I had; I just missed out on even more of the joys I could have had, if I had been more awake at the time. And it was not until I had a dream towards the end of my teaching career, that I did not understand at the time, that I realized where I was headed. I had walked into an old deserted turn-of-the-century home. The huge old farmhouse was empty of furniture but I walked into the front room and found myself walking straight through it to the back door. Yet as I walked through, the place became crowded with little children. They had no faces and no hair on their heads, but I knew I was to touch as many of them as I could on the top of their heads with a firm wide spread palm. But I also had to keep at a steady pace and could only place my palm on those closest to me before I reached the back door frame and walked out the back and down the steps into nothing at all, as I woke up.

I also had to heal with my own family, my parents, my brothers and sisters. I needed to love them and let them go. I began blending all of the parts of myself together. I merged my teaching, my writing and my metaphysical/spiritual senses all into one, and I let go of past yearnings, past relationships, past egos and competitions, and anything else that a healer has to do before they can set themselves up to assist others in their own life journeys. Not that I am finished by any means, but at least I am on the right track now with more healing layers yet to unfold themselves within me and along my path, without.

But at the same time, I did not quite heal my physical body. When I reached the end of the holistic world, I then, finally, took responsibility for my own health and began to put together what had worked and threw out what had not. I put together a package for myself and began wailing in the dark to others that this really was the secret to health and not running about looking for others to heal yourself for you. I tried my hardest to "believe" I would heal. Although I also knew, that sometimes these aches and pains are part of life, or at least the process of life, and can be a powerful example for others to work on their own healing as well. If I heal – great and if I don't heal - so be it.

"Pain seems to me to be an insufficient reason not to embrace life. Being dead is quite painless. Pain, like time is going to come on regardless. Question is, what glorious moments can you win from life in addition to the pain?" (*Cordelia's Honor: Barrayar by Lois McMaster Bujold, p. 534.*)

After all, the body is merely a vehicle for the soul and the spirit powers the soul. When the body dies, the "soul" dies with it, having been the center and supporter of the body. As the "soul" comes out of the body in white light and essence, it joins into the essence of the "spirit" that is emerging from the crown of the head. The "spirit" then takes the time needed to re-form into the "spirit" body of light and essence. Once the "spirit" is fully formed, and moves on, it is powered by the frequency or vibration waves of energy. We become energy and essence and travel on these frequency waves into the multi-verse and join communities of our choosing or travel around a myriad of worlds quite different from our own. And as a psychic or intuitive, I have envisioned many a time the process of death, where we go and how we get there, through the eyes of other's journeys, in a sort of parallel near-death experience, as I inhabit souls temporarily, both living and dead. This then was the answer to "What did I believe?"

Over the years as a teacher, however, I was getting very discouraged with what was out there for children in general, and especially for intuitive children. There are lots of books and articles on theory, philosophies, research and case studies. One can read case study after case study and still it may not resonate for a particular set of parents of a particular child. I should know, with much more than a thousand encounters with "case studies" of my own while working in the "trenches." I could tell you dozens of stories but it would not help you and your children except to offer you comfort that you are not alone. When I began my workshops for parents of intuitive children, I wanted to find a book that would not only give me the basics in forming an integrative picture of a child, give me help in where to go and who to ask for assistance, but also one that would provide lots and lots of ideas for how to help each individual child. In the end I decided that the only way to find such a book was to write one, using my own experience, expertise, intuitive knowing, what the experts say or have researched, and the common sense that my own parents taught me.

One day a young psychology major at the college where I was teaching in a demonstration school for severely multi-handicapped came to me after attempting to test several of my students on the command of his professor mentor and said, "Can you help me? This child cannot have an IQ of '0'." I took a look at his test and told him it was totally inappropriate to be giving a normal children's test to children functioning below the three month developmental level and that this test was the wrong kind to be giving to little Gerald. He scratched his head and said, "What can I do? I absolutely have to give these tests to three of your students or I won't pass my class." I looked at him amusingly and suggested that he ask me the questions and I would give him the answers for the child. After all, the tests were already invalid. And I figure that that young man learned something important that day anyway, but more importantly, he was able to look beyond his task and really see and feel, children like Gerald.

Secondly, where were the solid, down to earth things to do, after the labels had been discovered and applied? Not being a doctor or psychologist or even a scientist or politician, having taught for 36 years meant that I did not know a thing about my profession. Yet there is such a thing as learning on the job and intuiting on the job, and seeing a young child's face when after being diagnosed as having attention deficit disorder, childhood depression and oppositional defiance disorder, it was discovered he was just plain brilliant, stubborn, bored, a confused visual-spatial learner, and an intuitive dreamer. Who wouldn't be depressed with all this, upon starting into the world of public schools? The day I finally found something he could hold onto, and it took a quite a while to do this, I looked down at his face after praising him for his beautiful poem and his chess win, and saw that smile on his face for the first time, and to quote old Chief Dan George in "Little Big Man," my heart soared like an eagle.

At the end of that year his parents wrote me this: "We are so grateful for your kind, loving and supportive education of Andy. You have truly changed our family forever. Your guidance has been patient and centered around his individual strengths and weaknesses. You are truly the reflection of an ideal teacher. We treasure the gifts we have received from you. Thank you for everything you have done. You have made a wonderful impact on our lives...." What I had done got me in trouble with the powers that be. When their child was diagnosed with all this stuff, I told them to get on a plane and go to Denver and have their boy assessed at the Gifted Development Center which Linda Kreger Silverman had founded. You'll read about her work in more detail a little bit later. Being a bit of a seeress, I also knew that this trip would dramatically change both of their children's lives sometime in the future. The parents came back very happy with the results. It seems that the boy I was teaching had such a high IQ that not very many people would know just what he was thinking nor just how to teach him. And this had given the parents the direction and focus that they needed. The point being that I and that student psychologist had something in common. We both cared and we both could and would, look beyond what was in front of us, and were also willing to bend the rules a bit for the sake of a child.

The third reason I wrote this book was that our world at this point has gone deeper and deeper into the notion that dividing is conquering. When I started teaching in resource, I was the only person there to make sure that each child got what they needed to succeed. I could go to a few experts but essentially I had to study and find out what to do on my own, just as I intuited what to do as well. When I left resource 12 years later, there were a half dozen experts on every case and endless paperwork (which is what the children came to be called, a case if they were still being followed, or a terminated one if they had left the school.) Not only did I have to consult with all these people, bring them in on the child's story, but the child also went to each of them for help. Unfortunately they did not work as a team, had egos about their expertise, and often ended up arguing among themselves on what was best for that child. Eventually I found myself going underground and performing covert operations to still provide each child with an integrative individualized program. In the course of doing this the children respected me and I loved them. This got me into trouble and very often I dealt with things like I was "playing" with the children too much and not "teaching" them, while I saw no difference between these two words. Or was I sure I was teaching what was appropriate or in the right way? Did I really know what I was doing and then the assumption was made that they needed to "teach" me because obviously I was either deluded or "attle" brained. And actually my brain was wired differently, but in a good way, because I had experienced what my students were experiencing, hadn't forgotten my childhood and cared whether they moved forward or not.

Having taught 12 years with severely and moderately multi-handicapped children, 13 years with behaviorally, mentally or learning challenged underprivileged elementary students K-6, and 11 years with gifted and talented students in a regular advanced placement classroom, I realized that I probably had a somewhat unusual training ground for working with children. Over the years I had managed to garner a lot of different certifications and attended a myriad of workshops and in-services, which kept me up with the latest research and information about children. Along with this, I had my own learning disability to deal with, my own gifted difficulties to deal with, and later I realized that I had always been dealing with my visual-spatial learning style, and, an overload of intuitive gifts and curses. It was all in how you look at it, I suppose, because in those days I hadn't a clue about my various spiritual emergences along the way. Fortunately, I also had the ability to celebrate for others, really listen to others, and as the Native Americans say, walk in the spirit lodges of others carefully, responsibly, and with both kindness and energetic force.

When I retired, I began giving workshops for parents of intuitive children, and for "wounded" intuitive adults, discovering that one group could help the other and vice versa. I had already been doing intuitive counseling sessions privately for the past 25 years, for those on a spiritual path. My teaching world, my writing world, and my spiritual world suddenly collided, and began merging together. I began to wonder why children when infused with self-worth, self belief, and knowledge of their own talents and abilities, at any level, began to blossom entirely on their own. I also wondered why so many of the childhood labeled difficulties were never addressed in combination with a child's intuitive talents, creative talents and type of learning style. My early training had been to look at the whole integrative and developmental child, before proceeding to work with them. Children are like Christmas packages, they had to be opened up one by one and examined carefully for all these things, minus any labels, including New Age ones. After investigating and researching all of the things that could form a picture of that child in the teacher's mind, then the teacher began to "teach" them. And when you had 25 or so students, this took a lot of extra work and a lot of intuitive guidance from whatever invisible forces were helping me or the child.

After retirement, I began to come up against a particular issue over and over again, when intuitively counseling parents and teens. Parents would call me, I would go through the file in my head, with a few questions and some searching around in my "files," I sent them in the right direction for the books they needed, the Internet sites they needed, and to various experts who could help them. But startlingly, what I had taken for granted from all these years of experience and training was both my intuition and my knowledge. I had a lot to share and a lot to inform parents about, when one or more of their children had what seemed to be problems in school or at home. And the experts out there were not addressing intuition because it is still in America, after all this time, considered a "belief" rather than a reality. The experts were still not addressing creative talents for children, because these talents were not considered important but mere "frosting on the cake," in terms of funding various arts for children. Very few were telling parents what combination of things would work for their child, especially learning styles and manifested difficulties that might not be coming from the child, but from those who taught him instead. And last, all of these things interacted with each other to form a picture of each individual child. No longer gagged and bound by the public education system, I could and would, now share what I knew.

When I worked with more severe children, who all suffered from sensory integration and developmental problems, a great deal of so-called "miracles" took place. Higher functioning children only expected to function in the multi-handicapped department, began to graduate to either the normal deaf school or the normal blind school. When I worked at a preschool for multi-handicapped, children brought in, wrapped in blankets and being carried by their mothers, eventually went into the normal handicap preschool and eventually on out into a normal preschool for totally normal children. What did these two programs have in common? The entire campus had an integrated curriculum, which for the preschool began developmentally on the one-month-old level and continued on up to a six year old level. At the deaf and blind school, curriculums which ended at the top level of the deaf blind multi-handicapped, then began at this same level in the deaf and blind departments, tailored of course, to the deaf students and the blind students. Social skills was addressed and supervised when a child was integrated into either the deaf or blind school.

Along with this was an expanded curriculum on every development level, or in the case of the older children, a curriculum which included adjustments to a new group of peers. A new teacher coming into the program, or a teacher's assistant, was schooled in these methods and techniques. No one was told, or was not told, that nothing could be done, that there would be no progress, and this was just a babysitting job. Even the chance to make this assumption, was taken away from new employees through training and insight. In short, unknowingly, I had had training that did not prepare me for traveling to a different state, and meeting those who saw severely multi-handicapped children as "pet rocks" or "blessed spirits," children who just had to be loved until they died. Nor was I prepared to meet teachers and staffs who saw resource children as the lower end of society, who were lucky if they graduated from high school. Nor did I think, that when I went into the public school system as a classroom teacher for gifted children, I would meet many people who either thought they were better than everyone else, because they were teaching the cream of the crop and therefore had the ability to judge their students too, or, teachers of regular classrooms, who did not see that these gifted children had just as many problems and difficulties as their own students and suffered just as much but in different ways.

In all the years that I taught, I only ever saw children. My expectations of them were always very high. And never once did I think I didn't have to work hard to figure out every child in every classroom that I had, whether severely multi-handicapped or gifted, poor or rich, black or blue or green, or having just arrived from another country, they were children. No labels, no judgments, and no preconceived notions from others who had taught them before me. I rarely looked at testing unless it was necessary for a particular child, and I rarely worried about my student's tests because I knew that if they had the self-esteem, the belief in themselves, understood what their gifts were, were instilled with these various beliefs, and I taught them what I was suppose too along with a lot of other things that I was not suppose to teach, but did anyway, like social skills and conflict resolution techniques, they would do well on their tests, and they did.

So please parents, look at each of your children as the special little people that they are rather than being thrown off base by what those around you ask you to believe, you know them best. I am giving you a smorgasbord of information and when you have the two or three possibilities about your child, read and explore further so you are ready to advocate for your child at school. You would be surprised at the amount of misinformation and judgments that are out there, even by the experts. And certainly with intuitive children, you have the problem of a lack of belief in what you know is happening to your own child. If you go into a meeting armed with the right information, you will have to be listened too, even if it is about the paranormal or the psychic and intuitive gifts of your child. At least now, there is a larger audience receptive to the idea that we all are intuitive in one way or another. Or even that this is something that needs to be addressed with all children, as a part of their entire "integrative wholeness" in the person they will eventually become.

Realize that your "tweens" and teens are still forming both physiologically and emotionally, and that they are not in their "terrible teens," but are instead in their developmental, historical, cultural, emotional and physical stages of becoming an adult. That all these many aspects are coming into play to form the adult that they will become in their style of learning and communicating, in their empathic and intuitive abilities, in the strengths and challenges they have come in with, and, in their evolutionary shifting which is in synch with the moving and shifting of the planet they live on and the animals and plants that surround them. Always look for another way in anything told you about them, another insight, another perception, another focus, another method or technique that will get them to where they need to be with the least amount of emotional pain, stress or physical trauma. Never judge what we cannot see, hear or feel. It is there anyway.

And do not forget the very bright learning challenged young men and women who hesitate to enter college each year because they have a hidden learning disability and only see this problem and not their true goals beyond it. Or the people who squeezed through school unable to read and have become excellent memorizers and verbalizers, still crippled by something, that even as an adult, they could overcome with the right methods for teaching them. The damage is being done every day in every classroom in America, in one way or another. Those of us who did our best not to damage anyone, in my case making math fun and interesting even though I secretly hated it, still could not entirely avoid it because the system itself forced us into positions where we were unable to avoid something with a child that we knew in our hearts was not the right thing to do. All that I learned from every single student I had, from the severely handicapped to the low-income resource kids to the so-called "privileged" gifted kids, made me a better teacher. Every parent I dealt with, taught me even more, and so did every administrator who either ignored me or challenged me and showed me what I did not want to be or what I might want to be. But it was the children who looked up at me with their shiny or grimy little faces, and suddenly realized that they had just gotten something, that made me stay. I knew that if they believed in themselves, no matter their circumstances, they had a chance to live a good life, and in some cases, even a spectacular one that could transform many other lives for the better too. And for the severely handicapped, there were parents and siblings who would remember what they learned and turn around and teach it to others.

A common problem I ran across when teaching the gifted and talented were parents who felt their children were perfect as gifted children, and did not need other remediation's to make them even more perfect. These parents found it embarrassing to face the fact that their child had some other problem going on besides a high IQ. And vice versa, parents of severely multi-handicapped children got caught up in the details of all the various diagnoses of their child, or why their child was handicapped in the first place, and neglected to accept their child just as they were. Or they did accept their child, and did nothing to help them move forward, because they believed that all a child needed was to be loved. In between this, was what I call the "throwaway children," who had utterly amazing potentials that needed to be constantly challenged and then they would never have to feel as though they were being "thrown away."

In my sixties now, I have at long last found my own intuitive soul and can see and feel that soul in others who ask me for advice and guidance. This does not mean that I have stopped questioning or doubting the road I take, or anyone else takes; it just means that in knowing my own intuitive soul, I can let those wiser than me from the many "other sides" around me, send their guidance through me to those seekers on their own journeys. These pilgrims on their own quests to assist many others knock at my door and I answer. And I also know that there are many others out there who are doing their part, quietly and without fanfare, as we go through the eye of the storm and await the other side of this storm to arrive. Children are our most precious resource they say in the physical world, and in the invisible worlds beyond this, they say that children are our intuitive inheritance, those who we must nurture in order for them to transform the world from which we have come.

> "Those who bring sunshine to the lives of others cannot keep it from themselves."
>
> --Sir James Matthew Barrie, author of Peter Pan

CHAPTER ONE

"The most beautiful thing we can experience is the mysterious. It is the source of all true art and all science. He to whom this emotion is a stranger, who can no longer pause to wonder and stand rapt in awe, is as good as dead: his eyes are closed."

--Albert Einstein

"Those who were dancing were thought to be insane by those who couldn't hear the music."

--Sufi Saying

A Bit of Whimsy

In the Wisdom of Fairy Tales, Rudolf Meyer addresses the idea that fairy tales do something else for children besides reflect who they are. They provide "...compelling evidence that the wild and nonsensical imaginings that kids love to engage in may well be picture-remnants of the soul faculty of clairvoyance. He demonstrates how fairy tales are teaching tools to help youngsters become more humane, handle relationships, overcome the lure of darkness and fear, gain respect for animals and nature, and adopt the refinements of good behavior. In other words, he found that make-believe is important." And more important, he gives credence to the idea that clairvoyance is alive and well in children. Folklore and fairy tales empower children, reflect who they are as individuals, and confirm the existence of their souls and spiritual knowings. They also confirm their intuitive gifts. (*Quoted by P.M.H. Atwater's book, The New Children, Bear & Co., 2003, pp. 209 – 210 and taken from Meyer, Rudolf's The Wisdom of Fairy Tales, Floris Books: 15 Harrison Gardens, Edinburgh, fourth printing, 1997.*)

The Empathic Psychic Children in Fairy Tales

Throughout history, and all over the world, folklore and fairy tales have told about the adventures of creative, intuitive, children. If scientists believed that this was confirmation for the existence of worlds beyond worlds, and various kinds of intuition, they would have had their confirmation thousands of years ago. As a child, this was my first experience in reading about children like me. Only I had no idea at the time, that that was why I loved these stories so much. My "vivid imagination" had not become "real" as yet. So let's look at a few such stories, such as Dorothy from The Wizard of Oz, Peter Pan, and Alice in Wonderland or Through the Looking Glass. A boy and girl from literature who epitomize the intuitive child, Dorothy and Peter represent all that intuitive children do and experience and encounter in their lives on earth.

The Wizard of Oz

> "When all the world is a hopeless jumble, And the raindrops tumble all around, Heaven opens a magic lane. When all the clouds darken up the skyway, There's a rainbow highway to be found, Leading from your window, To a place behind the sun, Just a step beyond the rain."

--the verse never used in the movie
from "Somewhere Over The Rainbow"
--lyrics by E.Y. Harburg

> "Somewhere over the rainbow, way up high, there's a land that I heard of once in a lullaby. Somewhere over the rainbow, skies are blue and the dreams that you dare to dream really do come true. Someday I'll wish upon a star and wake up where the clouds are far behind me. Where troubles melt like lemon drops away above the chimney tops. That's where you'll find me. Somewhere over the rainbows bluebirds fly, birds fly over the rainbow. Why then, oh why can't I? If happy little bluebirds fly beyond the rainbow, why, oh why can't I?"

--movie version of "The Wizard of Oz"

Dorothy was an empathic intuitive and all of the characters in her physical world were Auntie Em who spiritually guided her there, the three farm hands who watched over her, the evil neighbor who frightened her or judged her and represented all her fears and doubts reinforced in the physical world. Then there was the traveling salesman who enticed her into exploring her gifts. The ruby slippers were her internal guidance system to turn her gifts on and off and the hot air balloon was her external guidance system. When she traveled to another world, she traveled either at night in a nightmare or night terror / the tornado – or in a song/day time dream "Somewhere Over the Rainbow." She got guidance from the other side or in her case, while traveling in the other side. The Good Sorceress of Oz, Glenda and the bad witch, which her house drops on and smashes represents the classic battle between good and evil, but also Dorothy's growing awareness of herself as an intuitive. She receives her ruby slippers from the good witch as she chases all her fears and doubts away and is rewarded by her spiritual guide in another world (Glenda) by getting her wings or slippers to "fly." She is now a "good witch" or empathic intuitive herself, so now she has to take a journey through many worlds to learn about herself and others.

On the way she meets the Scarecrow who will help her gain "thinking" skills to analyze what happens as she travels and to use her common sense. The Tin Man helps her to have "heart" or compassion and understanding as she steps into other's shoes to walk in their path. And she also meets the Lion who gives her "courage" to face her fears and doubts when she returns to the physical world. The Wicked Witch of the West represents her facing her shadow self, conquering fears and doubts, and overcoming them by melting this part of herself. The flying monkeys represent her powers in other worlds that must be translated to her physical world, going from the dark to the light which the storm brought on at her original home. She bridges worlds in her hot air balloon and she turns her intuitive talents on and off with her ruby slippers (originally silver). By the end of the story she is ready for many more adventures in other worlds and dimensions as an astral traveler, empathic intuitive and has telepathic conversations with those she meets along the way. Is it any wonder that a lot of us so-called intuitives loved The Wizard of Oz and many of the other books in L. Frank Baum's series, when we were young?

Peter Pan

> "So come with me, where dreams are born, and time is never planned. Just think of happy things, and your heart will fly on wings, forever, in Never, Never Land."
>
> --Peter Pan

> "You know that place between sleep and awake, the place where you still remember dreaming? That's where I'll always love you."
>
> --Tinkerbell

So now let's takc Peter Pan. He is from Never, Neverland, and is often in a battle of some kind, making him more of a shamanic warrior. The story even begins with Peter looking for his lost shadow self, having a spiritual crisis over this, as he yearns for the things he cannot have as an immortal boy. Wendy is his bridge person between the physical world and other worlds, but Tinker Bell is his spiritual guide while traveling in other realms. No wonder they are jealous of each other! Although, Wendy being the more spiritual one, ignores feisty Tinker Bell as she tries all her little tricks and taunts. Wendy's two brothers are her guides and protectors and the Lost Boys are led by Peter, who is their shamanic guide in alternate worlds. He teaches them how to travel and return without being harmed. Captain Hook is Peter Pan's occult teacher and nemesis, while the crocodile represents all those fears and doubts which both Hook and Peter must conquer. Deciding to never grow up, because you can be a better intuitive if you remain child-like, Peter Pan prefers to wander in these other worlds rather than come home. The crocodile also represents traveling in various times and dimensions without fear. Peter Pan is not only a great shamanic teacher but also has pretty much chosen to "translate" into other shape shifting forms, coming back from time to time to teach others. And even though the Native Americans in the original story are generically and ethnically typecast, they still represent the teachings of nature and spirit in the story. "Tink" could be more of an elemental than a fairy and the Croc could also be the fears and doubts of living a shamanic life which is often perilous and scary.

Alice in Wonderland & Through the Looking Glass

> "Anon, to sudden silence won, in fancy they pursue. The dream-child moving through the land, of wonders wild and new. In friendly chat with bird or beast – And half believe it true."
>
> --Alice in Wonderland

> "To the Looking-Glass world it was Alice that said, 'I've a scepter in hand. I've a crown on my head; Let the Looking-Glass creatures, whatever they be, Come and dine with the Red Queen, the White Queen and me!"
>
> --Through the Looking Glass

A much deeper tale and more for adults than children are the stories of Lewis Carroll and the beautiful illustrations of John Tenniel. The characters in these two stories really tell of the worlds most of us have forgotten as we grow older. Alice's adventures in these books are to the intuitive mind and heart, quite real. They are just dressed up a bit, so it is harder to recognize them in today's world. There is Alice, the intuitive, empathic, kinetic, shape shifting, night flyer, whose dreams are real whether they are in the day or at night. A powerful "light being," Alice represents all of the traits of the "super psychic" child. She has them all, clairvoyance, clairaudience, clairsentience, and many of her various abilities are reflected in the characters she meets in the other world. She even has a balance of left and right brained skills, making her a "whole brainer!" She is a shaman who uses "tools" to assist her in her travels into other worlds and she is a warrior when it comes to battling evil and sorrow in people's souls. She is a storyteller and eventual wise woman, who is always alone in her travels unlike Dorothy who has companions who help her, or Peter's "Lost Boys" who care a lot about their leader. She has strength and wisdom and bravery in facing those on the other side of the mirror, or those who play against her on the "chess board" of life.

She distains the "Antipathies" or people full of hate and aversion who walk upside down blind. But she does have some help in Wonderland, the White Rabbit is like a guardian angel and the Mad Hatter who has two cohorts, the March Hare and the Dormouse who could represent Alice facing her shadow self in several forms. And while the White

Rabbit is her travel guide, the Cheshire cat, in the book, confuses her with his directions, a sort of trickster spirit guide. In Through the Looking Glass, the White Knight takes the place of the White Rabbit, as a guardian angel. Still none of them were consistently loyal to her, as exampled in Dorothy's animals and family, or Peter's Lost Boys and Wendy's family. Alice is essentially alone; constantly shape shifting and always meeting creatures and people that she has to outsmart to survive. The mouse, the duck, the dodo, the Lory, the eaglet and even the serpent and the pigeon all lead her to the Caterpillar, the wise shaman holy man who uses drugs to have his otherworldly experiences and then dispenses his advice from the universal consciousness to Alice. In the physical world of Wonderland Alice deals with the Duchess, the pig /baby, the frog footman messenger, the Red and White Queens, the King, the card soldiers or knaves and all the rest of the not so pleasant "real" world of Wonderland.

In the end she defeats them all with her childhood naivety and innocent wisdom, and some of Carroll's subconscious feelings emerge, that children are the only ones to be trusted and that only very young girls can be beautiful and honest and clever enough to outsmart everyone on the chess board and win the game. And when the Duchess gives Alice some advise, we get a clear picture of what Carroll thinks of most people, and also just how special Alice is as a master intuitive: "Be what you would seem to be - or, if you'd like to put it more simply - 'Never imagine yourself not to be otherwise than what it might appear to others that what you were appear to others that what you were or might have been was not otherwise than what you had been would have appeared to them to be otherwise." He ends his first tale telling us just how he views little Alice: "Lastly, she pictured to herself how this same little sister of her would, in the after-time, be herself grown woman; and how she would keep, through her riper years, the simple and loving heart of her childhood: and how she would gather about her other little children, and make their eyes bright and eager with many a strange tale, perhaps even with the dream of Wonderland of long ago: and how she would feel with all their simple sorrows, and find a pleasure in all their simple joys, remembering her own child-life and the happy summer days." (Alice in Wonderland and through the Looking Glass *by Lewis Carroll, J.J. Little & Ives Company: New York, Deluxe Edition, no date given, p.85 & p.115.*)

In Through the Looking Glass, Alice ends up being crowned the new queen after going through the looking glass into an alternate and reversed world. She meets another spiritual teacher, the Gryphon and an assortment of animals and people who are downright silly such as the Jabberwocky, the Tiger-Lily flower, the Walrus and the Carpenter, Tweedledum and Tweedledee, Humpty Dumpty, the old lady sheep and of course the Lion and the Unicorn. My favorite lines in this tale about the silliness of people is the first stanza of the Walrus and the Carpenter poem: "The time has come the Walrus said, to talk of many things, of shoes - and ships - and sealing wax – of cabbages – and kings – And why the sea is boiling hot – And whether pigs have wings." The White Knight is her protector spirit guide in this world and this entire tale is based on a chess game. Alice learns her math and the "History of England" too. And as she plays the game she outsmarts everyone and gets her golden crown as the wise woman intuitive that she will become. "In Wonderland they lie, Dreaming as the days go by, Dreaming as the summers die. Ever drifting down the stream, lingering in the golden gleam – Life, what is it but a dream." So in the end of both tales, Alice will grow up to live alone with all her spiritual riches and intuitive gifts, teaching others and shining her light out for those who seek her, having learned about life from those women who came before her, the White Queen and the Red Queen, learning all about good and evil in the physical world and all the other worlds that she has been too. (*Ibid., p.164 & p.244*).

Empaths & Folklore & Fairy Tales Around the World

One can take almost any fairy tale and find the fable of the intuitive life within it, especially in such other tales as "The Snow Queen" and "Snow White and the Seven Dwarfs"or in tales like "The Little Mermaid" or "Beauty and the Beast." In my favorite tale, "The Snow Queen," Gerda has to look for her friend Kay at the Snow Queen's ice palace. The Queen has kidnapped Kay because the devil's demons broke a mirror onto the world and whoever got a piece of the mirror in their eye and heart, forgot everything and became cold as ice in their heart, nor did they have vision to really see the unseen worlds. She goes through many lands and adventures with both physical and otherworldly creatures, who either try to make her forget or help her. Finally after all her growing up years, she finds Kay and her tears melt his heart and they are reunited. She has all the knowledge and tools from all of her adventures to now be a powerful intuitive in the world, but in her case she gets the guy too! But not without a very lot of suffering on her part! Not a likely scenario for two powerful intuitives to be together!

"The magic mirror that never lies" is one of the best metaphors for a dream process from yet another fairy tale, "Snow White and the Seven Dwarfs." Dreams reflect our shadow self as well as anything disturbing or distressing that we have encountered in the physical world and always speaks the truth. Anything we don't like in ourselves is reflected in the many mirrors of our dreams. In Snow White the wicked queen looks in the mirror and says, "Mirror, mirror on the wall who is the fairest of them all?" knowing full well that she is aging and young Snow White is much prettier than she. It is nature and her animals which aide Snow White from being murdered by the evil queen. The magic mirror lies to the queen every morning just as our dreams may lie to us every night. We face unpleasant truths from our subconscious about ourselves and others every morning, just as we may have wonderful and beautiful dreams scattered in our night dreams too. "The reflection in the magic mirror is always true and accurate, but we do not wish to acknowledge its relevance to our own interior lives." And even though some of our dreams reflect this, we can learn from our dreams to improve our lives as we can learn from fairy tales to guide us in our lives. (*<u>The Wisdoms of Your Dreams</u> by Jeremy Taylor, Penguin, 2009, pp. 39-40.*)

In "The Little Mermaid" it is a much more likely scenario when the mermaid sees her handsome prince, sacrifices her ocean life for very painful land legs that hurt when she walks on them in the physical world. And after all her trials and tribulations of even rescuing him but being unable to speak – her penance for being a powerful intuitive and immortal – she loses her handsome prince to a beautiful mortal princess as well as all her intuitive powers. She returns to the sea, having lost everything, but especially her chance to have a voice in the matter, by bargaining with a sea witch, and ends up becoming sea foam on the waves of the ocean (or universal frequencies of the multi-verse) for all eternity. Disney, of course, didn't like this particular Shakespearean tragedy from Hans Christian Andersen, and so he changed it and many children today are only familiar with the movie versions.

In "Beauty and the Beast" Beauty saves her father's life by going to live with the lion beast who has been shape shifted by an evil witch. And by learning to love the beast who is not beautiful on the outside but very lovely on the inside, except when he is mad, she eventually gets her reward, but not without almost losing him. The beast becomes a handsome prince again from the love she had for him and the inner beauty that she also had. I myself liked Peter Pan the best, probably because of the night flying in it, which must have been my way from the time that I was little! Peter is able to travel to so many places both real and imagined, while Alice, powerful, strong and beautiful, a super psychic; has to live alone and separate while always celebrating for others, rarely for herself.

Many of my intuitive friends, however, just loved The Wizard of Oz and all the subsequent books in the series. Dorothy did not just fly over the rainbow, but had many other adventures in other lands and actually my favorite of the series was the one where she went under the ground and slid from one place to another in glass tubes. Dorothy always had friends and companions wherever she went. Peter Pan came in second with them, but the others were mine alone to contemplate and enjoy. "The Snow Queen" was my all time favorite, because one really has a choice in life between becoming a Snow Queen or a Gerda, when dealing with powerful forces that many people do not sense or see. It is quite a job to come in with things, gain things through a spiritual crisis or near-death awakening of one kind or another, gaining the insight and knowledge to both control and use these things for good, and, merge all of this together to forge some kind of a mortal life to help and assist others on their paths without judgment or control. Life is never really a fairy tale, nor is it what we hoped for. It is what it is, and so much more!

But are these tales just fables and stories or vivid imaginings? Or did their authors really understand this intuitive life quite well, experiencing it for themselves quite often? Probably, but don't ask me! I was told while young that my made up stories were constantly irritating for my brothers and sisters, drove my parents nuts and had them worried about me all the time. Would I ever grow up and learn to function in the physical world properly? Or would I be made fun of, function poorly, or be considered mad? In the end I shifted all this to storytelling, found people who I did not irritate, and became a writer, simply because making up all these stories gave me an excuse for my "strange" behaviors. By "channeling" what I envisioned and felt, I was writing instead. It was not until much later that I realized I was "channeling" or "inhabiting" the people that I wrote about. And by the time I realized that a lot of my experiences, all my life, had been real and not imagined, I had been deemed sane enough, grounded enough and educated enough to believe in what I saw and experienced, without needing so much confirmation. I just kept irritating or even scaring, those with blinders on! So now, let's get to it, what even the planet is now showing us is real in terms of either a brain shift or a rise in consciousness, or both! The old merges with the new, "the shift" brings in all the good ideas that were left behind but in a better form, and the new ways of seeing. The new ways of being have been coming in for quite a few years. It is just that we did not recognize them until now. Communities of spirit are coming, and how we look at them will be entirely different than what we perceive now. No one will stand alone.

Rudolf Meyer's Spiritual Take on Fairy Tales – A Child's Soul Connection:

The inherited "blood-memory" of mankind has slowly been expelled by the "head-memory" of the present, in other words, history has been rewritten to exclude our ancestral intuitive experiences and only include the mental or physical world experiences and memories. "When ancestors still spoke in the blood, when memories of past generations flashed up from the depths of the soul like memories of childhood days, then the soul became wise." Bearers of a much more comprehensive consciousness, ancestral forces stored up in primal wisdoms, gives to every child born, an ancient lineage and heritage of spirit. Fairy tales help all of us to rediscover our eternal childhood, whether these tales are in books, told verbally, viewed on a screen, viewed as a performance, or enacted. The mode of transporting these tales doesn't matter, what does matter is that the stories continue to be told. The resolution of inspired consciousness still works through the holiest of forces in these tales. The soul can acknowledge its descent and origins through the self-awakening of fairy tales." Teachers call this story time. (*Meyer, Ibid. p.21*).

In these tales there is a deep connection with all energies on the earth, whether man or beast, plant or earth energies. The soul life, rejuvenated in sleep and awakened by ancestral memories, can lead each child into a world both imaginative and creative. Fairy tales are a reflection of a child's nourishment and animating force on the earth. In imaginative knowledge, children can experience all of the life forces of the earth, the seasons, the four elements, etc. Remaining united with the spiritual world as well as the physical one, helps children to understand their own soul and meditate on this while they sleep. This releases the chains of self-perception and creates a deep community with the earth that helps children unite with others rather than feeling separate and alone. As Christ said, you will never enter the kingdom of Heaven unless you become like children, and remaining child-like is an essential element of the intuitive life. Remembering the spiritual power of our childhoods can continue the magic of life into our adult years. Weaving its home into our physical bodies, the spirit creates a dwelling place for itself from our heritage, generational memories, childhood and spiritual emergences over the course of our life. Fairy tales are our first recognition of all this as young children. So it is no wonder that even today, many little children remember their story time with their parents and teachers in a much deeper way than one would think, even those perceived not to be listening at all!

Fairy tales point to the soul mysteries we face as we grow up and denying our natural clairvoyance for physical realm prisons as adults, keeps us not only from our own souls but the soul connections we can have with others. These tales teach us about child-like soul qualities: courage, generosity, compassion, and appreciation of the spirit. "It requires a considerable strengthening of the will to awaken the hidden self that lies enchanted in the weaving of dreams...A dreamlike, backward-looking life is set free, and can bend its vision forwards,: a 'prophetic' spiritual power that points to the future, is born." Diluting the darker powers and characters of these tales, denies children the ability to learn and to clearly perceive the good in human hearts over the evil in the world. The rescue of children through learning from these tales can help in a small way to keep the suffocating death of selfishness and materialism, from clouding the ancient and ancestral knowledge of their own souls. Fairy tales and their morphed versions of today can help children form their soul lives for themselves and with others. (*Meyer, Ibid., p, 123*).

Serialized tales like Harry Potter or The Chronicles of Narnia, help to continue this tradition. Many other child and teen series, in print or translated to the screen, provide this same fairy tale format for children and even adults. Even in Hollywood, those who produce these versions of the original books, manage to hang onto what Meyer was talking about. The diluted versions become either horror films or whitewashed with no evil to overcome in them. But most of them still provide the journey that children need, to understand how to be the hero or heroine, even in some of the graphic novels brought to the screen. One has to weed out those that make no sense or have absolutely no cohesive story on the path through the dark forest to that happy ending where good defeats evil. Without this journey and the inevitable overcoming of evil ending, the child has been given nothing, watched nothing, and learned nothing. Children need these good versus evil tales to not only recognize what evil consists of, but to gain skills in how to confront or overcome such evils. They must also understand and recognize good in the world and how to find a balance towards the "good" in the gray areas of their lives. Fairy tales and many other types of tales can help them to gain these insights.

What We Already Know:

"If the world wanted to feed starving children, it could do so easily. If the world wanted to outlaw acts of war against children, it could do so easily. If the world wanted to provide homeless children with shelter, it could do so easily. But children are not a priority in the world, and never have been...We don't need to start still one more angry movement, or one more angry letter-writing campaign or one more march on Washington. We must simply begin – today – to cherish and protect our children in our own homes, our own schools, and our personal lives. Within a world that has done very little for children, that is at least something. It's a starting point. And who is in a position to know the effects of just one parent, or one couple, or one schoolteacher learning to see and enjoy children? ....In many ways a teacher is a parent, a coach is a parent, a counselor is a parent, a politician is a parent; even a mere voter is a parent. We should all think of ourselves as a parent in the gentlest sense of that term, as a guardian of the young...If our relationship with children is a sacred trust – and that is the premise of spiritual parenting – in no circumstances can anything be more important than protecting and nourishing the children in our care...None of the heinous acts in history could have occurred if children had been the world's priority."

--Spiritual Parenting, Prathers, pp. 3-4

"If you do not believe in magic, your life will not be magical. Magic is part of the unknowable – that which you cannot describe, but which exists and makes your life extraordinary. It is part of the goodness of your spirit. It is the mysterious and intriguing part of your spiritual life. Magic is what we all are looking for, but if you try to hold it and name it and describe it, you will lose it. You must talk around magic, describe what led you there, and give thanks for that part of the universe that is unknowable...Out of relationship comes magic. Out of friction and remembering comes magic. Out of the mists of dawn and the mysteries of creation comes the magic that we call life...."

--"Magic" The Power Deck by Lynn Andrews

"Fairy tales have a profound influence on the developing mind of the child. They envelope the soul in a magic which is a necessary and counterweight to the increasingly powerful effect of a technological society in which children become intellectual and awake to the earth far too early," said Rudolf Meyer, who died in 1985. But what he was not around to see coming in, was a new wave of children "brain-wired" quite differently and evolving just like the planet is. Fairy tales themselves are still quite alive, but they have metamorphized into a new and quite technological visual-spatial problem solving form. On the other hand, we have to hope that the ancestral heritage connections are also kept alive as these new forms of "fairy tales" and storytelling emerge!

--The Wisdom of Fairy Tales by Rudolf Meyer, p. 181

"If you want your children to be bright, read them Fairy Tales. If you want them to be brilliant, read them even more Fairy Tales."

--Albert Einstein

CHAPTER TWO

Who Are Psychic, Empathic, Intuitive Children?

"The best and most beautiful things in the world cannot be seen, or touched...but are felt in the heart."

-- Helen Keller

"We are confronted with insurmountable opportunities."

--Pogo

Who Are Intuitive Children?

In Catherine Crawford's book the highly intuitive child, she presents twenty questions to find out if your child is intuitive or not. A lot of these questionnaires often include all children but there were a few of the questions I think are worth mentioning here to help you in your quest to understand your child or children. For example, some of the best questions would help those who are not so sure of their own intuitive gifts and need some guidance in sorting out all the parts of their very integrative son or daughter. These are: Does your child consistently finish your sentences for you, thus reading your mind? Does your child sometimes tell you about things before they happen and then they do happen, does your child pick up on tensions or atmospheres in places or with people, and do crowded places produce anxiety reactions such as stomachaches or headaches? Does your child have a fascination with deeper issues and concerns for world events way beyond his or her years? Is it hard to keep secrets from your child or does this child show a high level of sensitivity? Does your child make emotional and logical connections way beyond his or her years? Does your child solve problems quickly and often accurately? Does your child have a vast inner life with astounding details for all of its supposedly imaginary inhabitants? And is your child unusually drawn to the natural world, demanding peaceful contemplation time, and also seems to be able to communicate with very young children and animals without speaking? (*Crawford, Catherine. the highly intuitive child, Hunter House: Alameda, California, 2009, pp. 17-18*).

Crawford also talks about what can happen when these parts of your child are not addressed, confirmed and empowered. "When intuitive children get the impression that the adults they depend on think they are overly sensitive, weird, occupy too much of their time, or should act more like other kids, they may be tempted to shut down. Unfortunately, as they suppress their gifts, they start to shut down other wonderful parts of the self. The cost is great for children who detect, register, and believe that their trait is too much for the people around them. In the child's mind, this is a message that the whole self is too much. It is at this unfortunate point that an authentic sense of self is injured and the child may begin to develop a pseudo-self to fit in with the world.

Ultimately, I don't think the trait can be squashed or taken away ... When repressed in childhood, these intuitive gifts wait under the surface until they can be seen, acknowledged, and given permission to be used again." (*Ibid, pp. 21-22*).

Thoughts on True Intuition as Opposed to Magical Thinking

"It is important to address how true intuition can be written off as simply magical thinking. If we lump all the child's intuitive impressions in the category of magical thinking, even when they are accurate beyond any doubt, we muddy the distinction between intuition and imagination ... Learning to tell the difference between magical thinking and clear intuition is not always easy, but you can help as a parent if you know what to look for ... Magical thinking can feel a lot like jumping to an intuitive conclusion, but it's different. Intuition has a distinct signature of arrival; the body signals a sense of inner knowing, even without necessarily seeing anything immediately – hair might stand on end on the back of the neck or a sudden image pops into mind. Magical thinking, on the other hand, seems to piece together details that create a faulty picture of reality. The child sees the outline of clothing shadows and soon is convinced not only of the robber but a full-scale assault on the family ... Ultimately, the way to determine the difference between intuitive impressions or a magical thinking tangle is to check the facts ... You can help your child out of magical thinking corners by gently having him work backward to check the facts and details of whatever it is he is convinced is occurring." (Ibid., pp.33-34).

Two Major Types of Intuition

When we experience an impression or sense what is outside linear thinking and does not seem to be a rational concrete process, we call it "intuition." There are two major types of intuition: Intuitive Thinkers and Intuitive Feelers. Intuitive Thinkers use their five senses to assist them as they move through the physical world and they most often focus outwardly rather than within. They have an auditory processing style of learning, fit into the existing school system and process information easily. Intuitive Feelers focus on their interior life and experience both this world and the multidimensional one at the same time. They do not process, integrate or download information as easily and have more of a visual-spatial learning style. Over two-thirds of our earth's population and over two-thirds of every classroom in the world, contains this type of VSL learner, so that rather than them having a problem, it is just as often, the people teaching them and counseling them that do not know how to work with them. More and more, these two styles of learning are either converging into whole brain thinking, or changing our world as technology and our information about brain function increases. (*Ibid., Crawford, PP.11-13*).

Both types of children are not necessarily exclusive of each other, all of us are along this continuum and share characteristics from both sides of the spectrum. Both types of intuitives also share the same anxieties, fears, doubts and lack of acknowledgement, yet many intuitive children find a way to thread themselves through the schooling system with certain modifications and confirmations, often with support from their parents, while many others suffer these fears and doubts quietly on their own. Intuitive abilities tend to run in families like a lot of other traits do. How parents and relatives, teachers and counselors handle this makes a big difference for each intuitive child. If by example, they see not to fear, not to doubt their abilities, and they receive feedback or confirmation of what they can do, and are somehow empowered as children, their journey to adulthood can be quite spectacular. There are many other countries that do this, but America's melting pot and backwardness in acknowledging this sort of thing, can also backfire on many of these children. There are many "wounded" adult intuitives still in recovery! Fortunately, many in raising their own intuitive children are often reliving their own upbringings and doing a great deal of healing along the way. (*Ibid, Crawford, the highly intuitive child, pp. 8-24*).

Intuitive Traits

Intuitive traits can encompass such things as worrying, anxiety, fearfulness, shyness, low sensory thresholds, low pain thresholds, empathic or deep feeling for others, reflective or contemplative abilities. These children maybe more aware than others in their emotional intelligence abilities, and they would often rather experience things than be told. They have sensitivities to their environment and the frequencies and energies that surround them and they are also very sensitive to other's moods and energies. They need to be inspired by their teachers rather than just take in information and they are often intelligent, creative and conscientious. They are also good observers and listeners. They learn through their feelings and process things through their body movements. Many of them are motivated to create and explore on their own. They experience dreams and flashes of insight as well as having access to other worlds both in a dreaming and waking state. And obviously these traits can integrate with other types of abilities with each child, such as a gifted child or a super creative kid, etc. Academic skills may or may not be important to these intuitive children, depending on how much investment they have in the physical world and how much they invest in all those "alternate" worlds.

In the Goode-Paterson book, they mention the following intuitive traits based on some research that there are around 75 million intuitives in the United States. This would be one fourth of the population, but how they got this statistic is hard to know. They say that these "… traits comprise a style of interaction with people and environments that can result in intuitively feeling like a round peg in a square hole. Exactly! Providing a person with a perception more expansive than that of the linear mind, these round peg traits are now valued. The right kind of nurturing and training empowers intuitives to be leading exceptional lives of contributions and service." They list the following traits: shyness, fearfulness, low sensory threshold, sensitivity to energies in the environment, sensitivity to people's moods and energies, reflective, empathic, intelligent, creative, aware, and conscientious. (*Ibid., Raising Intuitive Children, Goode & Paterson, 2009, p.37*).

Dealing with Multiple Worlds

Psychic children also deal with three main worlds at once: the physical world, the non-physical world or worlds and the spiritual world. Imagine trying to sit in a classroom and concentrate on your studies while experiencing all three? The teacher is giving the lesson and while this lesson is being delivered in an auditory processing learning style, this visual-spatial learner's mind wanders out the window where he or she sees things others do not, or hears things others do not, or is touched by something that others are not aware of? Perhaps the child's paper and pencil begin to move on their own because that is where the child is focusing. Or perhaps the object that a friend gave the child is speaking to him from inside his desk or he has it in his hand and is receiving information from a past or future event. Perhaps the tree outside is talking to him or one of his friends is sending a telepathic message to someone else and he is distracted by this two-way conversation? Perhaps a dream about a natural disaster kept him awake last night and he is worrying about the people involved in it. Or perhaps he is so bored by the lesson, that he finds himself floating off right in the middle of the day in a real or imagined daydream. The possibilities are endless, until adults understand what all those possibilities are!

Dealing With Space, Time & Distance

Regular time is not intuitive time and is sometimes experienced as hectic and fast paced or is sometimes slow like a silent movie in slow motion. "Pop-Ups" and "hits" sometimes arrive instantly and they are immediate flashes of information. Not knowing how you arrived at the solution to a problem is a trait not only of intuitives but also of visual-spatial learners. So these intuitive "knowings" can actually bypass linear time quickly or come as a precognition or futuristic prediction. These leaps of thought or visions, can be lost by doubting one's first thought or flash, or by having others say no, that cannot be true because they do not experience these flashes. "Intuitive knowing about people, places, animals, and even world events can come at an astonishingly rapid speed. Sometimes intuitive leaps, including predictions, frighten children who suddenly can intuitively see things for which they don't have a context. When this happens, they can outpace the child's emotional development. Whether it is experienced as an acceleration of personal understanding or getting a read on something related to other people or even the planet, the child might feel scared and overwhelmed with the knowledge. Adults can support children in these experiences by listening attentively, reminding the child that there is nothing wrong with having these kinds of insights, and offering comfort if the child is upset at what she sees." (*Ibid., Crawford, p.169*).

Imaging Travels through Time and Distance

In one of Atwater's books she talks about levels of imagery found in otherworldly journeys such as near-death experiences, as well as all the other types of spiritual emergencies that will be discussed later in this book. She identifies four levels that include Personal imagery, which are images taken from your own life, Mass Mind imagery, which are collective images that reflect the human condition, Memory Fields, which are archetypal images that are universal in nature, and Truth imagery, which is difficult to describe in words because it is a "knowing" rather than a "seeing." She states that this type is a "... consistent, stable reality that undergirds and transcends creation and all created things." For those who do intuitive readings, this is a perfect description of the types of images that one receives as information for the person sitting for the reading. (*The New Children by P.M.H. Atwater, Bear & Co., 2003, p. 26*).

Avery says that waking dreams can come individually or in patterns over a longer period of time. He says that they can confirm our path or warn us, protect us or offer us guidance. They give us insights about our lives or they can become an initiation of some sort to towards an expansion of consciousness. They can predict the future and give us a "knowingness" for our own inner communications. They can comfort us or offer us great spiritual awakenings. They can offer us insights about the cycles of change in our lives or help us to interpret night dreams that we are having in conjunction with our day dreams or "waking dreams." And it is well known in New Age circles that these waking dreams can come from the other side as well, like seeing something that is not there while driving, and when you return what you saw or what you thought you saw, is no longer there. Or after death visitations from loved ones that whether dreamed, imaged, really seen, or offered to you, can confirm something for you, or simply offer the unconditional love that you have yearned for from this loved one. (*The Secret Language of Waking Dreams by Michael Avery, Eckankar, 1992.)*

I'll use a couple of examples from my own experiences to explain these more clearly. A personal image might be seeing a woman, perhaps your own mother, holding a baby, or you. A mass mind image might be seeing a cartoon or advertisement of women with their babies. A memory field for me is seeing a walnut/pinecone in the womb which indicates a baby or a pearl for a special baby. A truth image might be seeing a woman floating on a giant lily pad, the giant leaves folding down from her in her sitting position on the lily pad. She may be floating down a huge river, which is the river of life, praying for a child to come to her. And I may see this image as a long drawn-out vision, with still more to come, as I float beside the woman in a slow moving silent film. Or, one sees a bird – and birds are always messengers – say a small live owl in one's mailbox one morning. The mail box is "personal," the owl is from "collective" imagery and one can look up the habits and life cycle of the particular type of owl. Then one can look up its meaning in a reference book such as Ted Andrew's Animal-Speak for the "mass mind" spiritual meaning related to you. And finally the "truth" imagery is the interpretation for the meaning in your life. Owls can mean a death or a rebirth or a dramatic change in one's life, so what would this be for you and how should you follow through to answer or understand the "message?" Sometimes these messages can come in sentences or in patterns of observations that happen over a series of days or weeks. These day visions or waking dreams arrive more and more frequently as one becomes more aware of them, especially now that the shift in consciousness or planetary changes are becoming easier to discern. Look for the unusual all around you, especially with animals, and then interpret what you have witnessed.

A good, more complex example of one of my waking dreams was related to teaching. When I was contemplating retiring - only I didn't know at the time that I was more likely changing professions – I witnessed several unusual bird messages over several weeks. I had a plan to work one more year which would give me my thirty years plus the other 6 that did not count in the state I was working in. So I knew that I was ready, although I was torn between my devotion to the children and my burn out with the system. I had one more year to go but that spring at the very end of school I fell down. I had been falling down once a year for the past five years due to my balance problems but was unaware that a single medication I was taking had increased the dizziness as I tried to work through my days at school. A week or so before this fall my husband was driving me to work because I didn't trust my balance at that time even while driving. I figured I had time to recover over the summer. We were a few blocks from school when a huge magpie flew straight down into our windshield from out of nowhere and broke its neck. This had never happened in my whole life as a driver or for my husband as a driver. A few days later I was at a quaint old-fashioned looking cottage restaurant with some girlfriends. The restaurant had one high ceiling room in it with high rafters. A small bird had somehow flown into the restaurant and was flying about the room dive bombing our food. The employees could not get it out of the room or the restaurant for that matter. They finally called animal control and we all sat in the room watching this man chase this little bird with a huge butterfly net. I couldn't eat for fear that the bird would be killed right in front of me. The man finally opened the emergency exit door at the end of our room and in a few minutes the bird found it and flew out the door unharmed.

A few days after this I was at another quaint shopping mall full of old transplanted houses from around the state surrounding an over one hundred year old mill. I ran into a woman I had done a reading for when she suddenly became a young widow with five children to take care of. I had been asked not to do any more such readings by a family member for any more of their friends or relatives because I was scaring them, and yet here was one of these relatives standing right there before me. Being curious, I asked if my reading of many years ago had been of help to her, or if it had scared her. She looked at me puzzled and then threw her arms around me and said that it had been the best thing for her at that time and she had really appreciated it. I noticed that she was buying lots of candles and knew that she worked in a different shop at the mall. I asked her why she was buying all the candles and she said that they had found a dead crow on the rug at the front of the shop and it had stunk up the building so badly, even with opening the windows in the place, that she had come over to this other shop to get candles to get rid of the remaining smell. Since all these occurrences were unusual and seemed to be connected together, I began to look up and interpret what these things meant.

Magpies, I found out, represented high intelligence, metaphysical knowledge, and use anything they find to help them out in discovering new ways to do tasks. They adapt easily to change and can help organize other birds. There is an old folk story that it was magpies that were the only birds that refused to get in Noah's Ark and perched instead on the roof of the ark. And from this came the folk myth that if you have magpies perch on the roof of your new house, it will never come down. Those that have this animal as a totem will enter the metaphysical world in an unusual way, and also experience these worlds in a different manner, just as magpies enter their homes from the side. But only seeing one magpie can be unlucky. On the other hand, magpies were often pets of alchemists or magicians and healers in the old days, so this magpie, having broken its neck, even had a message for me in that way, my protections were huge! But the questions on seeing this bird were right on for me. "Do you have knowledge and are not using it? Are you employing whatever skills you have to give the most you can? Are you using your knowledge and skills inappropriately?" Was I in a field where I was now not being allowed to help little children in all the many ways that I could? And with the spiritual and intuitive counseling that I had now attained, could I help a great deal more children and their families in a different way? Had I outgrown my usefulness in a system that restrained and imprisoned my ability to reach those who perhaps needed this knowledge and help? (*"Magpies," Animal-Speak by Ted Andrews, Llewellyn Publishing, 1998, pp. 165-66.*)

So I realized that the magpie had given me a message that if I kept teaching in public school I would not only really get hurt physically but also lose my spirit in the process. The second bird looked like a starling or a wren to me so I looked both of them up and gathered this information from Andrew's book also. Starlings are social and like to hang out in large flocks. They can teach you how to be more effective with groups or in communities of people. The thoughts that came up were things like feeling as if life is ganging up on you or that you are being mobbed by the crowd you hang out with. Being able to communicate in various ways or in many languages can help one to communicate more clearly and effectively. Wrens can outsmart other birds easily and make themselves invisible in a crowd. These birds are constantly singing from dawn to dusk, have lots of confidence and will easily confront other birds. "Are you using the resources available to you? Are you so wrapped up in daily worries that you are forgetting to sing? Are you not staying grounded? Are you not seeing the forest for the trees? Are you not attacking your life with enough gusto?" The second bird had found an exit door after a terrifying flight from what it surely thought would be its demise. It had found a way to escape from an imprisoned life, in a place where it no longer belonged. My only chance for spiritual freedom was to first find the exit door and then fly out it.

It took me a while to figure out the last one and being as it was a crow, this was quite significant. Crows, with great mysticism and mythology behind them since the very beginning of mankind, are guardians of the dreamtime. They are also sentinels to warn others of approaching danger from unseen worlds. They have a complex language in which each caw has a particular meaning. They can predict weather changes, warn others of approaching troubles and are closely associated with the magical worlds around us. Symbols of creation and spiritual strength they remind us to create magic in our daily lives. Keepers of sacred laws they can shape shift into whatever will aide them in their astral travels and find or create medicines to help heal people. An omen of change, they can see the interconnectedness of human laws and the laws of the Great Spirit. Crows can see the past, the present and the future simultaneously. They always stand in their own truth. "Be willing to walk your talk, speak your truth and know your life's mission, and balance past, present and future in the now. Shapeshift that old reality and become your future self. Allow bending of physical laws to aid in the shape shifting world of peace." (*"Medicine Cards by Jamie Sams and David Carson, Bear & Co., 1988, p. 133-134.*)

That the crow was found dead in this shop and at the same time I had run into a woman who could confirm my abilities as an intuitive counselor who worked in this regular gift shop, was very significant. The old me, as a teacher in the physical world, was now dead. I know knew that an absolute total change in everything I had been and done was coming, and it did. Yet it took me a while to understand that I was still a "teacher." Only now I was free to teach in a myriad of ways and had really not left the children behind. They were now, instead, even more available to me, as the new children coming in and changing their own ways quite dramatically. I, as an older woman, had been given the opportunity to fly with them, with the otherworldly knowledge that I had, the bravery that I had, and the expertise from many worlds and experiences that I had acquired over the years. I would not "die" on that front door mat, but instead, I would find a way to light candles - candles that would lead me forward to assist and help these little children and their families navigate the unknown territories that were coming. So I did not break my neck when I fell and I did not go back to teaching after that summer. I did accept my physical body for what it was, no more, no less. When I recovered I spent over a year reflecting on my spiritual and intuitive life. I did fly out the exit door offered me, unharmed. I did begin to accept my night classes and my teachers from the other side, and I found my spiritual "place." And finally, I accepted that I was indeed, a "teacher!" In the acceptance of this intuitive life, I found peace and comfort and joy, even though I realized that I would essentially walk this path alone. But I had friends, you just sometimes couldn't see them!

Since then I have collected my own vocabulary of images from my own experience (personal), the experiences of others (collective), and universal symbols from cultures all over the world (mass mind). The (truth) imagery comes from both the universal stream of consciousness and the beings who deliver messages to the person sitting in front of me. I am merely the vehicle in all of this. But there are reference books where one can look up animal, plant, and tree imagery interpretations, color and iconic symbols from around the world when images arrive in one's intuitive reading. As an intuitive counselor I have my experience, common sense, training and listening skills to guide me. But I also get this "channeled" information to take me down the right pathways for each person that I see. Along with this are images and silent movie pictures which I follow and also let lead me. Much more rarely, a person I am seeing has a visitation, brought by an angel or light being on the request of a relative, ancestor, or loved one, because the crisis they are in is very severe. What is essential to know is that it is all in the interpretation of what one sees or hears or feels or touches. The information is never wrong, but the interpretation can be. One must have no doubt, no fear, and no hesitation, and persist until the information is interpreted as accurately as possible at the time.

I find it best to simply convey the information and let the person interpret this with only minimal assistance from me, if the person is in touch intuitively. When they are not in touch, it is much more difficult to do this. But I know I have to give the information to the person anyway so that I will not carry it emotionally. Perhaps this will help you understand just how your child feels when the first awakenings come to them and they are frustrated and confused by these images. And I only mention this because these challenges could be happening in your child now, and think how overwhelming this can be. Many of the new sets of children coming in are more advanced and things may be happening much more quickly for them without an intuitive compass to guide them. Discussing the details and going over and over such experiences can really help. When I woke up again, I read as many biographies and autobiographies of psychics as I could find and this helped to guide and comfort me, as I knew at the time would.

One year a young woman from South America came to this country for three months to receive medical and holistic help for her serious injuries from a car accident that happened when she was a teenager. She was 26 years old and could not pay for any of these services. So her friends in America put together a "team" of people who never met each other who volunteered their time. She saw medical doctors, chiropractors and others for her treatments and I was contacted to be the intuitive counselor for her because she was very intuitive herself and had obviously had at least one near-death experience already. I saw her several times over the three months. When we started out she had to have an interpreter come with her and finding out that she liked to draw, I handed her a drawing pad so she would not be bored while waiting for the interpreter to interpret her words. During our sessions, she learned to speak English and the last times I saw her we could converse without an interpreter, but she continued to draw.

As she drew, I began to realize just how intuitive she was. And as she asked me questions more and more clearly, I was astonished at what she needed to know from me and at the depth of her questions. Not only did we eventually speak mind to mind telepathically, but her drawings amazed me. She had drawn for example all of the icons and universal images from every major religion in the world but did not know what she had drawn. I only recognized enough of them to know that this was what she was doing, and I can remember wondering if some of the symbols were from lesser known ones from the past or even some from other worlds that neither of us knew much about. She also drew an upturned palm with a geometric shape in the palm and inside this was a triangle and inside that was a flame which I recognized as a healer's hands. The young woman wanted to marry, but I felt she had a larger mission through her near-death as a spiritual teacher, though perhaps she could do this while married. When she left she had gone from a wheelchair to walking without her crutches for short distances and I felt privileged to have known her. I have always felt that she was going straight to "the Source" as it is called and what she intuited were "Truth" images all the time.

Developing a Family or Tribe of Intuitives

In the book Psychic Families by Casandra Eason, the author talks about fifteen ways of encouraging positive psychic family bonds. Obviously this British psychic might have been born into a family of psychics in a nurturing and creative atmosphere. And there are many such people, such as John Edward and Sylvia Browne, who did not have to experience being wounded or having to find their own way through things such as only child, Lisa Williams. But many others were wounded and Eason tries to address what should happen for an intuitive child. These are her suggestions for the openly psychic parents and their children, or even more rare, the psychically aware family. She says to keep a Psychic Family Book which can contain family legends, and everyday examples of telepathic predictions. Even natural cures for illnesses can be kept in this scrapbook. Dreams and stressful situations and how the family solved them, can also be chronicled in the family book. Part of this book could contain a baby scrapbook. That includes the mother's precognitive experiences before she had her baby, as well as incidents with the infant, as the child grows up that were paranormal in nature.

Eason also suggests trusting one's instincts and tactfully making inquiries of another family member who may be having some difficulties, at any age. She says to save these interventions for those times when one feels an instinctive right to enquire, or a family member feels that something is wrong. She said, it is important to protect the family against hostile vibrations from the outside world, or fears, which could conjure up anxieties within. Making a specific time every week, when all the family can link up either in the physical world or through mental telepathy, can remind all of the family members, that they are not alone and they can gain a few extra positive vibrations from each other. She also suggests that the family spend time together and not just dash from one activity to the next. During this time, the family can reinforce the family history through telling famous family stories, folklore, and especially stories from the older generations that can be told to the younger generations.

She also suggests that one doesn't force a child to be independent from the home before he or she is ready. She encourages family members to discuss all kinds of experiences so that the children can feel that family members are open to hearing about their otherworldly experiences, and include discussions about near-death, death, and the afterlife. Always accept dreams and visions, not as prophecies of doom, but as clues to the inner dynamics of the family. Encourage simple family rituals for each member of the family, letting children pick instinctively the things that may help to drive away a headache or a nightmare, etc. Cut down on the second-hand living with television, DVDs, computer games, etc. and let the family get to know each other as real individuals. Concentrate on priorities in family life, and remember that time is infinite. Value the unique qualities of each family member and make sure that everyone understands that true togetherness does not mean conformity.

Always include new family members in the psychic and emotional life of the family, such as stepchildren, in-laws, and new partners after a divorce. Don't try to be too perfect as a parent, grandparent, child or partner. Anxiety, guilt and unrealistic expectations can actually block one's thinking and other insights. And last she says, that even with all of this, there will be family members, who will sow the seeds of their own self-destruction. Parents can have the attitude that they only believe in what they see and prove, or they may forbid the child to speak of intuitions in or outside the home. They may say it is all in the imagination of the child or that such talk is evil. They may worry that others will think the child crazy. They may be afraid for their child in terms of scaring others away or think the child has no way of knowing such things. Some parents really instill fear in their children by telling them never to speak of such things again, or anything like this is the work of the devil. Children who experience these sorts of things without ever being able to change their situation, and really trying to change it, just have to walk away when all else has failed, and create or find their own psychic family, rather than be destroyed. (*Psychic Families by Cassandra Eason, foulsham Publishing House: London & New York, 1995,pp.177-182*).

Generational Intuitive Families & Cultural Intuitive Groups

This also brings up the topic of families of intuitives or even cultural groups where these awarenesses are fostered or have been fostered historically. After all, primitive people were much more in touch with the natural world than we are today and therefore much more in touch with their intuitive natures. For example, in the Huna culture in Hawaii, centuries ago, those children discovered to be intuitive were sent to live with a known intuitive family in the village for several years while they learned the proper behavior for using their talents with others, and then they returned to their own family for the rest of their upbringing. Still, I was baffled by something else I had observed in my various classrooms over the years. I wondered why I would get certain children from a certain ethnic group who seemed to have an innate intuitive ability that could not have come from their cultural, ethnic or even their family and community upbringing, perhaps because they had been adopted, or perhaps because they showed no signs of having been raised to know anything about their own cultural background. Where did it come from then I asked myself? And I have absolutely no proof of my own theory on this except my years of experience as a teacher of all ethnic and cultural groups in my various classrooms over the years.

But taking the example of Native American children born in the city and never having any training in their background as far as how Native American groups educated their children through nature, these children would come into my room still learning in these ways even though schools never accommodated this style of learning. Of course some of their parent's up bringing could have rubbed off on them along the way, but still, they almost seemed to have a cellular memory of how they should be taught and this was the way I had to teach them in order for them to learn. Perhaps "the calling of the ancestors" in many primitive cultures still has an important place in the minds, hearts, and cellular memories for our future generations, whether we are aware of this or not! But it is my thought that we should be aware, that we have an obligation to be aware, and that the fifth world coming, according to the Hopi elders, will be one with this evolutionary knowledge already in place.

"Filling your own intuitive cup, and knowing what it feels like to be witnessed and supported is also fuel for being able to do the same for the child in your life. It is never too late to fill this cup for yourself and harness the creative power of this trait in your life. In addition to the relationships that can heal old wounds from childhood, you can also benefit from building an intuitive tribe. These are people who share or at least value and can appreciate your intuitive abilities. These are friends with whom you don't need to worry about sharing the depths of who you are. You don't need to hide. With these kindred spirits, you can share the ups and downs of living with heightened abilities and enjoy the support of others who know the lay of the land." (*Ibid., Crawford, p.185*).

Specific Types of Intuitive Children

The easiest topics to cover first are the types of intuition, which Goode and Paterson cover in their book Raising Intuitive Children. Rather than naming the better known sensory gifts of clairvoyance or visual impressions; clairaudience or hearing sounds, tones, voices; clairsentience or touch impressions; and clairkinetic or feeling and moving things; they name them in a better way. They call them: Physical Intuition, Mental/

Creative Intuition, Emotional/Social Intuition, Psychic Intuition, and Spiritual Intuition. Physical Intuition means exceptional motor skills, awareness of body movements and positioning in space, these people often become athletes and dancers. Mental/Creative Intuition encompasses daydreamers and inventors who are the internal geniuses who can focus on a problem and solve it faster than anyone else. These people often become pioneering scientists, engineers, mathematicians, inventors and are often influential and very self-sufficient. Emotional/Social Intuitives can read others, feel others, they also have good emotional intelligences and management skills. These people are often motivational speakers, counselors, teachers and healers who have excellent people skills whether shy or outgoing. Psychic Intuitives use all of the sensory gifts mentioned above, but have particularly sharper skills in some areas over others. They can be visual, hearing, tactile, sensing and kinetic. They have an expanded awareness of non-physical worlds and energy fields, etc. Spiritual Intuitives walk that bridge between the physical world and the non-physical worlds, explore inner worlds and foster better communications between cultural, ethnic and theological groups. These people often seek a deeper meaning in life, have a greater sense of inner peace and can internally center themselves. They will become either a spiritual teacher, clergy, or have a reclusive spiritual life. So obviously, these types of intuitives can also merge or be integrative with more than one "type." (*Goode, Caron B. and Paterson, Tara. Raising Intuitive Children, New Page Books: Franklin Lakes, New Jersey, 2009, pp. 28-29.)*

Spiritual Intuitives & the New Children

In Raising Intuitive Children, Goode and Paterson say that children who are in this category can find doorways to interpret and connect with inner worlds. They believe in a power greater than themselves and have a special connection to nature. Spiritual beliefs can be gained through a spiritual crisis experience or through training within a family, community, or culture. Concerned the most with their inner life and deeper insights into various levels of consciousness, they are very aware of their relationship to the transcendent. This spiritual intelligence can give these particular intuitives, an "old soul" appearance. They have a wisdom and goodness beyond their years or peers. They instinctively trust in the mystery and magic of life and they have a great concern for people, animals, and the earth itself. Goode and Paterson also offer some tips for spiritually connecting with your child, no matter what your belief system is, your particular culture dictates, what religious beliefs you hold, or family values you subscribe too.

These tips include viewing your child as a whole being, a child with understandings way beyond their peers, and a child who connects with his or her parents in a reflective manner. Learn to follow your child rather than leading your child and pay attention to your child's behavior when they are around other people. Be able to nurture your own feelings and emotions while still guiding this spiritual child, who can really sap your energy, because they are so intense in everything that they do. These children need special help with identifying their functions or ways to cope with life. Always acknowledge their true feelings, and expect them to behave. Consider the qualities that you want your child to have later in life and help your child recognize and foster his or her intuition and other special gifts by teaching awareness and living in the present moment. These children need to develop a warning system to keep them from being too trusting. But of course like all empathic children, they need to know boundaries between their feelings and something else that they have connected themselves to. (*Ibid., Raising Intuitive Children, pp.147, 155, 156, 157*).

Tuning In & Out of Intuitive Channels

With having more "channels" open than the less intuitive person does, the psychic child has to learn to tune in, tune out, slow down, or lower or raise the volume on their own personal "radio." These children are not only tuning into the regular channels but the family, peer, school, community, country and planetary "channels" and have to learn how to differentiate between all these channels, but also how to manage this flood of information, sorting it all out and only allowing in what they can handle at any given moment. Their life can really be complicated when they cannot learn to do this. Catherine Crawford says that the three most important channels for children are the "Family Channel," the "Peer-Classroom Channel" and the "World Channel." With each of these channels the child may pick up on other's feelings, accidentally connect channels together, pick up on worries or disasters, and know information about others.

Beyond these three basic channels that children usually deal with are many more "channels" or radio stations. The child must learn methods for switching off all these other channels when they need to focus on the physical world. As an adult they will be bombarded with many physical world channels and many alternate dimensional world channels, all at once. If they do not have guidance they will think that they are going crazy or be accused of focusing on too many negative outcomes, or sometimes even be diagnosed with an obsessive-compulsive disorder, when in reality some may have started out instead, with an undiscovered intuitive talent which has bombarded them to the point of obsession. All intuitives share the same empathic characteristics which appear to others as being spacy, distracted or unable to follow directions, because they are channeling information from other realms, while trying to remain focused on the physical world. For me, I find keeping to a consistent chronological order concerning the person's life while doing a reading, helps to keep me on only one channel and I don't drift off too far into a brother or sister's channel, etc. Nor do I drift off into a peer or world channel so readily.

When Gordon-Michael Scallion began to receive terrible images of natural and man-made disasters from all over the world, 24 hours a day non-stop for several years in a row, he found a way to turn this into something positive rather than succumbing to what was suddenly bombarding him. He began a newsletter with his predictions in hopes that he would help those who lived in these areas prepare themselves anyway they could, but he also got his many confirmations that a majority of his predictions were accurate. When this "channel" closed up abruptly, just as it had come on abruptly, he was well on his way to receiving much more positive information from various other "channels." He originally found ways not to fear or doubt what was happening to him, which then led him to the right questions and details that would confirm his abilities. However, he was an adult when this happened to him, and still went through a huge spiritual awakening that affected every area of his life, including his health.

Think what a child might go through when confronted with this sort of overwhelming incoming information, once they are not in their trance-like state of those early years in childhood before the age of seven. Developmentally they are prepared for this imagination time in the pre-school years, but when they are supposed to move on into their "mind" time in the elementary school years and there is no one there to guide them through these intuitive "mind fields," all sorts of internal and sometimes external things can happen with the intuitive child. The mixed messages they receive from their caregivers can be very confusing. It is absolutely vital for caregivers to help them to learn how to tune in to these channels and how to tune them out when necessary, even if the caregivers don't experience this or even believe this is happening to their child. Empowerment for the child comes from acknowledging something is going on, discussing every incident or experience chronologically and in detail, and devising ways to manage these channels by whatever means, such as visualizing a water faucet turning on and then turning off, a radio being turned on and off, putting a hat on and then taking if off, etc. Focusing on one channel persistently and in detail can really help.

Here is an example of floating off into a world channel. It is also my own theory that our individual experiences and interests are what are most likely to interfere with staying focused on one channel at a time. I was in a reading once when suddenly a Chinese Buddha figure floating in a golden triangle appeared in my mind's eye, a ridiculously oversized bullet shot through the center of the Buddha's chest and red streamers came out the other side like those on a fan. This figure was floating in the air and had nothing at all to do with the reading I was doing except that the theme at the time was fathers and sons. I returned to the reading and completed it. A few days later I heard that Bruce Lee's son had just died and later heard one of the conspiracy theories on Lee and his son that included a secret organization in China called The Golden Triangle who had not liked Lee bringing the secrets of martial arts to the United States and threatened to kill Lee and any sons he had, or at least put a curse on them. Of course his son was killed on the set of a movie by a gun shooting blanks and one of these blanks strangely misfired. I have always wondered if Brandon Lee was shot in the chest. It took me even longer to try and figure out why I would pick up on this particular tragedy when I was "open" and on a different "channel." I concluded that I loved martial arts movies, had some sort of affinity for things Chinese, and the reading I was doing at the time did have a connection concerning a son learning to understand his father's actions after the father had passed on and not wishing to repeat his father's mistakes with his own children.

Sometimes one wanders off channel in a dream. I had a day vision where I was with many other people wandering around through hundreds of clotheslines with giant ribbed pieces of wet cardboard hanging on them. We were all in a daze and trying to find our way out of this maze. A few days after this there was a very large Tsunami reported somewhere in the world, I forget where. I knew the dream was connected to this but did not remember that there had to be a huge underwater earthquake for a Tsunami of this size and magnitude to happen. At school we taught about earthquakes every year as part of the science curriculum. I always used pieces of ribbed cardboard to demonstrate the types of faults and each of the children made their own "fault" cardboards. When I realized this, I then had to figure out if I had had a dream, a premonition or had really been there with the other people right after the disaster, or all three. I concluded from the intensity and lucidity of my feelings that I had dreamed about it ahead of time and had perhaps experienced being there with the survivors of this disaster while it was actually happening. But I knew for certain that I had gone from a world channel into my teacher classroom channel in a waking dream.

A third kind of example is where the connection was more obvious and closer to home, a young teenage boy had gone down a dangerous old mining shaft on his own, and had not come home. The news broke on the television that they had found him and he was down there alive waiting for the rescuers to reach him. This rescue went on for days and the mine was so dangerous that the rescuers were afraid of killing the boy by trying to rescue him with all of the dangerous debris and collapsing tunnels, etc. All during this time I could not sleep, had a terribly uneasy feeling and finally had a dream about the boy. I knew I hated closed spaces, that he was still alive, and that being underground was smothering for me. I floated into the tunnel and straight down the slowly inclining shaft, until I reached a shelf where the young man lay face-up on this shelf. His face was like a white mask and I had seen this before on beaches where people were crossing the great water or the river or lake or ocean of death, crossing over to the other side. But the dirt around his face was moving which indicated to me that he was unconscious but still breathing.

As I looked down at him I saw that one of his sneakers was lying away from his body on its side with the strings ribboning out from it on the ground. I felt myself being very anxious and upset until I looked to the other side of the shaft and there floating in the air was a 12-foot high light being or angel. This androgynous being had long blonde hair and was really handsome. The figure looked at me very piercingly and lovingly, then raised its arm and pointed to where the boy was laying as I floated in my mind's eye above the barely alive young man. I suddenly felt relieved and comforted, that this being was letting me know that the boy was not alone, that he was with him and that I did not need to worry any longer. I woke up sweating with tears on my face, and yet I felt at peace about this boy who I had worried about for days down in that shaft because I knew he was still alive. A day or two later I was actually walking downtown on a busy street and I suddenly stopped in the middle of the sidewalk and knew at that precise moment, that the young man in the mine shaft had just stopped breathing. Because of the dream, I did not mourn, but instead felt the burden of knowing about this young man's still breathing, lift off my shoulders. I felt a strong sense of relief for both for the boy and for myself when I felt the young man die. It was over, and he had never been alone at all, down in that shaft. This "being of light," that looked like an angel had been with him all the time.

I told a friend about this dream and a couple of days later she called me early in the morning and asked if I had read the paper yet. I said no and she said go get it and read it and call her back. It seems that when they had called off the search, his uncle had secretly gone down the shaft and brought the boy's body up from a 30 feet deep pile of debris at the bottom of the shaft, late the night before with the help of other family members. All of the times had been connected somehow to the number ten and I had told my friend this. Around ten o'clock at night was when the two rescuers went out there, the first attempt by the family had been around the same time the night before, and several other events were connected to that number. This uncle had been unable to sleep too, knowing his nephew was alive. And this would have been it except that I caught a late night interview program on TV totally by chance, although I even wonder about this, where a newsman was interviewing this uncle. What the man said was never in any of the papers or on the news. He had taken oranges with him for his water and food and had gotten to the bottom of the shaft where the body had fallen and it was under about thirty feet of debris. He had to dig for a long time but said he had dug about ten feet into the debris when he found his nephew's body and as he tried to pull him out, one of his feet was stuck and for a while he thought he would have to cut the foot off in order to get the rest of his nephew's body out. At that moment I felt as though a knife had gone through my heart and I had chills running up and down my spine. This huge, strong man began weeping just a little and so did I. There was the sneaker lying on its side with the shoe strings ribboning out, only there might have been a foot inside the shoe had things happened differently.

The biggest difficulty for me was knowing a different scenario than the one the media told, that the boy had fallen all the way to the bottom and had died on impact, face down and immediately. What I saw was the young man, face up and barely alive lying on a shelf and when the rescuers tried to get down the shaft, the whole shelf collapsed and the boy fell to the bottom. This was what killed him. It was no one's fault. The old mine shaft was dangerous and unsafe and sure to do this anyway, disturbed even a little bit by several men trying to get to this boy. It was all very precarious. As an empathic person, the hardest part was carrying around this feeling of the boy being alive and knowing I could do nothing. As an interloper on the scene in my dream, the angel had let me see his comforting and steady watch over the boy – I had always seen the angel as male in this case, even though I knew he was androgynous – and this vision had allowed me to begin sleeping again at night. It also allowed me to stop on that busy street when I knew the boy's heart had stopped and feel this great sense of relief, although I stood there silently weeping inside and probably looked a bit strange to anyone walking by.

Nowadays I am much more capable of tuning in and out. But those connections are still there and my theory is that the reader has a special connection to certain people and events because of their own life experiences. I have a special connection to children, PTSD and soldiers, and animals, among other things. So when being "flooded" by a lot of people in a large space, knowing when to "tune in and out" has to be developed as an art form for one's own safety and peace of mind. However, you can be taken by surprise upon occasion, and maybe even often, if you are in a line of work like Nancy Weber and Allison DuBois, solving crimes with the police. In which case, you have to be doubly careful to focus on the details and remain on only one "channel" at a time, keeping your emotions in check as much as possible. A gimmick of some kind to remind you to pay attention, and focusing on the details nearly always works! On even rarer occasions you may have to forcefully extricate yourself from the "scene!"

How Others Belief Systems Can Shut Down an Intuitive Child

Messages of protecting your child from becoming "crazy" or at least looking crazy in front of others is a great way to push your intuitive child into hiding. A message that you want your child to be able to function in the physical world regardless of where that child might be coming from can also help your child to wear a mask in order to be accepted. Dismissing your child's abilities as a vivid imagination or even saying proudly to others that your child is gifted as a storyteller or writer, can still cause the intuitive child to shut down. Remaining neutral towards your child and saying that none of this stuff exists or simply saying don't talk about such things, can also shut down your child. And scaring them is one of the worst forms of denying them their own power as an intuitive, such as the idea of the black and white concept of good and evil, rather than life's "grays," or with the fact that your child is burdened by everyone's emotions and therefore many will either not understand them or fear them, etc. Simply acknowledging the possibility of things that cannot be proven is a great start and as Catherine Crawford states: "I know of no greater gift that can be given to children than their knowing they are loved and accepted for being themselves. It is like bedrock for the personality, like a deep well to drink from and a gift that no one can take away." (*Ibid, the highly intuitive child, pp. 49*).

Supporting Children When They Are Intuitive

Pre-school children, who receive support, progress with their specific gifts, no matter what they are, whether intuitive, creative or anything else. They really do not move into linear thinking and cognition until they are around seven years old. Since their intellectual development takes over at this time, they have to set aside their intuitive intelligence for a while. However, psychic gifts have to be utilized and supported, or they will disappear for quite some time. While the child is developing in school, you can still support their interactions with worlds beyond and their empathic, intuitive nature. In this way they can develop the vocabulary that they need to describe things that are happening to them. These children can bond with animals and nature and continue to keep their imaginations and intuitive experiences, alive. They often find an art form that they love and continue to development their emotional empathy for others. This is also the time that children are developing their mental telepathy skills. Interactions with the nonphysical world can be either fun or frightening.

The childhood years are an awesome time for these types of things to develop. Just be sure to really listen to the things that they tell you and help them to differentiate all of these experiences. On the other hand, if children are discouraged from speaking about these otherworldly experiences they can find these particular years very difficult. Children want to keep their sensitivity, but may also be told by teachers and other children to put their imagination away and focus on their schooling. They may be pulled between these two worlds, their rich emotional life and their intellectual common sense. They can become either emotionally sensitive or emotionally volatile as they take this journey into the school years. They really need to learn to manage and organize their lives to balance the intuitive with the intellectual.

What Causes Intuition to Develop Beyond Genetics?

Most people know that super psychic talents run in super psychic families and some people know that it can often skip a generation or at least be suppressed by individuals in a particular generation for a myriad of reasons. But there are lots of other theories on why psychic abilities suddenly improve or broaden, or even just appear out of nowhere! Being struck by lightning or having a long illness, being in a car accident or going through a spiritual crisis of one kind or another can make one not only more aware of one's own abilities, but also increase one's abilities as well. Meditation is a powerful way to broaden, increase and deepen all of one's intuitive talents. Exposure to these types of things and training in them can also increase one's psychic abilities. The cultural beliefs of a nation of people can either foster these abilities or bury them, or living in a particular community can foster their growth. The new wave of brain shifted children coming in will demand our attention when it comes to intuition.

> "From the left side of your body comes your female energy, whether you are a man or a woman. Within this femaleness, this feminine consciousness lives your intuition. Intuition is the intelligence of your body-mind, rather than know what is true with your mind. Intuition does not have the clouds of accumulated knowledge to distort your vision. Intuition simply sees what is truth. With intuition you can feel the source of your being filled without reasoning it

away and being filled with doubt. Doubt destroys intuition. Find your power always in balance between mind and intuition."

--"Intuition" The Power Deck by Lynn Andrews

"We urge you to take your experiences of your child's deeper nature into the quietness of your heart and learn from them...Spiritual parenting is based on the river of God, the love that flows between hearts...But in the heart of God no child is assigned a role that is spiritually less important than the role of any other child...How do we work to bestow such an inheritance on our children? We love them; we understand them; we respect them; we honor them. We commit absolutely to never losing sight of their basic nature, no matter what age or stage they are in...We do not forget who they are."

--Ibid, Spiritual Parenting, pp. 23, 34,38, 64–65.

"You are being given the doorways to forever."

--Ibid., p.110

Chief Seattle's Prayer

"Every part of this earth is sacred to my people. Every shining needle, every sandy shore, every mist in the dark woods, every meadow, every humming insect. All are holy in the memory and experience of my people. We know the sap which courses through our veins. We are part of the earth and it is part of us. The perfumed flowers are our sisters. The bear, the deer, the great eagle, these are our brothers."

"The rocky crests, the juices in the meadow, the body heat of the pony, and man, belong to the same family. The shining water that moves in the streams and rivers is not just water, but the blood of our ancestors. Each ghostly reflection in the clear water of the lakes tells of events and memories in the life of my people. The water's murmur is the voice of my father's father. The rivers are our brothers. They quench our thirst. They carry our canoes and feed our children. So you must give to the rivers the kindness you would give any children."

"Will you teach your children what we have taught our children? That the earth is our mother? What befalls the earth, befalls all the sons of the earth. This we know: the earth does not belong to man, man belongs to the earth. All things are connected like the blood which unites us all. Man did not weave the web of life, he is merely a strand in it. Whatever he does to the web, he does to himself."

--This shortened version of a much longer speech, was given by Chief Seattle to the white fathers in 1855 and adapted in the present by Sarah Judith Cole

"A human being is part of the whole called by us universe, a part limited in time and space. We experience ourselves, our thoughts and feelings, as something separate from the rest. Which is a kind of optical delusion of consciousness. The delusion is a kind of prison to us, restricting us to our personal desires and to affection for a few persons nearest us."

--Albert Einstein

"When we play with the Little Ones, the angels play with the stars. The power of play opens up the play gates of the universe where we all play with the Creator – a joyous play, a game of love, giving and receiving. Honor and learn from the Little Ones intent to play. They will teach us the innocence in their hearts that embrace unconditional love. They shall inherit the earth with this love… Through peace they are teaching us a greater understanding of humanity."

--"The Power of Play: Gateway to the niverse," the indigo Children, p. 125

CHAPTER THREE

MOST COMMON MISLABELINGS ATTACHED TO INTUITIVE ABILITIES

"It is better to build children, than to repair men."
--anonymous

"The beginning of wisdom is calling things by their right name."
--Chinese Proverb

"Every young thing…is incapable of remaining calm in body or in voice, but always seeks to move and cry: young things leap and jump as if they were dancing with pleasure and playing together, and emit all sorts of cries."
--Plato, The Laws

Types of Mislabeling

We must also briefly cover the topic of mislabeled children, or at least the forgotten types of problems that can come up for intuitive children, rarely addressed by doctors, counselors or in the schools. A very good exception, written by two doctors, Brock Eide and Fernette Eide, The Mislabeled Child, uniquely addresses correct assessments of various childhood difficulties and even offers interesting ways to find solutions. Often due to lack of funding or ignorance on the part of school specialists and teachers, or perhaps even laziness in seeking specific information these areas are: "Mislabeled Attention Deficit children or dreamers; mislabeled Attention Deficit/Hyperactive Deficit children who are too active to be tolerated in the school systems as they are structured at present. Then there is Oppositional Defiance Disorder and Obsessive Compulsive Disorder and these are the ones we will discuss in depth in this chapter concerning intuitive children. I will discuss Aspergers or Autistic or Autistic-Like challenges related to intuitive children and sensory integration a little later.

Attention Deficit & Attention Deficit Hyperactivity

ADD or ADHD are the most often diagnosed difficulties for children and children are usually showing the symptoms before seven years of age. This is mainly a childhood difficulty because most adults who continue to have these problems find other ways to cope with the things that interfere with them being able to function in their daily lives. Around 5% of American adults live with these two difficulties. About 5% of the children of the world are diagnosed with this problem and around 16% of school-age children are diagnosed with these two parallel problems globally. The attention deficit/hyperactive type is diagnosed two to four times more frequently in boys than in girls. No one knows for sure if this because boys cause more problems in the classroom bringing attention to themselves, while girls tend to go inward and display regular, attention deficit disorder with no hyperactivity. When these types of disorders became popular in the 1970s, they soon also became controversial. Everyone was arguing about whether this was really a disorder, what caused it, and should medications really be used for it.

There are actually three types, the first is called <u>hyperactive-impulsive</u> in which at least six symptoms are predominant, along with displaying the symptoms for more than six months in two different settings. Symptoms for this type of behavior include: fidgeting and squirming in their seats, nonstop talking, dashing around, touching and playing with things obsessively, trouble sitting at home, at school and at story time, constantly in motion, and difficulty doing quiet tasks or activities. The second type is called <u>inattentive</u>, but once again, the child must have six or more symptoms for longer than six months in two different settings, but these children are less likely to act out or have difficulties getting along with other children. Some of the symptoms of this type include: being distracted, missing details, forgetting things, difficulty focusing, bored with certain tasks, poor organization, trouble completing tasks, difficulty listening, day dreaming, easily confused, difficulty processing information, difficulty following directions, and changing too quickly from one activity to another while some of the symptoms for hyperactive-impulsive can also be present in the child with inattentive difficulties. The third type is called <u>hyperactive-impulsive and inattentive</u>, and this type is a combination of the other two types with the acting out behavior added onto this. This is the mega type, which includes all of the other symptoms along with impatience, blurting out inappropriate comments, showing their emotions without restraint, acting without regard for consequences, and having difficulty waiting for things. But these problem behaviors must appear before age 7, and then continue consistently for over six months. These behaviors must also interfere with two or more of the following settings in the child's life: classroom, playground, home, community, and social settings.

Medical conditions that could cause similar symptoms in children, which are not related to a diagnosis of an attention deficit problem, include: hypothyroidism, anemia, lead poisoning, chronic illness, or vision impairment, substance abuse, medication side effects, sleep impairment or child abuse. Other types of conditions that may be triggering these behaviors and show that the child does not have ADHD include: a sudden change in the family, a death or divorce, seizures, an ear infection, a learning disability, anxiety disorder or depression, sleep disturbances and child abuse. 60% of children diagnosed continue to have symptoms as adults. Adult ADHD sufferers most often find a variety of addictions to anesthetize their chaotic and disorganized lifestyles. They may also begin to show a higher incidence of such things as depression, anxiety disorder, bipolar disorder, substance abuse or a learning disability. But again, was the learning disability always there and simply manifested itself in adulthood? Or was the learning disability caused secondarily by the ADHD? And the same with all of the other psychological disorders that manifest themselves in adulthood, do they accompany the ADD or manifest later?

These particular behaviors or disorders exist separately, and only in about a third of the children diagnosed with ADD. The other two thirds can have an additional or even more than two types of diagnosis. Those that appear the most frequently are: oppositional defiance disorder which includes other behaviors such as stubbornness, aggression, frequent temper tantrums, deceitfulness, lying, stealing or a weak sense of right and wrong. There is also borderline personality disorder, which seems to appear more in girls than boys. Other types of things that appear frequently, alongside ADD include something called primary disorder vigilance, which simply means poor attention concentration skills, as well as difficulty staying awake. And last, are the mood disorders, bipolar obsessive, obsessive-compulsive disorder, and anxiety disorder, which seem to appear more in girls. The only one of these that has a genetic component definitely identified with it is obsessive-compulsive disorder.

There are some studies that support the idea that the child's learning style, when addressed and adapted for, can help the child to avoid taking medication while in school. One study says that if the child is allowed to move about the classroom or stand at their desk, it will help them stay alert enough to complete tasks and focus on their schoolwork. There are studies to support this idea. There are some recent studies which also indicate that there may be some neurological developmental damage, or even just neurological damage contributing to this need to be constantly on the move. Another theory proposes that ADHD children who need that excessive activity are actually using self stimulation to pull themselves out of a low arousal state. In other words, they cannot attend to things without using environmental stimuli. Children with ADHD cannot self moderate their attention to tasks without enough stimulation from the environment and therefore they must walk about and talk to induce the ability to attend. There is also some evidence that this particular need is caused by abnormalities in neurochemicals in the body which may have caused the neurological damage in the first place.

"ADD and occasionally ADHD share a couple of characteristics in common with some intuitive children; notably, distractibility and occasional spaciness. The two are quite different, however, as are their remedies. It is widely believed that symptoms of ADD are caused by an imbalance of chemicals in the neurotransmitter fluids in the brain, and because of this, treatment is targeted at rebalancing these levels, usually through psychotropic medications. The occasional spaciness or distractibility that comes with being highly intuitive, empathic, on the other hand, stems from dealing with things like multiple intuitive impressions arriving all at once. Researchers are trying to figure out where a sudden empathic pain or transmission is coming from." Young children with past life memories can also display many symptoms of ADHD, because they become distracted and obsessive about this other life that they remember. (*Ibid., Crawford, p.63*).

It also becomes obvious that children can be mislabeled or misdiagnosed, especially highly intuitive children, or any child for that matter. Intuitive children certainly have sleep difficulties, which can make children very irritable, anxious or depressed or moody. Problem solving and memory skills can suffer when the child is not getting enough sleep which can be caused by internal or external disruptions, or both. Some research suggests that the central nervous system centers, that regulate sleep and also regulate attention arousal, is playing a role in the ADD symptoms of inattention and poor behavioral regulation. Sleepiness in children ranges from simply yawning and rubbing their eyes to the extreme behaviors of impulsivity, hyperactivity, aggressiveness, moodiness, and inattentiveness that denies the child sleep. However, later in this book, there is an entire chapter devoted to all of the sleep difficulties that intuitive empathic children can experience and what to do about them. Many of the exercises and activities will help any child with a myriad of sleep difficulties.

A combination of factors is being studied for causes of ADD and ADHD. Among them is a genetic factor, which many experts agree might be the main cause for 75% of the cases. There is even a theory that these children retain evolutionary "hunter" characteristics in their genetic makeup, which is manifested as searching and seeking rather than staying put in one place. Other studies show that manifestations or causes of these disorders include mothers using alcohol and tobacco while they are pregnant, pregnancy and birth complications such as infections, head injuries, exposures to certain insecticides and pesticides, and food colorings. Studies have been done in other countries on particular artificial food colorings, which were dangerous enough to have those countries begin to phase out these particular artificial food colorings from processed foods. The food products containing what the United Kingdom calls the "Southampton Six" are: sunset yellow FCF (E110), quinoline yellow (E104), carmoisine (E122), alura red (E129), tartazine (E102), and ponceau 4R (E124). Britain is phasing these out, but the United States and the FDA have only taken the following steps: artificial food colorings must be approved by the FDA, colors must be indicated on the food package or at least the numbers for the food colorings must be present on the package. Since this is quite recent information, be sure and check the labels on all processed foods that you may be feeding your children, whether they have been diagnosed with ADD or ADHD or not. (Check out the bibliography for several sources on nutrition and herbals concerning ADD children and also check out Phyllis Balch's section in her Nutritional Healing book on ADHD and ADD.)

Social-emotional factors include such things as family dysfunction, post traumatic stress disorder, and something, I as a teacher was well aware of when teaching, children with this disorder also have sensory integration problems. It is interesting to note, that foster children have a much higher number of these symptoms, as do children who suffer violence and emotional abuse. In other words, not bonding with parents or other vital care givers can produce most of these symptoms without an official diagnosis of ADD or ADHD. And as I already mentioned, the controversies and arguments continue about whether these two particular types of non-attending, should really be diagnosed at all. There are many experts in many fields, including adults who suffer from these supposed disorders, who feel that this is simply a difference and not a disorder. That learning styles should be addressed, both at home and at school, and adaptations should be made for these problems by those who care for them and teach them. Relate this to intuitive empathic children, and one has a lot to think about concerning this in terms of whether these children are simply intuitive, have an additional difficulty to cope with, or are simply invisible in the classroom.

And last, a warning about the use of stimulant medication in young children with any form of officially diagnosed attention deficit, and here are some of the facts. The longer the child takes the medication, the more likelihood of addiction. And the more likely of continued addiction to various drugs or alcohol, in adulthood. Children and adults feel really good on these medications, and don't want to give these up. Most ethical doctors will prescribe them short-term, either during school hours or during the home hours, depending on when the child is most hyperactive. Although this is often needed more in the school setting than it is at home, and it is the parents who deal with the most difficult part, this can sometimes put the child at risk according to how each family functions. On the other hand, it is proposed that 70% of children improve after being treated with stimulants short-term. But it is also proposed, that behavioral and psychological treatment can be equally successful in the early childhood years. The United States and Canada account for 95% worldwide, of Ritalin consumption, which makes one speculate that perhaps controlling the child is easier than teaching that child to manage his or her own behavior and doing this extra work as parents and teachers, to accomplish this.

There is one last thought to leave you with, that is that the adults who were diagnosed with some form of attention deficit in childhood, are found to have an extremely high continuation of various addictions, the highest being cocaine and alcohol. They are also at the highest risk of abusing pharmaceutical stimulant prescriptions. These studies have generated an even bigger controversy over the use of stimulant medications for the treatment of ADHD. It is also well known that children diagnosed with ADHD have much more complex difficulties as adolescents and adults, regardless of the treatments that they receive. Few ADHD students graduate from high school, and fewer still graduate from college and the effects of these difficulties produce diverse and serious impairments. The good news is that only 30 to 50% of diagnosed cases persist into adulthood, because many adults find more appropriate coping mechanisms as they mature.

One very interesting and thought provoking fact, concerning athletes, is that in 2009, 8% of all Major League Baseball players had been diagnosed with ADHD as children. This is a huge proportion of baseball players as compared to the percentage in the general population. When the League's 2006 ban on the taking of stimulants came out, it was revealed that many of these baseball players were taking them. Does this mean that taking these stimulants came from the childhood "feel-good" drugs, which these athletes possibly took when they were young? Or does this indicate that many athletes were directed into sports, because they needed to get up and move around in order to focus and attend to the task at hand? The final question being, that if the athletes had been directed into sports because of their need to move, their motivation to move, and their natural talents as an athlete, without taking drugs as a child for ADHD; what had they needed stimulants for? Pain mediation maybe, but perhaps not stimulants. Maybe the stimulants continued to help them focus on the game?

Those who contend that attention deficit is a difference and not a diagnosis, state that the whole diagnosis is a fraud perpetrated by the psychiatric and pharmaceutical industries. They also state families that are anxious to understand their children's behavior might be being duped and being given inadequate information about their children's "difference." The whole, integrative package of each child being divided into "parts" that various experts only look at from their individual perspectives is an American disease of gigantic proportions. It is also considered laziness on the part of caregivers to take the easy way out and fit the child to the system, rather than to tackle the system and change it. Adapting to learning styles and modes of learning is a great deal more work and a lot more difficult than it is to pop a pill and see a miraculous but often temporary improvement either physically or behaviorally. I ought to know, that after all those years in the classroom and from one end of the child scale to the other; the amount of work needed to meet their individual needs was stupendous and I only had them for 6 hours each day, parents have this responsibility for the rest of the time.

Oppositional Defiance Disorder

Since there is a 20 to 25% incidence with ODD in children with learning disabilities and also with children who have a form of attention deficit, it is easy to see how all of these particular labels are tied together. Oppositional defiance disorder is only one more popular school diagnosis, which involves a pattern of disobedience, hostile and defiant behavior towards authority figures, stubbornness, temper tantrums, stealing, bullying, vandalism, and a weak sense of right and wrong. Of course all of these behaviors disrupt not only those around the person, but the person himself. The same controversy at this even being a diagnosis exists as it does for both Aspergers Disorder and ADD. The question with this disorder is, is it separate from conduct disorder and does it need to be? There is evidence that over 50% of young children diagnosed with ODD, will move into the diagnosis of conduct disorder as adolescents, and then as adults. By focusing on positive approaches to increase compliance behaviors, several treatments have been highly successful. Among them are parent training programs, individual psychotherapy, family therapy, cognitive behavioral therapy, and social skills training. And perhaps a restructuring of the education system too!

Obsessive-Compulsive Disorder

An anxiety disorder in which intrusive thoughts produce uneasiness or fear and worry, OCD symptoms include repetitive actions or rituals, thoughts or ideas. Symptoms can cause the person to be alienated from others, embarrassed by their behaviors, or cause emotional stress and financial difficulties. Sufferers recognize their obsessions which causes them further stress. The fourth most common disorder, this is equally spread among children, adolescents and adults. These thoughts that recur or persist cause the person to perform tasks over and over again. While these notions do not correspond with reality, those on the less severe end of this disorder feel that these compulsive actions will help them escape from their obsessive thoughts. But these rituals or routines provide only temporary relief from their obsessive thoughts. Many OCD sufferers use rationalizations for their behaviors, but these aren't often that logical. There is also a subgroup called "Pure-O's," or those who show no overt compulsions and strive to not display these compulsions openly, so that they suffer even more from the extra effort it takes to live a personal and private life without the OCD openly showing up anywhere.

Theories on the causes of this disorder involve the idea that this disorder is a combination of evolutionary changes from past requirements to survive and the biological irregularities of the neurotransmitter serotonin, which regulates anxiety. And this is why anti-depressants are often recommended to correct these irregularities, because a class of these drugs includes serotonin regulation. One other theory is that OCD is a genetic mutation, since 45 to 65% of the childhood cases develop into adult OCD, although environmental factors also play a part. Many children in having a strep infection can have rapid onset of OCD afterwards, which is an interesting factor. Diagnosis is based on the severity of the compulsions that drive the person to perform rituals or routines over and over again. The amount of time each day spent on these routines is also a factor in diagnosing just how interfering this is to the person's life in general. Unlike the more severe personality disorder of OCPD, OCD sufferers are perfectly aware that their behavior is not normal and quite unhappy about the anxiety it produces and derive no pleasure from what they do, as an addictive personality would. Early intervention through behavior management and parental support can help children alleviate or at least manage this behavior effectively. 80% percent of the cases are present before 18 years of age and studies suggest that these symptoms are worldwide regardless of culture and geography. ("*Obsessive-compulsive disorder," Wikipedia, the free encyclopedia*)

So like all of the disorders I am talking about here, this can also go hand-in-hand with intuitive abilities. What has to be recognized is if some of these thoughts are powered by real intuitive feelings, visions, and sensings, rather than delusions. Perhaps a person is obsessing on an upcoming natural disaster that has not occurred yet, because of their past experiences with intuiting such phenomena. They are on an intuitive channel which is receiving detailed information in the form of pictures, impressions or feelings and therefore seem to be obsessing on them. Or perhaps after the disaster happens, they continue to obsess on the dangers of this natural or manmade disaster, because they are literally inhabiting the disaster intuitively from past experiences or even in the present incident? Determining this is done in the same fashion as previously mentioned, do your homework! Go to the library and internet to check out historical evidence. Really dig into the details of the natural disaster the person is obsessing on either from the past or the present, to see if they are receiving accurate information from across the planet or even across time. Discuss the details carefully and fully with the person and help them to determine if they are obsessing for a reason, or simply being compulsive. If the differences can be weeded out, this may help the intuitive person to compartmentalize the real intuition from the compulsions by checking the facts and accuracies of their impressions.

Intuitive Children & ADD, ADHD, ODD or OCD

With intuitive children, the question is, have these children sometimes been mistakenly diagnosed with ODD or OCD as the primary issue, when in reality, there is a side issue as well? And in this side issue, are they also simply distracted by the nonphysical world around them or quite gifted and quite bored with their school setting? There are so many other perspectives that can come into play, when the intuitive child copes with home and school, that are not always recognized, especially when the child has a set of gifts or abilities, which are not addressed because intuition is not understood or recognized as real. These childhood diagnoses are very real, but perhaps there are other factors at play here that are not addressed at all, in addition to the disorders themselves. It is in the details and diagnosis by professionals that one will find the answers in this unrecognized field of study. These highly intuitive children also have the additional burden of being invisibly gifted in our American society. If they can draw or write, produce music or graceful movement with their bodies, they become visibly creative. But if they claim to see things, hear things, move things without touching them or even feel or sense things out of the ordinary, they must have mental or behavioral problems of one kind or another. In the end, it always comes down to looking at each child individually and understanding every aspect of that child's gifts, talents, and skills and then making them aware of them, and honoring them for having these gifts, while working with any challenges they may also have.

Latest Guru in Raising & Educating Autistic & ADHD Kids

Dr. Stanley J. Greenspan has written many books on parenting and mentoring both autistic, which includes Aspergers and Autistic-like kids, as well as ADD and ADHD children, teens and adults. It seems that there is a rise in these less interfering childhood difficulties and the more severe handicaps are on the wane due to many medical advances keeping more children alive as well as less likely to be born with handicaps. However, many more young parents are now facing these lesser but still very overwhelming and exhausting parenting issues due to among other things, the pollutants and toxicities in our poisoned environment which effects the foods we eat, the water we drink and the air we breathe, just to name a few. However there is also research which indicates that there are several factors contributing to the increase of these less severe difficulties from genetics to neurological changes in the brain, etc.

Dr. Greenspan suggests something named DIR - Floor Time as an answer to parenting these more difficult children. And many parents are now arriving at the same conclusions that I had learned in my early training with very severely handicapped children through Jean Ayer's pioneering developmental stages work and Van Dyk's integrative programming for deaf-blind multi-handicapped children from Holland. Their model or curriculum introduces an easily applied integrative program that is begun in infancy and continued into early childhood with parents as the immediate caregivers and trainers. The program is expanded upon later with the support of all of the specialists needed for cognitive development and motor planning, behavior management and overcoming difficult symptoms. These "special" children require a developmental profile, an in-depth sensory integration assessment, and a really detailed behavioral management intervention program with down time for the parents and siblings, while letting the child lead with what he or she displays as interaction with people and their environments. Exactly the same as those techniques I learned so very long ago and used successfully with all children in many modified and adapted forms over the years.

To learn more about this, please look in the Sensory Integration or Out-of-Sync-Child chapter where I address the Autistic-Like and Aspergers special needs in more detail, as well as Greenspan's how to follow a child's lead approach. Many of the children I worked with in those days, while dealing with sensory deprivations with their sight and hearing, really dealt with autistic, autistic-like, and probably Aspergers, long before this term reached the USA. Parents of these types of children will understand my own personal frustrations on moving to another state where things were so compartmentalized, upon arriving at kindergarten with their autistic-like child who has already taken the lead and has already begun an integrative program addressing all of the child's needs, but not in "sections." The compartmentalized programs are at long last on their way out, but not yet! Giant clipboard displays of individualized programs that I saw in hallways completely took me by surprise! So don't despair parents, with a little searching and a little investigating, the right combination of things for your child will appear, especially if you let this child lead the way!

The "Gay" World & Intuition

I thought long and hard about this one and where to put it in this book. While "gayness" is not an affliction, a disorder, a belief, or a mislabeling, or even should be a "label," it is the world's problem, history's problem, organized religion's problem, a country's problem, a community's problem, a family's problem, and an individual difficulty for both gays and straights. And while it shouldn't even be a problem at all, it is. I am mentioning this in this particular chapter because it has been my experience as a teacher – and excuse me for generalizing here – that every year when the little children walked in the door, I would first assess them on paper and then in my intuitive mind. There were always a few I knew were gay, whether they knew yet or not, or if they did know, before they would decide to tell everyone else. More importantly, I also noticed that these little ones were much more in touch with their intuitive natures. For better or for worse, they were nearly always "sensitives." Nearly always empathic and sensitive to their environment and the people around them, they were already suffering even as young children. They knew they were "different" but unlike ethnic or cultural differences, it was harder for them to determine just why. And they had no group that they could choose to identify with, unless, like intuitives, many family members were gay and already "out-of-the-closet," in which case the child just maybe was getting some group support.

Whether this was cultural or innate didn't matter, as I know the "gender scale" goes from heterosexual to bisexual to homosexual. We are all on that scale, whether we know it or not. I often wonder if there is such a category as bisexual, and if instead, one is either gay or straight and then at some time in one's life the person has to choose one road or the other. This might be where the misconception came from that gays can choose to be straight. How painful would this be to have to choose worlds when maybe both seem equally enticing? When these little ones came in and I knew their gender orientation in my own mind and heart, I tried to treat them with kid gloves, kept my mouth shut of course, and hoped that I encouraged their intuitive gifts along with their creative and academic ones. There are so many people out there that still believe that one can choose to be gay or straight, it was useless to even broach the subject with adults. But I could see the suffering and did my best to encourage and instill these children with as much self-worth and "being true to one's self" as I did for all my students. Yet I knew in my heart what the future could or might hold for them, and I wept inside for what they would have to endure from every culture, every faith, every country, every family, and every individual that they came across in their life, until the evolutionary consciousness picked them up too and we really were that "rainbow" of people we are suppose to be.

I needed to address this because as a group, the majority of gay women and men are quite intuitive, and gay men in particular often show their intuitive and empathic gifts more openly than straight men, who often see intuitive gifts as a sign of weakness rather than strength. The Hopi say that the fourth world that we are in now consists of each individual standing in the center of their circle of consciousness and slowly rotating to defend themselves from any intruders. They say that the fifth world coming will consist of communities of people standing within each circle and welcoming in others of all kinds and varieties of beliefs, gender orientations, and ethnic and cultural backgrounds into each circle, even though each circle of people might have their own individual belief systems already in place. The Hopi Elders say that as the shift in consciousness takes place, we will be required to go inward, keep to whatever spiritual path we are on, assist others, and pray or meditate for the rest of the world in any way we can, to help the energy shift in the direction of community and peaceful communications.

My hope for those little boys and girls then, was that they would find a place to belong, live their truth as a person, and stay in the physical world to experience life, no matter how difficult this might be. I could see death approaching them and I hoped for them, that they would escape this by the choices they made in life to find support, their own personal truth, and self-love as a worthwhile and very psychically gifted human being. Sensitives are much more likely to succumb to physical and mental illness, addictions and depressions, and feelings of despair, isolation, and loneliness when they do not find a supportive family, a supportive group of like minded people, or an even larger group pride with which to identify. And it still is my hope, that these children and the adults they are today or will become tomorrow will contribute a lot to society, especially in the intuitive worlds coming. Let's not lose any more of them to an international "shunning" of any kind.

But on a lighter note, here is something to really think about, concerning the connections between the gay world and the intuitive one. I can remember interviewing a gay male couple for a story I was doing in one of my ghost books. As we walked out of the restaurant, I joked with them that I had just come out of the closet too. They looked at me startled momentarily, until I explained that I was letting people know about my intuitive abilities for the first time in my life. They laughed and laughed about this ridiculous notion, to them anyway, that gayness had anything to do with intuition. I looked back at them and said, "Why do you think I am interviewing you two about the paranormal happenings in the canyon where you want to live? Do you know anyone else who would have these experiences, actually notice them as odd, and then be brave enough to not only make the necessary connections but also to tell them?" And as intuitives know, while our "closet" is not so deep and long suffering, it is more likely invisible to others, or even something thought ridiculous or suspect or silly, even maddening or downright scary. Talking about one's other worldly visits, is not done in "polite society." Even in this day and age, we see programs on the intuitive world, entirely missing the point and presenting an absurd collage of disconnected topics, rather like it was for the gay community some years ago. Both groups are still an embarrassment for those somehow disconnected from the circular motions of their own hearts and minds.

Ethnic Identity, Status, Difficult or Not so Difficult Upbringings

Everything in this book is for all children, in all families with a spectrum as broad as the planet itself. There is nothing that cannot apply to or be adapted to the cultural background, religious persuasion or belief system of any family or child. I wrote it this way because I will not presume to know all of these things for all children. However, each parent, each family, each coach, each counselor or therapist, each teacher or religious clergy, and all others who guide and love children sincerely, with true light and clear intent, guiding them on their way, should find it very easy to adapt any of the thoughts and ideas and activities for the children they are assisting. Whether you see intuition as a belief, a practical every day phenomenon, a special gift, or a brain function that we do not understand as yet, the important thing is to foster these abilities balanced with all the other talents and needs that each child presents to us. These abilities should not be over focused on, or under focused on, but simply part of the balance in all the other dimensions of each child's soul.

The "whole brainer" (which many more children are coming in with now) is also the person who can balance their physical, emotional, mental, energy body and spiritual self to the warp and weave of all the rest they must balance in their everyday lives. Many children have a lot to deal with, other children have more difficulties than most, some have an easier time of it and some find their way out of horrendous situations to lead a very good life. We as their guides and mentors have a responsibility to do the best we can for them, planting seeds and thoughts wherever we go, in hopes of easing their trials or inspiring them to have a ripple effect on others. It is always a great deal easier to build children, than it is to repair adults.

We really are all children of the earth in the garden of the world, under God, or a universal life force or whatever one chooses to call this presence or process. There are no "weeds" in God's garden, or anywhere on the earth for that matter. In Native American cultures there is no word for "weed" because all plants are equal and revered for their healing properties. Perhaps we should just be proud that we are all one diverse "garden" and should be more concerned about taking care of this garden before we lose it altogether. Letting children lead the way is a given. We as adults just have to catch up to what we are learning about our own childhoods and those of children today. Even the most intelligent researchers on this planet have finally figured out just how little we know about your world or other worlds, be they dimensions or travels through time, etc. Even atheists know we have comforting images fed to us when we die, and I suppose they wonder about why this is, too. There is so much we don't know, that what we do know, is nothing more than a speck on a fly's back. But someday, we will know much more than we do now.

> "The brain and mind are beautifully interwoven. Our feelings, thoughts, and actions can only occur through the complex actions of the brain. Any changes in the brain, even subtle changes, can have a major impact on our feelings, thoughts and actions."
>
> --Carol Stock Kranowitz, Out-of-Sync Child, p.ix

> "Recent studies of how experience, at all stages of life, can change the structure and function of the brain are giving increasing support to the changes in autistic children...Newer brain imaging techniques are documenting these changes. They are beginning to offer concrete evidence of the way certain experiences can affect not only the child's ability to relate, communicate, and think, but also the very architecture of the brain."
>
> --Greenspan & Weider, Engaging Autism, p. 8

> "You must never allow another's diagnosis or opinion of your child's personality, IQ, or health, color your knowledge of our own child's inner spirit. Whether the opinion is that one of your kids has attention deficit disorder, attachment disorder, a terminal illness, 'doesn't consequence well,' is overly needy, is learning disabled, is a bully, is possessed, is dyslexic, or is just 'a little strange,' don't start looking askance at your own child. No matter what is going on within his or her body or brain, in this child's heart there lies the quiet memory of God. That memory will eventually awaken...Children are not given to us by God to mold and define. They are already created."
>
> --Spiritual Parenting, pp. 108- 109

> "A label is not a phrase or a word; it is a thought...Once a child is labeled, he is seen either as doing the behavior or not doing the behavior – but now everything is defined in terms of the behavior...Know your child. Knowing calms you. Knowing comes from listening and watching, not from deciding, classifying, and categorizing. Knowing is an open, ongoing process that is able to see change as it occurs, whereas making a decision about your child's character or personality type can blind you to what is happening now."
>
> --Ibid, pp.108-09. 129. 145, 160-61.

CHAPTER FOUR

Intuitive Children & All That Anxiety & Panic & What to do About It

"Walking with a friend in the dark is better than walking alone in the light." "Everything has its wonders, even darkness and silence, and I learn whatever state I may be in, therein to be content."

--Helen Keller

"When darkness comes, light a candle."

--anonymous

Stress in Intuitive Children

Learning how to spot stress in intuitive children before it becomes an anxiety attack or worse, is a bit tricky. Sometimes not enough stress can cause people to be bored, while other times, too much stress can make us freeze shut. The right amount of stress seems to be a person being able to be alert and awake while not damaging the chemical interactions in their "stress body." Intuitive children can tune in to all kinds of conflicts in all areas of their lives that other children can often ignore, unless of course, it entails severe emotional trauma and abuse. Some of the things that a child will do when experiencing stress is have an implosion of emotions which often brings about a total shutdown of the body, a sudden burst of emotion, which can help the child to shake off his or her anger, inexplicable emotions, where the child is feeling an emotion that can't be described or understood, and something Catherine Crawford calls, "psychosomaticizing." This means that the child has absorbed the emotional state into their physical pain. When a doctor cannot identify any physical causes, and the child is experiencing headaches, stomachaches, or other migrating aches and pains, then it is probably the child's empathic abilities causing the pain.

Some of the other stress factors, that Crawford mentions, are a hyper vigilance, in terms of seeing or imagining problems when there are none. The child will adopt this self protection to control intuitive surprises that don't feel good. They may also misinterpret social situations and events and draw the wrong conclusions. These particular issues must be discussed in detail with the child to help them to understand what is happening to them. Associated with this are clouded decision-making abilities where the child tends to pay more attention to other people's opinions and feelings than they do their own. Then the child is unable to honor or know what he or she wants, or the child can be unable to express his or her own opinions. The child can also be very distracted and unable to focus because of too many emotional and intuitive signals in their environment. This can also make the child appear spacey, because they are lost in other interests outside the classroom or involved in problems they are trying to solve in some other area of their life or dimension.

These stressors can lead to anxiety because of premonitions, intuitions or worrisome interactions with others which they feel they can't control. Along with the anxiety can come depression and exhaustion, and these are the major feelings that lead to actually experiencing an anxiety attack, and the more severe panic attack which can follow this. When children are depressed, it is often because they feel they cannot exert any control over the stressful situation and this loss of control robs them of their vital energy. If the child is than judged, ridiculed or shamed for any reason, this can lead to depression. Because the child is being robbed of his or her energy, they will feel very tired and exhausted. And sometimes, working too hard and being involved in too many extracurricular activities can produce this exhaustion. Stress that goes on and on can cause an overload on the nervous system, as well as anxiety, which can sometimes lead to panic attacks.

Asking for help can also be difficult for any child, but especially intuitive children. Intuitive children are quite perceptive, and they want to feel special in the eyes of their parents, like any child does. But the intuitive child is at risk for putting too much of themselves into others' emotions. They may use entirely too much energy to please others and deplete their own reserve. They may feel that the only trait they have, that the parent pays attention to, are their intuitive gifts. So as Crawford says, parents are also at risk to unconsciously respond to their child's gifts with either too much or too little attention. When the child's intuitive gifts can be responded to as something normal and natural, then both parents and children can have a healthy relationship.

Crawford, a marriage and family therapist advises that you do the following when assisting your child through stressful situations: "Stay calm and try not to match the child's stress or fear. Give permission for the child to express her feelings. Evaluate for sensory overload, and help reduce sensory inputs. Take a few deep breaths together and clear conflicts if necessary. If the child is caught in a random intuition, help to release it. Practice saying, 'Is this mine?' and look for ways to shift gears and orient to the present moment." (*Ibid., Crawford, pp. 45-49, p.57*).

Stress & The Healing Code

Since stress and inflammation are the two main causes of all illness, reducing the toxins in your environment and building up your immune system are the two mega background players in stimulating the immune system and then using the frequency or energetic healing techniques to not only reduce or eliminate anxiety and panic, but also to heal the physical body. Once you have eliminated the toxins that you can in your environment and then the toxins in your body through diet and exercise, you have set the stage to heal both emotionally and physically, since stress is interconnected with both. I have found Tapping is great for reminding the organ - acupressure point connections to remain strong in the physical body. And it is also great because of its built in positive affirmations to rejuvenate the physical mechanics in your body. Some medical research has shown that the Tapping procedure is great maintenance for the body's various systems that need to keep flowing without blockages: the lymphatic system, the blood system and the nervous system. Americans especially, have sluggish systems due to what they eat and how much they do or do not exercise. By including Tapping simply for maintenance of these systems, one can reduce this sluggishness and invigorate the body's systems, regardless of any other claims for self-healing.

The Healing Code technique is great to fit perfectly with the Tapping point routine, as the etheric body – spiritual frequency healing connection to reduce and hopefully eliminate stress, anxiety, fear and physical symptoms for any of the above. Together, they are the perfect pair! Although of the two I feel the concrete physical actions involved in the Tapping procedure work the best for reducing a panic or anxiety attack. It is like getting busy when all else fails, and "working off" the panic, only you are also actually doing something in addition to diverting your attention into something physical. You are powering up your body's liquid and electrical systems like the oil and gasoline that a car needs to function well. This body maintenance is absolutely vital to any other self-healing technique, as is the healing code procedure for all of your vital organs and the energy body that goes through and surrounds them. And there certainly are no side effects to worry about, unless you don't follow the two golden rules in all health avenues, and that is rotating foods/herbals and using moderation in all things.

While The Healing Code by Alex Loyd and Ben Johnson, Grand Central, 2010, is the latest fad in the holistic world and claims to heal everything just like Tapping does and many other such methods and techniques. But what I like about both of them is that they are teaching people to do self-healing for the tremendous stress we deal with each day that we are often unaware of in our lives, but also for their value in taking command of our own healing. We can become managers of our own network of things that work for each of us to reduce inflammation in our bodies and to reduce the amount of stress we deal with daily. These two techniques are easy and simple and fit together perfectly. Done together on a daily and consistent schedule, but with the creativity of varying what we say and think to heal ourselves, they become a powerful way to heal our lives and bodies. Add daily meditation to this for a powerful threesome, especially if you have to avoid medications and herbals altogether!

In The Healing Code, they talk in a common sense manner about balancing everything, understanding your stress control centers and how they work, that stress is caused by an energy problem in the body, that emotions cause stress and eventually inflammation in the body if left to its own devices, that we let viruses attack us because we do not take control of our own health, and that belief is vital in self-healing. For example, one method of healing may work for one person and not another because they believe in the one method and not in the other. They also talk about the head and heart being in conflict with each other and that we have to learn to get our head and heart together in order to heal. They claim that four etheric points can deactivate stress over a short period of time and open these main energy points for both emotional and physical healing. They say that these four points correspond to "master control centers" for every cell in the body. This is nothing new in energy work, but it is new in terms of simplifying and focusing the energy, just as Tapping has now been simplified for everyday use in a short and easy format. And done together two or three times a day for as little as 16 minutes each time, this combination of things really is powerful for many, many people.

These two "coded sequences" are twice as powerful done together. The removal of emotional and physical stressors (Healing Code) and the maintenance and building up of the immune system (Tapping) paired with decreasing toxins in the body and in one's environment combined with daily meditation, is indeed a powerful package. Apparently one can access deeply guarded memories, experiences and hidden stressors by "broadcasting" these frequencies to the body. With the ten minute Tapping session and the six minute Healing Code session, combined with affirmations, visualizations and belief, self-healing can begin at no cost to anyone, except for the commitment it takes to time, repetition and creative variations. For the self-healing universal "code" look right behind the Tapping information (#4) for the four major energy points (#5) and how to do them in the correct sequence in conjunction with Tapping in the next chapter. However, unlike Tapping, which needs to be compacted in order to be usuable, you really do need to get the healing code book and read it. Why Meditation is an essential ingredient in the balancing of our daily lives is addressed in Chapter Fifteen.

Anxiety , The Pre-Panic Attack

There is some brain research that explains why some people are more empathic than others or sensitive to other's feelings. Apparently there exists something called mirroring neurons which mimic or make a person actually feel the emotions of others more strongly than most of us do. The mirror neuron system is a group of brain cells that actually mimic the actions and feelings of others simultaneously. This sensorimotor activity seems to be automatic in some people and not so automatic in others. Communication and empathy between human beings can affect children in the same way that that one catches a cold, thus partially explaining degrees of empathy among adults and children. Higher levels of mirror neuron activity can be equated with higher levels of empathy for others. So that what is perceived as being overly sensitive or too sensitive by some is actually partially caused by a brain function. I can remember saying to my brothers when they said to me, "If I was as sensitive as you are I'd kill myself," I said, "If I were as insensitive as you are I'd kill myself," in jest of course. This was how impossible it was for one group to understand and communicate with another, where sensitivity was concerned.

Crawford uses the terms "ducks and sponges" to help children understand the two major types of intuitives. A scale of sensitivity from "water runs off a duck's back" to sponges, who soak in all the emotions of everyone around them, can be equated with auditory processors or left brain thinkers and visual-spatial communicators or right brain thinkers. These two scales can easily be superimposed, and we are all along these scales somewhere. Thus learning styles and sensitivity are closely tied together when it comes to communication. The "duck" uses terms like "I think..." or "I am of the opinion..." or "I am sure..." And the "sponge" uses terms like "I feel..." or "My heart tells me..." or "I sense...." The supposedly highly emotional "sponges" become some sort of high maintenance for the "ducks," and the "ducks" become people who don't even know when they have hurt themselves physically, or are "insensitive" to people's feelings, from the "sponge's" point of view. Understanding these different perspectives and honoring them while figuring out ways to meet halfway, even just verbally; could really solve some major relationship difficulties for couples, bosses and employees, and parents and their children.

I know I drove my mother absolutely crazy with all of my childhood sensitivities. And I carried on about them, especially where my low pain threshold was concerned, while her other children who seemed stoic to me, skipped along, hurt knee and all, seeming to never even notice that they were hurt. In other words, I could have spent all day long with that "flower in the woods" story, worrying about its lost petal and trying to fix it while crying! (See activity section for "flower in the woods") There are sensitives who say they have a higher pain threshold, but that does not mean they don't have a myriad of other things, like allergies or sensitivities to smells, environmental pollutants and medications or herbs, etc. My favorite story about this was my one day trying out aroma therapy. I took one whiff of the lavender as the directions stated and the 36-hour migraine that followed was just searing through my brain. On the other hand, the humor in this is that the lavender aroma is suppose to attract the opposite sex, so I guess I am out of luck all the way around! But there are sensitives who seem to fare better with their health, so perhaps genetics plays a part in this, as one can compare very health conscious people and find within this group those whose pain threshold varies or whose sensitivities are minimal compared to others. I only know that in my case, and I do know a few others, I was always the one in five thousand, with physical proof of this too. I guess you could say I manifested these things, or that I set myself up to fail, or any number of other speculations could be made, however, I know my own body and the truth is, I am way over there on the "sensitive" side, rather "holistically!" So, you may ask, what does all this have to do with anxiety and panic attacks? A lot!

When a child is so sensitive towards others and even other living things on the planet, he or she experiences such things as sudden mood changes, sudden explosions of emotion, a shutdown to emotional overloads, emotions that seem to come from nowhere and have not been brought on by anything the child has experienced. Picking up on emotions can then be perceived as causing physical pain for the child, and becoming what appears to others as spacy, distracted or unable to focus on the task at hand. These children may not be able to make good decisions or may draw conclusions that are based on their emotional radar rather than logic. And finally they may become depressed, fatigued or anxious. In the extreme they can even be diagnosed with childhood depression, emotional exhaustion or with anxiety that then may eventually become the more severe panic attacks. Panic attacks supposedly run in families as well, although a lesser form can be tied to a certain set of temporary circumstances and the person more likely just suffers from anxiety. But a panic attack can really overwhelm an individual with irrational thoughts of danger and stress, which is often treated with an anti-depressant medication taken regularly or just at the onset of the panic attack to reduce the symptoms.

Whatever the intuitive child is experiencing it is closely tied to using their sensory gifts to the extreme and not understanding that they are in sensory overload. This constant stress can bring about an overload on the nervous system and also cause tiredness and anxiety. One of the things that can happen to such empathic children is that they can learn to use their abilities for attention from their peers or parents, or they may over extend themselves in this manner, to the point of physical illness or emotional exhaustion. Learning to control and use this particular gift in moderation can really help the child not to be diagnosed inappropriately and can often explain too many absences from school in a way that teachers might not have thought of. Empathic teens often stay home not because they are lazy or truant, but because they are on overload from having gathered and owned, all of those emotions that are not really their own. Overloaded with this constant bombardment of emotions from others and from the environment itself, they become afraid or are too exhausted, or at least very reluctant, to go to school. They literally inhabit the souls and emotions of others and sometimes take a "crash" dive from the overload of emotions.

If the child does go to school under these circumstances then one can easily see what looks like depression from not fitting in or exhaustion from overload or anxiety. Many of the tips and exercises you will find in Chapter Fifteen will help with these issues, especially a good diet and methods for reducing stress at home or at school or even during after school activities. However, another set of issues that are very common with intuitive children and really a lot of children in this day and age of high stress, are those methods for pushing children to become adults too soon. Due to the influence of the media, children are often the "pushers!" And before considering a drug with multiple side effects and often worse possibilities than the problem itself, or herbal remedies that are not often tested enough, mixed together so you can't figure out which one is bothering you, and can cause just as many side effects for sensitives as the prescription drugs, there are some things to consider. Popping a pill or taking a multiple combination herbal remedy or several such remedies can really cause more problems than they are worth for people who are so sensitive that the world is like a huge tainted environment of confusing "triggers" for physical inflammation. And physical inflammation is the root cause of many lesser illnesses which then can lead to more serious illnesses.

I remember taking a ghost investigation class at a local high school where a young man had recently committed suicide right in front of his locker and classmates at the school. So naturally our first "ghost investigation" was not in some distant location – of which we had several later – but right in this high school. After the teacher trained us on the equipment and distributed it to us in small groups, we were then to go out and see if we could get anything to register on our various machines. It was an evening class but there were sixty people in the overflowing class and other night classes going on all over the school. Being an intuitive I knew that this was an entirely impossible situation, as you need absolute quiet to really pick up on anything. As I rounded the corner with my group and saw the long corridor of lockers, running the entire length of the school, I was literally blasted backwards – internally anyway – with the flood of emotions emanating from all of those lockers. The rest of my small group went running around erratically testing this and that while I stood frozen in place at the end of the hallway with a tsunami of emotions flooding over me from all those lockers. I was transfixed by the many high schoolers not only contemplating suicide, but their thoughts about harming others, the bullying and the hormonal tidal waves of crushes and yearnings. That was as far as I ever got on this investigation, because what was coming, was a great deal more overwhelming than what had already passed.

My favorite philosophy and theory on how to deal with all of these physical sensitivities when one takes responsibility for one's own health, takes more work and attention than running to the doctor or the chiropractor or even the homoeopathist, naturopath, acupuncturist – the list is "end" list and expensive! Doctors are good for setting a bone, giving you a pill, performing a surgery, suturing something, or sending you on to other specialists, the experts who charge you more money or say there is nothing they can do for you. These specialists instill a sort of overwhelming fear into your soul that is insurmountable. However, there are doctors who find you the kinds of experts that you need even though the costs are exorbitant. Alternative health practitioners are in two categories, those who make you co-dependent and those who enable you to find the right kinds of help. Insurance often does not cover their services however, leading the seeker back to the pharmaceutical companies, medical insurance companies and hospitals in a sort of "round robin" merry-go-round.

If you are like me with decades of chronic smaller type ailments, you reach the end of the medical world and then the end of the alternative health world, and that is when you begin to take responsibility for your health and manage things the very best that you can, as well as being brave enough to tell all these experts what you intuitively know you need. So back to the philosophy! Get on the internet, look up what you have if you know it and find websites where people who have had this or that, are talking back and forth about the remedies and management techniques that they have found successful for them and try them all, one at a time of course! This gives you a starting place and helps you to begin to put together what works specifically for you. This will also tell you what alternative experts you might seek out and try very cautiously, to see if for you, their methods can enhance and assist what you already know. When new cures or remedies or machines come out, gather more specific information, because you may find out that you have already tried this under a different name or in a different form. No sense in "reinventing the wheel" on your own physical body, which could cause setbacks as well.

Do all the other things recommended by others who have gone through the same thing, especially the ones that cost very little, then meditate daily, shed the negative energy daily through a brushing technique or some other method that you already know, use affirmations, do relaxation exercises, do a form of personal exercise such as yoga or tai chi or whatever appeals to you, get on a good and moderate in aspect diet, give yourself quiet contemplative time, and do the techniques I mentioned for maintenance and building up the immune system. But I can just hear you now, "What, all this with the life I have to lead?" I told you, for chronic, highly sensitve ailment people, getting and staying well, takes work and prioritizing and keeping your triggers below threshold at all times. The example you set for your children is an added bonus. Then read Dr. David Buchholz's book Heal Your Headache: The 1-2-3 Program for taking charge of your pain. What the title should be for Buchholz's book because "headache" is misleading, is Heal Your Physical Inflamation in the Only Way You Can or What Are the Only Two Things You Can Control in Our Polluted World of Today? When you walk out your front door you only have control over two things, your emotions and your diet, everything else is out of your control and therefore polluting to you. Read more about this in the nutrition and health chapter, this is really the one to help you out with anxiety and panic attacks in terms of reducing outside factors in your environment and then those inside your physical body.

Panic Attacks

Most people think that anxiety and panic attacks are the same, but they are not. We all deal with anxiety from time to time or maybe even most of the time, but a panic attack is much more severe. It is an intense episode of fear or apprehension and dread that affects you physically and you feel completely out of control of your body and emotions so that you can experience what seems like life threatening physical pain and doom. Attacks can last from fifteen to thirty minutes and peak within ten minutes of the start of the panic. However, some people experience cyclic episodes that can last for hours. I remember one friend telling me that she finally went to sleep in the middle of a panic, only to wake up the next morning, peek out from under the covers and realize that she was still in the panic mode. In these longer episodes, the person will experience anxiety and limited anticipations of the next "peak" panic still to come. Fear of a heart attack from heart palpitations, or a nervous breakdown from the entire nervous system making your hands and feet or even your whole body shake involuntarily, can occur in first onset situations or in other panic attack episodes. These attacks are self defeating because each time you anticipate one coming on, the anxiety from this adds to the strength and length of the ensuing panic attack. One person joked that when they were old and dying they would have the biggest, longest panic attack that they would ever have.

Feeling that you are dying, going crazy or having a heart attack certainly doesn't help a patient in the hospital when they show up to emergency for the first time and are made light of or even ridiculed by hospital personnel who do not understand what is happening to their patient. Nausea, numbing sensations, feeling faint, hyperventilating, tunnel vision due to blood flow leaving the head, and hormones flooding your body because you are thrown into a fight-or-flight mode, is not something anyone would wish on anyone. Trembling, chest pain, hot and cold flashes, dizziness, burning sensations, tingling sensations, a feeling of being choked or choking can also occur during the panic attack. Now add to this the intuitive empathic child, who does not understand any of this happening to him and who is on sensory overload anyway from real or lucidly vivid experiences, and you really have an anxiety ridden, panicking child!

Causes of these attacks are hereditary or have nothing to do with this. Twins seem to share a higher rate of this together. More women than men have them, just like more women than men are empathic. However, it is possible that more men than women don't recognize these episodes as panic attacks and just work their way out of them. Onset is usually in early adulthood although children can experience them too and people of above average intelligence seem to have them in a higher incidence. Other emotional causes can be post traumatic stress disorder, obsessive compulsive disorder, phobias, trying to avoid panic attacks and causing them instead, lack of assertiveness, and short term or "situational" bound trigger causes. Other particular physical or medical problems that can cause them are hypoglycemia or hyperthyroidism, mitral valve prolapsed, inner ear problems, vitamin B deficiency, drug withdrawal, side effects of some medications, and chronic or serious illness. What a merry-go-round that is! The child tries to avoid them with anxiety and makes them worse or the child who is sensitive suffers from chronic ailments and then brings the panic attacks on. Just reading the above symptoms can bring one on too!

Agoraphobia or the fear of open spaces or fear of panic attacks in open spaces speaks for itself. Housebound people need to read all this too! Panic attack disorder has one major difference from all these other forms of anxiety and panicking. There is often no identifiable "trigger" and they are often sudden and unprovoked. In other words, what cannot be seen can cause a panic attack. Picking up on another's strong emotion cannot be identified either, and yet both could happen to an intuitive child who then panics and is told he or she is imagining this. And being an intuitive adult, just writing all this, gives me a lot of anxiety! Especially when reading all of the symptoms, 20% of all adults experience this stuff, stress and environmental pollutants are increasing in our whole country by leaps and bounds, and, that everything I read on the treatments for this medically was rather bleak. There was a tiny little section prescribing a pill and "emotional support?" Only one medical article had a big section and this consisted of all the many types of pills and their side effects! In short, not much help available, medically, but lots of help on the various personal websites! Counselors can help, although panic attacks have a physical basis too.

Speculated Causes & Effects of Anxiety on the Body

First, however, we need to look at what the experts speculate may affect or even cause panic attacks. Many think that these attacks are caused by a change in brain chemistry, where the brain sends and receives false emergency signals. Women seem to have genetic factors much more strongly than men to come into life with an anxious temperament. A major enzyme which controls chemical messages sent to the nervous system called COMT has been found to be low in women with this sort of temperament. Therefore these particular women experience larger amounts of anxiety than their male counterparts. While 20% of Americans experience panic attacks, there is a much larger population of women within this 20%. "This is a complex, involuntary physiological response in which the body prepares itself to deal with an emergency situation…The increased production of adrenaline causes the body to step up its metabolism of proteins, fats, and carbohydrates to quickly produce energy for the body to use. In addition, the muscles tense, and the heartbeat and breathing become rapid. Even the composition of the blood changes slightly, making it prone to clotting." In a crisis survival time, this is normal and natural, but taken out of this context, this experience is distressing, frightening and very real. (*"Anxiety Disorder," Prescription for Nutritional Healing by Phyllis A. Balch, Avery, 2006, p. 205*).

Over time, if these measures are not taken, in terms of nutrition, exercise and energetic/meditation work, a person can begin to have accumulative problems such as overall aches and pains, muscular twitching. Stiffness, depression, insomnia, nightmares, with abnormal amounts of constant tension, and lowering one's ability to really know how to relax their body and mind, all contribute to panic attacks. These long term effects can be triggered by high stress, illness, a hidden food allergy, high caffeine or sugar levels, or simply a pile up of various triggers which brings about a sudden and often surprising onset of anxiety which then turns to panic. In other words, what the experts say about sudden, inexplicable panic attacks is really a lack of a certain chemical in the brain that many are born with. And if one continues to remain oblivious to the things that have been found to trigger this reaction, one can continue in a never ending cycle which increases in its symptoms over time.

Holistic Help for Anxiety & Panic Attacks

Nutritional Foods

Holistically, there are many things one can do to help prevent anxiety or panic attacks, nutritionally, herbally, and physically. So we will start with nutritional ideas. Phyllis Balch is a nutritional expert and this is just an example of the many chronic and even severe illnesses that she tackles with good foods, vitamin and mineral supplements, and herbs in her amazing and huge reference books which every parent of any child should have on hand, especially the nutritional book. You need to check her books for dosage levels for adults and children and of course make sure you have the appropriate guidance when trying any of these supplements. On the other hand, eating the right foods is the best place to start and this anyone can do safely. And even Balch states that eating the proper foods is always the safest place to start with everyone. All of the following foods supply valuable minerals and vitamins not only to improve one's diet, but also to lessen anxiety: apricots, asparagus, avocados, bananas, broccoli, black strap molasses, brown rice, dried fruits, figs, garlic, legumes, nuts, seeds, whole grains, yogurt, dulce, fish (especially salmon), brewer's yeast, soy products and green, leafy vegetables. Use the foods that balance the PH in your body; 60 percent alkaline and 40 percent acidic to avoid inflammation. Attend to how these various alkaline foods can mix with acidic foods and drink plenty of alkaline water in the seven point range for a normal body system.

Some of her other suggestions include eating frequent small meals to keep the body's systems balanced all day and all night and limiting the animal protein, eating complex carbohydrates and vegetable proteins instead. Eliminate as much refined sugar as you can and reduce or stop all caffeine intake (including chocolate if you can), which stimulates the nervous system to produce even more "panic." Reduce or stop all intake of alcohol, tobacco and carbonated soft drinks. Another dietary change is to increase or change the type of fatty acids you use and the same with amino acids.

Vitamins & Minerals

As far as nutritional supplements to reduce anxiety, and remember to check dosages carefully and under the guidance of a holistic professional such as a homeopathist or naturopath or nutritionist, she suggests these supplements: a multivitamin with a mineral complex first and then calcium and magnesium. Second to these are the vitamins C and E, a complex of all the B vitamins and the minerals: zinc, chromium and selenium, but especially zinc. If all of these do not improve things then there are several other more obscure supplements such as floradix iron, liquid Kyolix with B-1 and B-12, and S-Adenoylmethi-

Anxiety and Panic Attacks

Touch For Health Holding Points

Rub holding points in small circles with two fingers or with whole palm.

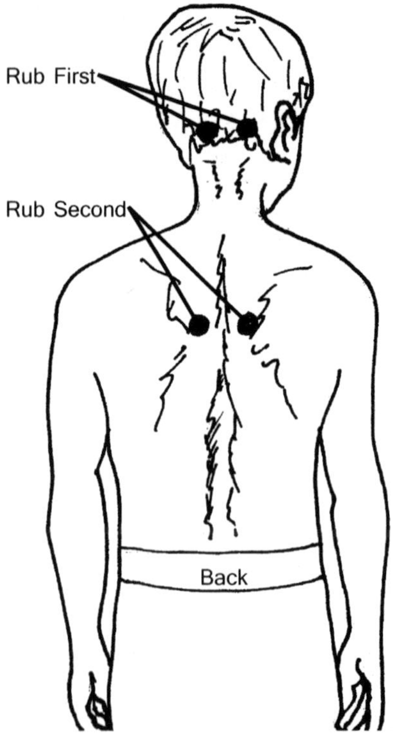

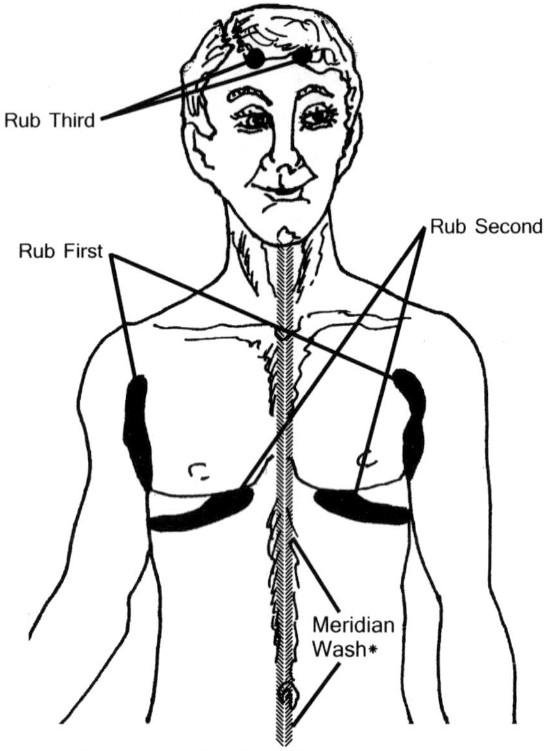

*Finish with a Meridian Wash or brush down the front of the chest three times.

Holding Points to Strengthen

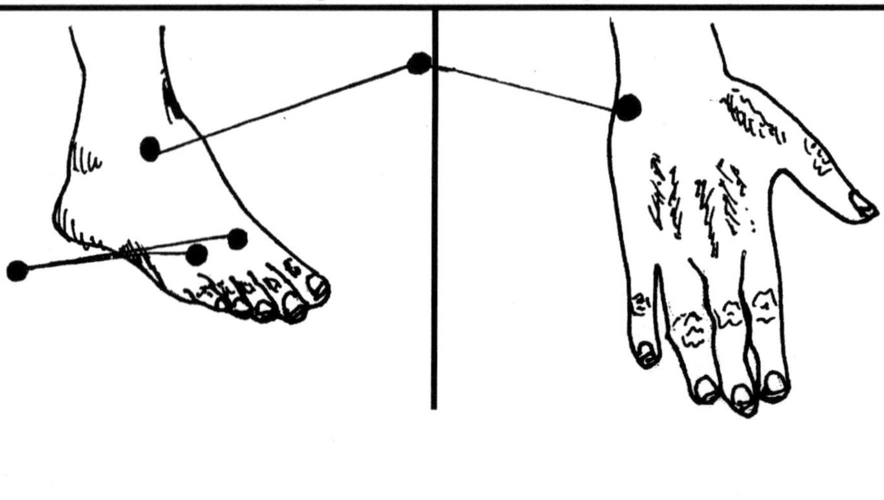

onine. Herbs that she recommends include seven or eight different types and combinations, all of which reduce stress, promote relaxation, reduce gastrointestinal upsets, eliminate headaches or reduce the number of migraines, promote emotional stability, help the person sleep, and alleviate oppressive feelings.

Physical Preventatives

Meditation, exercise, biofeedback, learning to relax techniques, adequate sleep, and in short, keeping a healthy lifestyle in both food intake and relaxation techniques can also play a major part in preventing both mild anxiety, major anxiety and even some panic attacks. Acupressure and acupuncture sessions will help, as will massage therapy appointments. Yoga, Tai Chi and especially Qui-Gong or Chi-Gong daily practices, as well as forms of karate will also help along with other kinds of physical workouts or even sports exercise. But all of these are, while preventative, quite expensive and require a commitment in your life, both emotionally and time wise. Those who select one of these and really commit themselves to this practice, really are ahead of the game where anxiety is concerned, but not many Americans can do this with the busy lifestyles that they lead, and even if they do commit themselves to one of these practices, it isn't always enough to stave off a huge anxiety or panic attack, by itself. Perhaps the nutritional things and the physical things combined will, or even a form of behavior modification or even counseling added on, will. But once again all of this costs a lot of money and Americans spend thousands of dollars every year to do all this stuff, although people often never follow through long enough for it to make a difference.

What Can Work When the Darkness of Anxiety & Panic Descends

So here goes what I have tried and others have by word-of-mouth that may be emergency measures when it is too late to prevent the onset. At immediate onset, grab some carbohydrates and eat a little, then use the breathing technique and then the tapping procedure you will find at the end of this chapter in detail. Integrate the Touch for Health holding points or acupressure circular rubbings and holding points with your tapping procedure in whatever manner you wish too. This gets the liquid, electric, and etheric systems flowing and builds up your immune system anyway, as an added bonus. The breathing technique is quite simple, inhale slowly through your nose, then count in your mind to 3 or 4, then exhale slowly through your mouth and repeat this procedure for about 3 to 5 minutes, and then go directly into your Tapping procedure and use the Touch for Health holding or rubbing points either with this or immediately after your several sets of Tapping. Repeat your mantra or affirmations in your head, quite a few times, while completing this procedure. Then eat a little protein and by this time it will be at least ten to fifteen minutes into the "attack." And if you can, begin the six minute Healing Code procedure, as an added measure.

Tapping procedures are in the next chapter but here are the acupressure holding or rubbing points from Touch for Health: 1) Supraspinatus/Central/Lymph Glands are the lymphatic points where you rub from armpits to the breastbone and then hold, Forehead two small circular rubbing points between the hairline and eyebrows on both sides, which stimulates blood and energy flow, Top of the Head small circular motion, directly in the middle of the part in the hair. 2) Pectoralis Major Clavicular/Stomach, hold points in the middle of the outer edge of each wrist, top of ankle on each foot in the center and hold, above each little toe about two inches and hold, and above the big toe on each side, and hold –no rubbing of any of these points. Rubbing points are back and forth below the rib cage with entire palm on each side and on either side of the 7th vertebrate in a small circular rubbing motion. Use the Tapping for maintenance, because EFT keeps you "physically" busy and incorporate the Healing Code if possible. (*See the chart on page 95 for help visualizing the healing code positions.*)

One should always muscle test before doing these various procedures to see if they will help to reduce stress or are necessary for a particular child or adult's anxiety. There are several techniques for muscle testing but the traditional one is best. Have the person extend an arm, breathe normally and ask if this is the appropriate thing to do for this body system. Then press very lightly on the wrist and if the muscle goes weak the person needs the procedure and if the muscle stays strong the person does not need to do this. It is all in how one asks the question so make sure your question is very clear and precise and so that only a "yes" or "no" response can be given. The body works like a lie detector to answer questions with a "yes" or "no" answer, if the muscle is strong it is "yes" or if it is weak, it is "no." You can also use the "finger cage" technique where you hold the thumb and middle finger together and then slightly press them apart for a weak muscle or "no," or you are unable to press them apart for a strong muscle or "yes."Or you can use the technique where you stand up and fall slightly forward for "yes" and slightly backward for "no." Or you can use a dowsing tool such as a pendulum, which is merely an extension of your weak or strong muscle answers in your arms and hands. Any of these methods can give you the answers you need, not only to try out the various techniques, but also to answer "yes" and "no" questions that will help to relieve your anxiety. (*Touch for Health by John F. Thie, 1979, pp.32 & 36*).

And then here are some other techniques you can use if they work better for you, or you can use after doing these other things in the first ten minutes. If you own a cat and it's a good lap sitter, grab it when the panic begins to descend. Scientists in Russia have discovered that cats – not dogs, although a faithful companion can help too – emit some sort of chemical that calms the nervous system and soothes the soul. They found out that cats can often help in the healing process after an illness or surgery and not just emotionally but literally physically with this chemical. But before you do this immediately eat some carbohydrates followed a few minutes later with some protein, then grab the cat and stroke it for all you are worth in between. Drink plenty of water, and then if you feel yourself going down, get very busy. Clean your house, do some yard work, go for a run, use your home gym or garage workshop, or do anything physical that will get your body pumping but distract you from the panic. It's already too late to get in the car to go anywhere so have these things available in your house or workplace, although if you are working hard you probably aren't panicking. Also, have a buddy who also has panic attacks to call any time night or day and have that agreement between you that you will always answer, and talk your friend down as needed. Perhaps you can avoid medication totally! But as a last resort only use the stuff as needed in a low dose and not all the time.

Fifty percent of panic attacks can disappear with the knowledge that you have them, have had them and will have them, how they make you personally feel, and knowing you are not alone. Information is your best defense because you can keep your anxiety from fueling them. Once the peak is over go into a meditative state or at least a listening to music state and stay there awhile. Now, translate all of this to your child in whatever ways that work for each child and you will have anxiety licked even if the panic attacks show up as they get a little older. Along with this and being informed yourself, have those talks about being intuitive, those detailed and specific talks about what your child is experiencing. Also check out the herbal remedies for lessening anxiety and try other holistic methods and techniques that seem to lower your particular stress level. There are many books on the subject and there does seem to be a correlation between anxiety and herbal remedies which really work for this, if you can tolerate them.

Herbal Remedies

According to Balch, the following herbs can really help you, but just like any prescription drugs, they have their side effects too. So it is best to try only one at a time to make sure that you are not having any of these side effects. A few days to two weeks can establish if you are not only doing okay on this or that particular herb, but also seeing results as far as reducing your anxiety or even the number of panic attacks. She says that stress makes the body vulnerable to damaging free radicals and that any of the following herbals used individually will protect your body from this additional stress: ginkgo, biloba, and bilberry. Milk thistle will not only protect the body from stress but also from damage to the liver. She suggests a host of herbs that will relax the body: catnip, cramp bark, hops, linden flower, motherwort, passion flower and skullcap. Chamomile or kava kava tea will also relax you but chamomile can cause allergic reactions and kava kava can make you too drowsy. For headaches associated with stress try: feverfew or meadowsweet teas. For stomach distress of varying kinds, use: lemon balm or willowbark or fennel teas or herbs before and after meals, however sometimes one of these may cause mouth sores or nausea. To reduce depression associated with anxiety, try St. John's Wort but read carefully about dosages. To sleep better, take valerian root. Taken from the peels of mandarin oranges, mandarin oil helps alleviate feelings of anxiety and depression. It can be rubbed on the skin, poured in the bath or used as an aromatic. But don't stay in the sun too long because it can cause brown spots on the skin. Avoid taking Ephedra as it can increase your anxiety, and just like prescription drugs herbals have side effects too! (Ibid., *Nutritional Healing, p.207.*)

Counseling Therapies

For empathic children especially, you can really instill in them very empowering techniques early in life to manage their own anxiety and panic whether there is a chemical component involved or not. Teaching them all the emergency procedures can not only be used when they panic in their daily life, but when a real episode where normal adrenaline is needed, they will be prepared for this. Projecting out of the body for very severe attacks might be a good protective measure but only in dire circumstances, projecting into a fantasy world might be a far less severe way to promote relaxation and calming down techniques. I would only use either of these after all the other physical and preventative techniques have been tried in an individualized and specific "package" for each child. For adults there is one other method that counselors and therapists use, and would also probably be used in a modified form with children who are really suffering from this in the form of night terrors or day time anxiety and panic. This is called Panic Control and involves a therapist to coach the child or adult who is suffering from long term panic attacks and the person is beginning to show all of the difficulties and debilitating physical effects on their physical body. Long term results have been seen with this type of coaching. Therapists coach their patients into recreating the feeling of the panic attack and then teach them how to deal with the symptoms, feelings or sensations this produces.

What Else Can You Do?

But remember to follow the steps! Prevention comes first and the simplest methods also come first as well. When dealing with anxiety, the best thing to do first is to eat a better diet and eliminate the trigger foods, while adding in the calming down foods. Also teach your children all the emergency concrete things to do that will help the physical body calm down when a sudden anxiety or panic attack begins. Then go to other preventatives, first foods and then vitamins and minerals, as well as other physical factors that have to be changed. Then go to the herbals and stronger techniques if the person really needs more help in managing these chemical panic attacks – use them all if you have too! Check the internet for more recent bloggings and information on what others have done. The trigger foods for controlling the inflammation that can lead to panic attacks, the tapping techniques, under #4 Physical, for physical healing and the energy healing code technique are in the next chapter on Health and Nutrition under, #5 energy healing. And most of all, realize that you are not alone, nor are your children. And good luck!

Also check out a great website on panic attacks by a sufferer of them at my-panic-attacks-.com and several other such sites that are tremendously helpful. Lately my orgone bars have also worked to relieve immediate aches and pains and used regularly over time for minor chronic ailments, these ailments seem to lessen. Read www.orgonite.com articles and others. Even after a lot of studying I cannot tell you how they work, just that they do with no side effects. There are recipes where you can make the stuff yourself or you can go online and buy the much more expensive ones encased in either copper or silver with a battery for a very weak electrical current to amp the conductor or collector. Look under "Zappers" for these. But the homemade ones seem to also work for anxiety attacks or panic, although they do not work for everyone when it comes to anxiety or the more severe panic attacks. Try them out and see what you think!

"Many of our fears are tissue paper thin, and a single courageous step would carry us clear through them."

--Brendan Francis

"Do not anticipate trouble, or worry about what may never happen. Keep in the sunlight."

--Benjamin Franklin
(Franklin definitely suffered from panick atacks!)

"Within each one of us there is another whom we do not know. He speaks to us in dreams and tells us how differently he sees us from how we see ourselves."

--Carl Jung

CHAPTER FIVE

Triggers/Nutrition & Herbs/Energy & Frequency Healing/Psychic Self-Defense

"The superior physician cures before the illness manifested. The inferior physcian can only care for the illness which he was unable to prevent."
--Chinese Aphorism

"A wise man should consider that health is the greatest of human blessings."
--Hippocrates

"The physician should not treat the ailment, but the patient who is suffering from it."
--Moses Maimonides (800 years ago)

What we do to avoid ill-health, maintain good health, and heal our bodies when the chronic ailments don't heal or turn into more severe diseases, we also do for our children. Extremely sensitive children will deal with more of this than most children, but all children are suffering now from the effects of what has happened to, or was done to, our environment. The following are ideas and methods or techniques that you may or may not know about, but the very best that I could find to help cope with chemical, mental, or physical disorders, fortify our children's immune systems and keep them as healthy as possible, including losing weight, as obesity is a national childhood epidemic now. And don't think I don't know what I am talking about, as I watched my very overweight mother die from this root cause of all her other diseases and having struggled with the weight issue all of my life. I have never been a "skinny" person who always says when you present food to them, "Oh, I just ate." But there are many thin people too, who have issues with poor nutrition and obsessive feelings about staying "too" thin. We all struggle with something when it comes to our weight and our health, in one way or another, and our children are struggling even more now than we have.

You Can Heal Your Life Affirmations

Louise Hay had an idea that many felt really helped them. She wrote a book filled with affirmations of all kinds and even affirmations associated with major organs of the body and what emotions we feel in connection to this. Her book is called You Can Heal Your Life. The following is a simplistic guide to what is out there that works and can help you, from the most easily understood to the more exotic types of healing methods, but with an explanation for what and why these practitioners are doing what they do. You can use Hay's affirmations in conjunction with all of these methods and techniques, along with dozens of other affirmation books available since hers came out.

Step #1 - Avoiding Bodily Inflammation through Trigger Reduction

Especially for dealing with anxiety, along with using herbals and vitamin supplements, is avoiding the pollutants in your environment. We have so many remedies now that one can be overwhelmed by all of the material out there. But there is a better way besides unloading those pollutants that are obvious in our homes, garages and backyards, etc. You can do your best with this but really the only things you can really learn to control or soothe, are your emotions and what you eat. Everything else is rather out of your control and every day when you walk out the door, you have to face emotional, mental, physical, energetic and spiritual "pollutants" of all kinds. So let's start with the best way to avoid these pollutants by talking about prevention. All of these "triggers" pile up on you every day, but if you control your diet you can keep these various "triggers" below threshold and feel so much better, eventually so much better that your immune system and your body will undergo a more permanent change. The best book on this subject is Dr. David Buchholz's You Can Heal Your Headache: The 1,2,3 Program. This book should be entitled How To Heal Your Bodily Inflammations by Keeping Your Polluting Triggers Below Threshold. But for one thing the title is too long and who would read such a book without having more information? Since nearly all ailments less severe and eventually moving to more severe without treatments, are caused by inflammation in the body. Without inflammation, our bodies remain healthy. And what is the number one indicator of inflammation or pre-illness? Headaches!

Buchholz's theory is that all of the chronic ailments not having to do with allergies or family genes or simply happening to you, but with inflammation in the body which leads to more inflammation overload until you are sick in the hospital with a severe illness. Buchholz says that we all have headaches all the time because it is part of the human condition on this planet, especially with all of pollutants we are exposed to everyday. We are just so used to them that we don't recognize them as such and to be entirely headache free would be quite foreign to us. In learning to manage headaches for his patients he discovered that most chronic disease could also be managed in the same way before they became major diseases that can incapacitate or kill us. He says these myriad of inflammations can be managed through diet by keeping our "triggers" below threshold and therefore not going into overload. You have to give up some foods, a lot of foods, while you find the ones your body can handle a little of and that are some of your favorites. It is a long, slow process to healing your inflammation "outbreaks" but over time you are not only managing your flare ups but also stopping them almost entirely, giving your immune system a chance to clear out and start over. Added to all the rest that you are doing for your emotions and a lot of high PH water all day, you'll have more money in your pocket and a much stronger immune system to fight off anymore inflammations.

Most of this is nothing new and I am sure there are plenty of other books out there saying the same thing in one way or another, but this book lists all of these chronic ailments and his theories on each one and how his patients did following the diet for each of these diagnosed ailments. Add to all this the specific things, holistic or medical, you may take or do for flare-ups, and some ideas for reducing anxiety and panic attacks, your intuitive children and you, may all find health and wellness, partially or completely over a little time and patience.

Intuitive empaths often deal with anxiety and panic attacks. Beyond what I have listed to do for your emotions (again there are many in Chapter Fifteen) and how to keep your environmental "triggers" under control, including checking your house and car and workplace for additional pollutants that you can change, here are some tips that I have learned to reduce or stop the pollutants around us. But first we need to hear what the medical, psychological and nutritional experts have to say about them.

Step #2 Fortifying Our Immune System through Nutrition, Vitamins & Herbs

Seeking & Using the Best Nutritional Guidance

Phyllis Balch is a certified nutritional consultant who was a leading nutritional counselor for over twenty years. She began researching her gigantic and really the best reference books there are, for both herbal healing and nutrition and vitamin healing, in the seventies. And she began her research because of several undiagnosed ailments that both she and her children suffered from. Doctors could find no illnesses and therefore did not recommend cures, and yet all of them continued to be sick. Balch began to determine that the medical world had something basic missing from its approach which treated the symptoms rather than the cause. She turned to the holistic healing world through her mentor, Paavo Airola, who was a famous naturopath and writer. She then began her own intensive journey into researching the science of nutrition, introduced some rather radical changes in her children's and her own diets, and got everyone healthy. She then opened a health food store and in 1983 published the first of four huge reference books on nutrition and health.

Millions of readers in countries all around the world have read her books, used them as reference guides for many ailments and sought cures or relief from the many chronic and even more severe ailments which plague them. She shared her knowledge with many others and even convinced many medical practitioners to incorporate nutritional healing methods into their practices. She lectured all over the United States, was interviewed on television and radio programs and produced four books in her lifetime, some of them close to a thousand pages and entitled Prescription for Nutritional Healing, Prescription for Herbal Healing, The A-Z Guide to Supplements, and Prescription for Dietary Wellness. Her books have been translated into several other languages and they are still the definitive reference books for both individuals and practitioners of all kinds. She passed away in 2004 while working on the fourth edition of her first book, Prescription for Nutritional Healing which came out in 2006.

In the front of each book she presents the elements of health, the disorders and then there is another huge section on remedies and recommended therapies for each one. Under each disease or ailment she gives a brief text of one to several pages, she then lists the nutrients needed in detail, and the corresponding supplements and foods, dosages and comments. She does the same with herbs recommended, dosages and comments. She then lists other recommendations and considerations, also in full detail. Depending on the illness, a single section can go from three or four pages to twenty. In her preface she quotes Hippocrates once and then Socrates once when he says that "There is only one good, knowledge, and one evil, ignorance." She says we have a responsibility to know and understand our own individual bodies and to be responsible for collecting and understanding all we can about how we each individually function physically rather than always running to this expert or that one, before we try what knowledge is already available to us, that the "cure" always comes from within. "All individuals should take an active part in the maintenance of their health and in the treatment of their disorders with the guidance of a health care professional." (*Ibid, p. xiii.*)

In her "How to Use This Book" section she discusses alternative medicine but stresses that all these methods should be used alongside the medical techniques and suggestions, but with the patient being the "captain" of his or her own "ship." She offers suggestions with simple diagnostic self-tests that can guide you to the right expert help as well. She also provides a list of current alternative healing methods and brief descriptions of what they do and offer, such as acupressure, acupuncture, aromatherapy, Ayurvedic medicine, Chinese medicine, Chiropractic, color therapy, fasting, glandular therapy, homeopathy, naturopathy, hydrotherapy, hyperbaric oxygen therapy, light therapy, magnet therapy, massage therapy, music/sound therapy, breath work, rebirthing, frequency healing, and energy work. She always prescribes eating a good balanced diet first, followed by supplements and exercise, etc. And she says that "The body is a complex organism that has the ability to heal itself – if only you listen to it and respond with proper nourishment and care." (*Ibid., p.3.*)

The basics are water, carbohydrates, proteins and fats. Selecting and preparing foods and foods to avoid and how to cook foods properly are points of discussion. What is safe and unsafe about processed foods and how to balance vitamins and minerals and select the right regiment for you. She discusses in detail each vitamin and mineral the body needs. She talks about pollutants in the air, spends a section on drinking and hydrating with water, amino acids, antioxidants, enzymes and natural food supplements and herbal remedies. And these two sections are quite extensive. She then discusses drug interaction difficulties, lists what she calls the "disorders" and then begins to discuss each one in detail. In other words instead of using hours of your time on the internet looking up each of these subjects individually or getting a book and only getting some information on a particular method, her books have it all, without any preconceived notions, judgments or money making schemes. I have the herbal one and the nutrition one and always look things up and try various methods that I think might work for me, very cautiously. But as I said, very little can go through my stomach without problems and my sensitivities are myriad. I had reached the end of both the medical world and the holistic one, so this was what I had left. You may be able to do a great deal more than I could in both these worlds!

Kids with "Labels" - Holistic Treatments & Do They Work?

There is some information on various kinds of vitamins, minerals, herbs and nutritional balances or special diets for attention deficit and attention deficit with hyperactivity, as well as forms of autism and Asperger's Disorder. Not as much for oppositional defiance disorder, but plenty on anxiety and panic attacks, although I think the things that have shown to be helpful would not only help with ODD and anxiety, but also childhood depression, since all these things are a little bit related. Beyond behavioral therapy to help kids cope, and pharmaceuticals to change the brain chemistry, here are the few things that have been discovered so far. Some of them would probably work for many other things as well, although the following ones have been shown to be directly linked to helping these particular disorders. A few good books are: Eating for Autism (and Aspergers, ADD, ADHD and PDD) by Elizabeth Strickland, MS, RD and LD, Autism Treatments and Therapies a free download from http://autism-treatments.org-types/diet-nutrition-therapy. There are many others listed but they all have the same therapies in them and Strickland is the big guru on these topics. Balch's section on ADD/ADHD is quite extensive in her nutritional healing and herbal healing books.

Attention Deficit and Attention Deficit with Hyperactivity

As far as ADD and ADHD goes the following studies have come up with several things as a result of the increased toxicities in or on our planet, which have led to a rise in this disorder and others: chemicals, other environmental pollutants and metal toxicity, especially lead, mercury, and cadmium. Genetics, infections and brain trauma also add to the causes of these disorders including autism and learning disabilities in general, but these are rare, where the following causes are very common. "...a dysfunctional home, heavy metal toxicities, nutritional deficiencies, food and chemical allergies. The majority of cases are caused by an immune defect and allergies in food additives, preservatives, chemicals and inhalants. To deal with this illness, we must address all these potential imbalances. Some of the nutritional deficiencies that correlate with LD or ADD are calcium, magnesium, iodine, iron, and zinc. On the other hand, high copper, lead, cadmium, and aluminum levels have also been seen in learning disabled children. Good nutrition during pregnancy and in the early years of the child's life may help in preventing ADD. Eliminating processed foods, artificial flavorings, colorings, preservatives, and sugars have been shown to help the hyperactivity aspect of the affliction." (*"Attention Deficit Disorder & Hyperactivity" by Dr. Allen Burez, Chiropractic doctor, National Health and Longevity Center, www.all-natural.com.*)

Dr. John Ott who is a pioneer in light deficiency disorders – read Dr. William Campbell Douglas's book Into The Light for more information – suggests that you replace all of the light bulbs in your home with full spectrum lights although Russian scientists say that these are dangerous too? Food additives research from Dr. Benjamin Feingold, MD, years ago, suggested that these were a major cause of various childhood disorders but especially ADD. This has also been in question but more recent research seems to support this idea too. Research on the dangers of Ritalin and Cylert and other such medications negates what the medical people say because of dangerous side effects including seizures, suppressing growth, angina, blood pressure problems and depression. Dr. Robert Mendelsohn along with the World Health Organization warns that over use of these drugs has reached epidemic proportions and states that these drugs have not proven over time to produce better academic success or better productivity from the child. These drugs simply make it easier for the teacher and the parents to manage a difficult child.

Nutritional approaches for ADD, ADHD, LD, Autism, and Aspergers, having been studied for their children's lack of particular nutritional substances. It has been found that these children are especially lacking in omega-3 fatty acids, magnesium, and zinc. The cell membranes and synapses in our nervous systems need to be protected by antioxidants or fatty acids, B vitamins, magnesium, zinc, and vitamin C. So supplements must be fortified with anti-inflammatories, antioxidants, vitamins, minerals and nutrients. Foods must include good fats such as olive, fish, canola and flaxseed oils, eliminate trans-fats or manmade oils and avoid food additives and processed foods if at all possible. Lack of these nutrients can result in impaired long and short term memory. Richest sources for zinc are meats, sea foods, whole grains and legumes or beans and peas, etc. Foods rich in the B vitamins must also be included in the diet along with some calcium and vitamin C. Amino acids are also important and one should avoid any type of artificial sweetener, especially in soft drinks, although even regular sugar sweetened soft drinks are very injurious to an autistic or ADD child.

Homoeopathists look at the whole system and then treat it accordingly with tinctures and herbal concoctions, but they also would use methods to rid the body of metal toxins and allergies. The lowering of triggers in the environment through a food diet can also help. Neck and skull adjustments can be done by a chiropractor for pressure and irritation on the neck as well as Spinal Touch treatment. Lessening dairy products, eliminating refined sugar, eating a high protein diet, eating fewer simple carbohydrates and more complex carbohydrates, and even drinking small amounts of caffeine seems to have helped eliminate many symptoms with especially ADHD children. Besides the Phyllis Balch materials, some of the best books recommended on these subjects are: Childhood Illnesses and the Allergy Connection by Zoltan Rona, MD, Ritalin Free Kids by Robert Ullman, ND and Help for the Hyperactive Child by William G. Crook, MD.

Autism and Aspergers or High Functioning Autism

Autism seems to have more things identified as holistic treatments for the various types of autism. Included in these are nutritional therapies of vitamin B-12, magnesium, gluten and casein - free diets, pancreatic enzyme's, colloidal silver, omega-3 fatty acids, calcium, Aloe Vera, lowering sulfur, and a couple of specific nutritional supplements called Dimethylglicine or DMG and Efalex Oil or DHA oil. All of these treatments are specific to individual children, according to the results that the child shows. The B-12 therapy is given as a series of shots, but there is quite a bit of research showing that vitamin B-6 has especially proven to show many positive results for autistic children. Many parents have experimented with many kinds of vitamins for their autistic child. But this is the vitamin that over time has accumulated quite a bit of evidence of dramatic success using mega doses of vitamin B-6. Along with the B-6, the children were given vitamin C, niacinamide, panthothenic, and a multivitamin in various studies to see what the results would show. There was a significant improvement in 40% of the children studied. The children showed less irritability, less sound sensitivity, and the bedwetting symptoms disappeared with the addition of magnesium added to this regime. No one was cured of their autism, but the children had better eye contact, there was less self stimulatory behavior, fewer tantrums, the children exhibited more speech, and had a greater interest in the world around them.

A lot of the other nutrients listed have to do with the poor digestive problems that most autistic children have. Because they had received repeated or prolonged courses of antibiotics for their many respiratory infections, most of the good bacteria in their stomach and intestines had been killed off. 90% of autistic children have chronically inflamed guts as a result of other types of infections as well. Restoring a healthy gut requires supplementing with digestive & other products that can help to heal the digestive track and promote normal absorption of nutrients. The gluten-free diet, pancreatic enzymes and fatty acids are all meant to help heal the digestive track. Colloidal Silver helps to control diarrhea, which is a common problem among autistic children as well. For the hyperactive children, improving blood sugar balance is absolutely necessary to reduce abnormal glucose metabolism. Three-fourths of all autistic children display, an abnormal glucose tolerance which means that they cannot maintain balanced blood sugar levels. Essential fats seem to be missing in autistic children, which means that they need a higher intake of fatty acids than the average person. And there is some research that autistic children in particular are lacking in iron, which is essential for vision and having healthy cells in the gut and brain.

Undesirable foods and chemicals often reach the brain through the bloodstream because of faulty digestion and absorption, which is a good thing for all of us to know if suffering from any kind of digestive problem. But wheat and dairy seem to be linked to autism and this of course suggests trying the gluten/casein - free diet to see if your child improves in this way. There have been quite a few dramatic results from this particular diet for autistic children. And since children with autism can have nutritional deficiencies, drug and nutrient interactions, food allergies, food sensitivities and intolerances, gastrointestinal disorders and feeding problems, one might want to try all of these suggestions one at a time to see which set of things seem to be helping your particular child. Most important though, is to keep a food diary and notes on your child's behaviors and symptoms. Alongside all of the foods that they have been eating, you can identify much more efficiently which food allergies that they may have. There is a great book for identifying allergies in children, entitled Tracking Down Hidden Food Allergy by William G. Crook, MD and Cynthia P. Crook, illustrator. It is written and illustrated for children to read and discuss with their parents and even explains the Cave Man Diet for children who have to go to this extreme to discern their hidden food allergies. I used it and it helped me to discover a few of my own! Drinking water all day long, especially one with a high PH content such as artesian water can really help most physical problems and if you are not close to a normal weight then divide your weight in half and drink that many ounces of liquid a day, preferably water. If your weight makes this an impossible amount to drink, then do the recommended amount of anywhere from 8 to 10 glasses each day in the 7 point to 8 point range of PH water.

Step #3 Acupuncture –Acupressure /Touch for Health/Tapping

Touch for Health &Tapping Acupressure Points

Acupuncture came first and has been used for thousands of years in China and Japan using needles and little glass cups. It is a very complex system and takes years of training to do it accurately and well, working with the over 700 meridian points located all over the body. Then came Acupressure Points where one holds these various points rather than using needles. Touch for Health is a more simplified type of acupressure or holding the points, but still takes a lot of training and is somewhat complex. One can train in these methods but there are many others out there too from both Chinese medicine and Japanese medicine. The "meridians" are points all over our bodies associated with specific organs and specific ailments and diseases. There are hundreds of them and one would have to study quite a while to understand them all and use them for both diagnosing and treating patients. Touch for Health is a sort of shorthand for lay people, and Tapping is an even briefer, quick way of working on ailments and emotional problems on your own. There are dozens of such touch therapies based on this system with a variety of names, but Tapping is the easiest to use at home.

EFT Tapping is simply a means to making the entire immune system sit up and listen by prompting better circulation in the blood system, the lymphatic system and the nervous system. Americans, especially, have very sluggish immune systems when it comes to the circulatory processes and paired with all of these positive phrases repeated over and over again, both a belief in wellness, and a belief in one's worth in the world are confirmed every day, day in and day out. Studies so far have shown that Tapping increases balance and healthy flow in all the systems in the body and has a positive ripple effect on the organs and our general health. It is simply a quicker, more efficient way to do acupressure points, thus energizing the body towards better health and well-being. Tapping the points seems to be stronger than simply holding the acupressure points with two fingers. And most important, you can do the procedure on yourself too!

There are also EFT or Emotional Freedom Technique facilitators who work with Tapping on deeper levels with many kinds of exercises and claim all kinds of healed illnesses with people who follow through on their exercises regularly. Read more about this on the internet and watch all the videos on it. Claims are that healing can take place on anything from health issues minor and major, solving emotional issues or stopping addictions, losing weight, being financially successful, and even healing the various energetic field layers around the body can take place. If you plan on trying it, my advice is to try a minor physical ailment first to prove to yourself that you do feel better after a few days, because the exercises seem silly and repetitive and most often people give up on them because they don't have the time, don't understand why they are doing them, or just plain find them silly. After two weeks of having to do the tapping procedure 5 or 6 times at each sitting, 3 or 4 times a day, my nerve damaged legs suddenly one day stopped hurting and continued not to hurt for several days. Some people claim to have cured a serious illness but not without constant effort to do this procedure over time or under the care of a facilitator. Try it first and see if this is something you think you or your child can feel or resonate with. It would be a fun thing to do together, especially for temporary things like anxiety or a panic attack, and the results can often be dramatic.

"TAPPING" Procedure

1) "Even though I have this ______________________ I completely and totally accept and love myself." Or "I love and approve of myself and am healing this________________________ gratefully. Or, make up your own phrase.

2) On a scale of one to ten in your mind, one being the best and ten being the worst,

Tapping Points

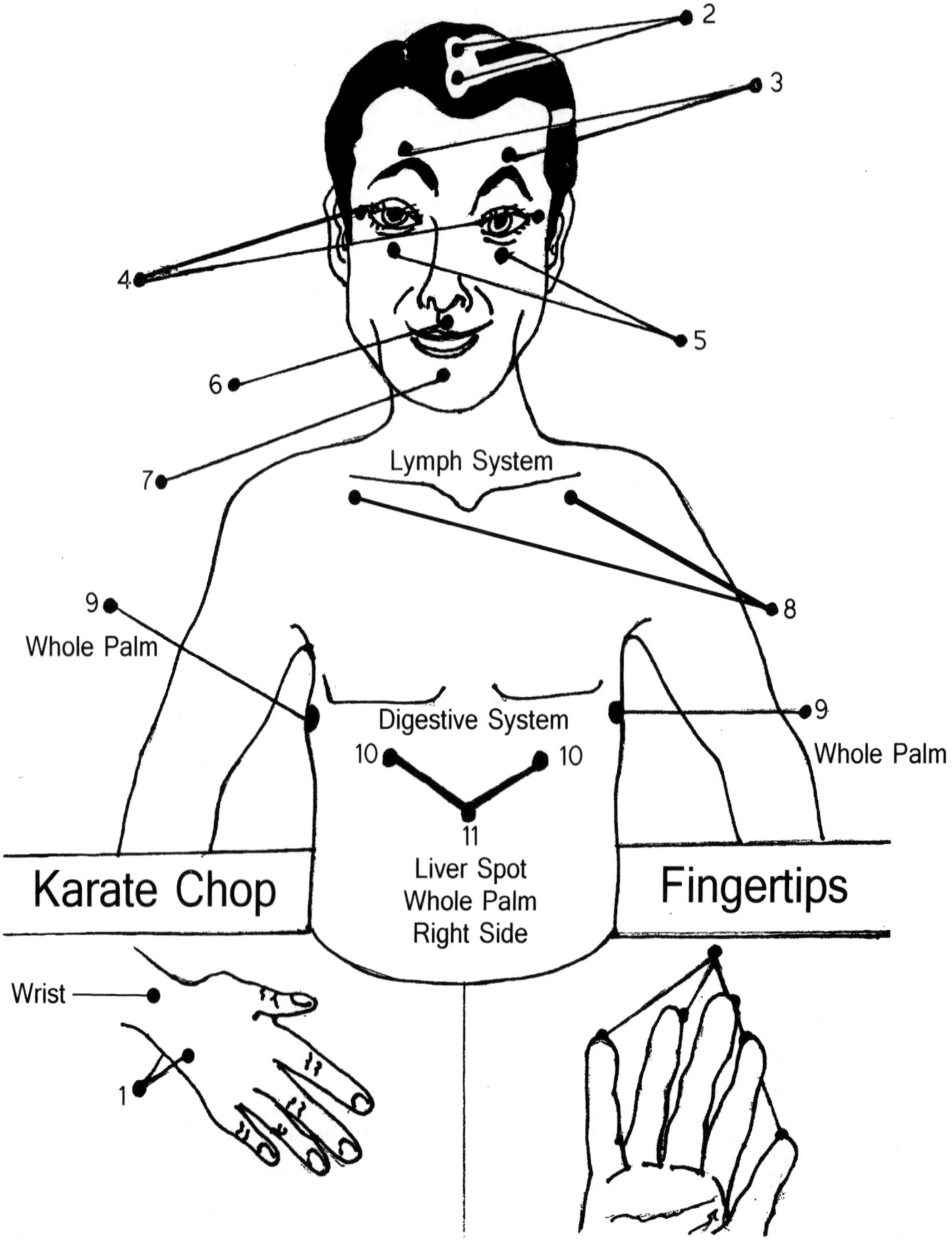

ask yourself "Where am I on this scale?"

3) Use reminder phrases (or a single word is best) for focusing throughout each repetition of the tapping process, each time you do the session.

4) Repeat the tapping of the acupressure points in a gentle rhythm of your own choosing and stop after each time to check your "scale" of 1-10.

5) When you are down to a 1 or 2 on your scale, you can stop for that session.

6) About three or four sessions per day would be best, spaced out over the day, and then in the evening of each day you can see how you feel if it is a health problem, or continue to do this procedure until you see a change in an emotional issue or request.

7) Only do one problem or issue at a time until you feel you have reached your goal on that one and then proceed to another one as needed and follow the same procedures as already mentioned.

8) Tap anywhere from three to seven times at each point if you are more left brained and if you are right brained follow your own rhythm.

9) Check out the websites on Tapping for more information. Watching the short videos provided will help you visualize what to do and also inform you as to what to ask for in a positive manner.

10) Remember you are really just talking to your own body and asking it to help you to feel better, reduce stress, offer physical comfort for a health problem or emotional issue. Whatever the claims for tapping, it really does improve your immune system and emotional state through the power of positive thinking and the repetitions of positive mantras for self love and healing.

Procedures for Simplified Tapping

1) Say the beginning phrase several times to yourself, placing in the blank the issue or health problem you are going to work on.

2) Visualize your scale in your mind and determine the number you are starting on, then begin the tapping procedure.

3) Side of each hand using two fingers, using the "Karate Chop," tap both hands

4) Top of head, tap rhythmically, alternating finger taps

5) Above the middle of each eyebrow – two finger tapping

6) Outside edge of each eye socket – two finger tapping

7) Tap under the middle of each eye

8) Tap upper lip below nose tap with one hand, two fingers

9) Tap on the chin below middle of lower lip, one hand , two fingers

10)Tap sore spots on either side of collar bone about eight inches apart

11)Tap under each arm pit about 3 inches down from each arm pit, alternate

12)Pat the "Liver Spot" or right side over the liver with the entire palm, tap lightly

This tapping procedure is a condensed version of many other acupressure trainings. Facilitators do various levels of much deeper work for individual difficulties and remediation's to achieve the whole brain functioning mode. You can download huge workbooks on this subject for free but you need an interpreter to use any of the material. With this simplified version, you can have a quick fix for your immune system. Be sure you repeat this procedure as needed until you are down to a 1 or 2 on your scale and then stop. Repeat the entire session at least two more times spread out over the day until the problem is reduced to a comfortable level or goes away altogether. Tap gently clockwise around an especially sore area several times, for especially tender spots.

Additional Tapping Points as Needed

For sore hands and fingers tap the tip of each finger from thumb to pinky on top of the fingernails on both hands and do two finger tapping, across each wrist for wrist problems. You can add in a tapping point below the ribcage on each side for digestive problems. You can associate a chakra with each tapping as you pass by that particular chakra, or even tap over each chakra to energize them as well.

Step #4 Maintaining Health & Wellness through Movement

Many of the movement forms of self-exercise are well-known these days. There are several in martial arts, Tai Chi from China and several kinds of Yoga from India. There are dozens of physical sports both team and individual that a person can use for their own well-being. However, in team sports there is a necessity to be competitive and aggressive, so it is better to do a more individual form of exercise to keep the body in good health, running, climbing, gymnastics, and other such sports are good for this. And even though meditation is not necessarily a movement sport like dance or mime, etc., it does give the body and the mind a spiritual shower all on its own. Choose your individual sport for well-being, and then choose the sports, according to how athletic you are, to do with others. Even a gym workout or a warm-up regiment can fulfill what the body needs to be in good health. Unfortunately, in our society today, the pressure to compete and win is so high that many athletes use stimulants of one kind or another, and of course these are not good for the body. Many a retired athlete deals not only with these sorts of addictions but also a battered body. As they age, many athletes then require both medical and holistic attention.

Step #5 Healing the Body through Energetic Healing Work

Based on the idea of "chi" or Chi-Gong from China, "prana" from India, or "breama" from Tibet, etc., the idea that we have a second body or energy body comes from very ancient beliefs and practices from such countries as Egypt, Greece, Rome, Japan, China and India. This second body is really not a second one but an integrated part of the human body and radiates out from the physical body and through it in all directions. This "aura" can be seen by psychics and Russia claims to have photographed it around all living organisms as well. A person's health or illness or mood will show in the aura and psychics claim to be reading a person's aura when they garner information about the person they are "reading." The Chinese developed acupuncture from this "Vital Energy" which has over seven hundred meridians or points on the body that were mapped out thousands of years ago on the premise that these points communicate with organs deep inside the body. These points on the skin also connect with the whole mental and physiological state of the person and the needles inserted into these meridian points to correct imbalances in the energy flow of the "chi." "Changing the energy flow on these points changes the Vital Energy deep inside the body." (*Psychic Discoveries Behind the Iron Curtain by Sheila Ostrander and Lynn Schroeder, Bantam Books, 1971, p.223*).

Not only do these points or meridians connect the body with the inside organs and internal flows of the energy systems such as the blood, nervous and lymphatic systems, but they also connect each body to the energies around them in plants, animals, other humans and the earth itself. All energies are integrated and interwoven together in the environment. The Chinese believers in Chi Gong say that "... If there is a change in the universe and environment, a resonance is produced in the Vital Energy of the human body which in turn affects the physical body." Therefore the seasons, the weather changes, the cycles of the moon, the tides and all other cyclical earth changes can affect both the emergence of an illness and what treatment the patient should receive. And these changes in the environment can bring about an illness as well. Russians feel that they have now photographed this aura and can someday use these constantly changing color flares or colors to diagnose illness or predict illness before it appears. They have matched their Kirlian photos to the very acupressure points identified in Chinese medicine and at the time were convinced that they had found concrete evidence of an energy body. Russian research scientists also felt that these meridians were the answer to not only mental telepathy but also a way to know details about a person through their auric field, as psychics have been saying for centuries. They felt that acupuncture meridian points could increase psychic abilities when stimulated because the points are related to brain and organ functions, although this evidence was discounted in many recent studies. (*Ibid., p.225*).

Healing hands or energy work materials are practically endless, and all the self-help ones always have a myriad of rules and regulations to follow. There are many healers and many methods, and so rather than wasting your time trying to talk about some of them I have selected some great books that you can use at home instead of, or in preparation for going to a massage therapist, energy worker, aura healer or chakra cleanser, chiropractor, etc., etc. Healers may or may not actually touch the body, and more often they do not. They are working on the energetic or auric fields that surround the body and go through the body or chakras. There is a lot of disagreement on what the chakras look like, and what the various auric layers look like as well. Many people cannot see them and many who do, claim to see very bright colors. For myself, I am of the opinion that they are much more subtle than this and look like steamy waves rising from a tea kettle. There is a color to them but it is very subtle and all the colors change by the hour or day, etc. so going and getting a photo of your aura will only show how you and your body are feeling at that particular moment.

There are dozens of variations on the chakras of the body. Most of the belief and philosophy concerning chakras comes from India, but there are others from other countries around the world as well. Chakras are the "controllers" of the energy field that goes around and through our bodies. Even though the colors of the chakras may vary according to the type of chakra system you get introduced too, and there may be from seven to twelve basic chakras going through the body, most people agree on the following basic seven chakras: the Root Chakra is red and is about at the tailbone, the Sacral Chakra is orange and is about two inches below your navel, the Solar Plexus or stomach chakra is yellow, the Heart Chakra is an emerald green, the Throat Chakra is a light blue, the Third Eye Chakra is in the middle of your forehead and is indigo, while the Crown Chakra or top of the head, is a light violet or metallic gray-white. Other chakras are added according to the system you study and some say there are even many more than just the twelve or seven. There are many CDs out there with guided meditation chakra cleansings but my favorites are "Chakra Balancing" by Stacey Dean and Gerald Markoe and "Journey through the Chakras" by Jackie Haverty. Refer to the chart for the additional information on the five chakras in the activities chapter on page 291, or for in depth information read The 8th Chakra by Jude Currivan.

Energy work is done either with a method like the best known one, Reiki, or by many other techniques both trained for and done without training from the intuition of the practitioner as a natural-born healer. This is cause for some lengthy discussions because some people train for years and others have no training except for their healing hands and experience. So you have to be careful and choose what is best for you and your own beliefs. There are many medical practitioners, many holistic practitioners and many religious practitioners to choose from. Even Mother Theresa developed a healing method of her own and trained her nurses or nuns, which was an energetic rubbing of the body, often in circular motions. It was used on many poor or starving children in her mission in

India with great success. From one end of the spectrum to the other, energy healers and workers are here to stay and can be seen working on hospital patients for a quicker recovery or in hospice, for a calmer and more peaceful death.

Here are some good books for you to use at home: Your Healing Hands: The Polarity Experience by Richard Gordon, Acupressure's Potent Points: A Guide to Self-Care for Common Ailments by Michael Reed Gach, Hands On Healing: Massage Remedies for Hundreds of Health Problems by the editors of Prevention Magazine, and my favorite, besides Your Healing Hands, is Gordon's Quantum Touch: The Power To Heal. Prevention Magazine has a good one to use for specific ailments, but Richard Gordon's are the best for teaching the basic methods and how to use them for all ailments over and over again. His technique is easy to read and follow. He explains what you basically need to know before attempting this sort of energy healing on your loved ones. In the middle range are books like Energy Work by Robert Bruce. Some that go quite a bit deeper for those of you who want to know more or get training in a particular method, or read life stories from healers and how they got there: Energy Healing: A Pathway to Inner Growth by Jim Gilkeson or the popular books by Barbara Brennan, Hands of Light and Light Emerging. The research in Russia on Kirlian photography and the energy body is quite interesting from Psychic Discoveries from Behind the Iron Curtain.

The Healing Code is a simplistic method for self-healing using energy work principles and also frequency healing combined to heal both physical and emotional issues. The explanation for why these four energy centers manage everything else in the body, is that the Bridge position heals the processes of the master gland or the pituitary gland combined with the pineal gland. The Temples help heal the processes of the hypothalamus and the functioning of the left and right brain. The Jaw Corners heals the processes of the spinal cord and central nervous system (the emotional brain) as does the Adam's Apple with the help of the thyroid. These are the major control centers for every system and every organ, much like acupuncture but in a simplified form. The idea being that a less complex holding point in the energy body is much more focused and powerful. Also each of these centers has a code sequence that will alter the cellular memories of the body and realign the "code" for better health.

Please read the healing code book if you need a lot more explanation than this and want to go more in depth. Combined with Tapping for body maintenance and done three times a day, stimulating the energy centers for frequency healing and realigning the body systems, can be doubly powerful. This six-minute healing code can be done using the same 1 to 10 scale just at the beginning as a visualization for physical or emotional pain. The same individualized affirmations or prayers can also be done to integrate the two sequences or techniques together. Varying what you think and visualize and say, keeps the procedure not only from being boring for you, but also for your body and beliefs and healing "codes" to remain powerful. The power lies in the combination of all these things.

HEALING CODE

Alignment Positions——Resting Positions

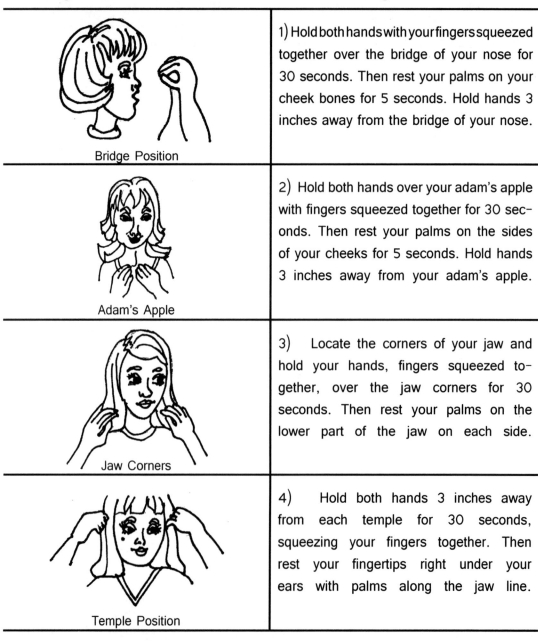

Bridge Position

1) Hold both hands with your fingers squeezed together over the bridge of your nose for 30 seconds. Then rest your palms on your cheek bones for 5 seconds. Hold hands 3 inches away from the bridge of your nose.

Adam's Apple

2) Hold both hands over your adam's apple with fingers squeezed together for 30 seconds. Then rest your palms on the sides of your cheeks for 5 seconds. Hold hands 3 inches away from your adam's apple.

Jaw Corners

3) Locate the corners of your jaw and hold your hands, fingers squeezed together, over the jaw corners for 30 seconds. Then rest your palms on the lower part of the jaw on each side.

Temple Position

4) Hold both hands 3 inches away from each temple for 30 seconds, squeezing your fingers together. Then rest your fingertips right under your ears with palms along the jaw line.

Do this procedure three times in a row.

In the Healing Code there are four points or healing centers: the Bridge is down from the invisible line between your eyebrows to the bridge of your nose and then do the resting position, do the Adam's Apple/resting position, Jaw Corners which is the back bottom corner of the jawbone or about three inches below the hinges of the jaw/resting position, and the Temples are about two inches away from your eye sockets on each side/ resting position. And finally hold your entire hand, fingers pinched together over this point about two to three inches out from the body doing the procedure in this order for 30 seconds each. Repeat in the same order three times, because including the resting positions, this is about six minutes altogether. This is supposedly the proper order to do this in, but I found this confusing and put them in order by holding my hands about three inches out from the Temples, and rest on the line of the jaws for a few seconds. After the Bridge position rest your hands on the side of your cheek bones. After the Jaw Corners, rest your hands on the side of the lower end of each jaw and after the Adam's Apple position rest your hands on the sides of the jaw. Use the pictures in the book to make sure you are positioning your hands correctly and do whatever order works best for you or refer to the following chart. I find that by the third time I can really feel the healing power or energies and the pain is temporarily gone even after each time you do the four positions. I assume that over time some healing can take place. There is a great deal more information in The Healing Code book, so be sure and most definitely read this one. They provide detailed charts on the holding and resting positions.

I say my affirmation first, think about my 1 to 10 scale of pain level and then visualize any emotional issues attached to the physical issue for a few minutes. I do my Tapping first, down to a one or two on the scale of pain. Then I finish off with the four healing code energetic points continuing to visualize and affirm as I do these points three times, holding my hands two to three inches away from the body over these points. Combining the two has an even more powerful effect and you will feel this. Some people find they actually heal within a few days, others within a few weeks and some within a few months. Still others do not seem to heal from this and instead of saying that you are "cleansing" and this is why you don't heal, the authors tell you to go back to the drawing board and check out what your Memory Themes are attached to this ailment. They provide a whole section on some generic emotional issues to consider. Whatever happens, the Healing Code is on the right track, the authors have great explanations for why you are doing this simple technique and you can do it on your own. They also provide various ways to heal emotional and physical layers of energetic memories in many other ways throughout the book. I have found that varying what I think in my mind for both the tapping body points and the healing code energy points does help. I do them regularly but I also keep my directions short, so as not to confuse the physical body or the energy body. For example, my back hurts and there are many past emotional issues tied to it hurting: all the back injuries, all the unreleased memories and incidents surrounding my back, etc. So as I tap I might say only one or two words but vary them, such as: back, reduce pain, strengthen spine, build tissue, cushion, ease pain, etc. As I do the healing code I might say:

strengthen, heal heart, support me, walk free, heal back, release pain, relax spine, etc. After this I do my daily meditation anywhere from ten minutes to 40 minutes, either guided or just with soft music or in silence. I might do a Self-Healing Draw (see chart on page 302) as well or my tachyon cells or orgone bars, etc. according to the level of the pain. It is the consistency of daily routine, the belief that one can heal, the repetition of affirmations, thoughts and phrases, and yet the creative variations on a central theme, that make these methods powerful in your healing process. (The Healing Code by Alex Loyd and Ben Johnson, Grand Central, 2010.)

Step#6 Vibrational or Frequency Healing

Healing Rays & Sound Healing or Toning

In ancient Egypt the priests and healers used a combination of sound and color and light healing to help those who were ill. They had special rooms painted a certain color that were associated with certain organs. The patient would be placed on a table in the room associated with the diseased organ and then a small opening from the ceiling of the room would allow the sun's rays to strike the organ being affected and hopefully the exact small color ray from the sun would bath the diseased organ as well. They would move the table to continue to have the sun strike that particular spot for the rest of the day. Then the healers would come in and use chanting and instruments that produced special tones associated with the diseased organ as well. At least this is what people in metaphysics believe or have channeled, as no one really knows exactly how healing was done in this culture. It is believed that many ancient cultures used similar methods to heal their patients, and from this have come the metaphysical sciences of "toning" or healing with sound, various light/color therapies and other variations on these sorts of healing methods. Drumming, chanting and playing crystal bowls and many other sound/light/color techniques, not only put the patient in an altered state but then are claimed to effect healing from facilitators acting as channels for the correct information to come through and help heal the patient or at least relieve the patient's symptoms. From these sorts of techniques and what scientists have learned about frequency or vibrational waves, pioneers in this field have developed much more specific types of healing techniques.

Crystal Bowls are my method for helping to reduce stress in people and help foster deep meditation states. There are those who also believe that the crystal bowl tonal waves can realign the waves of energy for individuals or even groups of people, but I have never done this type of work unless I am unaware of it and my guides are doing this for me. I trust that I am being directed when this is done, but also believe that the person needs to seek and have diagnosed, any medical condition first, besides these general kinds of therapies, seek the appropriate healer for a much more specific type of healing than a crystal bowl. The ancient healers and shamans still have great knowledge concerning both herbal and sound/light/color healing methods, but today with the computer age, much more specific meridian point healing can take place using these same methods, but in a more detailed and accurate way. It is my belief that these various techniques will be developed and begin to show their power in a medical setting, with a more acceptable method of transmitting healing to patients in a hospital setting and that what science and medicine have learned will eventually merge with sound and frequency healing methods which pinpoint the problem and work in conjunction with what we already know in the medical field. These will be accomplished through precisely calculated computer programs already developed and being refined in other European countries, but especially in Holland.

Crystal Bowls were developed from the metal meditation bowls used in China, India and Japan. Someone got the idea to merge the sound healing and altered state techniques used with metal bowls into crystal made bowls which hold more light and color, and in fact attract light and color rays. One can buy a set of chakra bowls associated with the various chakras and go from there. While this technique, like many others, is great for achieving an altered state to begin a meditation, it is not specific enough for actual healing work. Where computer generated programs along with equipment for the various tones and frequencies for light and sound and color, are, like the I Health program. Tuning forks are also used in the same manner with various tuning forks associated with various chakras, and the same with drumming and chanting. All of these techniques came from ancient shamanic methods eventually integrated into the so-called "New Age" methods, and then began to become more and more specific as these various techniques continued to be associated with the meridian points, chakras and auric fields, and finally various energy rays and frequencies.

<u>Frequency & Energy Waves – Does This Work</u>?

The father of this research in our country was a man named Royal Rife. His story is a very interesting one and one even less well-known than Nickolas Tesla's. Both men were discredited by the huge corporations which did not like some sort of energy being available to the masses for free. Tesla's inventions would have given free electricity to everyone at least 80 years ago. Rife's development of a more precise microscope that did not kill pathogens or bacteria with heat or magnification, would have given us the beginnings of medical research by many others to cure over time, many major diseases through the idea that every cell in our body emits an electromagnetic pulse or frequency. A lower frequency allows pain and a higher frequency can heal it. His microscopes allowed him to determine the electromagnetic signature of most diseases and what precise frequency could kill these various pathogens or bacteria. If the person's body can reach a higher frequency then healing begins. And today there are many variations on Rife's work using frequency healing associated with either cellular level alterations or using the Chinese meridian points or killing the malignant cells through frequency wave therapy. There are medical and university research facilities working on this in many countries around the world now, using other names rather than Rife's "MORs."

Dr. Rife, a pathologist and bacteriologist, stated in 1938: "We do not wish at this time to claim that we cured cancer, or any other disease, for that matter. But we can say that these waves or the 'ray' has the power of devitalizing diseased organisms, or killing them, when tuned to an exact particular wavelength, or frequency, for each different organism. This applies to the organisms both in their free state, and, with certain exceptions, when they are living tissues...." Rife claimed that he could find any mortal oscillatory rate or MOR for various pathogenic organisms, and directed his research accordingly, culturing and testing various pathogens with his Universal #3 microscope, he then directed radio frequency energy through his 'beam ray' tube machine. Rife claimed to have documented the precise frequencies, which destroyed specific organisms." Rife's newer type of microscope was able to clearly show that destroying or weakening pathogens could take place by introducing or inducing destructive resonances in their constituent chemicals. (*"Royal Rife" in Wikipedia, the free encyclopedia at* http://en.wikipedia.org/wki/Royal_Rife.)

Rife's work was 98% successful in a study done in 1934 under a grant from the University of California where last stage cancer patients from the Pasadena County Hospital were taken to Rife's lab in San Diego for a ninety day treatment using his pathogen killing treatment. After ninety days 86.5% of his patients had been completely cured. He continued to treat the other patients for four more weeks adjusting the treatment for each individual patient. After the additional four weeks, 13.4% of the remaining patients responded to treatment, although not entirely cured. Many doctors and pathologists worked with him. Yet by 1939 most of those who had worked with him were denying that they had ever known him. Because of the many slanders that his 50 years of work received and the many watered down frequency techniques modeled after his work and in some cases prosecuted for fraud, in the years to come, Americans did not get to see his work embraced by science and medical researchers, thereby possibly proven to be a very viable foundation to more extensive discoveries and cures which I believe will eventually come to fruition regardless of the powers that be, and Rife's pioneering work will be exonerated as it already has been in some European and Asian countries.

Obviously these two men were lost to history because the electrical companies and all the other financial uses for electricity would have been out of business, with Tesla credited rather than Thomas Edison, as the father of electricity. And the pharmaceutical companies, medical insurance companies and medicine itself as it is today, would all be altered financially as well as professionally, had Rife's research and testing continued in the medical field. One might say that Rife's rudimentary invention could have taken us as a nation down an entirely different "disease healing" path as early as the forties or for sure the fifties, because the intrusion of World War II would have taken the entire country's attention and put it elsewhere. There has been a more recent revival of Rife's work in the holistic healing field with mixed results. On the one hand, variations on his findings in the field of healing have surfaced in an ever expanding "theme," and yet on the other hand, his findings have continued to be harassed as he was years ago, but this time by the law for fraudulent health marketing. Rife died of alcoholism, valium, and a broken heart, when he realized that his work was never to be taken seriously, and after a series of disasters which one group says was a systematic discrediting of his work. While another group claims that modern day interpreters of his work are breaking the law and fooling the public through fraudulent health practices, which in certain cases is still true if the frequencies have been watered down or used incorrectly, or even not at all.

The truth is somewhere in between these two groups, but only more time and more research will prove his theories, that very well could have cured many, many people by now. During Rife's lifetime certain groups attempted to pay him off, he suffered a series of robberies where his vital and meticulous work evidence was taken, and when he tried to replicate what had been taken he then had his precious virus microscopes vandalized. A mysterious fire destroyed his lab and then the police confiscated the remainder of his 50 years of research because of a lawsuit which was only vaguely related to Rife. The American Medical Association refused to publish anything related to Rife's work, and what work he had published was stricken from the records. His boss suddenly retired and moved to Mexico with a quarter of a million dollars in his pocket, and other professionals who had endorsed his work, also denied having ever worked with him or even to have known him. Rife was a broken man. A few who had worked with him preserved what they could and continued on. But decades later, a woman wrote a book on his materials and a lot of good intentioned people but also many con artists explored his work to make money. Had his work simply moved into the research field, we would probably have had cures for some diseases today, but now we will have to wait for medical science to catch up to his groundbreaking start.

Variations on his work claiming to heal have produced many fraudulent techniques so that the real research has been buried by those using his ideas but not honoring his meticulous 50 years of research. Several people running companies and offering devices based on Rife's ideas were prosecuted in Wisconsin and Minnesota in 2002. In 2009, another man was convicted of offering Rife related machines. Some other companies continue to offer different products that enhance or magnify a particular ray activity for healing. Still others, who are on the right track, offer light, color and sound healing through identified meridians associated with organs and healing, and these facilitators have had many successes, confirming Rife's initial results, such as the I Health program from Holland. One group wrote a fiction book on computer healing called Sanctuary and they keep their locations secret so they can continue to offer distance healing via sound and light waves on the computer. It is indeed sad, if not criminal, that some place between what Rife discovered and what medical researchers will soon discover, the truth about frequency healing will bring about the use of a major healing tool in the future. And as soon as the powers that be find a way to market this and make money off it, we will all have amazing and quite sophisticated healing for many diseases, along with entirely different perspectives and directions in medicine. Taking a pill will become an occasional support, instead of a major money making industry.

Step #7 Protecting Ourselves from Psychic or Energetic Attack

For centuries now, people have talked about ways to protect themselves from psychic attack but most people do not have this happen to them, even though whole countries, cultures or communities and individuals have dealt with energetic "attacks" since the dawn of man. Interestingly, for those who have experienced this sort of thing and probably kept quiet about it, there is more help available on a more practical level than there ever was before. If you think this section is "crazy" then just skip it and go on, but if you have personally experienced a psychic attack and you know you are not "crazy," keep reading. Psychic attack is when an unseen force seems on the beginning level to be bringing you more bad luck than you think is usual for you. A more severe form can bring on illnesses, nightmares or even night attacks that seem downright impossible. I won't even begin to address this here. I will simply recommend you read up on the types of psychic attacks, get some good books on how to ward these things off, and consult the experts who have been there. Practical Psychic Self-Defense by Robert Bruce is my favorite but I am sure there are many more out there as well. In Bruce's book he devotes the first part to the relationship between humans and unseen spirits and then he talks about the signs and differences between having your life disturbed just by regular stuff or mental illness, and actual "invisibles." The last part is devoted to countermeasures of various types of disturbances or interferences in your life. If you have eliminated every other possibility and you feel you are left with something that is impossible to explain then read this book and use what you think will work for you or your child. Bruce's book certainly helped me out when I needed it and he does devote a whole section to children.

Step #9 What May Be Coming Healthwise If We Make the Right Choices

Being a science fiction reader and great fan of Rod Serling and his other writer's stories, there is a "Twilight Zone" episode that sums it up for me, after technology and spirit meet and agree. An astronaut crash lands on what he thinks is another planet in another galaxy or even universe. He is certain that he is mortally wounded. The people live in grass huts, wear plain woven garments and herd goats while growing their own food. They do not have the technology to save him. They pick him up and take him into one of the huts and lay him on a simple handmade wooden table. One woman puts her palms on either side of his face and his whole body becomes numb to the pain. Another woman puts her palms on the bottoms of his feet to establish a circuit of energy healing through the body. Another man monitors all of his bodily functions with his mind and hands and then another man begins to reach inside his body, breaking apart matter to perform the repairing surgery that the astronaut needs. A last woman uses her mind to quicken the healing after the surgery. The astronaut is completely healed in a day or two and he realizes that the inhabitants who found him, rather than being very backward, are way ahead of humans on earth. Eventually he finds out that he has merely time traveled and actually is on earth many centuries into the future.

And even this is going to take decades still, before the far future that this episode demonstrates, combines and merges with technology when mind power will join fully in our future practices of "medicine." This would be after we have learned all we can from technology, merged this technology with ancient knowledge in a new form, and created small medical centers with easy access from our homes and with very low cost healing and cures available and lots of portable equipment that doctors can carry with them to once again visit us in our homes for the lesser ailments. Along with these medical healers will be energy healers to ease physical reactions, pain, and to speed up healing. Telepathic communicators will act as therapists as they speak to the patient verbally and in their minds. Healing and surgeries will become painless, quicker, and a team of both medical people and holistic health people will work together as equal professionals, with each patient's needs the center of their focus, since pay and prestige will be equalized.

Nutrition will have been taken care of through adequate education and things that we can take internally to supplement our healthy diet. No one will deal with being either too heavy or too thin, there will probably be pills or frequencies for this, or even better, foods for this. Those with a genetic predisposition will suddenly be "equalized" with those who do not struggle with these sorts of issues. One will have a choice of either seeking a spiritual beauty ideal or the physical beauty ideal will become what we all look like. Or we will have reached a spiritual level where inner beauty is the ideal and outside beauty is not found as attractive as it was. Our children will come into a world where many things will have been taken care of. They will also become much more responsible for their own neighbors and all other communities of people. Communities of all kinds will live and work together with a lot less strife or disagreement. Those who struggle in our society will no longer have to do this, as people and diseases and differences will not disappear, but instead, become neutralized and invisible. That is, if we choose this path and not the self-destructive one that we seem to be on now. The best of all ethnic cultures will also be preserved and differences of all kinds will be honored and celebrated, if they are good for the communities. We will arrive at these conclusions on our own, and take action, or we will be forced to, through brain and soul evolution, planetary shifts and natural disasters, and whatever else it takes to become spiritually awake and involved.

CHAPTER SIX

Depression, Mental Illness - Spiritual Awakening & Emergence - Teens

"Mental illness is nothing to be ashamed of, but stigma and bias shame us all."
--Bill Clinton

"We are asleep with compasses in our hands."
--W. S. Merwin

The Mystery of Mental Illness

All children are just waiting to be listened to, understood, and taught to play in a structured environment. All of these things empower children and obviously every child is an integrated, multi-faceted being. Can we have a child that is gifted, creative and intuitive too? Or can one have a child with sensory integration difficulties, a slight learning disability, and yet that child is extraordinarily gifted as a psychic? Or maybe one of these labels is absolutely right but only defines a small portion of who that child is? And of course the answer is a resounding yes! Treat your children like gift packages and open each one carefully and thoughtfully, determining each integrative element that makes up the whole picture of each child. Do not allow labeling of any kind to affect how you deal with each child, including New Age labels. They are, each one of them, their own individual "package." And in most cases, how you treat them, teach them and love them, will determine how they turn out. Perhaps a small percentage really do have developing chemical and mental problems, but then one wonders, even with this topic, what the fine line is between insanity and creativity and intuition? Is it merely repetitive motion or being unable to break out from the same patterns repeated again and again? It is a very fine line and one not currently addressed as "real," unless genetic or chemical or brain damage is involved.

Childhood Depression

After discussing anxiety disorder and panic attacks, which are vital topics concerning intuitive children, we need to now discuss a little bit about depression in children.

Childhood depression is something that can be easily identified with a set of characteristics or symptoms. However, childhood depression can also be pervasive across every label we are discussing, including empathic intuitive children. Symptoms of classic childhood depression are: irritability or anger, continuous feelings of sadness or hopelessness, social withdrawal, increased sensitivity to rejection, changes in appetite, changes in sleep, vocal outbursts or crying, difficulty concentrating, fatigue and low energy, physical complaints such as stomachaches and headaches, reduced ability to function during events and activities, feelings of worthlessness or guilt, impaired thinking or poor concentration, but the most severe symptoms are thoughts of death or suicide. Children under 12 rarely attempt suicide, unless chemically influenced by a side effect from a drug they are taking for some other issue. There are some children who attempt suicide at a younger age on impulse simply because they are very angry or upset. Symptoms in children vary and it is difficult to identify whether children will become clinically depressed adults.

Obviously intuitive children could become temporarily depressed over many issues such as boredom at school, difficulty with a teacher, parent or other caregiver, peer difficulties, lack of sleep and falling behind in their school work, a loss of some kind such as a grandparent or a pet dying, an invisible friend deserting them, dealing with or hiding their difference from others, coping with an awareness that those around them either do not acknowledge or are shut down from, not understanding why other children are not experiencing what they are and coping with more than a psychological disorder. Above and beyond their intuitive abilities, children are often dealing with nightmares and night terrors and all the other night time difficulties that arise in the dark, while often coping with intuitive gifts. And these are only a few of the problems for intuitive children that can result in feelings of depression, loneliness, and isolation from others. The biggest issue is abuse of any kind that can be perpetrated on children. And there are a few children, who most often hang themselves, that are under the age of 12, although suicide is mainly an older teen and adult problem that is on the rise in many countries around the world, especially in the United States.

Spiritual Awakening or Mental Illness?

Children can often be mislabeled when it comes to childhood depression and other lesser mental illnesses, and as always, there may be several integrative difficulties going on for the child. In each section of this particular chapter, I have tried to give an alternative way of looking at what might really be going on for each child. Transpersonal psychologists and other experts in the fields of psychiatry and psychology have had another view of the difference between mental illness and what is termed a spiritual crisis for the last 40 or 50 years. "Throughout history, people in intense spiritual crises were acknowledged by many cultures as blessed; they were thought to be in direct communication with the sacred realms and divine beings ... The often colorful and dramatic experiences were nourished with the trust that these individuals would eventually return to the community with greater wisdom and an enhanced capacity to conduct themselves in the world, to their own benefit as well as that of society." (*The Stormy Search for Self by Stan and Christina Grof, MD, Penguin Books, 1977, p. 2.*)

"Psychiatry found biological explanations for certain mental disorders in the form of infections, tumors, chemical imbalances, and other afflictions of the brain and body. It also discovered powerful ways of controlling symptoms of various conditions for which the causes remained unknown, including manifestations of spiritual crises. As a result of these successes, psychiatry became firmly established as a medical discipline, and the term mental disease was extended to include many states that, strictly speaking, were natural conditions that could not be linked to biological causes. The process of spiritual emergence in general, along with its more dramatic manifestations, came to be viewed as an illness, and those who demonstrated signs of what had been previously thought of as inner transformation and growth, were in most cases, now considered to be sick." So while clinical and laboratory tests don't support an automatic medical problem, some of these people get classified into the same category as those who do, if they have emotional or psychosomatic symptoms. (*Ibid., p.2.*)

The Grofs contend that most non-ordinary states of consciousness are then considered pathological and treated with traditional psychiatric methods which include suppressive medications, counseling and sometimes hospitalization. So while there are many who are mentally ill, among these people are those who are going through a natural healing process, or a spiritual emergency because of a crisis in their lives, creating difficulties for their family and friends, or having a temporary inability to function as they normally do for over weeks or months or even a few years. One person I can think of historically, who went through this sort of rather dramatic process was Mary Todd Lincoln. Both she and her husband were interested in Spiritualism, were highly intuitive and empathic, and went through long grieving stages upon losing several people close to them. Lincoln also had two near-death experiences as a child and had many prophetic dreams. They held séances at the White House and the Lincolns were advised by more than one trusted psychic. Up until now, the biographies of Lincoln blamed all of this on Mary Lincoln. And while Mary did display the characteristics of a maniac depressive later in life, becoming more and more paranoid and obsessive, she certainly had many reasons for this grieving and political paranoia especially being of an empathic and intuitive nature. Mary lost her real mother at 6 years old and had a pretty desolate childhood with her very severe stepmother. After losing three of her four sons, going through the Civil War with her president husband and losing him, while having brothers and other relatives fighting against each other, many of whom died, she then remained in a never ending grieving and spiritual emergency process which probably drove her crazy! She was deemed incompetent by her only remaining son who had her committed to an insane asylum in her old age.

Regardless of how a crisis manifests in a person, it is worth our while to talk about the process of a Spiritual Awakening, which begins as a Spiritual Crisis and then becomes a Spiritual Emergence. Neither a medical nor an emotional problem, Spiritual Crisis is its own natural process which has occurred throughout history. While adults go through this type of thing, on a much deeper and more expansive level than children, to a child, the crisis is just as real, just as terrifying and just as vivid. A child's rich fantasy life and the real intuitive experiences contribute to this. When a child goes through a spiritual crisis, due to a near-death or the death of a family member, or even the loss of a friend or the loss of a pet; they too, are in crisis. All of these issues, severe or seemingly slight, can result in the child experiencing deep stages of grieving as well. This spiritual crisis can also cause a much more difficult issue such as childhood depression or staying in one particular stage of grieving. Looking at types of adult spiritual crisis can help us understand a child's crisis and find ways to help them. The aftermath of the crisis can also manifest characteristics and can indicate ways of dealing with the spiritual awakening before the person "emerges" in a new way. The intuitive child will have more to deal with when this happens because of their lack of awareness of their own intuitive gifts and how to manage them.

The experts on this particular topic are Stanislav and Christina Grof, who coined the term Spiritual Emergence. The definition of Spiritual Emergence or its end result, a Spiritual Awakening is "the movement of an individual to a more expanded way of being that involves enhanced functional and psychosomatic health, greater freedom of personal choices, in the sense of deeper connection with other people, nature, and the cosmos. An important part of this development is an increasing awareness of the spiritual dimension in one's life and in the universal scheme of things." These transformations can take place several times throughout a person's life. (*www.spiritualemergencenetwork.com*).

But before we go into the causes for such an experience, we need to make clear the difference between a medical or physical condition, deep emotional problems or mental illness and a spiritual crisis or emergency. The Grofs, provide in their book, The Stormy Search for the Self, a list of these differences. The criteria or assessments of a medical nature include such things as a clinical exam, laboratory tests, specific psychological tests, observation on how the person is functioning in the world, and a look at past functioning and diagnosis. If all these results are negative, and all the characteristics of a medical problem don't seem to be there, such as additional confusion, disorganization, impairment of memory, poor coordination, poor communication skills; medical causes can be ruled out.

Identifying and assessing problems of a psychological nature include compiling a personal history, which shows serious difficulties in relationships, poor social adjustment, and a history of psychiatric problems. Poor organization skills, unexplainable changes of emotions and behavior, incoherence, autistic withdrawal, aggressiveness, behavior that interferes with good working relationships or endangers one's health, confusion between the inner experiences and the outer world, excessively blaming others, acting out, mistrust and paranoia, neglecting basic hygiene rules, destructive and self-destructive impulses or acting without warning, and not being able to work and cooperate with others, etc. Another strong characteristic for mental illness is repetitiveness or the inability to break the cycle of patterns the person finds himself in. If most of these things are not apparent and the person is able to function in the world inside the parameters of what is considered normal behavior, then the term spiritual emergency can be looked at when the person seems to be in crisis. This type of emergence and its preceding crisis can occur for days, weeks, months, or even a few years, but is not a lifelong problem.

Spiritual Awakening : Spiritual Crisis to Spiritual Emergence

The Grofs have identified 9 different causes for spiritual crisis. There is the Shamanic Crisis, which is fostered in many countries throughout the world, but also sought out by people who become shamans, even in the Western world. For example, the younger men of the many Native American Tribes went on a vision quest as a rite of passage towards their manhood. Most of these types of rituals are in a sense a trial by fire, dangerous and frightening. The second type is the Kundalini Awakening which involves an energetic awakening of "chi" or "prana" depending on one's belief system. This awakening can be powerful, sudden or over a long period of time, and the magnitude of this particular crisis can be both embarrassing (because of its sexual connotations) and terrifying (because of its sudden onset and other types of overwhelming energetic sensations). The third type is called a Peak Experience which is the most esoteric of all the types because it is the balancing of yin and yang, a return to the wholeness and unity of both mind and spirit and experiencing mystical encounters that put the person outside the realm of the physical world. This is also called Unitive Consciousness and can also mean falling back in love with one's planet, community, family and the self. Reuniting with all that there is and will be, on a heart to heart level, can also include religious or mystical experiences, upon occasion.

The fourth type is called either Psychological Renewal or a "return to the center." A person having this type of spiritual crisis will find themselves contemplating such things as their own personal history, the history of their family and the generations that came before this, major issues of life and death, good and evil, etc. This type of crisis will eventually lead to increasingly pleasant experiences and a gradual resolving of these issues. Although initially, there will be much conflict and confusion, the end result is something called the "sacred marriage" or finding one's ideal partner, whether person or purpose in life. The fifth type is called a Psychic Opening and it is exactly what it says, the person becomes more aware of his or her own psychic abilities and begins to use them more as these gifts increase in size and scope. The sixth type is the Near- Death Experience and this one it is pretty much self-explanatory, since there is so much written about this subject. But this subject is so vital to those many intuitive children who have had this experience, that I devote a whole chapter to this topic for people to gain a broader understanding of these experiences.

The seventh, eighth and ninth types are all interconnected with whether the person experiencing one of these is believed in the particular society in which they live. These are the people who are sometimes misdiagnosed with a mental illness, because the parameters of belief interfere with whether what is happening to them is real or imagined. The seventh type is communicating with spirit guides or Channeling Spirits, the eighth type is experiences of Close Encounters with UFOs, and the ninth type stretches between Transfiguration experiences sometimes leading into Possession States. Different things can also trigger a spiritual crisis, such as intense spiritual practices, extreme stress, physical or emotional shock or trauma, severe illness, childbirth or intense lovemaking, addictions which alter the state of consciousness, time of life where either destiny seems to call or a desolation descends, and surgery and near-death experiences. I have had several spiritual emergences so far in my lifetime and don't expect them to stop any time soon. However, they were four to twelve years apart and lasted roughly from several months to two years. I can talk about them a little because I was old enough to handle them by the time they happened to me, and though sometimes frightening, the quantum leaps forward were highly rewarding and positive. In each case however, I had absolutely no one to help me, but I was wise enough by then not to talk about them and relied on a few friends I opened up to and what I read in books or on the internet to assist me through them along with a few workshops. I suppose too, that I had all that spiritual emergence stuff filed in my head from years back and paid attention to this material and any others I had learned over the years, subconsciously.

However, people who go through intense trauma, physical and mental abuse, substance abuse, a sudden accident or a near-death, etc. have a great deal more to deal with when the spiritual crisis occurs and not only do they need lots of confirmation that yes, indeed, they are going through one, but also mentors and friends who believe them and inform them. So now let's take the topic of empathic, intuitive children who seem to be "crazy" yet may be instead, going through a childhood spiritual crisis. A lot of the treatment is the same; it is the attitudes of those offering these treatments that need to be different. Is it you, who is in crisis rather than the child? Is it the child's teacher who is in crisis with themselves or your child, or both? Are the parents in crisis with each other, with the children caught between them? Who really is having a spiritual crisis? Is the entire family having a spiritual crisis? First, determine who's involved in the crisis, and then if it is only the child, everyone around that child will be drawn into it. And certainly if the child has had a near-death experience, this crisis will be profound.

Transfigurations or Possessions – Are They Real?

> "It is wonderful how much time good people spend fighting the devil. If they would only expend the same amount of energy loving their fellow men, the devil would die in his own tracks of ennui (boredom)."
>
> --Helen Keller

Transfiguration, for our intents and purposes, means that a person is momentarily or for a brief period of time, possessed by a spirit. The entire posture, facial features and mannerisms will become foreign to the person that you know and it really looks and feels like another person has decided to inhabit your friend or acquaintance. This is not necessarily a bad thing because the spirit may have entered you or another person's body simply to deliver a message to a loved one. On the negative side, if the spirit happens to be where you have gone and picks up on your intuitive abilities and enters you just because they are lonely or bored, this is another problem altogether. On the other hand, even transfiguration can be negative and one really needs to guard one's self from this sort of thing by asking the person or spirit, who has entered you uninvited, to tell you their name or even commanding the spirit to leave, politely and firmly. If this is only transfiguration then this is all that needs to be done. If a living remote viewer or even an astral traveler is trying to manipulate your feelings and emotions, then this will be more difficult. Living people are much more deadly to deal with than those not living, as well as one's own mind deluding you. The intuitive, creative soul walks a fine line here between sanity and illusion, or even delusion.

However, in rare cases, a real Possession takes place where the spirit wants to stay with the other person or "piggyback" for as long as it can. If the person is too psychically open or easily possessed, then the problems begin. And not just problems of a real live possession, but also determining what is drama and playacting, what is mental illness, and what is an actual possession? And unfortunately, it can sometimes be all three of these things and determining how to move forward is quite difficult, especially with the variety of belief systems that may be surrounding this so-called possession, both in the people's minds around the possessed person, and in the possessed person's own mind. There are deeply religious people who believe that all spirits are evil and that possession can literally kill you. There are also children raised with these beliefs that have learned to play act quite skillfully, not necessarily for the notoriety it might bring them, but in a way to survive family trauma and abuse. They learn to disassociate or literally "fly away" as a form of protection, even to the extent of astral projecting out of the situation. You have therapists who feel the person has a definite mental illness and priests who believe that only an exorcism will release the demon or evil spirit from the child and free him. And then you have the spirit itself, is it a real demon, a trickster spirit getting off on all the drama, or is it the child's belief in this demon that fuels it, or once again, all three? Unusual displays, such as levitation or throwing one against a wall can still be coming from the "possessed" person because of our own lack of knowledge about paranormal phenomena and how it is produced. Since some spiritual masters, saints and even a few magicians have throughout history achieved such things as the art of levitation, I suppose anything is possible!

Determining what to do can be a major problem and often the best thing to do, after you eliminate a medical or psychological problem, is to cater to the person's belief systems. In other words, if you believe in a Vo Doo curse or a Kuhuna revenge, then it is possible it can kill you, simply from your own belief. If you believe that the only thing that will work is hours of physically taxing drama and attention from others to release a demon, then an exorcism is the thing to perform. It could work temporarily, for a long while, or perhaps forever. If you believe that your house is part of the possession, then having someone clear your house may also work, although attached spirits often come back a while later after those clearing the house have left, so be sure all objects left behind from past owners are cleared out too! It has been my experience that traveling tricksters just like to mimic whatever the person responds too to toy with the person's fears and emotions, often for pure entertainment. More serious spirits seem to be very attached to the person or the place which they loved or experienced tragedies. Spirits just passing by can be extricated, but those quite attached to a place just hide out for a while and come back later when those who tried to remove them have left. Really "clearing" a place entails removing objects or sets of objects that may be causing the paranormal activity as well.

But whatever the possessed person believes will work for them and anticipates will work for them, is your best option. Before a person arrives at the place where they will be de-possessed, clear the place and this just may work too. For myself, I am of the opinion that in many cases the person being possessed is often a younger person who has the energy and desire to put on such a spectacle or just a person with either a great imagination or slight mental problems, who sincerely believes in what is happening to them. However there is a small percentage where something has escalated so deeply that evil is able to enter not only the minds and hearts of the "possessed, but also those entering into this "play." Evil of any kind - and evil is the desire to control, manipulate, or possess or seek revenge on others, having little or no conscience, and a selfish and narcissistic soul, can come from any direction! Many of us cope with this sort of "evil" from time to time in our lives but without the drama. Belief is a powerful tool for both good and evil, unfortunately. As Helen Keller so aptly puts it, put all of your focus on the good in the world and perhaps the devil's power will shrink a little or even a lot. And if under attack, do not revel in it, let it slowly dissipate of its own accord or command it to stop, and get help from those who have dealt with this before, only when all else has failed.

My advice is to first, just walk away when you are near such feelings and don't be intrigued by these things or stay near them. Second, call them out and demand their name and if they don't leave, politely ask them too. Third, if they don't leave, command them to leave and then you leave the area too. Fourth, ignore the behavior of the possessed person and don't fuel it or the spirit, by giving it any attention. Then send them out the door as quickly as possible and let some other foolish person take this on! I have had a couple of experiences of this type of person coming for a reading, and quite a few surprise experiences while visiting places for my ghost book stories. Some people who came to see me, had a whole entourage of people, living and dead with them, and were anticipating some sort of ritualistic de-possession. When they didn't get it they wanted to leave anyway, whether they were mentally ill, it was drug induced, or a real spirit was with them. A real spirit wants all this attention too, as does a super psychic person unaware of their own abilities or perhaps even very aware. If you cannot leave your own home or workplace, then it takes time and patience and a lot of good acting to get the negative energy or entities to leave. While ignoring them to the best of your abilities, you have one more, and the most powerful resource available to you, which is love. Sending love to evil not only confuses it, but also brings in all your guides, angels and any other positive energy available to rid you of these kinds of unwanted visitors. Sending love and understanding to someone or anything can deplete nearly all negative energies over a little time and patience.

When taken by surprise by ghosts or spirits in a home or commercial building or just outside in the "elements," I simply told it to get away from me or moved away from it. If it followed me, I left the entire building or area. If it came home with me, I politely ask it to leave and if it did not, I did my best to ignore it even though it really was frightening at the time. I used a few psychic self-defense things but found in the long run that negative energy and negative "spirits" want to fuel up on your emotions and they absolutely love fear. When you give them nothing, no emotions at all, and ignore them and don't respond to them, they will eventually leave of their own accord. For those of you who think that maybe I have not had something really harrowing happen to me, you are wrong. It took a lot of time but eventually they left and I moved on, and I had to do this alone or it would have lasted longer because of the attention it would be getting from others. I often wonder if this is not one of the lines between intuitive experiences and mental illness, the person's inability to distinguish between real evil and simple drama or delusion. There really are things around us all the time that we are unaware of, and being aware is one's best defense, whether it is coming from the living or the dead. No matter how afraid you are, you must pretend to ignore these energies, anyway! "Negs" as Bruce calls them, are then given absolutely no fuel on which to manifest, irritate, or even frighten you. And if you can, send them a very big dose of love energy, this always confuses evil and takes the wind out of its sails, depleting its power over time.

UFO Abductions & Channeling Spirits

But there are things one can do to protect oneself and Robert Bruce's book on psychic self-defense is one of the best. UFO abductions and experimentations fall under this category too, and as a way to be sure that nothing else is going on, follow the same guidelines. If you feel that you have done this and there is no hint of childhood trauma and abuse involved, find a support group where you can share your experiences safely, and keep your journal full with details. If you have seen the therapists and doctors, and then the dream interpreters and psychics, and you still really know that what happened to you is real, then begin a regimented meditation and energy rejuvenation course for yourself and try to find a place of peace within yourself. Perhaps what you understand about your experiences is different than those of the abductor's perceptions, or perhaps they really are evil and you have to face it head on in order to continue to live your life. But do not give up by any means! You have a special knowledge that the rest of us don't have, and this in and of its self can be empowering too. Sometimes, ceasing all spiritual practices for a while will work along with keeping yourself clear and focused and not numbed out by an addiction or two.

Also, be quite cautious in channeling spirits or using automatic writing. There are a lot of trickster spirits about who just want to dabble with you and see this as a strange form of entertainment. They may be pretending to be UFO abductors, ancient far eastern gurus or Native American holy men, or even demons, just to fool around. It makes one wonder if many of the ancient sorts of invisible world beings just simply like humans and love to entertain or be entertained by them in negative ways. In the physical world, you would be foolish to just talk to an absolute stranger on the phone and invite them to your house or start an e-mail relationship with a stranger who claims to be all these things that he or she is not, without checking them out first. So why, in visiting the otherworldly places, would it be any different? Always check the facts and records, both historical and present day, for intuited information, and get confirmations when possible. Robert Bruce told a story of working with what seemed to be a possessed little boy and after days and weeks of getting nowhere, he finally just threw his hands out and said, "Oh, just take me instead!" He ended up in the Australian desert for three weeks and could not remember a thing he had done until he wandered back to civilization and swore never to invite such a thing into his own soul again!

Guidelines for Making it Through a Spiritual Emergency

Some of the things that can affect a child or an adult while going through such a transformational crisis are a bombardment of inner experiences and old beliefs and ways of being that are being challenged. There are also difficulties in coping with the demands of everyday life, a difficulty distinguishing between the physical world and the visionary world and physical sensations from forceful energies. There can be a strong urge to communicate with others what these experiences are, and sometimes one can become out of touch with reality temporarily. Many sensory changes take place; one can have unusual or strange thoughts, intensive emotions, strange physical changes, a stronger feeling of oneness with nature or the universe, a feeling of actual psychological death and rebirth, and even encounters with other realms. In other words, in the wrong hands of powerful manipulators and without specific investigations of medical and psychological difficulties being ruled out, a child or an adult will not be assisted in the correct ways. Once guided through a spiritual crisis, the spiritual emergence and overall spiritual awakening can become a dynamic and fulfilling rebirth into a better life.

Guidelines for making it through a spiritual emergency include simplifying your life, limiting your use of all stimulants and seeing if you can stop the over the counter medications you use, or at least reduce them if possible. One must create a sacred space where you can journal and contemplate what is happening and discontinue spiritual practices for the short-term. Finding a means of expressing your experiences through some sort of artistic avenue or movement technique is important and finding one good friend, spouse, therapist, etc. to confide in is essential. Finding a way to flow with the process and not fear it is also important. Knowing your limits, both physically and psychologically and getting outside help if the experiences are more extreme will also help. However, if you are an intuitive person, visits from outside realms where you either go there or they come to you, can be quite frightening and downright terrifying. If you do not understand what is happening to you and do not know how to deal with such things, as most children would be, it is up to the parents to assist the child through such a crisis and of course a Transpersonal therapist could help mentor both you and your child through this experience, since they accept as real experiences what many regular therapists will not or cannot. And there are many others who may step forth to help you in a synchronistic way.

However, there is a huge website called the Spiritual Emergence Network, which the Grofs founded, and this network can supply you with ideas, information, chatting with others who have been through this, possibly with their children too, and they may provide ways to locate a therapist in your area. As for me, Robert Bruce's Astral Dynamics (the original version) and his psychic self-defense book helped me a great deal as did one little article you can find on www.Pharrah13.com entitled "Spiritual Awakening" on the list of Pharrah's finds, which provided specific questions and answers addressing the physical side effects of a spiritual awakening. Although there are several articles available now, this article specifically addresses the intuitive perceptions towards these various physical experiences and what to do about them. This can calm a child down quickly and eliminate the high anxiety of this crisis, when addressed in this manner, "No, you are not crazy. You are having an experience that many people go through and these are ways to understand and cope with what is happening to you." While some people balk at there being another explanation for emotional turmoil, others will see the value in checking out various websites on the current ideas of spiritual awakenings.

Physical & Emotional Symptoms that Appear & What to do About Them

I want to mention some of the more important physical and emotional reactions that both adults and children can have when dealing with a spiritual awakening that may be even more traumatic for psychic, empathic, intuitive children. These ideas are a combination of my own experiences and those referenced in the article "Spiritual Awakenings" that has no original author sited. The ways of telling if you are having a spiritual awakening and ways of coping include first and foremost a dramatic change in sleep patterns. Restlessness and waking up several times each night can occur, as well as waves of energy running into the body from the crown of the head. This can feel like sprinkles, tingling, itching, and crawling sensations along the scalp or down the spine. One can wake up; vibrating internally or externally and this could be quite frightening for someone who has never had this happen to them before. Journaling about this, meditating, reading poetry, or even just gazing at a pool of water or the moon when you can't sleep are ways of making peace with this new and temporary shifting that will become permanent later. Of course, with children, they need to be comforted, told this will pass, and helped to go back to sleep again. One can also experience pressure on the top of the head and this simply means that your head is opening up to receive divine energy. Or you may be actually going to a permanent higher vibrational frequency and this being a new sensation, takes some getting used to.

Sudden changes in emotions can happen and with this an emotional roller coaster experience that often includes episodes of pressure on the chest. Core issues can come up or old unresolved issues, so just feel assured that you are being guided to release these issues. One can have a weight gain or weight loss in an attempt for the body to ground itself while experiencing a spiritual awakening. There could be changes in eating habits or the person can be either not as hungry or hungrier, so go with the flow of what's happening and realize that it is temporary. You can develop all kinds of environmental sensitivities and food intolerances that you have never had before. This has to do with cleansing toxins from your body. Your senses can be amplified, and you may have increased sensitivities to lights and sounds, etc. Your vision may be slightly altered, because you are experiencing new ways of "seeing" so drink lots of high PH water and avoid those activities that you are more sensitive to for the time being. Rotating the kind of PH water you drink can also help those more sensitive to everything around them, following the "golden rules" of any regiment: "everything in moderation" and a constantly rotating schedule of foods and drinks. You may also be hearing strange noises in your dreams, or even in the daytime, because your ears are adjusting to new frequencies. Smelling, tasting, and touching, in fact all of the senses, become much more acute, and your likes and dislikes will change.

There can be skin eruptions of one kind or another as you heal an issue from the past, or even many issues, which are shedding toxins and emotions you no longer need to carry. The intense energy can put you in a pattern of physical highs and lows. If you are a person on a spiritual path you will find that there are changes in your prayers and meditations. You are beginning a partnership with spirit and power surges in your body can produce a certain coldness or heat which may become too intense for you to handle. Ask those who guide you on the other side to slow down the process to a level that you can handle. You can have a variety of physical feelings such as headaches, back aches, neck pains, flu-like symptoms, digestive problems, muscle spasms, numbness or pain in the limbs and even an occasional involuntary vocalization or body movement. Be sure to check any of these symptoms and make sure that there is not a medical reason for them before deciding that they are part of your spiritual awakening.

You may also begin to look younger than you have and your dreams may be much more vivid and lucid. Some major changes are on the way in many areas of your life and you will be asked to examine them. These are forces that you cannot ignore. There may also be a strong desire to break free from restrictive patterns. Solitude or contemplation will help with all of these changes. There will be creativity "bursts of energy," the feeling that time is speeding up, and an anxious feeling of something about to happen. An extraordinary and overwhelming deep yearning for meaning and spiritual connection can overtake one. Or a feeling that your life is different and you are different and you may have many teachers appearing to help you through your awakening. Also, to protect yourself against changes from the other side, blessing where you eat, sleep, play and contemplate, would be a good idea. Synchronicities and waking dreams and visions abound! Listen to your heart, tell your truth, and release those who are no longer good for you. Remember that electrical and mechanical equipment will be affected around you at a more intense level than is normal for you. The feeling of being out of control can be quite unsettling and sometimes scary. Just remember that "this too will pass."

On the more far-out side, for those of you able to acknowledge these things, there will be visions, illusions, and sometimes even delusions. Sometimes it will be hard to distinguish between them but remember that they too are only temporary. So here goes, these are all the more out there things that can happen: invisible presences, channeling, a unification with spirits, a sense of unity with all, high moments of joy and bliss, a feeling of integration, both within yourself and with the world at large, feeling closer to animals and plants, seeing beings from other dimensions, seeing a person's or shape shifter's true form or seeing loved ones with a different face, etc. Psychically, you will be physically manifesting thoughts and desires more quickly and efficiently, and all of your intuitive knowings and feelings will become much more pronounced and accurate. Your creative talents will begin to blossom. Some other rather odd physical side effects can be dizziness perhaps even causing you to fall, heart palpitations, your hair and nails growing more quickly, third eye or chakra muscles and nerves may twitch, or you may have tension or tingling sensations at the third eye location. And if you are a healer, you will feel energy surges coming from your hands or out from the center of your palms. Memories may surface in all different kinds of ways. Things that you have done in the past to calm yourself down, such as meditation, massage, chiropractic work, medications, or dozens of other things that you have done will now not be working for you. Or they will be working so well that your rollercoaster emotions are frightening you. Eventually, however, you will grow use to your new emotions, vibrations and awarenesses, and the spiritual rewards will be spectacular. (*"Spiritual Awakening," from the website www.pharrah13.com*).

The most important thing to happen in a spiritual emergence is coming to feel that you must be living your purpose in life and really haven't been. Friends will leave you or go to a different place in your priorities, and new friends will come in, your work may change, and your isolation and loneliness may increase for the short term while all of this change takes place. Your intuitive awareness will also become magnified. You may be afraid to confide in one person but you really need too, and your perceptions about yourself and the world in general will be greatly altered. In short, you are a new you! You will become much more aware of the energy fields that run the world and other worlds as well. But when children experience one of these spiritual awakenings they need help in understanding all of these things both physical and psychological. And especially if their spiritual emergency is quite dramatic, they may have had a near-death experience or they may have been in an accident or they are dealing with a severe illness.

Also, as you become more sensitive to all these things you can have experiences which may make it difficult to differentiate between a higher frequency level and a visitation done on the vehicle of a higher frequency level. When my mother died there was nothing until a year and a half later when a little oval picture appeared one day in my mind of a younger, happier portrait of my mother in her lilac colored sweats but with all her make-up on and her jewelry. She was smiling and younger and thinner and happy. That was it! Years later when my father died in the evening on Christmas Eve, the next morning I woke up absolutely startled by a huge energy surge through my body that lasted for about an hour and a half. It was downright terrifying because of the magnitude of what should have been a comforting visit from my dad. I was ecstatic to have the visit but overwhelmed as well. It was the most intense feeling of love I had ever felt, an all encompassing farewell from my father. By then I seemed to be much more aware of the energetic world than I had in the past and perhaps this was why my father came in this particular way because it was easier to get my attention.

"Loneliness is another intrinsic component of spiritual emergency. It can range from a vague perception of separateness from other people and the world to a deep and encompassing engulfment by existential alienation. Some of the feelings of inner isolation have to do with the fact that people in spiritual emergencies have to face unusual states of consciousness that they may not have heard anyone describe and that are different from the daily experiences of their friends and family …This is what it is like to be in the middle of a spiritual emergency and still try to operate as usual in your ordinary life. This is how it feels to attempt to live in two worlds. One world is the ordinary, familiar reality in which you have certain expectations to fulfill, roles to play, and obligations to meet. The other is the domain beneath the everyday layer, the vast pool of the unconscious, which contains unknown possibilities. When the inner realm becomes increasingly available, it intrudes into the ordinary awareness, and the separation between the two domains begin to crumble." (*The Stormy Search for Self, p. 52 & p. 158*).

Very Young Children & Spiritual Emergence

On the other hand, children, especially very young children, can handle and resolve such "emergencies" much more quickly because they do not have all the adult world judgments and perceptions that we have. Still, I am providing this information on coping with an "emergence" for the adults who are assisting their child through such an experience. Talking about these things can be very reassuring for the child but it is up to you whether you broach these particular topics or not, whether they are appropriate or not for the situation, and whether your belief system allows for this type of discussion. Whatever you do, dozens of suggestions for what to do, can be found in Chapter Fifteen. The worst thing you can do is to do nothing. Young children can be supported in many ways because they are so open to what you present them with. However, they also need to be protected because of this openness and trust.

Adolescents & Teens - Spiritual Emergencies

Adolescents are dealing with a few other things such as a search for their real identity. They are trying to integrate everything they've learned and everything they have been in their childhood, while also dealing with social roles, ego identity and their spiritual values. They have to make a lot of choices, while having many conflicting interests and loyalties. All of this is what leads to their moodiness. "In the United States, one adolescent attempts suicide every 90 seconds. One is successful, every 90 minutes." Adolescents have to deal with kundalini awakenings, perceptual changes and also psychokinetic phenomena. While all of this turmoil is going on within them, they may experience not only the movement and rearrangement of matter through energy bursts, but also what many people call "the dark night of the soul." How adults deal with these things, whether confirming and honoring these experiences, or instilling fear in one's own children, can really make a difference for these teens' mental health. (*The Call of Spiritual Emergency by Emma Bragdon, Harper & Row Publishing: San Francisco, 1990, p.57.*)

Adolescents can learn to ground themselves, empower their own choices, find outlets for their excessive energy, find a soul connection to a higher power, create positive outlets for their creative and intuitive abilities, and learn to show affection through touch that is not sexual. Most teens seem to avoid hugs from those who care about them and lose out on how to develop their own physical boundaries. Balancing out their attraction to the occult or darker arts, adolescents can learn to understand, control, and use their intuitive and psychic gifts in many positive ways that not only empower them, but also affirm their self-worth. Curious and "dabbling" by nature, many psychic teens need to understand and be guided into discovering their own types of intuition, safely and appropriately.

Goode and Paterson say that all teens that have had a near-death or any other kind of spiritual emergence and are coping with intuitive gifts anyway, could use the following supports provided: taking a quiet time for reflection, being appreciated for being the individuals they are, and being encouraged to not be afraid of their talents or how this empowers them. They need a mentor who will listen and encourage their creativity. They also need creative projects and service projects to focus on helping others. They need someone who complements their traits, and someone who celebrates their achievements. They need to learn how to manage their money and all the other adult skills that they will need out there on their own. But they also need parents, who will set boundaries, while at the same time understanding their viewpoints. Most important they need to be able to share their thoughts on the transcendent and the shifts of consciousness that occur somewhat randomly at their age. (*Ibid., Raising Intuitive Children, pp. 79-80.*)

The pressure to conform in the teenage years is overwhelming. A lot of times, teens will look to us as if they are regressing, not only from their intuitive gifts, but from the children that we knew. Their intellect becomes so strong that if they had profound intuitions as children, they either lose track of these things or set them on a "shelf," until later in their adult life. Those children, who strongly hold onto their intuitive talents through the teen years, tend to either come from intuitive fostering families, or these teens use their intuitive talents to escape from the not so good reality that they have to live in. The drive to get along with their peers is so strong and there are so many other things, that adolescents have to deal with, that parents often choose not to encourage teen's intuitive gifts, because this just adds one more problem to the mix. So the best way to handle this is to ask your teenager if they have an interest in these things and want to develop their own talents, first. Let them choose, and only go as far as they want to with this topic at this time in their life.

If teenagers are having some of the other problems such as depression and anxiety, their medications can numb their intuitive abilities and separate them from their inner voice. Using alcohol or taking drugs can also numb one's intuitive talents, or even, cause the person to misinterpret what they are intuiting. These addictions will take away from the true beauty of the intuitive life. So working with teens through counseling and mentoring, as well as determining the psychological or biological factors for what is happening to them, can help teens to get back in touch with their own intuition. On the other hand, teens can sometimes become depressed because they have lost touch with their intuitive abilities. It really depends on how strong the need to fit in is, in the adolescent or teen. Empathic teens have the worst time, because they pretty much soak in the emotional energies of other people and as a result of this they can develop physical complaints from headaches, to stomachaches to more severe problems like anxiety and depression.

"… parents could really help the teenager be okay with going home, sitting quietly, or walking in a garden, or whatever they want to do to ground themselves. Teens must know they're not weird or strange when this happens. Parents can help them understand that some people have the sensitivity. From the beginning, teens…with intuition have to learn how to take care of themselves and realize it's a form of great sensitivity that has its pluses and minuses. It's a gift. When you have that sensitivity, you have to take care of your energy. That's all there is to it, and that's a good thing... It's a form of self-care to teach teens how to set boundaries and limits. They have to know how great it is to be able to say no to somebody when they don't feel like going out. They might need to stay home to replenish and learn to say no to set boundaries if things don't feel good. They need to learn how to find a safe place where they can replenish their energy and all that. It's a very useful education, early on." (*Ibid., Raising Intuitive Children, pp.194-196*).

Latest research has unlocked some secrets about the teenage brain that can help to explain why teens act the way they do, as well as looking at how we have as a culture come to treat and perceive adolescents. Remember that those who research children, especially intuitive children, have discovered that whatever talents children have intuitively are basically mentored and fully developed at 12 years of age. After this, these skills will go dormant for a while, while other adolescent developmental qualities are being cemented and refined. When these abilities and thinking processes come to fruition in their twenties, the intuitive talents will begin to resurface as well, and continue to be refined, clarified and enhanced. However, there are more and more children coming in, who do not set their intuitive skills totally aside and this is very conflicting for them as all the rest develops.

Brain-wise, the teen brain is still a work in progress. Teens are still not adults as far as the brain is concerned according to current PET scan and MRI research studies. While some brain processes equal an adult's abilities such as motor coordination, the abilities to plan ahead, weigh priorities, organize, form strategies and control impulses, are still in the process of developing in the teenage brain. For example, Dopamine levels are not yet at their optimal level like they are in adults. This means that this chemical messenger is not consistently allowing teens to figure out what to pay attention to, as opposed to background noise or the incorrect details in any given situation. Teens would have difficulty deciphering and interpreting their options when trying to solve a problem.

Adolescents need from 8 to 10 hours of sleep, while adults need 7 to 8 hours of sleep. The sleep promoting hormone melatonin rises later in the morning for teens than it does for adults, in other words, teens need to stay up a little later and sleep in a little later, in order to function at their best. High school students often fall asleep in their early morning classes at school and some researchers have found that if the high school started an hour later, the drop-out rate and reports of depression decreased. Until recently, the brain wiring surge and processing of all these changes, that was thought to happen only once in childhood, has been discovered to have a second big surge right before adolescence. A process of "pruning" these synapse connections happens a second time in the early teen years and this process continues throughout the later teen and early twenty years, turning each child into the complete person that they will ultimately be.

Teens respond to simple requests and often misinterpret innocent comments as well as body language, because their brains are not yet ready to interpret facial expressions and voice inflections. For example, I had a very large sixth grade student in my resource room that had only been in my class for a couple of days when a little fellow Asian student came into my room to relay a message from his regular classroom teacher. I didn't know this student very well yet and the other student had come in with the message and delivered it when my back was turned. I turned around and both of them were gone. I walked out in the hall and halfway down the hall this very large student had the littler one, hanging by his neck against the wall with his feet dangling off the floor. I walked up casually and very calmly asked my student to put the boy down while we talked about what had happened. Fortunately, and perhaps because of my calm and respectful manner, he did release the choking boy from his one arm grip and let his feet descend to the floor. Once we got it all straightened out, the smaller student had simply come in to tell my student where his class would be found when he was finished in resource. The smaller student had a bit of an accent and between this and the larger boy coming into our school having been teased a lot about his size, my student thought the other boy had said something derogatory about his size. Violence and misunderstanding could happen that quickly, especially with my resource students.

Teens use different areas of their brain than do adults to process what they are feeling. "Teens rely much more on the amygdala, a small almond-shaped region in the medial and temporal lobes that processes memory and emotions, while adults rely more on the frontal cortex, which governs reason and forethought." This explains many incidents that come up in a household or make their way into the news, such as the student who posted a video of his roommate in college kissing his boyfriend, probably not thinking about the consequences of this act, just as the boy committing suicide because of his gayness exposed, feeling his life ruined and full of shame, possibly never thought about the worse pain that his parents and family would suffer when he was gone. Or a person I knew who, at fifteen, in a fit of anger with his father, got his father's hunting gun and shot himself, only to permanently paralyze himself instead. Less likely to understand and control these stresses that come up in their lives, this could also partially explain the high suicide rates in teens, as well as the high violence statistics in our society as a whole. Statistics state that fourteen to seventeen year olds murder 165 percent more than they did ten years ago. Juvenile arrests have skyrocketed and eighty three percent of juvenile offenders who were incarcerated in juvenile halls, own their own guns. One in every five crimes is committed by a juvenile and thirty-five percent of those incarcerated said that it was okay to shoot someone to get what you wanted. (*"Inside Your Teen's Head" no author, Parade Magazine, November 28, 2010, p. 5 and Mind in the Making: The Seven Essential Life Skills Every Child Needs by Ellen Galinsky, president of the Family and Work Institute, Harperstudio: New York, 2010*).

But there is another factor as well, which the Prather's in their book, Spiritual Parenting, address. This fact is that teens today have been culturally ostracized by the very people who are supposedly raising them. The mind set now is that "you are not your child's keeper" just as "you are not your brother's keeper." That we do not have to always take on the responsibility of loving, protecting, mentoring, rescuing, teaching or befriending our own children. Talents and abilities that teens display, once channeled correctly into younger sibling responsibilities, hunting and gathering skills which provided all the excitement and skills of a "warrior" to test their abilities and limits, initiated them into a society which honored them as coming into adulthood, no longer exist in our society today. Instead, teen's ability to do hard work, their fearlessness and love of danger, and their intuitive and individual talents, have all fallen into other ways of manifesting these things, often, not in safe or appropriate ways. There is no community to recognize and honor them as coming into their own, thus making way for positive advancements as teens and young adults. The fostering of selfishness and materialism in many societies, makes for a dangerous mix, with teenagers, for many reasons.

Hugh and Gayle Prather suggest that rather than making generic statements about those "horrible teenage years," those who raise them begin instead to look at these assumptions in a different and more positive way. They present Ten Assumptions made about teenagers and then how to change these assumptions. They also suggest that those of us working with children and teens are not only more than our child's and brother's keepers, but that we are our "brother." We are raising future adults, not children, and how the planet, nations, communities and families, respond to this call, will be our future too. Assumption one, they are just trying to see how much they can get away with, instead of looking at this as their time to make mistakes and learn from them. Assumption Two, they are just rebelling against their parents, rather than they are testing their limits and abilities to process the rights and wrongs of any given situation. Assumption Three, if we don't intervene, teens will act that way the rest of their lives, rather than asking yourself, did you continue to act a certain way after your teenage years? Assumption Four, teens are overly dramatic, but do we not present to them a world of overly dramatic multi-media addictions to drama? Assumption Five, teens are capable of shouldering more responsibility, but not according to the brain research and the developmental stage they are still in – not an excuse, a fact.

Assumption Six, there are always best punishments to use, however, those your parents used or those you would use on your own friends and neighbors often backfire, yet we try and use them on our own children. Assumption Seven, as a parent one must set limits and always have consequences, and yet adults have a different vocabulary for the mistakes or moods they have, blaming things on a "bad day," yet teens are 'misbehaving'– unequal treatment will always be challenged. Assumption Eight, you can only get through to a teen through anger, which in turn makes the child feel guilty and he or she can only perceive this anger as an attack, abandonment, overwhelming them or manipulating them. Assumption Nine, teens are only a bundle of hormones, emotions and peer pressure, however, research states that developmentally and brain wise this is true, so judging them doesn't help. Assumption Ten, cooperation and trust is the key to family bonding, in other words, we'll wait until the child's behavior is under control and then "bond." Bonding and a sense of community comes first, not after the fact, because we are our brother's keeper and we are our brothers. (*Ibid, Spiritual Parenting, pp.225–273.*)

Read the Prathers' book because they will give you other ways of working with your teens. What I want to focus on is how one perceives all this in relation to the very sensitive and intuitive teen. Surrounded by all of this chaos and growing violence both in the media and technological toys which all teens have, or even more deadly, can only desire, are the set of teens that are suddenly awakening to their dormant intuitive skills. These are skills which most of them laid aside on entering elementary schools, at least in the United States. Often told by the adults around them that these particular childish fantasies should now be forgotten, their confusion upon "awakening," must be overwhelming. Especially now that all around them are the beginnings of an interest in the inner journey, exploring the unknown and unseen, and the realization that many are having now, that we really do not know our own limits and capabilities either in the brain or in the world at large. Physicists are researching and challenging much of what we thought had been settled and defined by past research. And the new generations of teens will be challenging such thinking and actions in the future. This "group" is growing by leaps and bounds and many of them will never lay aside their intuitive abilities like those of us who did in the past. This can cause them huge problems as the world is not ready for their inner changes and is not evolving as fast as they are, although everything else is evolving around them. Some believe that evolution comes in spurts with no smooth transitions in between, and this would be one other explanation for many teen's confusion and how they sometimes choose to go on a wild "surfing" ride with their emotional "tides."

An additional factor is that the children of tomorrow are challenging much of what we think we have progressed into, while changing the entire face of the world. We merely have to honor and provide a rite of passage for these children to find their own way into a future that we can only dream of. It isn't even really hard to do this, because confirmation itself is a powerful tool. I once had a student in resource, part Native American, who loved to draw. One day we were on a lesson and all the other students were complaining to me that he was drawing instead of working like they were. I walked over and looked at the most beautiful, colorful and very detailed and accurate drawing of a Chinese dragon I had ever seen. I asked him to repeat back to me what we had been talking about and he did. I turned to my other students and said two things, one, that this was his way of taking notes and second, that he was very intuitive, so he had a right to draw as long as he was getting what we were talking about anyway. The smile on his face said it all. And perhaps a few of the others went home and tried to draw too!

A little space, a little extra time, a little acknowledgement, and a little honoring, and the intuitive child is awakened. The mentoring, at least in what we have to work with in the schools now, will have to be done outside them for a while. No child is ever "left behind" as long as we are running beside them, spiritually and academically. It is only when rigidity and inflexibility is the rule of the day, which promotes fear and its many attributes, that a child's self-esteem can be damaged. The art of teaching has always known this, but the process of teaching has always been self-defeating in our country. Testing, grades, cook book curriculums and step-by-step instruction, kill creativity, intuition and real learning. It was Mark Twain that said you should never let your education interfere with your learning. "Accountability" is often in our country, just another word for coming up with a way to turn childrearing and child "teaching" over to anyone that will take it on. The corporate fixers and the political lawmakers who want "good" workers, forget that what makes a "good" employee is all the training spiritually, emotionally, physically, mentally and even etherically, that they as children can acquire while growing up. They also forget that team work, hard work and even communities of workers require loyalty, trust and a great deal of laughter and play, even for adults. If these attributes were in place, money and material goods would not be such a lopsided issue in our world. But then the new world coming, will change all this, work will become play in disguise.

And please, do not forget the Grieving Stages when talking about spiritual emergence to intuitive children, or any children for that matter. These stages can come in any order, and will be coming up too as anyone goes through a spiritual crisis and at any time in your life when one occurs: Shock and Denial; Pain and Guilt; Anger and Bargaining; Depression/Reflection & Loneliness. The last three stages are all of the positive steps towards reentering your life once again: The Upward Turn; Reconstuction and Working Through, and Acceptance and Hope. These stages can take weeks or months or years to be completed and reconciled, after or during a crisis as it occurs. A loss of one's soul or a shift of that soul, or even a rebirth of the soul, will have the grieving stages accompany these dramatic changes. Children who have near-death experiences will also experience the stages of grieving but probably not as intensely as an adult. Some adults even re-experience their childhood near-death as an adult, sometimes more than once, increasing the number of spiritual crisis events in their lives. Any addiction is a disconnection between the mind and heart from the soul.

Do psychics also experience some of these spiritual awakenings much more deeply than therapists do for their own patients? Perhaps because psychics truly inhabit others as they read for them, empathically. I know that people have told me that when I write my biographical sketches of actors and actresses or my carefully researched historical ghost stories, that I am inhabiting the souls of these people from the past, and that is why I feel so attached to their life stories. So it seems that doing a reading for a live person might bring about the same result. And finally, when parents lose a child tragically, they are still going to go through a spiritual crisis and all the stages of grieving as well. They may also have metaphysical, spiritual or religious experiences – depending on what vocabulary they use for this. These after death experiences of losing a departed relative or friend can be painful, uplifting or even humorous, especially when a parent sees or feels something from a passed child. Whatever the feelings and experiences, they are all meant to reach one end, acceptance, hope and healing.

"Children's openness with a parent grows out of trust, the deep recognition that no matter what mistake they make, there always remains this one person who is forever committed to them, that nothing they can do will end the love of their mother, their father, or whoever it is that assumes the role of guardian in their lives." In this way a parent models love for one's self, for others, and for a higher purpose or source, as well as providing for the idea of family and community in a world that only displays separation, compartmentalization and aloneness. Even if a child has passed from this world to the next, or has done such a heinous crime that it is a massive death of the soul, the memories of this child remain steadfast and loving in the minds and hearts of those who loved them. (*Ibid, Spiritual Parenting, p.192*).

"Insanity is doing the same thing over and over again, but expecting different results."

--Albert Einstein

"The only devils in the world are those running in our own hearts. That is where the battle should be fought."

--Mahatma Gandhi

"Like the giraffe and the duck-billed platypus, the creatures inhabiting these remote regions of the mind are exceedingly improbable. Nevertheless they exist, they are facts of observation; and as such, they cannot be ignored by anyone who is honestly trying to understand the world in which he lives."

--Aldous Huxley, Heaven and Hell

CHAPTER SEVEN

Childhood Near-Death Experiences & Our Cosmos Children

"We sometimes congratulate ourselves at the moment of waking from a troubled dream: it may be so the moment after death."

--Nathaniel Hawthorne

"In the beginning there was a river. The river became a road and the road branched out to the whole world. And because the road was once a river it was always hungry. In that land of beginnings spirits mingled with the unborn. We could assume numerous forms... We knew no boundaries...We played much because we were free... and we sorrowed much because there were always those among us who had just returned from the world of the Living... There was not one amongst us who looked forward to being born. Living in the midst of the simple beauties of the universe, we feared the heartlessness of human beings, all of whom are born blind, few of whom ever learned to see."

--"The Famished Road" by Ben Okri

In this chapter we will discuss a slightly different take on spiritual crisis and emergence by reading about what the experts of childhood near- death experiences have to say about what is really taking place for the whole planet in terms of a consciousness shift and a spiritual and brain shift within each of us. Their premise is that those who experience any of the kinds of spiritual emergence types, especially a near - death experience, are the forerunners of what is now occurring across the globe in the incoming generations of children. That what people are labeling Indigo or Crystal or Starseed children, etc. are really just all children experiencing in many different ways various changes from past generations of humans. And there is a lot of research to support these theories that should make parents really sit up and take notice, because they are the ones who will have these children and raise them. They are also the ones who will be first in line to say, "Wait a minute, what you are telling me is not true for my child," and then will be looking for what else might be out there for them to understand just who they are raising. Whether you believe any of this or not, the changes are coming anyway and you will be the ones needing to adapt and adjust to whatever comes down the pike!

When Spiritual Emergencies Go Wrong

Emma Bragdon in her book The Call of Spiritual Emergency, says that, "Young children, especially before the age of seven, are close to dimensions of reality in which they feel the unity of all things... They are not bound by linear patterns of thinking, by having to be rational. Time and space are fluid. Creative expression is not bound by self-consciousness. As a result, the whole world is magical... Their world is full of fantastic phenomena. The child's mind is absorbing new information at a fantastic rate. Many children are effortlessly clairvoyant. They have not yet defined their personal limitations."Recent research has confirmed that even infants are smarter than adults. Children up to the age of six or seven have the ability to process information from anywhere and are wide open to the sensory, frequencies, and energies around them. In other words, they are capable of seeing and feeling what we have to struggle to re gain and their brains are receptive to using every sense and faculty available to them. But what has startled researchers is that infants can do all this too.(*Ibid., Bragdon,pp. 52-53.*)

Bragdon also says that the spiritual life of children includes many subtle level experiences. They have many memories of having been one with their mother and are not caught up in their own ego as yet. The kind of spiritual experiences that children have involve a direct knowing that includes abilities of clairvoyance, clairsentience, clairaudience and clairkinetics. Children before the age of seven can be very psychic. They may even have past memories, be able to read minds, and perceived energy that is invisible to the adults. They have a direct line to the universal consciousness and a creative problem solving ability that increases throughout their adult years. This cognition of truth begins to fade when children become more interested in critical thinking. As the child becomes more involved with the physical world, spiritual experiences can begin to generate fear rather than joy. Children who had invisible playmates begin to drop their contact with these other realms as conventional reality takes their place. Their spontaneous cognition and intuition go underground at this developmental level, yet they continue to be more accommodating to spiritual experiences with an openness and flexibility that adults have lost. One can observe this constant entering and exiting in a trance-like state, written on little children's faces!

The only time that spiritual experiences can become a problem for a child is when this child retreats into the subtle realms to protect themselves. Children who experience sexual or physical abuse, often develop unusual psychic abilities. They may also experience out-of-body as a defense mechanism against the physical and emotional pain that they are experiencing. By leaving this world and becoming preoccupied with the other intuitive worlds, these children handle their stress and anxiety in this manner. If children are taught coping skills, and how to handle their intuitive abilities in a positive manner, then children can learn to trust their own perceptions. Most importantly, is to affirm these abilities and honor them. The lucky children, who are able to maintain this connection with their spiritual life, are much more likely to have fewer spiritual emergencies in their later life. They can learn to use their intuition for themselves and others, in a positive manner.

What Are Near-Death Experiences?

There are many differences between regular spiritual emergencies in both adults and children, and the crisis of a near-death. Causes of near-death experiences range from accidents to birth problems to an experience that is really not a near-death and yet the child can have the same lifelong patterns as if they had had one. Some experts think that these are caused by the other types of spiritual emergencies already identified, while others just say that the causes are simply not from a near-death. One young seven-year-old boy told Elizabeth Kubler-Ross what heaven looked like: "It's sort of like if you went through another passageway... You walked right through the wall to another galaxy or something. It's sort of like walking into your brain. It is sort of like living on a cloud, and your spirit is there, but not your body. You've left your body. It is really like walking into your mind." This boy, after a three year struggle with leukemia, had just asked his mother to turn off his oxygen. (*Morse, Melvin. Closer to the Light, Ivy Books, p.126.*)

Those who study the brain offer this information. That in order to survive after death the mind has to establish some sort of connection with a source of energy that has nothing to do with the brain. Perhaps it is that energy from without that can then reach a person's brain, so that when the body dies, the mind has to rely on another source of energy for its existence. Most brain researchers continue to search for the source of spiritual experiences inside the brain. Some claim that they can stimulate particular areas of the brain, and re-create psychic abilities as well as near-death experiences. The right temporal lobe of the brain has been described by many researchers as "the seat of the soul." The hippocampus is the brain's master controller for sensory input, and it also contains our unconscious desires and our ability to dream. There is even a proposition from an anesthesiologist with thirty five years experience, who claims to have located the "soul" as a material in the body unaccounted for like the 21 grams theory. He cannot prove it, but is absolutely sure himself that this material continues to survive and operate when patients are under anesthesia or in a coma and therefore survives as a consciousness during a near-death experience and probably after we all die.

Dr. Michael A. Persinger is the leading researcher in the brain theory of re-creating near-death experiences by stimulating the Sylvia Fissure in the right temporal lobe. And while he could re-create some of this experience, he failed to induce anything other than a generalized pattern of imagery, a basic template or "blueprint." Other researchers have been unable to replicate his findings. He claims to have recreated religious and mystical experiences through stimulating the temporal lobe function, thus saying that all such experiences are merely a brain function. While this may be upsetting too many religious people, gurus and mystical teachers, I myself do not find this upsetting because eventually we will realize that all the great religious and spiritual healers and avatars were using "brain function" to accomplish all that they did. This does not mean that we do not require a spiritual life or a community effort to heal ourselves and the planet. It does not mean that man's brain does not evolve both spiritually and in the mind as well. Personally I think his research is probably under fire from two directions, the science worshippers and the religious worshippers, who in the future will be in the same camp because of "brain function." The brain itself, in order to operate with all of its power, must be a spiritual and energetic organ, vibrating to the universe as well! (*Persinger, Michael A. Neuropsychological Bases for God Beliefs, Wikipedia – the free encyclopedia.*)

Science still looks at near - death experiences nebulously, but cannot explain mysterious brain activity that goes on when a person dies. There are many questions and mysteries about what these children and adults uniformly see and feel in their near-death experiences that science at present cannot explain. Doctors and medical researchers do attempt to explain certain things however. For example, a lot of people who have a heart attack have near-death experiences, and this could have to do with the change in their brain waves as they experience a heart attack. These experts think that perhaps endorphins may have something to do with the visions that people have when they are dying. They propose that perhaps these endorphins are released in excess to make the dying process more pleasant. Today, many more doctors and researchers are now attempting to actually research and study those who have experienced near-deaths in terms of brain research. (*Ibid., pp.198-199.*)

My Own Experiences with Visions of Death

I can remember once when the woman I was reading for asked me the question, "What did it feel like when my mother died?" Instead of getting the answer that the woman probably wanted, I got a literal visual answer, which a doctor later told me, was a perfect description of what happens to the brain when a person dies. I followed along beside the woman's mother as she slid through a giant snail shell that had opaque walls. Bright light was coming through the walls as we went round and round through this snail shell as though we were in an enclosed waterslide. Finally we jettisoned out of the bottom opening of the shell, feet first. Then as I watched her body float towards a huge circular docking station, feet first and lying on her back, I noticed that, there were dozens of other people, floating out from lots of other giant snail shells towards this docking station, where their feet would lock into a sort of socket. Above this huge station was a gigantic very high and round, but very bright white light, and one could look at it without discomfort, even though it was huge and white-yellow in color. I knew there were things going on inside that light, but it was so bright you couldn't see anything, even though the light did not hurt my eyes at all when I looked directly at it.

That was the end of what I saw, and this doctor said that we had slipped through the convolutions of the brain going down to the stem of the brain, which is the last to die when the brain dies, and that was when one saw the white light, which was the only thing left when the brain died. Yet many spiritualists in the 1800's felt that when a person died the soul and the spirit separated, just like the placenta fell away at birth. The body no longer needed the soul and the light from the soul came from the solar plexus and joined in with the spirit as it left from the crown of the head in a bright white light. Spiritualists said that the appearance of the light being or spirit could take three hours to three days to form out the crown of the head before the essence or energy spirit left the body for good. The spirit body could be seen forming in the white light. Whatever the answer was to what I saw that day, it brought up for me the thought that psychics and intuitives who "read" for others and have these sorts of visions, might well be privileged to see parts of near-death experiences all the time, depending on the questions that the sitters ask of them. Since there is no time, space or distance, when remote viewing is used in an intuitive reading, then one can see beyond death as well, even without a near-death experience, and I certainly have had many other such visions in readings, although I always knew that I could go just so far, and then go no further.

I have also had many times where I watched people either getting in boats to cross the great water, dancing along the shore with white death masks all around them on the beach, or walking single file up into a huge tower-like rock, climbing many stairs and then walking out of the top onto a ledge of rock like a diving board and then they continued to walk up into the sky and disappeared. But one of my most profound experiences concerning death came years ago and did not get confirmed until many years later. In this experience was a two-fold vision for a woman I had seen a few times before this experience happened. This woman had come to me in the darkest time of her life and had asked me two questions, if her grandmother had seen her bringing her own children into the world, and if her children would come back to her.

In the first vision I saw a black funeral train leaving a station and an old woman let go of a little girl's hand and boarded the train. Everything was in silhouette but the sky behind them was a brilliant golden and amber sunset. The woman said afterwards that she had lived with her grandmother until she was eight and then her grandmother had died and she went back to live with her mother. Her grandmother was the only one she felt had really loved her. Her mother had never wanted her. Years later when she had her eight children, raised them and then had them taken away from her by her husband, who claimed she was unstable, she wept for their return. But instead she continued to live alone while her husband worked diligently to turn her children against her. Not the least bit crazy, she was instead a victim of circumstances, and added onto this she had been released from her religion. As she asked me the second question, a vision appeared that I did not entirely understand until many years later after the woman had passed away and I attended her viewing.

But something extraordinary had happened in the reading before I even began to transmit the vision. As I sat next to the woman, about six feet away from her, I suddenly felt myself temporarily frozen in one spot, my arms on my legs as though encased in a narrow tube. I knew that I could move but also knew that I was not supposed to move. Then I felt the atmosphere in the room change. A beautiful loving feeling filled the room and began to build up into a huge and powerful feeling of presence and love. As it did, I felt and saw in my mind's eye a shower of golden glitter rain down on me as though a narrow curtain of light that surrounded me. The rain of light just kept coming and more and more of it poured over my head and body until I realized that this woman's grandmother had entered the room. I first felt her hands on my shoulders from behind me and then I felt her sit down inside me and I began to have this vision, which I then proceeded to tell the woman as it grew before me.

In the vision a giant man/woman appeared floating in the sky. She looked like those very masculine women in old Russian posters looking robust and with strong, muscle bound arms. But I only saw her from the waist up. From the waist down was a giant circus tent whose walls were made of veils of golden white light. Her arms were outspread as if directing the formation of the tent of light, like a very wide skirt. I floated inside the tent and saw eight pathways going out like the spokes of a wheel from a giant center where a large black pit was located. At the end of each pathway stood one of each of her children with a large pillow on their backs tied around their waists with a huge clear ribbon in a bow. The woman was on her knees in the center pit with her face buried in her hands and crisscrossing her body were bars of black light from the many pathways. I did not tell the woman that this was a death scene or that the middle pit looked like a grave. But at the time I though this woman or angel with a skirt made of light, represented my sitter's grandmother. I told her that her grandmother had indeed been present at the birth of each grandchild.

Once the vision ended, I then felt the grandmother stand up out of me and walk or float slowly over to where the woman was sitting. I was so very entranced that I was not conscious of the room around me until that moment. It was then that I opened my eyes and realized that I could hear the woman weeping loudly. I could still feel the gold glitter surrounding the woman and I asked her later if she had felt anything but she was so overcome with the experience that she could not say. Then just as quickly as it had come, it dissipated from around the woman, the beautiful and loving feeling began to lift off both of us and the grandmother was gone. I never told the woman that she was in a grave under those tent walls of light and that the bars of black that crisscrossed this grave seemed to represent a prison. I certainly did not understand the large pillow that was buffering each of her children from the walls of light.

And then fifteen years went by, I lost track of this friend and one night quite late we received a phone call from one of her children. This child had been the only one at this low point in her life to continue to really support her. She said that she had been thinking about the friends she had made during this lost period in her mother's life, friends that her mother had lost touch with after this. She said that she was calling them to tell them now that her mother had passed away and letting us know where and when the viewing would be. We went to the woman's viewing and realized that many things had changed for her in the ensuing years. She was back in her church, all of her children had come back to her, because we watched the video of her life, and she was happily spending time with her many grandchildren. Her quilts and doilies and such were displayed all around the church and while she had put a lot of weight on and the cancer medication, which had made her face puffy, she was just beaming and quite happy in her coffin. You could see this contentment on her face and the fact that she had been quite loved by members of her faith. I went home and realized that the rest of the dream had come true, that that had not been grandma holding up that skirt of light but an angel or light being and a quite powerful one at that. She was showing this mother that all her children were protected, buffered from death, and her death in particular. That this angel had brought her grandmother to each birth and that her grandmother was waiting for her. That this angel had brought this grandmother in her granddaughter's darkest time, to comfort her in a room full of light and love. To tell her that her children would return to her before she died and would mourn her passing. I found myself crying too, and was very startled at the whole thing happening. It was my first experience with this and I would have a few more in the future that I would understand much more fully after this first one.

What the Metaphysical Experts Say about Death Visitations

I felt privileged to even have this experience and quite a few years later I read a small passage in Robert Bruce's Astral Dynamics (the original version), explaining what had happened and realized that I was not the only one to have this happen to me. Reading the visual pictures for the first time sent chills up and down my spine, when I realized that I had actually seen the angel or light being in my vision. At the same time I felt the spirit of the grandmother come through me to her granddaughter. Death had touched me and I had seen death, yet I had experienced at the same time, love in its purest form: "Angels and advanced beings…do not appear limited to any particular plane or dimension level. They have the ability, I believe, to manifest in any level. They have the ability to enfold lesser beings in their energy and temporarily transport them into other dimensional levels…they will often be seen helping the spirits of deceased people to manifest temporarily in the…physical dimension itself. This kind of thing always has very good reasons behind it, although those reasons may not be apparent at the time."

"Typically, a spirit manifestation like this will begin with a strong buildup of energy in the room, accompanied by many silver motes and tiny sparkles of light. A tangible aura of power and presence spreads throughout the room and the atmosphere becomes electric. A narrow, vertical shaft of brilliant-silver light then appears and quickly expands, as if curtains of light were being drawn apart just wide enough for a person to walk through. A huge gush of brilliant-silver light, along with a tangible feeling of power, excitement, and love spills through this parting in the dimensional veil. The visiting deceased spirit then simply walks through this opening and stands inside the room, bathed and held within this pool of light."

"At this time, if you have the sight and you look further back into the light behind the deceased spirit, you will usually see at least one advanced spirit being or angel standing there, as if patiently waiting a dozen or so feet behind the spirit visitor. A deceased relative or friend of the visiting spirit will also often be seen standing just behind and to the side of the spirit visitor, often holding a hand or resting a hand on a shoulder." All these years later I was reading about what had happened to me years before. But the angel being had stood behind me the whole time so that I would never see it, although I sensed her hands on my shoulders. My body had been the vehicle or shaft of light through which the grandmother had walked. I have had other experiences since with some of these aspects repeating themselves, but never one so profound until my own father died years later. The major difference was that rather than sensing or seeing the light being, I had had this translated into a vision that I could comprehend.

And in this case I was able to get resolution and confirmation about this experience when the woman passed away. I would never have told this story even now, but I am more comfortable being considered balmy, than I was many years ago. I can remember crying as I read these passages in Bruce's book for the first time, and feeling not so very alone to have experienced such a wonder. "Only very rarely will projectors (astral travelers) come across advanced spirit beings, or even more rarely will they encounter angels… Angels, and other advanced spiritual beings, seem to make themselves visible only when they have a very good reason for doing so. They are definitely not the type to stop and chat in passing." (*Astral Dynamics by Robert Bruce, Hampton Roads, 1999, pp.480-481*).

And then many years later I had a second such profound experience. It began with a dream six days before my father's death. I watched this dream from where I sat on a sofa on the twelfth floor of a big fancy retirement home. Dad came down the hall with his walker. He was a bit younger and a bit better off physically, but his dementia was complete and he was totally out of his mind. He walked towards me and when he got close to where I was he tripped and fell. He was carrying a big square box of popcorn, which then fell out all over the floor. But I was shocked to see that instead of the cardboard container flinging kernels of popcorn on the floor there were little pieces of chicken or at least flesh all over the carpet. Dad then miraculously sprang to his feet and walked without his walker over to a very deep window ledge and leaned against it, staring at me.

But it was his stare that got my attention. His silly, humor-filled, yet dementia held mindless look was gone. His eyes once again housed the powerful and penetrating look of a very brilliant man. They were the eyes that he had always glanced at you with, probing and questioning, trying to understand from which perspective you were coming. Then, suddenly, down the hall came two young teenagers, young, thin, pretty girls, skipping and laughing. They sat down at my feet, wrapping their arms around their knees and stared up at me. They thanked me for watching over all the supplies that began to spread before me on a slowly appearing coffee table. They said that they were with the rock band that was playing at the nursing home in another part of the building and had been entrusted with the band's extra equipment which they were suppose to watch over until the concert was finished. But they had instead, gone off to the concert and forgotten all about guarding this equipment. When I looked down and only saw stacks of notebooks, no guitars or drums, I was puzzled. The girls picked the notebooks up and skipped off, laughing and giggling some more, and I woke up.

And then, as I said earlier, the next morning after my father died, on Christmas Day, I woke up at the same time he had died the night before, to a huge surge of energy in the bedroom. It was all around the room and once again built up to a higher and higher pitch of loving energy. However, this time it was so overpowering that it began to scare me. I was sure it was my father but still it began to frighten me. I felt surrounded in a powerful energy that began to wrap around my body, all over me in equal amounts like a huge blanket. It was like I was a child being "hugged" by this energy. There were no visions at all and I knew my father was giving me a "feeling" hug and telling me in this way that he had truly loved me. I tried to think through the fog to try and ask that the level of this energy be tuned down to something I could handle and in the midst of this I did see an empty journal, its pages flipping back and forth. All the while the huge surge of energy continued to be all around me and my ears were ringing and throbbing like they do when I sense spirit energy around me, only much louder and more intense.

During my meditation the next morning I realized that this high energy had lasted so long to get my attention and I felt myself forgiving my dad and myself, for any grudges that I was still holding. Awakening from an altered state, I realized I was saying I forgave him and loved him out loud. By then I knew who would come for him because a couple of pictures of family members had fallen off the wall the day after the dream. And then the last piece of understanding came to me when I learned that for his urn, my father had selected a book, the "popcorn" container for my father's life on the "stage." I was continuing my father's legacy of writing and researching books about the past, but with a twist, they were about a spiritual and metaphysical past. I had been brave enough to truly be who I was intuitively, and yet I had written about subjects that would be targeted by some as only my vivid imagination. Yet the waves of energy and the frequencies of these waves, had literally "swept me away," as I was now more capable of sensing energies, especially one surging and building for an hour and a half.

A few days after my father's death, the interpretation of the entire dream fell into place. When dad fell, he had died. What spilled out of the book-like container was what was left of him in the physical world, his ashes. As he leaned against the window he was in spirit, his intelligence was back and his consciousness was simply displaying a picture of himself for me to see. His piercing eyes were observing the scene with an awareness that he had not had for seven years. I had come to see those who have passed on with a small round light in their eyes that is shiny and piercing. This is how I can know ahead of time that they have passed on before someone tells me. The two teenage girls were my sister and I when we were teens or they represented the younger women that I would teach in the near future. As sisters we were the groupies of an "academic rock star," in both positive and negative ways. That we were beautiful to him was a simple message that we could either believe or discard, because as still living beings, few of us have experience with unconditional love. Being the guardians of the family history and heritages, it was the two of us who made a huge memory book about our father for all our siblings and this he was enjoying. But I was the lone teacher - writer – storyteller and spiritual seer, although our parents had both revered the profession of teaching and the art of historical research and writing. And last, dad was back to let me know that for all my differences, I had been loved as much as any of my siblings, even though all of us often got lost in the shuffle of so many adoring "fans." I alone was a "groupie" for my academic rock star father.

Second-Hand Near-Death Experiences Psychically

So does the psychic experience what the sitter is experiencing, as deeply and profoundly as the sitter? I think so, especially if one is quite empathic or feels very close to the sitter. Does this experience equal a near-death experience? Probably not, but it does stay with the reader for a very long time, a lifetime I think. And if one gets lucky enough to get resolution, confirmation and completion in the same lifetime for such an experience, it can become like a near-death, mirroring the person's experience and profoundly changing the reader too. And last, I have seen many times in the last 25 years, what Andrew Jackson Davis – the great American psychic - described as the death process in many varied ways in my visions for other people. When I read his description of what happens in this process, I began remembering seeing this but not recognizing it for what it was. He was able, after he became a medical doctor, to witness in his mind's eye, two deaths where the two men were side by side in the hospital and they passed away an hour a part. Each man took approximately a little less than three hours for their spirit bodies to form, Jackson claimed.

A mist or light began forming from the solar plexus and he described this as the soul leaving the body because it was what fueled the physical body and it was no longer needed. This smaller mist then joined a similar mist or light coming out from the crown of the head, where the spirit of the person was forming inside this light as a representation of the spirit body. Jackson recorded it in detail but never seemed to make it clear whether he actually saw these two transformations or just viewed them in his mind's eye. But the process was identical in every way, he said. Nettie Colburn Maynard, the Laurie's and occasionally Andrew Jackson Davis, well-known psychics of the era, consulted with Abraham Lincoln, along with many other Spiritualists. Lincoln had had two near-death experiences as a child, lost his mother at a young age, lost his first true love to illness, and a few years later lost his beloved sister. Later, Lincoln lost two of his boys before he was assassinated and also watched an entire nation at war with itself, in which thousands perished. Lincoln was a highly intuitive prophet in his own right, but had to hide this from his public as President of our country. He made many accurate predictions, could read people quite easily, and was said to have wide mood swings where in an instant he could emerge from hours of silent sad contemplation on his own, to become a smiling, charismatic and charming host in a crowd. He displayed all of the characteristics of a near-death experiencer, an empathic intuitive, and a prophet of the future, with his brilliant mind and compassionate heart, while in constant mourning for all those he had lost. But none of this information can be found in older biographies of Lincoln, because these things cannot or would not be verified by historians as a real part of the true mystic and genius that Lincoln was.

Lincoln envisioned his own death. He died before seeing his poor wife supposedly go crazy from all the many deaths of loved ones that she had endured and a very plausible belief in various conspiracies against her husband even after his death. Lincoln often dreamed answers to important decisions he had to make and his hold on the American public is not just because he was one of the most important Presidents in the history of our country. It is beyond this, it is spiritually powerful. If you want to know more about Abraham Lincoln's own intuited experiences as well as the mystical experiences that surrounded him, Mary Todd Lincoln and Spiritualism, and the many ghostly events that happened after his death, including his haunted funeral train, read <u>Andrew Jackson Davis: The First American Prophet and Clairvoyant</u> by John DeSalvo, PhD which explores the connections between Davis, Lincoln and Coleburn, or read both Troy Taylor's <u>The Haunted President</u> and <u>The Psychic Life of Abraham Lincoln</u> by Dr. Susan B. Martinez on the intuitive powers of Lincoln and he and his wife's explorations with Spiritualism.

Another famous mystic that most people would think I was crazy for mentioning him as one, was Charles Darwin. There are many parallels in his life with those of Lincoln's, except that Darwin lived his whole life and did not make his mark on history until he was much older, even though his ideas had been formed and written about when he was a young man. He was waylaid by the same sorts of tragedies as Lincoln, losing three of his children to fevers and wondering if genetic factors had been involved as he had been a "sickly" child himself, when ironically he could have brought "foreign" fevers home to his own children from traveling the world. His oldest daughter Annie, died when she was only ten and he was closest to her, as Lincoln was to Willie Lincoln, who died of a "fever." Mirror reflections of their own father's spirits, genius, intuitive abilities and strange quirks, both sons who were now fathers themselves were haunted by their favorite child's ghost and suffered from severe mood swings for as long as they lived. And while Lincoln held this nation together, Darwin discovered the connections in the natural world. They both dealt with death, loss, chronic illnesses and with their own intuitive and isolated souls, extreme mood changes and pure genius, always ahead of their times with others. Darwin was a passionate scientist whose "Ah Ha" moments were intuited, or at least I believe so. And even though many would say that he was a left-brained scientist "duck," and not a visual-spatial "sponge," I believe he was just the opposite, although closest to the in-coming "whole brainers" of today.

In my own intuited experiences with death I would see the mist coming out of what I thought was the lower end of the breast bone and then see a miniature of the person as they had looked when they were alive, from inside this mist. So I actually saw this from the bones of the person either in relation to a missing person's bones, a crime scene, or historical events such as locally, the Mountain Meadow's Massacre or nationally, at Gettysburg. Then this mist would join another mist and form the full person inside it, growing to a life-size image. The answer to the question was always the same that it did not matter how they had died but that they had been saved by death and were okay now. It mattered much more that they were comforting their loved ones still here, or honoring their descendants who came after them in a "spirit picture" of themselves that the living could accept and see. I stopped doing this sort of thing, crime investigations and missing persons, not because of the dead, but because of the living, who were still being affected by this death and I could do absolutely nothing for them but carry around these images of really bad things that would haunt me instead, especially where children were concerned. So do I personally fear death, absolutely not! Experiencing it second-hand has helped.

The Pre-death Vision Experiences of a Near- Death

Dr. Melvin Morse in his groundbreaking studies said that he noticed that many children reported having a precognitive vision of their own near-death experience. Some of these visions told of a miraculous recovery before the doctor found this unexplainable change in the child's body. Others had a vision where someone appeared and told them they were going to die and they did. Others saw some form of Heaven before they passed on, or saw a preview of Heaven and then made the decision to return to finish out their life. Morse felt that in some cases the child having this vision before he or she did die was very comforting for the family and relatives if they were allowed to hear this description from their own child. He wondered if this was supposed to be a part of the natural death process that medical science has eliminated from our culture over time. He felt that the pre-death vision was meant to be and offered a short healing process for those left behind. He also felt that this was only one stage in a whole process of dying that ancient man had just accepted and experienced as part of his natural world, and that modern man has tragically forgotten.

On the other end of this, are the small group of people who have memories of being in their mother's womb or even having a near-death experience either before they were born, when they were born or shortly after this. There is limited research on this and yet people do have these experiences. It has been my experience that I need to talk with people who come for a reading about this time. We seem to come into the world in "herds" or with certain personality types. We also seem to be in certain categories as to experiences we have in the womb, at birth, and shortly after this. How the parents were feeling, how the infant is feeling in the womb, what the pregnancy was like, what the birth was like, and how we thrived or did not thrive right afterwards, really can give "readers" insights about their clients. Add to this a near-death experience while in the womb or at birth or shortly after this and you have even more to think about. One theory states that the person who has this sort of experience, while not always aware of it unless their mother told them, may already decide they don't want to be here. They may view suicide as a pleasant and loving experience rather than an awful choice, while those around them do not understand this. They may even, years later, choose to go, while those left behind see this as a selfish choice.

I see images of these transitions and see children coming out of the womb tap dancing, clinging to the walls of the womb, or even fighting their way out, etc. All of these factors contribute to the type of person we already are and the type of person that we will become. Looking at this time in the person's beginnings of life, can really have quite deep connections to how they live their life later on. And, I find that by bringing these things to the attention of the sitter, "seeds" can be planted and open old rusty doors of thought towards much bigger and more positive changes in these patterns that we develop either from our genetics or from our environmental adaptations or both. These are often more negative than positive patterns that people develop from their incoming personality type and their ways of communicating with others is often not helping them to live the best life they are entitled to live. Having information about one's birth process, time spent in the womb, and adjustments to life right after birth, can profoundly change patterns that people discover later, they do not want in their lives. Perhaps these patterns or reactions to things are interfering with relationships or causing problems in their work, or they are unhappy in the lives they are leading in general. Patterns which can influence choices we make that can have either negative or positive consequences do come in with our personality type. For example, if I see a person unsure about coming out. They may have trouble with sudden changes in their lives or not feel very secure in life. Or if I see a person fighting their way out, they will probably assume that they have to "fight" their way out of everything else. A person thinking they have to entertain everyone to be loved, may find themselves afraid of commitment or intimacy, etc.

A child in England suddenly announced to his parents when he was five-years-old that he remembered that he had died when he was very ill and only nine months old. He just announced it one day in a matter of fact statement to his parents, "Did you know I died?" His heart had stopped when he was in the hospital as an infant. He remembered the tunnel, the bright light, seeing his grandfather and mother standing with all the doctors and nurses. An invisible hand lifted him up when he grew tired of crawling down the tunnel and he had begun to float down it. He saw white robed people, a golden road and even God. He was asked through mind thought if he wanted to return and he said that he had thought in his mind that he wanted to stay there. But God said he had to return and suddenly he was back in the hospital and had been in a coma for three months after this. His parents at first did not believe him but he supplied so many accurate details about the whole experience in the hospital they became convinced that their little son had really had this near-death experience. (*Children of the Light by Brad and Sherry Steiger, Signet Books, 2005, pp.114-115.*)

What Do Children Uniformly Experience in a Near-Death?

"There is a sensation of floating out of one's body, passing through a dark tunnel or black space and ascending toward a brilliant light that seems to exude an overwhelming feeling of love. The light can be looked at without harming one's eyes and as the person ascends towards it they will hear and see loved ones or beings made of light. And while most adults have a panoramic life review speed past them, most children do not, probably because there is not that much life to "review." There is a sense of no distance, time or space and a wonderful feeling of peace and calm. Most of all there is a reluctance to return to earth and a great disappointment on being revived." (*Atwater, P.M.H., Children of the New Millennium: Children's Near-Death Experiences, 1999, p.53*).

Children also seem to have experiences with animals and pets on the other side much more than adults. Many children seem to go through an "animal heaven" before they can go to the "people heaven." In relating their near-death experiences to adults, they quite often mention how meeting this animal or pet had a great effect on their decision to return, if they were given this choice. Experts don't know whether this is symbolic or a projection from what children experience in the physical world. Many adults also report meeting a deceased pet, who assisted them in understanding their near-death experience. Adults reported this as always being symbolic and metaphorical for them. And some even reported spending time in what the children described as "animal heaven."

My favorite story about "animal heaven" is from another "Twilight Zone," when an old backwoods man, out with his hunting dogs, falls over and dies but doesn't know at first that he is dead. He begins walking down the country road with his dogs in tow.

He runs into a charming young man sitting on a log, who invites him to come down the road behind him to Heaven. When the old man finds out that he cannot take his dogs with him to Heaven, he absolutely refuses to go down that road and continues on down the wider path until he gets to another fork in the road and meets an older man. The older man invites him to go down the road behind him. The deceased man thinks he is going to Hell now, just to be with his dogs. The old man asks about his dogs and the man tells him that he can bring them right in. The deceased man tells this man waiting at the start of the road about the younger man he ran into down the road a piece and asks why he couldn't take his dogs in there. The older man at the "gates" to Heaven replies, "Oh, that's the devil. He's always trying to fool people before they get this far down the road."

Atwater, in her forty years of research, also described four types of near-deaths that she came across in her case studies for both children and adults: Initial Experience which means an experience that is limited and not defined except by a feeling, a friendly voice or a brief out-of-body, etc. In this first experience, 76% of children had this type of experience to report and only 20% of the adults studied reported this type of experience. The second is an Unpleasant or Hell-like Experience which only 15% of adults had and only 3% of children had. The third type was a Pleasant or Heaven-like Experience and 19% of children reported this type while 47% of the adults reported this type of experience. The last type was a Transcendent Experience, or visiting alternate realities, expanding one's awarenesses or even transforming one's life. Only 2% of children reported this type and only 18% of the adults studied reported this type of experience. Atwater also states that she discovered that many of those in her studies experienced more than one type in the same near-death experience. (*Ibid.,p.55.*)

Atwater also gives a different perspective to these four types of near-death experiences when she talks later about the transformative process of consciousness. In other words what are the transformations that take place in the spirit/brain shift that the child experiences in a near-death? Besides a "type" of near-death, these four can also represent a shift in a child's perceptions of the physical world and the multidimensional worlds. These transformations can occur for most who have experienced spiritual crisis and spiritual awakenings. In the near-death experience or the spiritual emergences we experience in life the Initial Experiences can be seen as an introduction to perceiving other ways of reality. The Unpleasant or Hell-Like Experiences can be seen as a healing or releasing through confrontation, those attitudes and beliefs that hinder our consciousness of a multi-verse around us. The Pleasant or Heaven-Like Experiences are a realization that the journey through life we each take is validating and confirming of how every decision or action we make for ourselves and others is of vast importance. And finally, those, in the smaller group, who have the Transcendence Experience, encounter a oneness with both the earth and all that is on it, and with the multidimensional worlds as well. They understand the collective whole of humankind and really do become more "enlightened."

What Are Some of the Signs That a Child Has Had a Near-Death?

Be on alert for some of these signs that may indicate that your child has had a near-death experience. Children may suddenly have a powerful need to have their own place to retreat too, whether it's a bedroom, a tree house, or at tent, etc. The child may suddenly want to have an altar of some kind in the "home." They may suddenly develop an intense curiosity about God, religion or spirituality. They may even want their parents to attend church with them when they may not have expressed an interest in this before. They may become extremely sensitive to sensory stimuli or develop allergies and have lights and sounds bother them. They may develop intolerances to over the counter remedies, prescribed medications, and holistic remedies. They may have become quite sensitive to people or animals being hurt, and especially have difficulty with the 'white lies' that people often tell. They may seem to have lost their understanding of boundaries when it comes to social skills and may have to relearn these boundaries. They seem to be able to merge into or become one with animals, plants, or whatever else they are focusing on at the time, even seeing auras within and around these objects, plants and animals.

There is a change in their sleep patterns, and a shift into becoming a faster talker or thinker, having a driving need to create, invent, read, and learn. They may show an earlier development than their peers in many areas and they may be deeply motivated to help others in some way. They will show an unusual interest in near-death materials, if they recognize their near-death as having happened. Or they may tuck the experience away until it is brought to their attention. They have a heightened awareness of the continuum of life and a heightened interest in mysticism and the paranormal. They have also become more psychic themselves and exhibit these abilities in one or many ways. With this shift in their sleep patterns, there can be many reasons for this. They may be unable to sleep, because of difficulties at home and school as a result of not being believed, or they are having nightmares or night terrors which need to be dealt with, or, they are having dreams and experiences that they cannot explain to others. Night flying, night travel, lucid dreams, and a myriad of other things can be happening to them, and they may not know how to explain them without being looked upon as crazy or at least deluded. Or, they may not even understand that others are not having the same kinds of experiences.

Diane K. Corcoran R.N., PhD and educator of medical professionals, says that "Children may not realize the things they are feeling are common aftereffects. They may be able to see things others don't, or they may at special times know things that are going to happen but find that nobody believes them. We need to listen to children. And we need to let them know they're okay." Especially when there is no dramatic sign exhibiting or indicating that a near-death has taken place. (*Ibid., Atwater, p.116.*)

What Happens After a Near-Death for Children?

70% of the children in these studies had angel visitations and these angels were either described as having wings and encased in a bright light, or they were just described as beings made of light. The children also saw deceased relatives and friends, animals and deceased pets, religious figures, and people who were very much alive in their lives on earth. One child described the experience as "I don't end or begin anywhere. I just reach out and catch the next wave that goes by, and hop a ride. That's how I got there." Thus children allude to the fact that they have experienced layered realms unrestricted by physical boundaries. This scares a lot of parents when their child reports such journeying in their near-death experience. Yet it tells us that they have now expanded their awarenesses of the multi-verse and they will not forget their experiences for a lifetime. The child returns from a near-death with a larger conceptual reasoning style, has gone from concrete to abstract thinking, and can go back and forth between the concrete and the abstract with ease. (*Closer to The Light by Dr. Melvin Morse, Ivy Inspirational Books, 1990.*)

After the near-death event, the child becomes a spatial – nonverbal – sensory – dynamic thinker. The child also becomes much more intuitive. "What I saw was what I call 'true genius,' where intuition is the equal of intellect; where the brain seemed to evidence parallel-processing systems, faculty enhancements, multiple sensing, the simultaneous presence of multiple brain wave patterns, and an ability to know things, unbounded by the constraints of past, present, and future, as if they could access and draw from a cosmic bank of knowledge." On the other hand, not so many develop and refine what they have achieved through their near-death experience, as adults. And part of the problem is that both at home and at school they are not encouraged to develop or enhance these new capabilities. Instead, they are often required to either withdraw, or exhibit feelings of anger or rage or resentment, because they are not believed or their visit to the spiritual dimension is discounted. (*Ibid., Atwater, p.80.*)

After Effects of a Near-Death Experience

Some of the elements of what some call a second birth are temporal lobe expansions though a reversal of the learning curve, IQ enhancements that include creative problem solving skills and a more visual-spatial learning style. There is also an awareness of the future and a deeper understanding of time and space. They also have the ability to sense multiple worlds. There are brain and spirit shifts that include advanced attitudes and behaviors towards social justice and moral integrity, as well as a higher level of compassion and caring that comes from the heart. Those who research, near-death experiences say that there are actually structural and chemical changes in the brain after the event. Long-term effects include an ability to desensitize the self from physical sensations, inability to communicate through nonverbal and auditory means and a partial loss of ability to indicate verbally what they need or desire. There are also problems integrating the ethereal self back into the physical self, and quite a few challenges interacting socially. (*Ibid. Atwater, p.103-104.*)

In other words, near-death experiencers learn to disassociate with ease. As the new lines of thought and creative imagination are being built inside the child's brain, a natural byproduct of this consciousness raising is to be able to literally step out of one's body and place one's awareness to the side of this body, temporarily. Without proper support and confirmation, a child experiencer can feel like they are either stupid or crazy, or suddenly quite different from everyone else. Some other aftereffects can include an increase in allergies, sensitivity to electrical storms or equipment, and some can even develop a serious illness. Some other common aftereffects that have been found in the studies include: an unusual connection to nature and animals, a greatly changed relationship with those around them, a new interest in religion or the spiritual, and a changed attitude towards one's focus and goals. As adults, other long reaching effects can be with marriage, attitudes towards money and jobs, suddenly having a particular mission to complete and a desire to return to the other side. But the most startling data is the fact that 73% of all experiencers have an increase in all of these after effects over their lifetime, while at the same time, only a few of them accomplish great strides in their lives.

On the other hand, 57% of those studied, stayed in long-lasting marriages, owned their own homes, and experienced a deeper contemplative life than their peers. 42% of the child experiencers had experienced parental or sibling abuse while growing up and one third of the children had problems with alcohol within 5 to 10 years after their episode. They said that the hardest thing was, that once they had experienced such a transcendent love on the other side, then abruptly lost it, it was not only very confusing, but extremely devastating to them. From the viewpoint of children who had experienced near-death, suicide was merely a pleasant journey to joining those in Heaven and not an end to life. They saw nothing wrong with going back to where they felt loved, and at one with the universe, and some of them felt that this was better than life in the physical world. They did not see leaving the earth as self-destructive at all.

In the Steiger book, Children of the Light, they list the following after effects including becoming more active or playful, having a great deal more or less energy, their boredom levels decrease or increase, and they seemed to be able to handle stress more easily. Physically, their skin brightened, their eyes sparkled, they smiled and, they had increased sensitivity to any light especially sunlight. They also had increased sensitivity to any form of sound and noise levels. But most importantly, their brain began to function in an entirely different way. People who had a near-death experience as a child, continued to have hypersensitivity to sound and light as adults. Extremely young children might have some post traumatic stress symptoms from their experience. For example, one five-year-old boy remembered crawling down the tunnel toward a bright light and when he grew tired, some sort of force picked him up and helped him to float the rest of the way through the tunnel. When his brothers and sisters attempted to help him crawl through any sort of tunnel on a playground or at an amusement park, he stubbornly resisted doing this and really got upset. (Ibid., "Chapter Five," Children of the Light.)

What to Do For These Children Besides All the Tips Coming Up

There are many near-death experience books on children and many of the coping suggestions in Chapter Fifteen will help too. But as far as what the experts suggest, there are the Transpersonal Psychologists who understand and will deal with this type of experience. They also suggest what kind of help adult experiencers sought: a Philosophical Counselor, a Life Coach, group intervention with other near-death experiencers, Spirit Release Therapy, Sound Healing or Toning or revisiting the near-death experience similar to having a Rebirthing or Breathwork experience. One very good suggestion for children however, is scrapbooking or journaling with a parent. This can go on for months and would really empower the child as well as validate his or her experience. It would also bring parents and children closer together as you deal with all of these new issues and experiences that the child is having. For many more concrete ideas for children on balancing the body, mind, emotions, spirit and energy body, check the activities chapter. You and your child can put together the best "recipe" for dealing with a near-death experience, empowering your child and you, in ways to not only comfort each other, but also "enlighten" each other in the process.

When a Child Becomes a Multi-Dimensional Traveler

Going back and forth from one world or worlds, can become a part of the child's near-death experience. For me, I discounted my travels as my own vivid imagination, for some they write or tell a story, and discount it that way. For others, they buy into the physical world or actually receive counseling for their "mental problems." Others keep quiet for fear they will be considered crazy. Some receive the confirmation and comfort in families who accept these strange happenings as normal perhaps because they are generational psychics. However the child copes with this new found skill and however he or she accepts these experiences as real or imaginary, the journey is the same. The descriptions of children who have had near-death experiences and those of marvelously intuitive children, become the same when referring to the journeying in other worlds, whether these children gained these abilities from some form of spiritual emergency, genetics or training. And the following characteristics are the same as well.

These "cosmos" children tend to live in their heads and often do not pay attention to the fact that their body needs to exercise to be healthy. They either learn basic skills quickly or much more slowly than their peers because they are busy with other things. I can remember that my parents waited and waited for me to walk. One day my mother was in the other end of the house doing something and I guess I got curious. Without much practice standing or crawling, I simply stood up one day and walked to the other end of the house to see what she was doing, without missing a step. My father and brother and sister were so amazed that they just all followed me as I walked steadily and smoothly down the hall. It was just time to walk I guess, and so I did it.

These multi-dimensional children pay little attention to social distractions, large crowds bother then, and even finding a boy or girl friend doesn't seem to interest them as soon as it does everyone else. They are very loving but also emotionally removed from others and life in general. They have a hard time understanding death or do not fear it. They are sensitive to all types of pollutants and sensory things like vibrations, odors, barometric pressure changes, sound volumes up or down, temperatures, etc., etc. This is why psychics are "sensitives." "The key to successfully raising multidimensional/cosmos children is to arrange opportunities whereby they can relate one object to another, relate one feeling to the next, each action to its consequence. Once they catch on to the basic maneuvering of physical matter and human behavior - it may take longer than the average child to figure this out – they more than make up for lost time in their rapid-fire manner of absorbing information." (*Ibid., Atwater, p.197.*)

Some have called this near-death experience for adults and children, a journey of both self-discovery, as well as "looking for the light on the other side of the mountain." But all experts who have studied and researched this phenomenon, especially with children, agree on one thing. These experiences are going to increase. Not only because of advances in medical science and technology which is keeping more people alive, whether child or octogenarian; but because many more people will be pulled back from brief periods in death. The other reason they will increase is that there is enough data and research out there to support the idea that an evolutionary process is taking place in humankind and on our planet in general. Many see it as a greater cosmic plan for humans or a blueprint on which human destiny is being acted out. Near-death experiences are seen by those who study them as "crash courses" in spirituality. This acceleration of consciousness is marked by a unity both on the earth and in the "heavens." No longer linear or sequential with no barriers of time or distance, no single entity will be isolated from another. We are all multidimensional beings and the near-death experiencers may be the first to know this.

Of course not everyone agrees that the soul even exists or that it is eternal. Nor do they agree that a person can be elevated to higher realms of consciousness and spiritual communion, before death or even after death occurs. Becoming one with "the Source" is still a New Age concept for now, at least in America. However, the signs and synchronicities are all around us, and wherever or whenever there is change, there will also be chaos and turmoil. It is all in how you look at it. Near-deaths can tell us about reaching that brink and what lies beyond it. As a psychic I have seen the process of death, the journey towards it and the aftermath in the "light." I have also experienced what death means in my heart, both as a teacher of the severely multi-handicapped and as an intuitive reader. As for a near-death, I simply don't think I have ever had a full one, but who knows? I only know that all of these characteristics apply to me probably through other types of spiritual emergences over my life, such as a severe illness and its ensuing spiritual crisis, as well as journeying with others who have experienced such things. For me, I don't need concrete proof, because nowadays my heart tells me.

Famous Near-Death Experiencers Talk About Their Transcendent Experience as a Child

After a transcendent near-death experience when he was seriously ill, Chief Black Elk began to hear voices and see spirit beings when he was nine years old. His mission was to try and save the world, a tall order for a nine-year-old. He was given 12 days of visions as he lay half-dead, and he emerged with the knowledge that all people should live as one. Later in his life he was to trust one white man, John G. Neihardt, a famous poet and writer, who took down Chief Black Elk's stories and published them in Black Elk Speaks as well as in many other of his own writings. Neihardt had also had a near-death at age twelve and had traveled the same roads as Black Elk, as one who had the "knowings" of a great intuitive and visionary of the future. Black Elk's visions were so spectacular that the tribe was gathered together and this little nine year-old boy told his visions to them all. He told of the Thunder Beings and the Six Grandfathers and the Riders of the Four Directions. He saw that "spirit" shapes all things and that all things were connected. He also saw the Tree of Life as a flowering tree there to shelter all children of the earth and that this tree was holy.

He went out of body and saw himself lying ill. "I could see my people's village far ahead, and I walked very fast, for I was homesick now. Then I saw my own tipi, and inside I saw my mother and my father bending over a sick boy that was myself. And as I entered the tipi someone was saying, 'The boy is coming to. You had better give him some water.' Then I was sitting up and my mother and my father didn't seem to know I had been so far away." Black Elk retreated from his friends and family, feeling that he was a stranger now and he longed to be back in the spirit world. By age 13 he was seen to levitate by some of the villagers and in telling his stories and visions to a medicine man, he was encouraged to act out all of his visions using other tribal members in costumes, etc. He began to have healing powers and would have many very accurate visions about the future, predicting the Battle of the Little Big Horn, etc. His intuitive powers grew ever stronger, ever deeper and ever broader as he aged and his stories became the Rosetta Stone of American Indian spirituality. (*Ibid., The New Children, pp.127-129 and Black Elk Speaks by John G. Neihardt, State University of New York Press, 2008.*)

John G. Neihardt's early visionary experience was the foundation for his lifelong interest in mysticism, as well as his lifelong friendship and interest in chronicling the visions and tales of Black Elk. "John came home from the 9th grade grammar school in Wayne feeling sick. His mother, much excited over his feverish appearance, put the 12 year old lad to bed and called the town physician, an extravagance that showed her great apprehension. The fever lasting several days was a thrilling experience to the inwardness of the boy. In it he seemed to rise up from his bed and fly headlong through space, so fast that the air beneath him felt to his prone body like a sheet of glass upon which he skidded through infinite space. The memory and the mood of the flight stayed with him all through his life." (*Interpreting the Legacy of John Neihardt and Black Elk Speaks by Brian Holloway, University Press of Colorado, 2003, p. 57.*)

"For a specific example of perhaps the quintessential child experiencer, consider Abraham Lincoln. When he was a child of five, Lincoln fell in a rain-swollen creek and drowned. His older brother Austin Gollaher grabbed his body and once ashore, 'pounded him in good earnest.' Water poured from Lincoln's mouth as he thrashed back to consciousness. Although there is no record of the young boy's confiding an otherworld journey to anyone, ample remarks were made by friends and family who observed his sudden craving for knowledge afterwards, his insistence on learning to read, and his going to exhaustive lengths to consume every book he could find. Five years later, just after his mother's death and just before his father remarried, he was on a wagon driving a horse and yelled, 'Git up,' when the horse kicked him in the head. He hovered at death's door throughout the night with his sister Sarah in attendance. On reviving, he completed the epithet aimed at the horse: '...you old hussy.' As an adult, and referring to himself in third person, he is quoted as saying, 'A mystery of the human mind. In his tenth year, he was kicked by a horse, and apparently killed for a time." (*The New Children, Atwater, pp.124 – 125.*)

"At the age of five, he (Albert Einstein) nearly died of a serious illness...Although speech fluency did not occur until around the age of ten (perhaps because of dyslexia), family members recalled how deeply he would reflect before answering a question – a trait that made him appear subnormal...Interestingly he learned the play the violin at six,... taught himself calculus at fourteen, and enrolled in a Zurich University at fifteen. Like Lincoln he was plagued with nervousness and stomach problems and nearly died from these afflictions as an adult. Also like Lincoln, the unusual characteristics of his temperament and talent trace back to the age of five and afterwards." (*Ibid., The New Children, pp. 125-126.*)

Dr. Raymond Moody found in his research of near-death experiences in children that quite a few of the great historical discoveries and inventions in world culture came from men and women who either dreamed their ideas or had a near-death experience as a child, or both. He traced many of the great discoveries back to sixteen particular people, eight of whom had had a near-death experience as a child. He felt that these eight people had used their near-death experience as a central theme in developing their concepts or ideas or discoveries. Among them were such people as Mahtma Gandhi, Mozart, Winston Churchill, Queen Elizabeth I, possibly Shakespeare (Edward de Vere the Seventh Earl of Oxford.) Of course these are only a few that talked about their near-death experiences as children and possibly connected them to their work in the world. There are probably many other great men and women who never recognized that they had a near-death experience because they were too young to remember such an experience and those around them did not recognize this as an important factor in their development as a person. Still others may have had one, even remember it, but do not see the connections with their own spirituality and unique ideas. And if Dr. Moody found that people can assist one in the death process, be they relatives or hospital personnel, they can co-live an individual's death by joining in consciousness with the dying individual; then is it not also possible that this same process takes place when a child is born? (*"Cases from History," The New Children, pp.123-132.*)

What Returning Children Learned on Their Near Death Experiences

Children, who have been on that journey and come back, state some of these concepts the best. They say that "…there is no afterlife, just an ongoing life stream we leave and return to as we take part in different experiences. God exists. We each have a purpose in a larger plan and it doesn't matter if you know what your job is or not. Worship is important, and churches shouldn't put people down. Prayer is powerful and you can see it and feel it. Food tastes better, if you honor it. We need to respect each other and animals are our friends. We don't need a body to see, hear, think, feel, touch, smell, and know things. We have the families we have because we need them. Mistakes can be corrected. Life can be pretty scary so getting in touch with the love that is inside of us can make the scary things go away. Work is important, and so is learning. You can't laugh enough. No one ever dies, and everything is made of light. We are stuffed full of love because God is." (*Ibid., Atwater, The New Children, pp.187-188*).

> "The things that I saw and the feeling that I had was like the feeling that you had when you close your eyes and it's dark but there are little bits of color as well. It was almost fluid-like in feeling too because it was so supportive – I wasn't feeling like I was in a body anymore…with no boundaries of where I ended and where the blackness was. It was the most peaceful and warm, totally comfortable experience that I've ever ever had. And there was nothing there except for tiny thoughts I would have about the environment I was in, but nothing else… Everything in my life now is so intuitive. So now when I get that sort of feeling about someone I feel intuitively that there must be an energy of some description manifesting inside that person that for some reason is readable by me."
>
> --Nicole, Children of the Light, pp. 106-107, struck by a car at 12

> "They do not always come back as beaming little wonder children. They too, have light and sound hypersensitivity; they too, experience bizarre electromagnetic problems. But perhaps the biggest problem that these children face, who do they turn to? Who will they get to listen to their incredible experience? They perhaps don't have the language to articulate what has occurred to them, and they may be very frightened."
>
> --Beyond the Light by P.M.H Atwater

CHAPTER EIGHT

Interfering Sensory Integration Difficulties: Out-of-Sync Kids & Autism/Aspergers Connections

"We first learn to move. So we can move to learn."
– Edu-K philosophy

"...When sensations flow in a well organized or integrated manner, the brain can use those sensations to form perceptions, behaviors, and learning. When the flow of sensations is disorganized, life can be like a rush-hour traffic jam."
--A. Jean Ayers, Sensory Integration and the Child

Aspergers Disorder & Autistic-Like Children

I need to briefly mention, what is called the broad spectrum of autistic disorders, which includes the high functioning autistic person at one end of the spectrum. Asperger Syndrome was identified only recently in the United States and many people believe that it is exactly the same as the highest form of functioning autistics. However, all identified autistic people display sensory integration problems from very severe difficulties to moderate physical difficulties. But in this section we are only concerned with the link between sensory integration and Aspergers. Since there is not only a controversy over whether Aspergers is simply another name for high -functioning autistics or HFA, and a second controversy over whether autism should be viewed as a disorder, at least on the less severe end of the autistic spectrum, there is lots to talk about. Especially since there is also a movement among autistic adults to do away with the label at all, if a person can function fairly well in society. But we are mainly concerned about how Aspergers can be tied to giftedness, intuition and sensory integration problems, here.

Asperger syndrome is characterized by social interaction difficulties, a lacking in nonverbal communication and awareness skills, having restricted repetitive patterns of behavior and interests, and appearing to have limited empathy with peers and exhibiting physical clumsiness or much more extensive sensory integration difficulties. Where people who have been identified as having Aspergers are different from the rest of those identified as autistic, is in the area of language and cognitive development. In this area, these children not only have the verbal and written skills as well as the appropriate language skills, but they seem to typically have intelligence quotients higher than average and are cognitively right on track. In other words they can function in a school classroom but not at lunch or on the playground. Aspergers begins in infancy or early childhood and as the child matures, while there are various changes in the systems of the brain, the disorder continues, throughout the person's life time. These developmental milestones take a wrong turn somewhere especially in the area of the abilities to "see the big picture."

Parents can typically see this syndrome and its development as early as 30 months of age. Diagnosis is made between the ages of four and 11, but misdiagnosis of Aspergers could lead to medications taken that increase the poor behaviors. Sometimes children can also be misdiagnosed as high-functioning autistics with social skills difficulties and sensory integration difficulties when they really do not have autism along with these other problems. There are those who believe that Aspergers syndrome simply exists as a diagnosis because an Austrian pediatrician named Hans Asperger, who had many of the same symptoms in his own childhood, coined the phrase in 1944. But this information did not reach the United States translated into English until the 1990s. Thus the popularity of the syndrome took over the previous popular diagnoses of a learning disability or attention deficit disorder in the public schools in America. But the controversy continues about it really being a syndrome rather than just a label, and autistic people functioning in society are very much advocating a shift in perception of autism spectrum disorders as complex syndromes rather than diseases that must be cured.

The most interfering characteristic of Aspergers for the child is the seemingly lack of empathy for others. These children also have an intense preoccupation with narrow subjects, give one-sided speeches when attempting to talk to others, and are poor readers of body language cues such as eye contact, facial expression, or gestures, etc. They are often withdrawn from others, are awkward in approaching others and this can come across as being insensitive to other people's feelings, when they are not. Some of these people may speak only to some people and not to others, which is very confusing for the person trying to communicate with them. They seem to follow rigid behavioral guidelines when it comes to communicating with others and feel a deep yearning for companionship, because they have failed so often to achieve communication with others. One of the myths about Aspergers is that these children can be violent towards others, when in actual fact; they are likely to be targeted by other children because of their inability to understand social language and skills. These children also collect all sorts of detailed information on narrow topics or use repetitive patterns while they continue to often obsessively study particular subjects. Other children often see them as odd or unapproachable and they become an easy target for teasing or bullying. So they may react literally or concretely to these instances with a violent reaction, because they do not have the social skills to do otherwise, as a child.

Sometimes called "little professors" they could certainly hide out in a gifted classroom and although they take language literally, their higher IQs mask some of this behavior. Their often poor coordination, uneasy gait, poor handwriting or visual motor integration can make them stand out in the crowd even more. They do have excellent auditory and visual perception. Completing or even just doing some sensory motor tasks can be difficult for some Asperger's children. They are very likely to be unusually sensitive or insensitive to sound, light, and other stimuli. They can also have sleep problems, and also difficulties in describing their own emotions. They can especially have trouble with understanding humor or irony. It appears there may be a genetic factor involved as one of the causes of this syndrome. Fathers tend to have had some of these characteristics in childhood, but fewer mothers have them. And as I have said in recent years there has been an increase in its diagnosis, although some did not have high level autism, but merely social and sensory difficulties.

Traditional therapies used with this disorder are pretty much the same as those used with attention deficit or oppositional defiance disorder. The children are trained in social skills; receive behavioral therapy, have occupational and physical therapy, speech and social communication, training or support for those who care for this child, and medications for other difficulties that may parallel Aspergers such as depression or anxiety. 20% of these children grow out of Aspergers by their adult years, but like the others, adults show an increase in psychiatric disorders such as depression, anxiety, and panic attacks. Teenagers have ongoing difficulty with their self-care, how to organize things, and often cannot leave home to marry or work independently. These parallel diagnoses probably stemmed from failures to engage others socially or being willing to have their routines and rituals altered. 65% of adults diagnosed with Aspergers developed these other conditions, and there is even one study that says that males have a higher chance of developing a non-verbal learning disorder and/or epilepsy.

Having seen a few of these students over the years before the diagnosis of Asperger syndrome, when students were diagnosed with some other label, it is rather confusing to figure out what these pervasive developmental disorders and autistic disorders have or do not have, in common. When I worked with the deaf blind multi-handicapped, many of these higher functioning children would have been diagnosed with Aspergers back then, if the name had been around at the time. Yet their physical loss of sensory integration skills in terms of hearing and seeing may have caused them to function in this way. And how many Out-of-Sync children really have Aspergers, or just have motor problems? These confusions could go on and on, that is why it is vital to look at each child individually, discover the various symptoms without labels, and go from there. After all, having all this information under your belt then enables you as parents, to put a program together for your child that has just the right fit, with just the right alternatives, to help your child reach his or her maximum potential personally, and in society. Can one have an intuitive Asperger child? Most certainly!

Today's Integrative Programs for Autism

It has taken decades for the programs that I trained under in my twenties and thirties, to come not only to fruition, but also to be made easy to apply for parents, siblings and all the other specialists in your child's life. And even today you have to search for them, as the era of new brain research shows that the compartmentalized programs for children with disabilities, as well as all other children, might have worked, but also ended up labeling children and holding them back from their own progress. Letting children lead the way is a new concept for us, in every arena of childhood, and a guided, integrative approach which should not have been new, somehow is. Dr. Greenspan's DIR – Floor Time approach is nothing new, and yet it is what all children need, except in different forms depending on their individual needs. Looking at this type of programming for Autistic-Like and Asperger children, is only one example of how any teacher or parent can put together a learning program for each child that will help every child reach their potential. Remaining open-ended is the key.

Understanding varied levels of progress is a concept for all children, as is the DIR concept that any child can be influenced or presented with a foundation for core developmental stages that will help them to relate, communicate and think, through the avenues of their emotions and affect. Specific myths about Autism are addressed in their programs, such as autistic kids cannot love, cannot communicate appropriately and cannot be creative. Other myths include the idea that these children cannot read emotions or think abstractly and that their brain is wired in such a way that they cannot change or grow or achieve. Most teachers can tell you that these are myths for all children and can probably address dozens more such myths for any "labeled" child. They can also tell you that observing the child for a while can give you reams of information about that child. It has also been known for decades that early intervention can really help any child succeed even more rapidly. Meaningful emotional exchanges occur both in their relationships at home and in school. For the autistic child, all of this is even more vital.

Interrelated progress occurs when a child can relate to his environment and other people, having the cognitive and sensory-motor processing abilities to do this. The DIR model stands for Developmental Individual difference, Relationship-based approach. And Floor Time is based on nine or ten developmental stages which create emotionally meaningful learning interactions. The stages are: developing an interest in the world, engaging and relating, establishing two-way communication, social problem solving and developing a sense of self, regulating behavior and moods, creating symbols (developing words and language), developing emotional thinking and logic, and developing multi-causal thinking as well as emotionally differentiated thinking. The first steps are laid out for parents and caregivers as soon as the child is identified. And then the parents are given activities to help develop: attention, regulation, engagement, relating, emotional interactions, problem solving, creating ideas, and facilitating logical thinking.

Along with this are the sensory integration activities, verbal and auditory processing skills and the gestures, symbols and words that will facilitate the developing communication and language skills. And these areas flow smoothly into the pre-school and beginning school years, if done correctly. Along with this is a developing desire to communicate and use imaginative play or develop one's own interests and explore one's feelings. Distinguishing between fantasy and reality is an interesting one to look at from the perspective of the intuitive child. Is teaching this necessary for an autistic child, or is allowing the creativity to flow a better option when intuition enters the picture? In a compacted version of the many sensory integration difficulties that can come up specifically for these children, parents can facilitate these areas much more quickly before the various modalities are explored in depth by the professionals.

But the best idea in this program is that everything is a family approach from parents to siblings to other caregivers, and ideally by the time the child enters school, any child would be ahead of the game, but especially children with special needs who have in the past been considered incapable of all this progress. However, in watching documentaries on individual stories of such children, one cannot feel that way too much still falls on the mother's shoulders in the early years and her own emotions and anxieties certainly need to be addressed and supported. Time as a couple, time for attention to other siblings and time for moms will probably always be a problem in any plan concerning the guiding and mentoring of a child, even after they enter their formal schooling years and especially a challenging child.

<u>DIR-Floor Time</u> for young children progresses from individual exploration and caregiver time to siblings and peers, and eventually to different environments and settings, culminating in school settings. Then as teens and young adults, <u>Floor Time</u> becomes developing communities and finding deeper ways of relating to the world. They address a model learning community as being a place that is constantly strengthening one's processing skills while constantly promoting functional emotional and social skills and building meaningful and appropriate interests. These communities focus on academic and life skills as well as lessening the inappropriate social skills and finding better ways of relating to others while sharing a group identity. Exactly Van Dyk's approach for deaf-blind multi-handicapped children under a century ago, I worked in a small house with my "group" and we taught them from the moment these children got up to the moment until they went to bed. We oversaw their programs in a dormitory setting that created an artificial

yet very real family for very severe children not expected to develop beyond the three month old level. There were three shifts, three different "parents" who teamed together for each child.

Our assessments were the same, involving observations, developmental histories – we wrote a detailed curriculum for this, reviews of what had been tried, completed parent interviews, had specialist consultations and intervention programs and had on-going medical evaluations of medications and physicals. We also carried out consistent small group team meetings for those in charge of each individual child. I was dormitory supervisor for two years and eventually became a classroom teacher which then led to parent training in a few homes when I then moved out of the state and taught in only a day school and did even more of this home instruction. The structure of the day was similar with short periods of individual interaction, communication and language arts, visual-spatial processing, sensory motor planning, intermixed with life skills in their natural order as the day progressed. Small group times were intermixed with individual times and after school activities continued until bed time.

In short, I read this book, Engaging Autism and others like it, which I listed in the bibliography, but was surprised to realize at long last my frustrations when moving to another state, which would have explained the differences at that time. Something I had known for years and used with every child was now mainstream, written about, talked about and presented to parents, although it seemed that schools were still far behind. Not really their fault, but due to the lack of funding, a lack of proper training and knowledge, it had somehow built an invisible wall between myself and many others in the teaching profession in a different locale. However, there were still those who found their way to all this stuff anyway and we had been islands in the storm, a storm that Neil Marcus Estonia writes about so poignantly in his play "Storm Warning." But he does not write about the mortal storm, the New Age Storm, or even the public school storm, he is writing about his own disease and really the crux of the matter, his own body which is in constant and various levels of motion. And while Estonia's difficulties are visible, Temple Grandin, a representative of the just different but more silent difficulties of Aspergers, I think would agree with Estonia's poignant remarks:

"I believe I have a voice, words, feelings, observations, perceptions, thoughts, that can move the world. I am a storm. A cyclone of ideas, thunder and lightning, a warm summer's breeze, a gentle spring rain.

Some people hide from storms. They close their shutters, doors and blinds. They seep themselves in their own darkness and rob themselves of the tumultuous journey and its exhilaration.

Some people, when they see my twisted frame, my distonic disarray, embrace the storm. Their eyes light up and they rush to hug me as a long lost brother. As if embracing a storm was food for their souls. I can teach you to read a storm."

Out-of-Sync Children & Sensory Integration Difficulties

Called SID for short, Sensory Integration Disorders can accompany other difficulties such as ADD/ADHD, ODD and Autism or Aspergers, but they aren't necessarily evident in all kids. The characteristics of these various types of difficulties can however cross between these various disorders, and often not consistently. It is important to understand that SID children are not doing the things they do, because they want to, but because they can't. There is a sort of faulty wiring in the brain. The second important thing to know about SID, is that we all have varying degrees of it, but when it's interfering with the child's life it becomes something important to work on. The child may be oversensitive in a particular area, or under sensitive in another area, or have difficulties in several different sensory areas. Some of a child's behaviors, which might often indicate other childhood labels listed above, might only be indicating this particular set of difficulties, rather than a more severe problem. Or the child may have another labeled disorder along with SID. Behavioral symptoms include an unusually high or low activity level, impulsive or distracted behavior, poor muscle tone and motor coordination, difficulty making transitions, resistance to new situations, and a high level of frustration. The child may have difficulty with touch, movement, body position, smells, sounds, tastes, and visual or auditory problems.

There has not been a lot of research on what causes Sensory Integration problems, but there is some research that indicates either a genetic predisposition or various pregnancy difficulties, birth traumas, and postnatal circumstances may be involved. When the brain is so disorganized that a person has difficulty functioning in the physical world, one can suspect SIDs. Many believe that children with these kinds of difficulties have been programmed by their central nervous system to respond to things in a certain way that is not the normal way in which the rest of us respond. No one part of the central nervous system works alone, messages have to go back and forth from one place to another. The body has to work in a synchronized way, so that we can carry out our daily tasks. If the brain is processing sensory intake effectively, we can process even more sensory information. If the brain is not processing sensory intake appropriately, this makes the person unable to deal with simple movements that should have been organized for them. This complex system must be wired properly. But this also explains why some children with SID might not exhibit every characteristic of every type of difficulty, or show some of the characteristics on one day and not on another. Since everyone has some small form of Sensory Integration difficulties, then no one is well-regulated all of the time.

Types of Sensory Integration Problems

There are five types of Sensory Integration problems. We all have them in varying degrees, most of us learn to function in the physical world by compensating for the less severe motor difficulties that we have. For example, I hate honey on my hands because I am slightly "tactilely defensive." But there are many others who suffer from more severe motor problems that interfere with being able to live their life to its fullest. These five are called Tactile Dysfunction, Vestibular Dysfunction, Proprioceptive Dysfunction, Visual Dysfunction, and Auditory Dysfunction. I will spend a paragraph on the characteristics for each one of these, but for more detailed information and checklists for pre-schoolers, elementary aged children, adolescents and adults, please refer to the following and best book and workbook that I know of that can give you this information before visiting or working with an occupational therapist if it turns out one of your children fits an amazing amount of the criteria for one or more of these areas. The Out-Of-Sync Child by Carol Kranowitz and teacher workbook, Answers to Questions Teachers Ask About Sensory Integration by Jane Koomer, Carol Kranowitz and Stacey Szklut. There are many other books on this subject available now, as at long last sensory integration comes into its own, but this is the foundation book to read for your child and then you can move on to all the others. Intuitive children can suffer from any of the following difficulties simply by being psychic or sensitive, but they can also have a two-fold difficulty going on with both sensory integration challenges as well as empathic ones. It is only the cause that might be different.

Tactile Dysfunction or sense of touch problems involve such things as spatial relationships, touching others or being touched by someone, an aversion to touching objects, textures or things that are cold or warm, etc. This is divided into five types of problems: Sensory Avoider, Sensory Disregarder, and Sensory Craver, Tactilely Unable to Discriminate, and Dyspraxia or performing a sequence of movements and poor motor coordination. Naturally the changes in weather can deeply affect such a sensitive child, the child can respond negatively and emotionally to touch, demonstrate a fight or flight response to being touched, be aversive to changes and exhibit behaviors that are stubborn, rigid, or inflexible. They may love to feel everything around them obsessively, or refuse to touch anything or anyone, or be touched, etc. They may have trouble forming warm attachments with others, i.e., also a symptom of some autism present, although not necessarily. They may love to make messes or avoid them like the plague. They may not like their "space" invaded or don't even notice when it is being invaded. They may not even notice when they have dropped something or been physically hurt themselves.

The types are: Vestibular Dysfunction involves a child's awareness of a position in space. Over Responsive or Intolerance for Movement, Gravitational Insecurity, Sensory Seeking with Increased Tolerance for Movement, the Sensory Fumbler or a Dyspraxia where the child exhibits poor motor planning and Sensory Slumpers with postural difficulties. These children are uncomfortable in closed spaces, cautious, may fear the dangers of children's playgrounds or may have a fear of falling, have anxiety if they are lifted off the ground, have poor visual discrimination or try to protect themselves from these movements by manipulating their environment. They may need to keep moving all the time, crave intense movement experiences or don't seem to get dizzy when spun around and around. These children may have difficulty organizing and carrying out a sequence of movements, get easily frustrated, have low self-esteem and a low tolerance for stressful situations. Some of these children can be fidgety and clumsy, have a floppy body, have difficulty with their fine motor skills, and even may have problems with digestion and elimination. Dean 'floats' by his desk...

Proprioceptive Dysfunction means that the child has difficulty picking up on sensory and motor information in his environment. The four types of this dysfunction include: Over Responsiveness to Input, Under Responsiveness, Sensory Seeking, and Poor Discrimination. Some of the characteristics are preferring not to move at all, becoming upset when moved, being a picky eater, having low muscle tone, breaking toys easily, bumping and crashing into objects, engaging in self stimulatory activities such as cracking knuckles, stamping his feet on the ground or kicking his heels against the chair. This type of child may also have poor body awareness and motor control, difficulty positioning his body in space, difficulty knowing where his body is in relation to objects and people, and difficulty going up and down stairs. These children may also flex and extend their muscles in excess while doing projects, hold pencils and crayons too tightly, break delicate objects, manipulate an object with less force or with too much force than necessary, and have difficulty lifting or holding objects. These children may also have poor posture, slump in a chair, keep one foot on the floor for balance sitting and often are timid in unfamiliar situations.

Visual Dysfunction involves these four types:, Poor Basic Visual Skills, Difficulty Modulating Visual Sensations, Poor Visual Discrimination, and Poor Visual-Motor Skills. These children may have headaches, eye strain, rub their eyes a lot, complain of blurriness or seeing double, and all the other kinds of skills that would denote needing an eye test and probably eyeglasses. But they can also have problems with sunlight, indoor bright lights, avoid direct eye contact, experience nausea or dizziness or headaches with using their eyes, can be unaware of movement around them, seek visual stimulation, and excessively squirm and seek bright lights. The child may have difficulty seeing objects in three dimensions for depth perception, and may have difficulty judging distances between objects or difficulties in team sports or school work, or are unable to form mental images of objects. They also fail to comprehend what is being read, and have a short attention span. Children with poor visual motor skills may have poor eye hand or eye foot coordination, sometimes have difficulty with fine motor tasks and overall gross motor skills, and they cannot do rhythmic activities very well. They may have poor coordination and balance or poorly orient their drawings on the page. But most important they will tend to withdraw from classroom participation for many of the above reasons.

Auditory Dysfunction includes five types: Difficulty Modulating Auditory Sensations, Poor Auditory Discrimination, Difficulty with Receptive Language, Difficulty with Expressive Language, and Difficulty with Speech and Articulation. These children can be distressed by loud noises or attracted to them. They can be distressed by inaudible low noises or high-pitched sounds which the rest of us cannot hear, and be distressed by sounds that others are not bothered by. They can also seem unaware of the source of sounds, have difficulty discerning sounds, be unable to focus attention on a conversation or story, and have difficulty associating some sounds too familiar sounds. They may have a short attention span, may have difficulty misinterpreting questions and requests and also may look to others before responding with difficulty recognizing rhymes or learning new languages. They might be a late talker, they might have a weak vocabulary, they might have difficulty with spelling skills, they may have a limited ability to do imagination games or fantasy play, use immature sentence structure, have difficulty with reading or singing a song, and often require more time than other children responding to the sounds of voices. Children with speech and articulation problems are usually identified and sent to the speech therapist. But some of the other types of speech problems that often aren't mentioned are things like a flat monotone voice, speaking too loudly or too softly, and speaking without an even or fluid rhythm, etc.

What to do for the Out-of-Sync Child

The good news is that most of these motor difficulties can be almost entirely corrected if caught early. Misdiagnosing this can however, add to the problem. Children, who develop normally as they should, first learn to roll, then creep, then crawl, then stand, and finally learn to walk as a "solid block," until they can learn to integrate both sides of their body and walk with balanced and integrated coordination. SID children do not follow this prescription in one way or another, and must be taught to organize their "brain directions" to accomplish these things. The people who are best trained in understanding these difficulties are occupational therapists, most of who are trained in sensory integration methods and techniques. However, there are less severe fine and gross motor difficulties that parents can work on at home, and really parents should work on these things as early as they can in addition to taking their child to see an occupational therapist. Physical Therapists may or may not have sensory integration training so check this out before you start. Occupational Therapists pretty much automatically have this type of training although you may run across a few who do not.

Unfortunately, many parents have some rationalizations as to why their child doesn't need this particular help. They believe the other types of labels that have been put on their child and don't want to look any further. They have never heard of it or they don't think it can be that important, or it's something that their child couldn't possibly have.

Some look at it as something that love will take care of or that if the child doesn't do what the other kids are doing, then they must be advanced for their age or their child will "grow out of it." Some of my gifted parents felt that the child's brainpower would compensate for this over time. Then there are other parents who think the opposite, that the child is so smart, why can't he or she do simple tasks, and put a lot of unnecessary stress on this particular child. Some even believe that since the child can do everything else really well, then the child is just refusing to do it. But the issue does not have anything to do with these rationalizations; it has to do with why the child needs help. Is this problem getting in his way, is this problem getting in other people's way, or does the child experience extreme frustration, because he cannot do what other children do "motor-wise?" In the long run, if nothing is done about this, the child will experience emotional upsets, frustrations, and quite often, social skills problems. Asperger children nearly always deal with SID in one or several forms.

When a child is found to have some of these many difficulties: occupational therapy, speech and language therapy, auditory integration training, vision training, psychotherapy, and physical therapy are recommended. According to the degree of severity, the child may only need one or two of these types of therapies. And yes, adults do learn to compensate for any sorts of sensory integration problems they might have. But having seen children suffer emotionally and psychologically in gym class, because they can't do what the other children are doing, seems to be proof enough for me that working with these children while they are very young could eliminate many of these difficulties. Not everyone is gifted with natural athletic abilities, but being able to do what the other children can do during gym period, even in a limited fashion, is well worth the extra effort on the part of parents, teachers and therapists, to help that child fit in. Having my own memories of gym class, I can remember dreading it. I wasn't very coordinated anyway, but my main problem was that "intuitive daydreaming" that often got me hit by the ball, or someone else's body colliding with my own. The distractions of my daydreams, storytelling and real intuitive experiences, did not bode well for me in gym class. Add on to this a child who absolutely cannot coordinate his or her body movements, and this is a social-emotional disaster just waiting to happen. So please do your "sensory diet" exercises with your child at home, because you are then protecting your child from damaging situations and overwhelming environments. Read and re-read Carol Stock Kranowitz's The Out-of-Sync Child for your "difficult, picky, oversensitive, clumsy or inattentive child." Her workbook will give you specific activities and also the assessment checklists to identify difficulties.

Educational Kinesiology or Edu-K for Kids

There is something else available that can help you with these types of problems. Educational Kinesiology might be compared to when you choose between going to a medical doctor or an alternative health person. Both people are really working on the same things, but they are coming from entirely different perspectives when they look at your child. Physical therapists come from a medical model, while occupational therapists come from a "how to learn to function in the world" model. Medical doctors tend to look at pieces rather than the whole child, while the Edu-K facilitator will look at the whole child, not only in terms of sensory integration, but also how children learn, what their academic skills are, and how their brain is wired in relation to both physical and academic skills. Edu-K is a tool to take the guesswork out of education and childrearing. One can recognize the early signs of learning problems and work with these challenges in early childhood to help solve problems before the child's self-concept is damaged upon entering school. But even older children and adults can improve their academic, physical and social skills by working with an Edu-K facilitator when they have difficulties that are interfering in living and experiencing a good lifestyle.

In the Edu-K or repatterning concept, certain muscle tests, corrections, and procedures are used to help a person to become educated to move correctly. The philosophy is that each person can depend on the facilitator to support and trust the wisdom of that individual's way of unfolding, rather than approach the child with any preconceived expectations about how he or she should evolve. The idea behind Edu-Kinesthetics is that every person has brain neurology from the left and right side of the brain, as well as the front and back of the brain. Every movement the body makes takes an integrated complex set of skills from all these areas of the brain. The whole brain experience can be very elusive for most people, although it is the ideal way to function. Edu-K facilitators believe that every person must actually experience whole brain movement in order to know what this feels like. That if people can be trained to be more balanced in left/ right brain functions through a series of exercises and thus be able to coordinate their bodies better in space and through motor planning skills, then they can do much better in their academic skills.

When this sort of thinking came out many years ago, it was not looked at as a legitimate form of therapy. Yet, Edu-K is still going strong today, has been integrated into many school district programs and I personally used these Brain Gym exercises with both my resource classes and my gifted classes. I found that overall, it was a great way to break up the day to get up and move and do Brain Gym simply for physical exercise, and simply the belief in these exercises empowered children. Many children improved academically, simply because of this. I also found that, in particular cases, there really was a dramatic improvement in reading, spelling, handwriting, or mathematics skills. These exercises were also a great way to improve social skills by teaching children various exercises that helped the students to have a better understanding of their peers and to have a better awareness of, and empathy for those around them. With children or adults who have more severe difficulties, an individualized program with a facilitator outside the school setting or the workplace, improvements can be quite dramatic in terms of reading or vision problems, especially. The Brain Gym exercises are for the classroom, while deeper Educational Kinesiology work needs to be done individually with a facilitator. They have also expanded their Vision Gym, to especially help children who have visual or brain/vision dysfunctions.

I really like some of their beliefs such as the fact that human beings are meant to live in an integrated state or that human beings, when placed in a nurturing environment, are naturally good. Growth and change are inherent in man's nature and each human being is involved in the growth of every other human being. Each person creates their own reality, and must accept full responsibility for their own interactions. Everyone has a responsibility to interact positively with others and no one person is ever complete as long as there are new things to learn and new ways to grow. As for the facilitators, they state that "intention" is the most powerful healing tool, the corrections that are made must be specific, and one can never stop learning. The exercises begin to really educate the body to function in midfield, where the two cerebral hemispheres work best together. The naturally integrated person has learned to use his two hemispheres together as a "whole" brain. The "switched-off" person cannot do this and may never have felt what it was like to function holistically and integratively in their physical body. In other words, a person can "learn" to be whole brained!

In one of my workshops, a young man about 20 years old who was obviously brilliant and had exceptional verbal and memorization skills, volunteered to pretend to be a child with a reading problem so that I could demonstrate some of the exercises and have the participants try them out. One often gets, at least a few people who have been functioning without all of their motor skills integrated and when they feel this temporary change in their body, they are astounded, and this was what I was aiming for in the workshop. Instead, I was astounded, when the young man could not read. This explained a lot of things, his distrust towards me as a former schoolteacher, his interest in all things intuitive, his fabulous verbal and memorization skills which had probably gotten him through school and the wonderful mask that he had fashioned for himself. But I was to learn that he had been homeschooled, probably because his parents had already reached the end of the expert line, early in their child's education. This meant that he had never even had a chance to learn to read, if by chance he had run across someone who knew what to do and cared enough to do it. Anyway, I gave him a simpler text and continued on. When we had all finished the exercises together and he began reading a different text, I said to him, "Do you feel the difference?" The look on his face was answer enough for me, and the young mothers there to find out what to do with their own intuitive children had also learned something profound. Probably for the first time in his life, he had actually "felt" what it was like to be in his "whole brain" and could see his improvement in reading instantly.

In Edu-K there is a lot of terminology that has to do with different kinds of remediation, for example everyone has a dominant eye and a dominant ear. One has to first find out which these are to determine hand and foot dominance. So the first set of exercises concern Blocked Dominance and this type of difficulty is broken down into such things as Language Blocked Dominance or other academic skills. Then there is Uniform Dominance and this is broken down into specific academic skills such as reading where the person may "switch-off" visually when crossing midline. Then there are difficulties with "switched-off" ear or eye dominance. The person is "muscle tested" using kinesiology to decide which exercises need to be done. In the last few years, the Edu-K foundation has continued to develop the visual aspects of motor-brain learning specifically. More and more school districts have been adopting these methods in their schools and having their teachers trained in the basic Brain Gym exercises for physical, emotional, and academic success.

Since its early days, the Edu-K founder's Paul Dennison and Gail E. Hargrove have continued to work with the schools and they have private facilitators all over the world. The exercises consist of Midline Exercises, Lengthening Exercises, Energy Exercises and Deepening Attitudes Exercises. Midline exercises are to help the person to learn to integrate their left and right brain command centers. The Lengthening or stretching exercises are really basic warm-up or cool-down exercises that all athletes do. The Energy exercises, and Deepening Attitudes exercises, are both based on acupressure points, combined with crossing midline exercises. So some of these exercises are quite similar to the latest craze of Tapping the main acupressure points associated with the main organs. These tapping points energize the bodies' nervous, lymphatic and blood systems to improve the overall immune system. A brief explanation of the daily energizing Tapping procedure can be found in Chapter Six.

In any event, Edu-K obviously is something that would help children with more severe sensory integration difficulties just as weekly occupational therapy exercises would. The difference being, that the occupational therapist is only looking at the overall coordination of the body and the mechanics of physical movement. While the Edu-K facilitator is looking at the connections between body/mind and academics. If you have a child who is having more severe sensory integration problems, then it would definitely be worth your while to check into the Edu-K process along with occupational therapy outside the school system. It was always my experience that inside the school system it was extremely difficult to get occupational therapy for even young students, especially if the child was bright. And there was never enough of the therapy available to really make a difference in the first years of the child's schooling. If you have financial help, it is much better to seek this help outside the school system if you can see clearly that your child needs a lot more help than this. To find facilitators in your area just go online to the Edu-Kinesthetics website and also order the book E-K for Kids, it's a great starting place to help children to understand just why they are being asked to do these exercises. This specific book is difficult to find but hopefully it has been integrated into other materials available on line at www.braingym.com or you can find a used copy online.

Brain Gym Exercise Titles

One always does the PACE exercises to get ready for any of the Brain Gym sets. The PACE exercises are shown on the following chart along with drinking at least one or two glasses of water before doing any of the exercises. I added an energy exercise to the PACE procedures to help the child be aware of their energy body as well. Reading & Vision Skills, Spelling Skills, Math Skills, Thinking Skills, Writing Skills, Self-Awareness Skills, Study Skills, and Personal Ecology Skills are the sets of exercises in Brain Gym. All of these skills are a combination of the type of areas already mentioned such as midline, lengthening, energy and deepening attitude exercises. The children really enjoy them and even my gifted kids liked the challenge of figuring out how to do them when they discovered that they could not coordinate their bodies as perfectly as they thought. These exercises would be really helpful for coaches in little leagues to train those little athletes motorically while helping out their academics unknowingly. If you watch what coaches have their teams do, they have discovered similar methods and already understand how to help their students out in this arena themselves. They have not however, probably made the connection that an integrated body "machine" makes for better academics literally, although they probably do know that belief in one's self can really make a difference in any team sport or life skill in general.

Out-of-Sync children with sensory integration problems may have these separately from any other problems and this may be all they need to improve both emotionally, socially, behaviorally, academically, and motorically. This particular problem does require the diagnosis of an occupational therapist specifically trained in recognizing, assessing and coming up with a set of exercises for the various areas. However, children can often have secondary or even primary problems along with this, so get all the other areas checked out too. But remember there can also be a lot of mislabeling going on concerning your child as well. It is more important to get the facts and then create your own "prescription" or "diet" for your child because you know him best. Once again, advocate for your children by being informed and speaking up when this or that doesn't seem to be the right fit, don't let the experts intimidate you because there is a lot out there that we don't know yet, or don't recognize as happening to children. Edu-K is another great way to do things with your child in a more constructive way than just regular exercises. It can't hurt and it may very well help, sometimes in a profound way.

Dr. Greenspan's various books on the subjects of educating children of difference, especially autistic children, can also be quite helpful to you as the parents or a parent of an out-of-sync child, as Sensory Integration seems to accompany so many of these other difficulties. His programs and ideas are helpful with behavior management and avoiding labeling such children. And he also includes in his assessments of such children, ways to integrate the sensory deficits into these programs and on different developmental levels. Edu-K Facilitators also try to include an integrative program individualized for each child that can accommodate the academic learning as well as promote it. A combination of all these things can really help any child dealing with these various difficulties, find success and independence in life. Either program will help your child, no matter the depth and breadth of their challenges.

Few people realize that empathic sensitives, a term which encompasses all the types of intuitive abilities, often suffer from many of the same sorts of sensory integration issues probably because of a slightly different brain wiring, but most assuredly from their daily experiences in worlds invisible to many. As one becomes more spiritually awake and more aware of one's own abilities, the senses become much more acute and much more discerning when it comes to the sound frequencies around us, and both auditory and visual stimulations can really overwhelm the intuitive. Even in terms of motor movements, motor planning and motor coordination, intuitives can suddenly find themselves at any given time, in a spiritual emergency which is causing problems that never manifested before, such as dizziness. Although often temporary, these motor sensory integration issues can interfere with functioning in daily life. The auditory and visual issues can become permanent or they can also manifest temporarily or even inconsistently in sensitive children.

Astral travel can affect one's sense of being grounded or even one's sense of reality and sometimes be diagnosed as a mental problem. The list is endless and confusing for most intuitives, so paying attention to the types of problems or issues that can come up in this arena, is your best defense. But most important, realize that you are not alone, and that all these "side-effects" are simply part of the journey to knowing your own intuitive abilities, and not so much a "curse" as a gift in disguise. While the causes of sensory integration problems can be entirely different for psychic children, how you work with these difficulties is the same. However, with intuitive children some of these so-called problems can become "gifts" in disguise and should be honored as such. Honoring these gifts while learning to live with them is a bit tricky and managing or balancing these sensitivities can be difficult. The biggest challenge is in keeping these various sensitivities from interfering in one's daily life while enjoying the satisfactions of having and using these "gifts" appropriately. So working with these sensory integration issues and learning how to use one's sensitivities to help others is a very difficult balance for these particular children.

Since Sensory Integration can be a re-wired brain, and since it can accompany other types of strange phenomena, the intuitive person may very well experience many of the same kinds of things with all of the sensate information arriving chaotically from all five channels, especially the hearing channel. As we grow old, many of these things can increase. For example as I grow more in tune with my spiritual intuitiveness, I cannot tolerate what I used to such as loud sounds bombarding me, chaotic lights flashing at me and jerky movements, all the things one experiences in going to an action movie at the theater. While this is typical for many people as they grow older, it is magnified for the intuitive. Even younger people who happen to have the sensitivities to the hearing "channel" will pick up on electric lines or earth energy fields whose sounds are supposed to be out of the human range of hearing, but are not for the intuitive. One can sometimes feel as if the sounds are driving one crazy until you modify your abilities to live with these sorts of things.

For example, my tinnitus that was once low grade and intermittent, is now much louder, interfering and constant, as I grow older. One of the ways I intuit spirit presence is by the increased buzzing or humming in my ears which is rather like the sound a huge shell makes when you hold it up to your ear and have the blood pumping through your ears echo back like the ocean. Nowadays the presence of spirit is just a lot louder and has a pattern to it that I can recognize over the tinnitus. I had to modify my ability to tune into this and recognize the sounds in a different way. I sometimes even hear the buzzing of the electric lines. Or the dizziness from my many inner ear infections that damaged my middle ears as a child is also the same way that I intuit spirit when in an antique shop and I pass by various objects with energies attached to them. If I get dizzy in these shops full of old things, I know that it is just too much for me to tolerate, but I also know that this only happens when in an "overload" of spirit energy around me. In other words, Sensory Integration skills for the intuitive are really quite similar to what Temple Grandin describes in her book for both children and adult Aspergers. Her detailed descriptions of these various sensate issues are vividly described and analyzed in her biography Emergence: Labeled Autistic, while she offers amazing and detailed advice for helping a high functioning autistic child in Thinking in Pictures and The Way I See It. There is a movie available about her life as well, which tries to demonstrate these various sensory difficulties.

> "For the out-of-sync child, sensory integration does not go according to Nature's plan. Somewhere in the circuitry of his sensory processing machine, there is a 'short.' For some reason the circuitry is inefficient…Unable to screen the irrelevant from the relevant, he seems to defend himself from most sensations. He may be negative and defiant, lashing out, or he may be fearful and cautious, shutting down…Unfortunately, symptoms of SI Dysfunction are often misinterpreted as psychological problems."
>
> --The Out-of-Sync Child, pp. 19 & 57

> "…no matter how much advanced brain power a child has, intelligence alone is not sufficient for organized daily functioning if the underlying senses are not integrated. Sensory integration depends on a sensory processing machine that is in good working order."
>
> --Ibid, p.277

> "Like many children, my sensory issues were not limited to one sense. When I was in elementary school, the sound of the school bell hurt like a dentist drill hitting a nerve. There are some individuals who have such severe sound sensi-

tivity they cannot tolerate public places such as malls and supermarkets and the constant flicker of fluorescent lighting was visible only to people who are visually sensitive."

--Temple Grandin PhD. Autistic Adult

Sylvia Browne says that sensory sensitive, empathic children when grieving a loss of someone experience this sort of visit from the other side like this: "...whether we're aware of them or not they leave us countless signs we can easily miss in the dark, numb pain of grief. Like all their beloved brothers and sisters in the spirit world, they might leave coins in the most unlikely places. They might turn lights, appliances, televisions and computers on and off. They might stop clocks, make phones and doorbells ring, play music boxes,..."make toys without batteries work, manipulate photographs, move car keys, make a seat on a sofa or bed, or "...send birds, butterflies and other animals to visit on their behalf. They can make you swear you felt a subtle breath on the back of your neck, or a tiny breeze in your hair when the air around you is perfectly still."

"They can visit or send signs at anytime, but pay special attention during rainstorms or in the early morning hours before dawn. Electricity and water, in the form of lightning, rain, humidity or dew, are conductors of energy. And spirits are energy after all. These conductors aren't essential to visits and signs... but they can make the trip between dimensions easier and increase the frequency with which they occur." These sorts of sensitivities can well make up for any inconveniencies the empathic child feels when trying to integrate their sensory abilities, finding that their "overly" sensitive bodies can detect what many others cannot sense or feel.

--Psychic Children by Syliva Browne & Lindsay Harrison, p. 246

CHAPTER NINE

LEARNING STYLES, GIFTEDNESS & INTUITIVE CHILDREN

"What happens to the rat that stops running the maze? The doctors think it's dumb when it's just disappointed."

--Mark Eitzel

"Showing up at school already able to read is like showing up at the undertaker's already embalmed; people start worrying about being put out of their jobs."

--Florence King

"Loneliness does not come from having no people about one, but from being unable to communicate to others the things that seem important to oneself, or from holding certain views which others find inadmissible...If a man knows more than others, he becomes lonely."

--Carl Jung

Learning Styles

A lot has been written about learning styles in children but it was not until recently that most experts in this field began to narrow down the types of styles along a much more simplistic scale, which is actually more complex now that the experts understand their own journeys. I will spend my time on one such learning style continuum that is associated with giftedness but not exclusive to it. In this way, we can study the traits and characteristics for the types of giftedness in association with the most practical and very rarely addressed learning styles which Linda Kreger Silverman calls Upside Down Brilliance. This includes a scale from Auditory Processors to Whole Brainers to Visual-Spatial Learners. The whole concept of a left out learning style in our own public school systems hugely affects the outcome for over half of all school children not just in the United States but all around the world. This also affects adults in the work world where over half of all workers find themselves unable to communicate with their co-workers every day of their work week, as schools specifically and the world in general, are built to cater to the auditory processing or whole brain learning style. This is parallel to those who are trying to function as intuitives in a physical world which is only meeting the needs of under a third of its population in their style of learning, let alone the invisible worlds that intuitives ponder and experience every day as well. Most intuitives are also functioning predominately in a visual-spatial style. The amount of VSL's has increased over time to much larger numbers.

Trying to accommodate the various learning styles in a classroom can be an overwhelming task. But the visual-spatial learning model addresses the different options of each hemisphere of the brain. The left hemisphere is sequential, analytical, time oriented and the right hemisphere perceives the whole picture, synthesizes, and understands movement in space. Linda Kreger Silverman was one of the first researchers to narrow down the many different theories and types of learning styles. She found a way to simplify these scales down to three types: auditory-sequential learning to the left, whole brain learning in the middle with a balance of both types of learning, and visual-spatial learning to the right. We are all along this continuum with skills coming from both sides of the brain according to where we are on this scale in our learning style. This placement also affects our ability to communicate with others because the two types of learning styles have entirely different ways of communicating as well as learning.

Silverman says in one of her articles that she began seeing around 1980 that some highly gifted children she was working with had a basic ability to solve problems presented to them visually rather than in the known styles of learning. These same children were also very good at spatial tasks. At the same time, however, she also noticed that the highest scorers were outperforming others in the visual-spatial tasks, but were also the lowest scorers in many other areas on the test. Highly gifted children tended to excel in auditory-sequential items, yet there was another group of bright children who had marked auditory and sequential weaknesses. She also recognizes that all children are along this continuum, not just gifted children. Although her research is at the forefront of gifted education, all children and their teachers and parents need to understand this material in order to understand these different types of learners and communicators. Being an auditory processing learner herself helped her in a way, because she was absolutely mystified by this discovery.

But this was when the idea of the visual-spatial learner was first identified and also the idea that schools and workplaces only addressed the other two types of learners. And because they did only address these types of learning, it was the visual-spatial learners who needed the most attention and help. Silverman discovered that visual-spatial learners had a different brain organization than auditory processors, and that they learned all at once, and permanently remembered what they learned. They needed to have the big picture before they could learn the details. They did not learn in a step-by-step manner, but yet arrived at the correct answers without taking steps. They found it very difficult to show their work, or to tell you just how they did it. They also seemed to have difficulty with easy tasks, but not with difficult complex tasks. They could orchestrate large amounts of information from different domains, but nearly always missed the details. They could not seem to organize their time and yet could spend endless time on puzzles, Legos, mazes, counting, playing chess, building things, doing scientific experiments and taking things apart to see how they worked. They were also very gifted creatively, dramatically, artistically or musically.

It was at this point, that Silverman began to work with others to develop techniques for working with these types of learners. At her gifted center, she and those working with her, developed a list of characteristics for both auditory-sequential learners and visual-spatial learners. The Gifted Development Center in Denver, Colorado, assesses gifted children in all the modalities and from all over the United States, and then makes recommendations to the parents for options on how to proceed in the education of their children. (*"The Visual-Spatial Learner: An Introduction" by Linda Kreger Silverman, at http://www.gifteddevelopment.com.*)

<u>Auditory Processors or Sequential Learners</u>

1) Thinks primarily in words and has auditory strengths
2) Relates well to time and is a step-by-step learner
3) Learns by trial and error and is an analytical thinker
4) Progresses sequentially from easy to difficult material
5) Attends to all the details and follows oral directions well
6) Learns phonics easily and learns languages in class
7) Can sound out spelling words and is good in spelling
8) Can write quickly and neatly and can show steps of work easily
9) Excels at rote memorization and has a good short-term memory
10) May need repetition to reinforce learning
11) Learns well from instruction
12) Learns in spite of emotional reactions
13) Is comfortable with one right answer
14) Develops fairly evenly and is academically talented

15) Enjoys algebra and chemistry and is good at arithmetic

16) Is academically talented and is an early bloomer

Visual-Spatial Learners

1) Has visual strengths and thinks primarily in pictures
2) Relates well to space and is a whole to part learner
3) Learns concepts all at once, and is a good synthesizer
4) Learns complex concepts easily; struggles with easy skills
5) Sees the big picture, may miss details
6) Is better at math reasoning and computation
7) Learns whole words, but visualizes words to spell them
8) Would rather follow a map, than listen to directions
9) Prefers keyboarding to writing
10) Creates unique methods of organization
11) Arrives at correct solutions intuitively
12) Learns best by seeing relationships between things
13) Has good long-term visual memory skills
14) Learns concepts permanently, does not like drill and repetition
15) Develops unique methods of problem solving
16) Is very sensitive to the teacher's attitudes
17) Must be inspired by their teachers, rather than simply taught
18) Generates unusual solutions to problems
19) Enjoys geometry and physics, because they are more visual
20) Develops quite asynchronously (not synchronistic)
21) Often has uneven grades based on their own interests

22) Masters other languages through immersion

23) Is creatively, mechanically, emotionally or technologically gifted

24) Is nearly always a late bloomer

Whole Brain Learners have a combination of skills from both the left and right side of the brain. And so a person would check both lists of characteristics and form an overall picture or sequence of the type of learning style that they have. In her book, Upside-Down Brilliance: The Visual-Spatial Learner, Silverman discusses all of the topics around this type of learning style. This book, although the definitive or core information, is out of print. You may be able to find it in a library, but I know the parents of my students could not find it that way either, because they had been stolen by other parents desperate for the information. The Gifted Development Center offers many articles on the topic but has not published a revised edition as yet. However, you can get a reasonably priced copy from Australia, as well as many interesting articles about this topic! And this is an interesting comment on the fact that other countries, in some ways are ahead of the United States when it comes to the education of our children and having materials available for parents. My two copies are like gold right now, so hopefully in the near future, the revised edition will come out. In the meantime, you can now download articles from many sources on the Internet or get a copy of the book from Australia.

In her book, Silverman introduces both the idea of the visual-spatial learner and types of giftedness. She talks about the plight of being non-sequential in a sequential world, as well as discussing the hidden powers of the right hemisphere. She explores this so-called underachievement in terms of educators and counselors and caregivers and their attitudes towards these children who only seem to not be learning. She talks about the types of physical things that can affect this learning style, such as early ear infections as a child, central auditory processing disorders, and additional things such as a learning disability, etc. She explores the topics of visual-spatial learners with dyslexia, attention deficit disorders, and levels of giftedness. She goes into great detail concerning these learning styles, and talks about how early you can identify a child with this particular learning style and how to assess visual-spatial abilities. She explores how these children compensate and how they look at their schooling.

Silverman then goes into comparing various additional problems for the visual spatial learner, such as being introverted or extroverted, and goes into much more depth concerning ADD/ADHD problems for VSL's. The last part of the book talks about the challenges parents of visual-spatial learners have to deal with, teaching techniques that work for this type of learner, and their continued research in perfecting identifiers for visual-spatial learners. Her very last chapter talks about visual-spatial adults and the future of education. The only comment she made concerning intuitive abilities in children, when she first published this book, was that 75% of all the gifted children they tested had a marked interest in the "paranormal." This is quite a high percentage, and probably carries over into all children's interest in these topics nowadays. Later, she had learned a great deal more about this topic through sharing information with other experts in related fields. It seems there is a connection with how smart you are, how intuitive you are, how creative you are and what spiritual emergencies you have along the way. All children have a combination of integrative gifts and talents and certainly a particular learning style. Every parent needs to be very aware of their own children's learning style, and just like every other issue we have talked about, if you even have one child with this style, there is probably a husband or wife with the same learning style. If you have two children who display this learning style, the possibility of both parents having this learning style goes up dramatically.

There are others who say that we have four basic learning styles, which really does make sense. Almine, who channels information, in her book called How To Raise an Exceptional Child suggests that there are the right brained (visual-spatial learners), the left-brained (auditory processors), the whole brainers, and what she adds to this are the Heptic Learners or Kinesthetic Movement Learners. She also quotes a couple of facts from others about how children learn: "90% of people do not evolve their mind past age 12. Everything they know is often learned by age 12." This also supports the fact that the super child psychics studied in China in the eighties were trained at one point up to the age of 12 in special schools and then returned to their homes. Research of psychic children in other countries showed that the so-called super psychics would have reached their maximum potential by this age and would also retain their abilities at maximum potential for the rest of their lives. "95% of all education taught at schools around the world, is taught in the mathematical-logic learning style. Only 5-8% of the population learn in this manner." This is a much larger statistic than mine, with a population in schools having an unrecognized, unique learning style; Almine says it is closer to 90%! (*How to Raise an Exceptional Child by Almine, Spiritual Journeys LLC: Newport, Oregon, 2010 or at www.spiritualjourneys.com*).

While some of Almine's advice is on the far side of metaphysics, she really has a lot of great and practical advice. Her book is worth having just for the childhood illness health remedies alone. And I really like her advice about learning in general. One needs to be in the moment, be present, open the hearing and listening channels, remain awake and alert, create a connection, open the communication channel, and be sure you rest and rejuvenate in between. Most of all she puts succinctly what often takes years as a teacher to learn in depth and figure out how to apply to a large classroom of children: ask each child how they like best to learn and how they want to be taught. Is it Show me or Explain it, or Let me try it, or Let my body move as I learn. Once you find the style of learning in each individual student you can then group them accordingly, and they can learn with those in their own style first, eventually being exposed to the other styles, all of which will help them understand and communicate with other children.

One year in the gifted program, I had a little girl who kept being threatened with expulsion from the gifted program because she wasn't high in her reading and language skills but was really high in her math and technical skills and a visual-spatial learner. Nearly all of the students got in on their language and reading skills and so this girl appeared "dumb" to the teachers. I fought to keep her in and got her parents involved in understanding about the visual-spatial learner, etc. One day, her father came in to get the title of the Upside Down Brilliance book because he wanted to get forty or so copies of it. Curious, I asked him why he wanted to order so many. He said that he ran a small computer company and that his employees had trouble communicating with each other. He was going to require them to read the entire book and then have a series of workshops where they would discuss learning styles, in hopes of improving the communication in the small groups that had to work together as they invented new computer games. I was astounded; a parent and company boss had gotten the idea better than my colleagues in the gifted program. He watched his daughter, looked at how his family learned, and then had realized that learning styles were very important in how people communicated with each other, especially in the work place. Sadly, after two more years of fighting to keep their supposedly "dumb" child in the program they pulled her out in sixth grade when they felt she might begin to be damaged by the attitudes that were being fostered around her. On the other hand, she got what she needed according to gifted research, skipped sixth grade, and was ready to tackle junior high and high school, which is when the experts say the gifted visual-spatial learning child is ready to find those teachers who will inspire them and find and focus on their own interests.

Types of Giftedness

> "Mildly, moderately, highly and extraordinarily gifted children are as different from each other as mildly, moderately, severely and profoundly retarded children are from each other, but the differences among levels of giftedness are rarely recognized."
>
> --Dr. Linda K. Silverman

Types of giftedness certainly affect the types of intuitive gifts even more than they might in a less complex child, although it takes simplicity for one to be even more in tune with one's intuitive skills. Those experts in the field of gifted education agree that if we have levels of those identified at the lower levels of intelligence at the other end of the scale then we should have identified levels at the upper end of the intelligence scale. It is only logical that each higher level of intelligence would also have specific characteristics, different for each level. People at the lower levels of intelligence are identified by IQ, and now, so are the upper end of the intelligence scale children. A 100 to 120 IQ is identified as the middle of the scale. A 120 to 140 IQ is identified as Mildly Gifted, 140 to 160 IQ is identified as being Exceptionally or Moderately Gifted, but with separate characteristics, and then you have the Profoundly or Highly Gifted at from 160 to 200 IQ's, with their own characteristics, and finally you have a very select group in the over 200 IQ range to at present 262, who are termed Extraordinarily & Profoundly Gifted. There have been some people identified in this range but very little has been done to study them as this is a new category of children as IQs continue to climb. This 262 is the most recently identified and highest IQ out of the 800 children assessed at the Denver center, so there could be other children in the world higher than this. Although one wonders how people with lower IQ's can assess those higher than themselves in this highest level of intelligence?

The point being that a parent should know an approximation of each of their children's intelligence quotient. And even though there is a lot of controversy over whether these IQ tests are very valid, especially the academic ones which you can study for, an IQ score can give the parent and the educator, a ballpark figure for understanding and working with a child at either end of the scale. Unfortunately there's a lot of prejudice towards identifying children at the higher end and lots of support for identifying children at the lower end of intelligence quotient scales. Everyone feels sorry for the people at the lower end, but everyone would like to be at the higher end, so they often develop a great dislike for the people in that little 2% of the general population range. I myself can vividly remember when I went from teaching special education to teaching in gifted education. My fellow special education teachers were downright vicious towards my going from teaching underprivileged severely and moderately handicapped children, to teaching "those privileged" gifted kids. They had no idea how many underprivileged gifted children were out there, many of whom also had other learning disabilities and behavioral labels, which kept anyone from identifying them as gifted. Nor did they realize that gifted kids in general have just as many issues and problems as the moderately handicapped do, and that my training in the 25 years of special education with the developmental stages of children, would be deeply helpful when I went to work with the so-called "gifted."

The way I looked at it, once I had worked in all three fields, in teaching severely multi-handicapped children, I was looking for milestones like toileting, walking and talking, while at the same time looking for "inches" and sometimes "feet." With the moderately handicapped in a so-called "tough" school, I was looking for an ability to have all the basic skills and be able to function in the world without insurmountable difficulties barring the way, in "yards" or "miles." When I worked with gifted children in an underprivileged school in a half-day pull out program, I spent my time simply identifying them and convincing those who worked with them, that underneath all that other stuff was a truly gifted child who might affect change from which many others might benefit. With the time I had with these particular children, which was very little, I did my best to expose them to all kinds of subjects and experiences they might not otherwise have, in hopes of motivating them to look for these things on their own. With the gifted children in the full day program, many of whom had the background and environment to at least be perceived as being privileged, I soon discovered that these children too, had a myriad of difficulties, especially when it came to social skills and either a lack of compassionate understanding or too much compassion and a lot of confusion about what they were supposed to be doing. I was looking for them to motivate others, but with the added ingredient of a drive to improve or inspire the world. In the end, they were all just children, and what they needed from the people working with them, was to be discovered, their "whole picture" unveiled, and then helped to blossom, no matter the "distance" they would eventually achieve.

If, after reading this particular section, and taking the checklist quiz, you find that one of your children or even more than one, and you yourself or the person you are married to, or both of you share these VSL characteristics, it's time to find this book no matter what! The Internet articles on Visual Spatial- Learners are really good and there are many website links to gain more knowledge about this topic, as well as learning techniques for coping with and teaching your children. However, Upside Down Brilliance is the "mother lode" basic book for anyone who discovers that they are this type of learner and also for parents of gifted children, and especially if you are way over on the right side of the scale. Psychic, intuitive, empathic children are very likely to be visual-spatial learners, en mass! So I who would suggest that in forming a "package picture" of each of your already identified psychic or intuitive children, you have a deeper understanding of each child's learning style, each child's learning difficulties, each child's behavioral difficulties, and each child's specific intuitive gifts and talents, as well as a ballpark I.Q. score. While I. Q. means less where intuition is concerned and yet research says there is a connection between the two, it is well known that intellectualizing will inhibit the development of one's own intuitive abilities. It is not necessarily blocking these abilities, although there are those too, but it can be a distraction from fully developing intuitive abilities.

Characteristics of Giftedness

Gifted children have unique learning styles and they learn in different ways from other children. They create at a faster pace and they solve problems quite quickly. They are usually developmentally advanced and are often better co-coordinated, healthier and physically stronger than their peers. They are quite curious and tend to ask complex questions. They also give more complex answers that show a greater depth of understanding of the topics than their classmates. They quickly recognize relationships and organize information in new ways that create new perspectives. They can see many solutions to a problem because their thinking is more abstract, which involves hypothetical possibilities, as well as present realities. They can see the ambiguities in factual information, and often have large vocabularies. They have excellent memories and are natural leaders. Just imagine what an all day gifted classroom would be like with 25 little souls, all natural born leaders, and then remember the old saying that "Too many cooks spoil the stew." Suffice to say; every day was a battle of wills, and a series of peace negotiations, as these children learned all about Cooperative Learning, Conflict Resolution and Socialization Skills. And going back to what they have now discovered about infants and very small children, isn't this a beautiful description of what may be going on in their brains before focusing on the intellect? This changes all this both developmentally and environmentally at six or seven.

They also enjoy working independently and are good at multitasking. They prefer to be with older children and adults and they are perfectionists, often refusing to participate in activities where there is a chance they might fail. If things don't turn out the way they expect them to they can become very upset. And they are often their own worst critics. Sometimes they like to brag about their own achievements and compare them to famous personalities that they have read about. Or they are rarely gifted in all areas and usually don't want any attention brought to their giftedness in a regular classroom, although occasionally in the classroom I saw exceptions to this one! Some of the difficulties they might have are in the areas of social skills, and additional learning difficulties either in an academic subject or with an additional diagnosed disorder. Since most of them will have the characteristics of a creative child and often an intuitive child, this not only complicates matters, but can cause various emotional difficulties as well.

I spent two years working as a resource teacher mornings and as a pull-out teacher of the gifted in the afternoons, on special funding, at what is known as a "tough" school. This was in addition to my eleven years actually teaching in the gifted program. A low-income, multi-ethnic group of children, most of my resource students lived in one big trailer court next to the school. My most gifted students in resource were caught doing things like lifting my entire grocery bag full of candy for rewards, stuffing it in a backpack and then later selling all of it for change in the field next to the school to the students of the school over a period of weeks, which allowed for the prices to go up instead of down. One of my other gifted students in resource fashioned a weapon out of broken off pencils which he then sharpened and drove the blunt ends into a piece of clay in a circle, tied a small rope to it and threw the sharp circle of pencil points at other children on the playground to keep his position as "bullying" leader. Sweethearts in my class, they were both positively and negatively creative outside my class.

When I began the gifted program I was required to test every single student and served them all in a half day program in order to keep my funding, which was taken away from me after two successful years anyway, because the principal did not believe in pull-out programs, the teachers didn't like losing their top students because they were great teacher aides and their model students, and some other "older teacher" I was told, was ready to have some time off by teaching art for a half day. As a result of this program other teachers nominated me for "Teacher of the Year" in a district where politically, the principal usually selects someone for this honor. That year when I was one of ten winners, I got a brass bell from my peers. When I lost the program, which nearly killed me, but was really an eye opener and great fun, I was taking my gifted endorsement classes and on the first day of the first class the teacher asked each of us to say why we wanted to get a gifted endorsement. I said that I wanted to work with the students who had additional learning problems or behavioral disorders and that came from homes where these kids would never get to a gifted program. The instructor said, without batting an eyelash, "You know of course, that most of those gifted kids will end up dead." This same teacher ended up not only inspiring me, but we also ran in to each other at a Gifted & Talented Conference and learning that we both did intuitive readings decided to skip a class and went out on the lawn and did a reading for each other. I got the gifted certification and when my funding was taken away, I went into the gifted and talented district program. And as for the psychic reading, she said I would fly parallel with other "teacher soul mates" occasionally, but would spend most of my life flying at a certain intuitive altitude alone.

What I learned in that two years however, stayed with me for my whole G/T teaching career. I taught a group of extremely gifted children in every grade who would never get to the gifted program unless a really concerned teacher pushed it with the child's parents. These children simply did not get all the opportunities their counterparts did and they were falling through the cracks. For some single mothers who would have jumped through all the hoops to get their son or daughter into the program, simply having no way to get their child to the satellite schools ended their hopes. I ended up with an assistant from the sixth grade who I hope I influenced enough that someday I will see her name in lights on a marquee on Broadway as one of the stars of the show. She was a natural comic. I understand that now, there are several districts across the nation who sponsor programs for underprivileged gifted children and provide transportation for them to attend all day G/T programs. It is too bad that there are prejudices of many kinds at both ends of the spectrum concerning children. Experienced teachers are rarely asked just how to achieve the best programming for their students, although they all have great ideas, if anyone takes the time to ask them and then listen to their answers and suggestions. And gifted students do to, they need ways to navigate in the world that is different for those on this end of the scale, no matter their learning style or any other challenges they may have. They are also in just as great a danger of depression or even suicide, as are children with horrific challenges in our society from abuse or neglect or poverty or even gender identification issues.

As I constructed this program I began realizing that even in such a short time as only a 45 minute time slot for the fourth through sixth grade twice a week and the same time slots two times a week for first through third grade, these children took off like rockets and really blossomed. They loved it, but everybody else did not. But I did feel intuitively, that even this little "seed" perhaps only "planted" one time might see them through to adulthood. I only hoped all that genius went in the right direction for them and that all the gifted children I taught over the years, did not wind up "dead," literally or figuratively. When I began to really see and feel the new waves of children coming in, I was given hope. They were smarter, better group and conceptual learners, and quite out spoken about what they needed, wanted and demanded at school and probably at home too. They were super creative, loved being worked with as an empowered person, and if you inspired them, they were more than grateful to produce results. No matter background, privileged or not so privileged, boy or girl, younger or older, ethnic or cultural background, religious preference, or even learning style or intuitively aware; they all were much more sure of themselves and wanted the kind of teaching that they knew would work for them, although they often had no idea what was going to work for them. But it was obvious that what was in place for them currently, wasn't working at all!

I was surprised when a "media darling" superintendent of a big school district, who got many write ups in several national magazines, for her innovations in education, was interviewed on a morning program after three years of extreme reforms in this district. She was leaving, and while having raised test scores, she had failed as a human being. She had had a lot of difficulty in the communication department because she felt that all that extra stuff was not important, just as long as the children got their academics and had good test scores and this would help them to function in the world. I can remember reading about her and thinking about a little picture book a young beginning teacher had given me when she left this rather tough school we were both working in. It is called My Great-Aunt Arizona by Gloria Houston and this teacher had written inside the book to thank me for my support and teaming, but especially about my "contagious laughing" through her wall. The book is about a rural one-room school teacher of 57 years, who always inspired her students to learn, to dream, to imagine, and to travel, although she never got to travel herself. And I realized that this superintendent reformer had missed a very important point, one can have all the best test scores in the world and fit well into the "machine," as one little unbroken piece that makes the machine work perfectly. But when that particular piece breaks down, you don't throw it away or get rid of it, all the other pieces of the machine come to its rescue and fix it, while learning a lot about themselves on the way. That is what children need to be taught, along with everything else it takes to function in the world. If we go to war, we all go to war, whether we like it or not, and the energy of the world demands this type of responsibility or we will lose everything, everyone, and our home called planet earth, if we do not learn this. This life force permeates every living thing and every inanimate object as well. Whenever it is wounded anywhere, we are all "wounded" in one way or another.

Many physicists all over the world have already learned this, that everything is connected to everything else and that if we affect change anywhere with anything, everything else is affected too. Physicists also now know that the knowledge that what we thought we knew about our planet and universe is fundamentally incorrect. For example, just recently scientists in Geneva, Switzerland have begun to question Einstein's theory of relativity. It seems that there is something that can travel faster than the speed of light. Subatomic particles called neutrinos are traveling much faster than the speed of light and this has so upset the scientific researchers all over the world, that they are asking others to independently verify the measurements. One scientist was quoted as saying, "It's a shock, it's going to cause us problems, no doubt about that, if it's true."These neutrinos were smashing past the cosmic speed barrier of 186,282 miles per second and this is 60 nano seconds faster than the speed of light. And if true, all of physics will have to be reexamined and physicists will have to question everything we thought was true in modern science. (*"Roll over Einstein: Pillar of physics questioned," by Frank Jordans and Seth Borenstein, Associated Press, The Salt Lake Tribune, September 23, 2011.*)

And put another way, I once observed something happening at a Native American Pow Wow, that as a teacher was quite refreshing. The little seven and eight year old boys division had danced their hearts out in the traditional competition (meaning traditional costuming from their ancestral heritages) but at the last minute they had lost to the other team who had won the competition. If you go to a little league sport of any kind in America now, you will witness all sorts of poor sportsmanship displays from verbal abuse to actual fistfights. You can see parents yelling at others during the games, and a few players role modeling their parents and coaches but not in a positive way. Some of the children even come up with their own ways of bullying others. But these little Indian boys had put on a pretty nasty display of their own on the field in front of the entire crowd attending the Pow Wow, because they had lost the competition. Later, when the dances were all over and most of the people had gone, but we were still sitting in the bleachers talking, when suddenly out on the field came a man at least six foot nine who was obviously the head honcho of the whole Pow Wow. A couple of minutes later, out came the same little group of boys in street clothes. This huge man gave them a very long and quite calm and actually gentle lecture on what they had done wrong, disgracing their clan and all. They then spent the next hour cleaning off the entire field with their heads down apparently well aware they were to be ashamed of their behavior. Some might say this was like the military, but it wasn't, there was no confronting, yelling or degradations and humiliations in this, it was simply modeling by their leader how one should behave in relation to the rest of the people they represented, both family and community.

In my dream in the field of education, learning includes identifying each student's talents and abilities and difficulties, fostering each student's creative and intuitive abilities, fostering self-worth, confidence and social skills, teaching conflict resolution skills while very young, and cementing the basics for academic success. Part of the day can be in a room where they simply get infused with information in a non-stressful, non-competitive environment with both a human teacher and a computer "teacher." The second part of the day can be spent in small cooperative learning groups where noise and explorations of new ideas and different subjects are allowed! And the other third of the day can be spent on exercise, gym, the arts, and everything else they need to know to have a successful life. And if the school has an integrative and developmental curriculum that fosters an individualized progression for each student with different teacher experiences, things can work out nicely. The teacher would be with his or her students every minute of the day, and then go home and rest! Teachers would have the assistance and help they need from both stay at home parent volunteers and seniors who make a small salary for their services. In this way, young children's awareness of and respect of the elderly would also be fostered. All kinds of exchanges and learning would be presented to the students, along with their academic skills.

Just look at the U.S. Enterprise from the Star Trek series, the crew is a multi-ethnic, multi-species, culturally diverse group who get along with each other most of the time because they are a part of the "Federation." A microcosmic community of this sort needs not just all of the above components, but it also needs a spiritual basis, a fascination with the unknown yet to be explored, and a constant balance of intuitive awareness. Researchers all over the world, who research both intuitive adults and children, have found that a calm, supportive environment is what produces the best results in all areas of the paranormal. Is this not true in all areas of education or even life in general? Of course we have a long way to go, but educational reform needs to begin now, in order for us to move in this positive direction. All this bailing out and in fighting, is not accomplishing a thing. Perhaps once we are in the "fifth world" from the shift taking place now, our own brain power will let us know what we need our body/heart connections to accomplish for both individuals and communities of people. Hopefully this change in our literal thinking will guide us to achieve such harmony. I know I was able to achieve this calm and harmony, most of the time, each year after the first two or three months of school. The mornings were calm and well organized for basics, while the afternoons were always small group, noisy but managed cooperative learning experiences.

The Connection between Giftedness and Spirit/Brain Evolution

One interesting fact brought up by those who predict a spirit/brain and planetary shift in consciousness, is that IQ scores are on the rise everywhere. Once thought to be static and stationary, IQ scores have risen by 24 to 26 points since the first half of the 20th century when the marker for genius was around 135. That marker has now risen to around 160, although anyone over 120 is still considered gifted. It has been noted by several experts that IQ scores throughout the developed world have soared dramatically to the point where an average school child is as bright as the near geniuses of a 100 years ago. Since the gene pool can't change that fast, experts speculate that improved schooling and better nutrition might be the cause. This may be true in underdeveloped countries, but in developed ones there has to be another reason. Actually, rote learning continues and acquired knowledge coming from schools has improved only slightly, while non-verbal and creative problem-solving abilities have soared. In more developed countries, I think the computer age has the most to do with these advancements. Hunger brings one closer to spirituality, while the distractions of technological toys pulls one further away from the inner life journey. So while we may have better nutrition and education is available to more people, it is a paradox that we will perhaps solve in the next century.

Interestingly, those children whom experts studied that had had a near-death experience in the last 25 years had a sharp rise in their IQ scores immediately after their experience. Since the other types of spiritual emergencies have not been studied as much, it is quite possible that many people who have a spiritual crisis and spiritual emergence have a small rise in their IQ score and one can speculate that perhaps we are finally learning or evolving into, the understanding and use of more of our individual brain power. But it is probably children who have a dramatic rise, no matter the type of spiritual crisis. The researchers of these children also found that besides this there are sudden higher abilities for creative problem solving. Children overall seem to have had an increase in nonverbal communication and a decrease in their ability to express themselves and socialize. On the other hand, perhaps the decrease in verbal ability has to do with all the technology now that doesn't require verbal or communication skills, and in fact, it is a sort of shorthand visual communication that is replacing person to person communication. This leads one to speculate that perhaps the ability to use mental telepathy is on the rise, although these children only "feel" their difference while still being perceived to be in a smaller group of "evolvers." The shift in consciousness that everyone talks about seems to have some evidence behind it in terms of humankind and the increasing IQs and brain changes taking place planet wide. In the New Age community, they say we have a whole world wide network or grid, not just technologically, but telepathically going on with our incoming intuitive children, and that this has been going on for at least the last fifty years. One thing is certain thought, the increase in brain power is parallel to an increase in psychic skills.

Linda Kreger Silverman contacted the author of the definitive book on near-death experiences among children, P.M.H. Atwater, after reading some of her books. She said that the work that they both had done in the last forty years did support a lot of the same data. In her forty years of research, Silverman had found that those children in the Highly and Profoundly gifted category (above 160) showed many of the same characteristics as children who had had near-death experiences. Many of them had also had birth trauma, which supported the idea that they may have had a near-death experience. Their mothers had either had an excessively long labor, there was a premature birth, or overdoses of a particular drug called pitocin had been administered. Silverman had also noticed that in their drawings and poetry, they had alluded to having had unusual or otherworldly experiences and nearly all of the children who had an IQ over 160 exhibited whole brain development. They were mature beyond their years, were very passionate about having a mission in life, and very interested in spirituality and human rights or environmental issues. Intense, compassionate, and sensitive, children of this group were dropping out of school more and more and being homeschooled or teaching themselves on the Internet. Many of these characteristics spanned the entire range of the eight hundred identified gifted children at Silverman's center.

Silverman was quoted as saying to Atwater, that "Even more remarkable, I've come across children who are so evolved beyond anything I've seen in my four-decade career in this field, and neither heredity nor environment can explain their achievement. The only explanation is evolution." So perhaps this is more proof that we as a species are in a fast process of growth that will advance humankind in ways that we cannot even imagine. Even Silverman, no longer sticks with her statement in her first book, that 75% of the over 800 children she has assessed in her center, seem to have an interest in the paranormal. She has now gone beyond this and realizes that, the word "paranormal" may one day be only "normal," the evolutionary world is coming, and the spiritual/brain shifts are on their way already. There is one other thing to consider however, and that is that the climate has changed both in research and the medical field, as well as the scientific techniques for studying such things. In the last twenty years I have seen the beginning of an openness to broadening our perspectives in many fields of endeavor. Plus better worldwide communication due to the computer age has made it possible to be better informed globally, and therefore, more aware of the changes coming in, both within humans and on the planet. This rise in consciousness is definitely being seen in our children. (*Ibid., Atwater, p. 168-169*).

Atwater addresses the idea of achieving a broader concept of intelligence and briefly mentions Howard Gardner and his now 12 types of intelligence which is written about in more detail at the beginning of the activities chapter. They are called <u>Multiple Intelligences</u> and we learned them in depth for our gifted classes, although they apply to all children. What Atwater observed in studying near-death survivors, especially child survivors, was the following: "What I saw was what I call 'true genius' where intuition is the equal of where the brain seemed to evidence parallel-processing systems, faculty enhancements, multiple sensing, the simultaneous presence of multiple brainwave patterns, and an ability to know things unbounded by the constraints of past, present, and future, as if they could access and draw from a cosmic bank of knowledge." She feels that all children are evolving into these capabilities at different times and at different speeds and levels, whether they had a near-death experience or not. However, child near-death experiencers seemed to achieve these new types of thinking much more quickly. And we can speculate also, that perhaps small infants and very young children have had some of these abilities all along, we as adults are just now becoming aware of them. (*Ibid, Atwater, <u>New Children</u>, p.59*).

Those who have studied children in many different areas, including those who study super psychic children in other countries, agree that something is going on with them. New Agers address this with a vanguard "fleet" of "Indigos" who just have more of every skill, new and different skills and are tough questioners and can telepathically communicate with each other. They are sort of like the dark eyed, dark haired warriors, who are the first wave of "new" children, according to New Agers. After them come the "Crystal" children who have blue eyes, fair skins and are the intuitive healers, very sensitive to earth energies, exceptional healers, and also telepathic. Some claim these two types of children have already built a grid or network of telepathic communication all over the world. Others say that there was an "advanced guard" which came in a few decades ago along with the "harmonic convergence." These were called the "Starseed" or "Skywalker" children just to name a few. They were a little less intuitive but a lot more "in tune" than the last few generations had been.

There are many books on these subjects and I listed a few in the bibliography if you want to know more. As for me, a practical down to earth Virgo, I think these children, all of them, have been here for years, they are and have been "coming-out-of-the-closet" for some time now, for decades now. It is a planetary evolution, a brain wave evolution, a spiritual evolution, and our internal physiology, external energetic fields, planetary environment and even how we interpret the multi-verse are all interpreted through physics, whose past foundations are constantly being changed now at the same time that mankind is evolving. It is all in the warp and weave of the evolution of the planet and the universe. Sylvia Browne says, stop all this nonsense and look at each child individually. After all, she was once a school teacher too. And I say, whatever you want to call them, they are here, we are here, and somebody has to help them adjust to the pain of the earth and contribute to its healing with practical methods and activities. Theories are great, but pioneering parent and teacher futurists and intuitives, are in the front lines and are helping these 'new' children in understanding just how to survive on a planet that is so very painful for them in many ways today.

The plight of the intuitive and that of being more intelligent than others is twofold. And apparently these two abilities can go hand-in-hand, it is just a matter of which way the scale of balance leans. To the analytical, logical and literal side leans the scientist, and to the intuitive, creative and spiritual side leans the mystic. I think one of the most inspiring stories from history for a mystic, is that of Charles Darwin who obviously was a whole brained learner! His book, The Origin of the Species considered the single most original idea completed by a single individual in the history of mankind, was conceived and basically written when he was a young man. But one big spiritual crisis threw him off his path for over thirty years. Darwin's young daughter died when she was ten, a mirror reflection of the great scientist her father was and she would have become had she lived. Darwin lost two other children to fevers, probably never realizing that his worldwide travels had infected him and probably his children. Darwin himself worried about the genetics involved since he had been a "sickly" child as well.

Darwin continued to write his many books as a recluse, often ill and imprisoned in the longest spiritual crisis that I have ever heard of. He was in mourning for his favorite child as well as the loss of two other children, with what he wondered at the time might be genetic, although the illnesses were labeled fevers. And this, as well as his wife's support in making sure that he had the scientific research to back up his startling claims at the time, was what delayed the completion and publication of Origins, which sold out in its first day in print. His wife was a very religious person but she was on the other hand his strongest supporter and eventually gave her consent for him to publish it when she felt he had sufficient data to back up what he was proposing. During these thirty or more years, and while another man almost beat him to publication with similar ideas, Darwin acted like a mad man, so distraught that he almost died himself, more than once, tortured by these losses and wrestling with his intuitive thoughts, nightmares and chronic ailments. Haunted by his daughter's spirit and separated from others by his genius thoughts and ideas, he was probably one of the most forward thinking and spiritual men I have ever read about.

A Thinking Intuitive, Darwin's great love for his family and wife, his compassion, intuition and sensitivities, were balanced out by his scientific reasoning and passion for studying the workings of the world. There are three schools of thought even today considering Darwin's ideas. One set of people still condemn his work from a theological point of view, one set still clings to the scientific method and cannot understand how those less literal can find a middle ground or any way of looking at Darwin's work spiritually. And then there are people like me who can see the energetic and literal connection between all things, which is what Darwin came to understand way before the people of his own time. The survival of the fittest was however, only a small part of what he envisioned. Those of us in this category stand in awe of the universe and its workings, and see the idea and conception of God or a universal force in all its functions yet to be understood. From the depths of the oceans to the far reaches of outer space, and from the physical mechanics of the human body and brain, to the soul, spirit, and energetic connections interwoven into this body, as well as every living thing on earth and possibly in the universe, we are sure to see, hear and feel God everywhere.

I am absolutely sure that true genius takes a balance of all left and right brained skills, an in-born gift of using more of the brain than others, an intuitive ability to be months or even years ahead of other people, the strength to find out who you are and stand by this, to discover and understand what you are mentally constructing and intuitively receiving, and, the ability to overcome one's shadow self as you journey spiritually towards new ideas and pathways and then somehow finish what you started. Carl Jung's quote about the loneliness of genius at the beginning of this chapter is extremely poignant to me, and is what helped me to understand those little gifted children just as deeply as I had those special education children in the first two-thirds of my career. True genius does not divide one from the incredible workings of our human body or the interconnectedness of everything on our planet. Instead, it makes us very aware of all this and what exists or will ever exist.

Darwin, like Lincoln, Einstein, Neihardt and Black Elk, might have had a near-death as a child, perhaps even more than one, because he was so near death with his various childhood illnesses. He also, according to author Frank Sulloway in his book Born to Rebel on birth order, family dynamics and creative lives, owed his rebellious personality to the family dynamics that shaped him. According to Sulloway, Darwin was born to rebel. Sulloway says that Darwin, along with the science of biology also contributed to the science of human behavior in his writings, particularly to the development of personality, and offered the best guide to the origins of creative achievement as well. In a letter to his son Horace, written in 1871, Darwin wrote: "I have been speculating last night what makes a man a discoverer of undiscovered things; and a most perplexing problem it is. Many men who are very clever – much cleverer then the discoverers – never originate anything." So saying that beyond a near-death experience, beyond a massive collection of spiritual awakenings, beyond brain power and intuitive abilities, beyond genetics, and even beyond an evolutionary shifting of the planet and the people on it, there are such things as how one is raised, the order in which one is born, the role modeling of parents or lack thereof, that also contribute to cultural development, and that is the finishing and distributing of what one has created or discovered. (*Born to Rebel by Frank J. Sulloway, Vintage Books, 1997, pp. ix-x.*)

What Parents of Great Creative Minds Have to Say About Their Children

"He thinks in three dimensions, and his first 'art' project at about nine months, was a mountain made of tiny pieces of masking tape piled on the coffee table. I carried tape with me all the time and he piled it on anything he could, but mirrors were a favorite."

--Upside Down Brilliance, Ibid., p. 7

"From nine months (he was) increasingly interested in spending time with books, also love of music, and interest in world map – which began an continuing interest in maps. As a three or four year old, he often used to bite his crackers into shapes of Greenland or India or Australia or Antarctica."

--Ibid., p.127

"He worries about everyone in the world, people dying, people getting hurt, or sick, he wants to make them all better. When he was four he got his preschool teacher to help him organize a toy/food supply drive. He saw the devastating flood in southern Ohio on the news. He was very upset that those poor children had no 'toys' and he packed up most of his toys and then asked his friends to send toys, etc. to the families in southern Ohio who had lost everything due to the flooding. He made the front page of the paper and they ended up with a whole semi-truck full of toys, diapers, food, etc., to donate to the victims of the flood."

--Ibid., p. 261

"At age four, she surprised me one day with a love letter that she had composed and printed on our computer. I never taught her how to turn on the computer, find the word processing program or turn on the printer and print."

--Ibid., p. 137

"At age five, we bought her a two-wheeler bike for her fifth birthday. She has never ridden a bike without training wheels. She wouldn't ride it. I thought she was afraid. Then one day, I looked out the window and there she was riding up and down the driveway, by herself. (Without any of us knowing, she had gone to the neighbors to borrow knee and elbow pads and was wearing them.)"

--Ibid., p.78

"At kindergarten graduation, M. had to tell what she was going to be when she grew up. She couldn't decide between a spy or a comedian. Since then, she has informed me that she will be a tooth fairy, but is a little worried about who will be teaching her how to fly."

--Ibid., p. 129

"My eight-year-old son ... remembers where he was when something happened, but has no concept of when it happened (if he remembers at all). This is almost funny. He has no idea whether something happened weeks or years ago, but can tell you where everyone was seated at the time."

--Ibid., p. 75

"It's beginning to make some sense now as to why he is often looking off into space when thinking. Especially when working with numbers. I'm always amazed at how he can figure his math problems without concentrating on what's on the paper."

--Ibid, p. xix

"At the start of each engagement, I would 'see' a cloud representing the problem to be solved. As the engagement progressed the cloud would gain substance and texture – become something I could shape and sculpt. In my mind, I could build a scaffold within the cloud and frame the shape of the solution, chiseling in details as my analysis progressed. By the time I had completed a consulting engagement, I had completed a 3-dimensional solid sculpture in my mind. Five years later I can still 'see' some of my 'sculptures' when I think of the projects they represent."

--Ibid., p.8

"Since coming upon your site yesterday I have been thinking of the impact and import of this way of thinking and it not being recognized...The fog and storms I suffered since a child have parted and I am able to see 'myself' for the first time."

--Back Cover of Upside Down Briliance,
no author sited

"I now understand why I have heard myself saying countless times, 'Can't you see it?' I would like someone to address the psychic pain we have experienced for trying to make ourselves 'fit,' and being largely misdiagnosed and misunderstood."

--Ibid., p. 334

CHAPTER TEN

Sleeping Peacefully Through the Night & Dream Interpretation

"Our whole life is a dream. The dreams of our present life are the environment in which we work out the impressions, thoughts, feelings of a former life. As we live through thousands of dreams in our present life, so our present life is only one of thousands of such lives which we enter from the other, more real life – and then return to after death. Our life is but one of the dreams of that more real life."

--Tolstoy

"We are asleep. Our life is a dream. But we wake up, sometimes, just enough to know that we are dreaming."

--Ludwig Wittgenstein

"A dream which is not understood is like a letter which is not opened."

--the Talmud

Topics Concerning Sleeping

Many children experience nightmares which are individual events or even night terrors which is a cycle that can last most of the night. And most children cannot differentiate between lucid or realistic dreams, regular dreams, and real events which they may be having occasionally. These dreams are either based on frightening events of the day translated into a metaphoric dream, or intuitive encounters that may not be believed or cannot be explained in any reality based way, but are absolutely real. But common sense says to at least check for the type of dream or even waking state before assuming any of these scenarios by talking with your child and getting all the details of what has happened. And make sure the child gets 8 hours of sleep each night. To induce this sleep, do careful planning, comforting exercises and interviewing, as each intuitive child as well as many other children deal with different degrees of fear in the dark, night terrors or even just expecting nightmares to come in the night.

Topics that need to be addressed before introducing the various strategies for helping your child with these night terrors and dreams are the various stages of dreaming, bed wetting, sleepwalking, sleep apnea, near-death experience in relation to sleeping and sleep or astral paralysis. Bed wetting and sleepwalking are both volatile topics for parents and opinions on these topics are quite "heated." However, issues of belief systems, theories, opinions and expert advice, can be dealt with in ways that will help the child regardless of their parent's views. On the other hand, if you as a parent do not believe your child's experiences might be real sometimes or even often, there will be a problem. So at least open your mind and heart to the possibility and that will be enough to both empower your children and love them at the same time. If they feel and see that you truly believe them, whether it is simply vivid imagination or real intuitive experiences, you will enable each of your children to find a way to function in the world on their own, and to come into their own as grounded and balanced adults.

Stages of Dreaming

Sleep is one long state of unconsciousness, but it's also broken up into several different stages. The average sleep cycle is 90 to 120 minutes. Past two hours our bodies go into deep sleep, or REM sleep. It is extremely hard to wake up from REM sleep and if by chance you do, you will not only feel sleepy and irritable, but may upon occasion wake up with sleep paralysis because your body cannot move during REM sleep. The average human being sleeps in a 90 minute to 3 hour sleep cycle, going through a complete cycle in a 90 minute to 3 hour time frame. The ideal is a 3 hour cycle in which you can achieve REM sleep comfortably and this stage is vital to having a good night's rest and also rejuvenating and repairing our bodies for optimum health. So the best way to sleep is in 3 hour intervals, which means that if you get your eight or nine hours of sleep you will go through three complete sleep cycles and feel rested and refreshed the next morning. Most people sleep the 90 to 120 minute intervals but will not feel as good as they would when completing the ideal but longer 3 hour cycles. One has to train one's self to actually achieve the 3 hour cycle by napping in the afternoon. Most people are not going to take the time or do not have the time to do this so most people sleep the 90 to 120 minute cycle, which means that they experience approximately 4 to 6 sleep cycles per night.

Generally there is REM sleep, or Rapid Eye Movement, and NREM, which is Non-Rapid Eye Movement. Within these two main stages, brain researchers have labeled these stages NREM1, NREM2, NREM3, NREM4 (although stage 4 is really a repeat of the activity in stage N2), and then REM or N5. These stages are in any 90 minute to 3 hour cycles, which repeat themselves over and over again throughout the period of sleeping. In other words, while the exact amount of time for each stage will vary, stages N1, N2, and N3 happen, then stage N2 happens again, and then the person is in REM sleep for a while before the cycle begins again. Stage N1 lasts only a few minutes and is basically the period of falling asleep. During this stage, a person can experience strange sensations, they may hear voices, sounds, lights, or even have the body's muscles twitch. Breathing becomes slower and more even, the heartbeat becomes regular, the blood pressure falls, blood flow to the brain is reduced and there is little or no body movement. This first stage only lasts about ten minutes ideally and the sleeper is easily awakened and may not remember that they were sleeping.

Stage N2 is when the person goes into total unconsciousness and is totally unaware of his or her surroundings, having fallen into a deep sleep. This stage lasts ideally for about 20 minutes and one is falling into a deep sleep, progressively being unable to be awakened. There are larger brain waves and occasional bursts of activity. Even if the person has their eyes open they will not see anything, although the person can be easily awakened by sounds. Bodily functions slow down including blood pressure, metabolism, secretions, and cardiac activity. Stage N3 is also known as the Slow-Wave State, which was once recognized as two separate stages. This is the beginning of deep sleep and happens about 45 minutes after you first fall asleep. Brain waves are very slow, larger and are known as delta waves. It is very difficult to awaken a person in this stage and it would take a very loud sound or heavy shaking to awaken the sleeper.

Stage N3 is also the stage in which one can be found sleepwalking, bed wetting, experiencing sleep paralysis or having night terrors. However, there are significant differences between these types of sleep reactions. Sleepwalking occurs before REM sleep when the person wakes up from deep sleep and begins an episode of sleepwalking. Generally young children and young adults deal with this problem because as we age, this activity lessens more and more. In bed wetting, this activity can occur in all stages of sleep but more often seems to occur in N3 or deep sleep. There is a controversy about this and researchers go back and forth on this issue of which stage bed wetting can occur in. Sleep paralysis occurs just after waking up from deep sleep or sleeping at all, but it can also occur just before going into deep sleep or Stage N3. Night Terrors also occur in deep sleep or Stage N3 sleep, while nightmares and dreams occur during the REM sleep or Stage N4. But Night Terrors are also thought to be a reaction to suddenly waking up in a transition from one sleep stage to another. They happen in the first 3 hours of sleep and children often don't remember them, whereas nightmares happen in the early morning hours and children commonly remember them.

Just after stage N3, the person experiences an additional N2 Stage or Stage N4, or going back into total unconsciousness again before going into REM sleep or the N5 sleep stage. But in this second N2 stage or NREM4, there are some more complex changes that take place. The brain waves slow down even more, become even larger, and show a jagged pattern on an EEG. The sleeper is oblivious to everything and both sleepwalking and bed wetting activity will actually begin in this stage and sometimes go on into the NREM3 stage too. Bodily functions continue to decline and this deeper sleep stage can make the person very groggy or confused if suddenly awakened during this phase. It may make the sleeper have to take some time before they are not disoriented or having what is called "sleep inertia" upon waking up so suddenly in this stage. After the first deep sleep ends, the sleeper returns to stage N2 just for a few minutes and then enters the first REM stage or NREM5.

REM sleep is when we experience lucid dreams and nightmares, and all the other types of dreams and cannot move. "In the first sleep cycle of the night, REM is extremely short—only a few minutes. But as the night goes on, you spend longer periods of time in REM, culminating in about 30 minute periods of time. Babies and children spend most of their time in this stage, but as we grow older, we spend less time in REM. If you are an adult, REM, comprises about 20-25% of your total sleep time. During REM sleep, your body causes the atonia or paralysis, of the skeletal muscles. This is a very good thing, because you would not want to be acting out your dreams in real life!" Since your physical body is still able to operate before this stage. ("*Sleep Stages," from Dream Views, http://www.dreamviews.com; Holisticonline.com; www.soundsleeping.org; and Kidshealth.org*).

The REM Stage is characterized by having small and irregular waves with big bursts of eye activity. The brain wave activity resembles waking more than it does sleeping. All the other stages lead up to this stage with more and more relaxation, and yet when we reach REM sleep, there are lots of kinds of activity going on. Blood pressure increases and pulse rates increase irregularly. This is the time for the greatest risk of a heart attack as well. Breathing becomes irregular and oxygen consumption increases. While the jaw and chin relaxes, the fingers, toes and face may twitch. Wet dreams can occur for both men and women and the larger muscles of the arms, legs, and torsos are unable to move. Our bodily temperature becomes irregular and may drift towards whatever the environment's temperature is around us. We may even shiver or sweat, although the first REM sleep stage is usually very brief and we may wake up before going back to sleep again. While a 3 hour sleep cycle is recommended for optimum rest, most of us experience a 90 to 120 cycle between 4 to 6 times each night. And after the first two cycles of sleep, the deep sleep stage lessens dramatically NREM3 and the REM NREM5 stage increases. Dream recall is higher when awakened from REM sleep because awakened in another stage, dreamers will recall very little if anything. Sleeping pills cause a person to become even more drowsy the next day, because as the person gets more REM sleep and less deep sleep, the body does not get the relaxation and rejuvenation that it needs.

"Experiments have shown that if sleepers are awakened as soon as REM starts, they enter REM sleep more rapidly the next time, and their REM is more intense. If the deprivation continues, they go into REM as soon as they fall asleep. It becomes impossible to deprive people of REM sleep with keeping them awake all the time. REM-deprived people can go into REM quickly in shorter naps." This is why researchers feel that they can train people to direct their dreams, especially if they take a long nap during the day. They also feel that people can remember all the details of a dream more easily this way, and if they are a believer in astral travel, people can be taught to direct their astral "trips" as well as remember them. But more about this later when we talk about this phenomenon and how it may be affecting children as well as adults. (*Ibid, "Sleep Stages," p. 2*).

Bed Wetting

It has been suggested that children punished for lack of bladder control when sleeping at night might have several reasons for this happening to them rather than their own lack of control. None of these reasons are under the control of the child and they cannot manipulate the surrounding circumstances either. One is that as the child falls asleep in the first two hours of the sleep cycle, he or she isn't having nightmares but is falling into the much more severe night terror cycle and upon waking up during the night terror or right after it, they absolutely cannot control their bladder. Two, even during a terrifying dream later in the night, one might be unable to control bed wetting like you could if you were awake and then the child unconsciously releases the liquid without knowing it. Three, the dream itself could cause this to happen and not the child. Most children have this happen once in a while but children who wet the bed have to deal with this often every night. Terrified of the night and terrified of the next day, whatever choice they make, they will most often be punished by the adults around them.

Intuitive adults who recall all too well the traumas inflicted on them for this, in terms of moral shame and self-deprecations, tell me that there is another emotional reason for what would happen to them at night. They would wake up and absolutely know that something real was down the hall by the bathroom, and even though they knew they had to go to the bathroom, they were even more scared to leave their bed because they knew they could or would encounter something they could not explain and could not deal with. So the choice between facing these fears and facing the morning's chastisements for having wet their bed was always a terrifying one in and of itself. More often than not they chose the latter, because at least the morning's punishments, whatever they were, were safer than what they just knew was down that hall or under their bed or in their closet. This leaves to the parents a choice as well. Even if you do not believe that whatever the child is experiencing is real, does it really matter? Either way, it is not the child's fault; it is rather the parent's abhorrence of having to clean it up or their concern for "normalizing" their child, etc.

Robert Bruce says that bed wetting, because it can occur at any stage in the sleep cycle, may be related to "false awakening" in which a real out-of-body experience is going on. He feels that the majority of cases may be caused by this circumstance. The child gets out of bed to go to the bathroom but then realizes that he or she is really having an out-of-body, if the child can distinguish this without being terrorized or frightened by this experience. Two different things can happen and in one scenario the child is actually not awake but lucid dreaming that he is going to the bathroom, thinks he is in the bathroom and wets his bed instead. In the other scenario, the child is actually in his astral body but there is no bathroom to be found, and so he wets his bed instead. Robert Bruce suggests that the child can be taught how to Reality Check, whether he is in a dream, having an out-of-body experience, or really awake and in the physical world. Reality check ideas are mentioned in more detail later in this chapter.

Sleepwalking

There are several theories floating around out there for what causes this phenomena and I will discuss these first before presenting you with the idea of "night flying" or astral travel. Sleepwalking is known medically as "somnambulism" and more modern research on the subject has changed our view of this phenomenon. Sleepwalking can last from a few seconds to as long as 30 minutes and while 18% or probably an even higher amount of children sleepwalk it is only present in about 2% of the adult population. However, these statistics are probably not very reliable as so many adults never report their sleepwalking, embarrassed by this particular difficulty. Also if one parent sleepwalked as a child then their children have a 45% chance of childhood sleepwalking and if both parents sleepwalked the chance rises to 60%. There is definitely a genetic factor involved, especially in the more severe cases and with adults who continue to sleepwalk. In other words, there are generations of families who sleepwalk. Most children supposedly mature out of this experience by the age of 15 and it is thought that sleepwalking is associated with an immature nervous system and/or breathing problems, as many people completely stop their sleepwalking when treated with respiratory medications, sinus surgeries or a CPAP (a night time breathing apparatus) associated with sleep apnea. Those who do not cease their sleepwalking with respiratory therapies have what doctors call a genetically linked "disorder" about which little is known, although most sleepwalking lessens as a person ages.

In the past, sleepwalking was thought to be associated with acting out a dream while the dreamer was in the dream. But now scientists know that dreaming happens in a different stage of sleep and actually sleepwalkers are multi-tasking because the human brain is capable of being awake and asleep at the same time when sleepwalking. In other words the brain is awake but the body may still be sleeping. One way of putting it is that we have a body that sleeps but also a mind that sleeps and when the sleepwalker is sleeping only the mind is asleep while the body acts out sometimes harmful actions. The state of being awake and the state of being asleep happens simultaneously. In a sense sleepwalker's eyes are open but their senses are shut down. Latest research has now associated sleepwalking with something called non-rapid eye movement arousal. If one were acting out a dream the sleeper would be in rapid eye movement stage sleep and not in his or her deepest sleep where dreams are not usually reported. Sleepwalking itself occurs during non-REM sleep which is stage N3 or deep sleep. The person begins their sleep walking episode upon awakening from deep sleep and yet they are still in a lighter sleep.

Other things that experts know contribute to causing sleepwalking are such things as having a slow wave sleep stage, sleep deprivation, a fever, excessive tiredness, stress, and of course, a developmental stage for all children that is slower in sleepwalkers as they mature. Children with an associated "disorder" such as sleep disorder with breathing or restless leg syndrome have a greater chance of also being a sleepwalker. Immaturities in mechanisms controlling sleep arousals and breathing problems are definitely a factor in sleepwalking in children as well. The theory is that most children have different systems in their body that mature at different rates and with the right combination of imbalances comes both sleepwalking and night terrors. Children usually have sleepwalking episodes, night terror episodes, and even bed wetting episodes in the first third of the night from which they wake up confused, with an increased heart rate and often screaming. They usually don't remember what happened but may have vague fears of monsters or other things that have scared them. This sleep stage, N3, is called the deep delta sleep. Both sleepwalking and night terrors are considered severe by doctors when they occur at least one time a week to one or two times per night. More boys than girls wet their beds and sleepwalk, and the most common age range is from 6 to 12 years of age, although the 3 to 7 age range has the highest amount of sleep walkers in it. There is a higher incidence of bed wetting among younger sleepwalkers and included with night terrors, all three tend to run in families.

Other stress factors specifically for sleepwalking children include stress and anxiety, sleeplessness, excessive sleepiness, needing to go to the bathroom, environmental noise, and fevers. Unfortunately, according to doctors, waking the child up during the first few hours of sleep can cause a child to sleepwalk. This is the direct opposite of the advice that waking up a child at the one and a half hour mark will interrupt the sleep cycle and stop the night terror cycle for the entire night. One young mother responded to her daughter's night terror by taking her young child to the bathroom and then holding her comfortingly until she was asleep again, thus preventing the return of the night terrors, and alleviating the fear of bed wetting which then doesn't become an issue for her child. This mother's closely "wrapped" child won't fear astral projection, either consciously or unconsciously, because of the holding, rocking, and then being placed in a slightly wrapped blanket from the chest down with arms free. The Native American plains Indians had it right when they wrapped their children in a cradle board, while the child's head might have suffered being on such a hard surface, he certainly felt secure all wrapped up like that. In the old days this was called swaddling the child and mothers often used this method to calm and quiet their children.

So I would say try waking the child up anyway at one and a half hours into their first sleep cycle and then you will probably alleviate the possibility of any bed wetting problem by making sure that they go to the bathroom at this point. Then watch to see if sleepwalking becomes a problem or simply does not exist for that particular child anyway. Know your child. If the child has all three difficulties then play it by ear and see if waking them up momentarily works or not! And please have the child keep a sleep diary in which he or she can not only record dreams that are remembered even partially, but also to see if there is a pattern to your child's sleepwalking and night terror episodes. You can mark the journal together and if the child cannot write, then have the child draw what is remembered the next day. This will help both of you to see the big picture of what is going on and even identify what is dreaming, what is sleepwalking and what might be real, or perceived to be real, experienced, as well as astral traveled.

The biggest problem for adult sleepwalkers is in harming themselves. Children tend to only sleepwalk inside their houses because they are caught by a parent or sibling before they attempt to leave by the front door. Since so many adults never talk about having this difficulty because it is embarrassing for them, no one really knows the actual statistics and many are now realizing that it is way over 2% of the adult population. There are stories of people stepping out of second story windows, stepping in front of oncoming traffic on a highway and even attempting suicide while the person is sleepwalking. This raises the question of whether there are many more suicides that were caused while a person was sleepwalking? On the other hand, we have no way of knowing if this was the cause, because of course they were "successful" suicides. Not many of the incidents involve crimes or violence, but there are a few famous court cases where the murderer used sleepwalking as their defense. Most children do outgrow this however. But if they don't, one has to wonder if this is also some sort of intuitive ability that going undirected can become dangerous for the child or adult.

Shelby R. Gunn and W. Stewart Gunn said in their article, "Are We in the Dark About Sleepwalking?," after having dealt with this trouble throughout their lives as father and son and having the problem never go away, not enough research has been done concerning this issue, especially for adults. It was this man's son who stepped out of a two-story window while sleepwalking. They are the ones that brought up the topic of how dangerous or even harmful sleep walking can be for adults and speculate on whether a lot or some of the suicides might have happened when the person was sleep walking. They also say ironically or perhaps sarcastically with a quote from Shakespeare, that sleepwalkers are "the merry wanderers of the night." Or perhaps they just meant that sleep walking is suppose to be great fun and yet it can be dangerous as well. (*May 1, 2006.*)

Sleep Paralysis/Astral Paralysis

Sometimes the person may become conscious of their muscles being paralyzed and this can be mistaken for astral travel paralysis, although researchers don't know enough about out-of-body experiences or OBE's to separate the two from each other. According to scientists an episode of sleep paralysis happens when you're either entering or leaving the REM sleep cycle and have become conscious during this time. They have actually divided sleep paralysis into two types, the one before going into a deep sleep is called hypnagogic and the one after a deep sleep is called hypnopomic. While the brain is awake the body is still asleep, as motor neurons inhibit the brain from being able to direct the muscles. As a result the person continues to dream and hallucinate or have visions. These delayed bodily responses eventually catch up and the body becomes synchronized with the brain once again and can then move again. Regular exercise is recommended to prevent this scientifically labeled "disorder." But is this a disorder, or something we do not understand as yet in the unexplored world of sleeping and traveling? When the brain awakens the body movement then can catch up, but are we missing something? And if we are, just what is it? Reducing stress and exercising the body may prevent this particular paralysis, but, on the other hand, are we missing something still considered "esoteric" just because we do not understand it? Rather than saying that having this happen to us often can lead to more serious ailments?

Traveling somewhere, out-of-body, a matter of debate for centuries, until recently, many people in the last decades have become much more open to the idea of astral traveling at night, including some scientists. When sleep paralysis takes place, researchers say that we can have hallucinations, feel vibrations, listen to loud ringing or roaring in our ears, have pressure on our chests, or even have choking sensations. There is often a fear of impending doom or terror if the person wakes up, and feels that they are momentarily paralyzed. In astral paralysis, which I talk about more in depth in the next chapter, the person additionally feels the body leave and return. So there are two fields of thought concerning this temporary paralysis, but how they interconnect is not known at this time, nor can astral travel be researched with current scientific methods. But this does not mean that astral projection does not exist or that sleep paralysis is not connected to astral paralysis. Others believe that astral projection during sleep, along with the occasional astral paralysis are deeply intertwined with each other. Having astral traveled most of my life, I don't have the luxury of non-belief, it just exists.

Near-Death Experiences & Sleeping

Most interesting are the powerful shifts that take place when the child is sleeping. This could involve dreaming about dying or having nightmares that could somehow be associated with death. And while these can often be healthy, a healing experience both physically and emotionally, at other times this can escalate into an unhealthy situation. Child near-death experiencers can go into a dream that is so real and so vivid that he or she is actually re-experiencing the near-death or having a second near-death that closely resembles the original experience. These near-death-like experiences match the overall pattern of the real near-deaths and researchers are baffled by these particular stories. However, they speculate that perhaps the process of dying is one we rehearse more than once in our lives and those who have been closer to death, revamp and make "course corrections" over and over again in preparation for the real thing later in life.

Also, because children not only tuck away their near-death experience, but are often also told to forget this experience and go on with their lives, they become subject to more dreams and nightmares because of this. They may also exhibit some night time experiences in the daytime and show reckless or what people call "death-wish" behaviors. There is a movie called "Fearless" with Jeff Bridges who is one of the few survivors of a passenger plane and the only one to escape without a scratch. It is a psychological study of this sort of thrill seeking behavior, because the character in the movie believes that having escaped death once, he therefore cannot be killed and confronts death endlessly to demonstrate this. These NDE children may become either excessively withdrawn or excessively reckless in seeking attention with their actions. They may sleep too much or not sleep enough, becoming irritable and appearing to be lazy. Add to this the developing intuitive and other worldly skills, and you have many reasons for child near-death experiencers to spend many sleepless nights, with many groggy mornings. They too need to find ways of calming their fears when going to bed, and ways of staying asleep after they get there. And in many cases their near-death experiences have been much more powerful than mere intuitive journeying in the night.

Sleep Apnea

There seems to be little connection between sleep apnea and intuition in children. This seems to be a physical problem according to doctors. Pauses in breathing occur while the person is sleeping and sometimes a dream can be connected to this because the person will wake up trying to catch their breath. No studies have ever been done to see if the dream itself brought this loss of breath on, or the body manufactured the dream as a manifestation of the sleep apnea problem. This problem is especially likely with overweight men or postmenopausal women who snore heavily. One can get migraines from this, never enough sleep, and feel very tired and irritable during the day. Some people will even fall off to sleep during their work day and not realize that they have until someone wakes them up.

However, I do remember reading in a folklore book that in Denmark they said that many people slept upright on pillows to keep their hearts from stopping. Perhaps there are genetic factors in this, heart factors or of course breathing factors that contribute to this. Perhaps in the old days people died from this condition in the middle of the night, and no one knew why they had stopped breathing. The question is can a dream or simple mind control be powerful enough to stop your heart or another's? Can a remote viewer be powerful enough to send mental controls to another and stop a person's heart while sleeping or while awake? A rather scary thought, there are those who say that this is possible. And does an intuitive person experience in the night either powerful or lucid dreams, or even night travel episodes that can affect their health this drastically? Not enough interest in this subject or perhaps the wrong kind of research into this phenomenon can't give us answers now, but others may be able to tell us these answers in the future. Are UFO visitations, dark forces possessing one, or other far out theories, really a little more right on than we suppose? Only time will tell on this one!

What Are Dreams?

Dreams are a succession of images, sounds or emotions that the mind experiences during sleep. The scientific study of dreams is known as oneirology. Physically, what is known about dreams is that they are a response to the neural processes during sleep. But psychologically, dreams are considered a reflection of the subconscious, while spiritually; they are seen as messages, either from the universe or from the inner soul. In ancient times, they were considered messages from the gods in many cultures around the world for centuries. These people practiced what is called "dream incubation," actually cultivating dreams either for messages from the divine or for prophetic purposes, often going on spiritual pilgrimages or vision quests. ("Dreams," Wikipedia, www.wikipedia.com.)

According to Jeremy Taylor, a forty plus dream researcher, dreams have ten assumptions. First, dreams occur for our health and wholeness. Second, dreams come to tell us something we don't already know. Third, only the dreamer can really interpret their dream in depth. Fourth, recognizing things in a dream are mainly due to our unconscious memories. Fifth, dreams never have just one meaning. Sixth, all dreams have universal metaphors and symbols. Seventh, all dreams represent facing and solving life's problems creatively. Eighth, dreams always reflect a dreamer's relationship to society. Ninth, dreams can improve all of the relationships in our lives. Ten, working with dreams in groups can help build communities and impact society as well. (*The Wisdom of Your Dreams by Jeremy Taylor, pp. 8-9.*)

Types of Dreaming

Types of dreaming include wish or fantasy dreams, falling or flying dreams, emotional release dreams or the anxieties of that day, information and problem solving dreams, predicting the future dreams or precognitive dreams, lucid dreams, nightmares and real night time experiences that should be addressed separately and carefully. There are so many books on interpreting your dreams you really have to look for the right ones. I have listed a few in the bibliography that I think are good along with the reference books for the symbols of animals and other things in nature. Your best bet is to use these books as a starting point or to get more specific information about a certain part of your dream, but really, you need to interpret them yourself, or help your child to interpret them specifically for that child. So that they can learn to interpret their own dreams as well as including what one or two others tell them about the symbols in a dream. I know I can often differentiate my dreams by color or no color. Everyday dreams are in black and white for me, while special and informative dreams are in full Technicolor, or perhaps I am only aware of the color in my important dreams. Recurring dreams happen in 70% of females and 65% of males. Apparently, children who experience past life memories, also experience recurring dreams and nightmares. And the best therapy for this is through interpreting the dream to make them stop coming back over and over again. For everything you ever wanted to know about interpreting dreams, pick up The Complete Idiot's Guide to Interpreting Your Dreams by Marci Pliskin and Shari L. Just, Alpha, 2003.

Lucid Dreaming

Lucid Dreams are in their own separate category because they are a dream, in which one is aware that one is dreaming. There are two ways a person can have a lucid dream: there is a dream-initiated lucid dream or DILD, and a wake-initiated lucid dream or WILD. In the first type or DILD, the person starts out having a normal dream, and then realizes that they are dreaming. In the second type or WILD, the person goes directly from a normal waking state into a dream state and there is no lapse of consciousness. Obviously researchers want to study lucid dreaming, because a person can be taught to not only be aware of their dreams and direct their dreams, but also induce their dreams consciously. On having a lucid dream, the dreamer has to be conscious enough to recognize his or her dreams. Many ancient practices have always included wake-initiated lucid dreams, such as Tibetan Lucid Dream Yoga.

Recent studies show that people who practice wake-initiated lucid dreaming, experience all of the aspects of out-of-body Astral Projection. This means that researchers now may have a way, to induce a lucid dream similar to a near-death experience or an out-of-body experience, in the laboratory. Lucid dreams are experienced as being real in every sense of the word; so many researchers feel that this is the explanation for such real feeling night travel experiences. Many who have experienced these sorts of travels would not agree, having had much more happen to them than mere hallucinations or sleep paralysis. The controversy is at least "real" now, where in the past, there was no controversy at all. Sleep was sleep and wakefulness was wakefulness and that was that. Nowadays however, science and mysticism seem to be merging just a bit, and what was thought mere sleeping or a mere brain function, is in question. Mere brain function is no mere subject now. It seems that brain function just might be tied to spiritual function, and we at present have no way to study the "ties." Although Russian scientists are on the brink of this, or may be beyond this brink, as their present research is not being shown to the world now. Rather than calling these fields, as the Western world does, paranormal or parapsychology or metaphysics, which are philosophical or psychological or even "magical thinking" titles, the Russians had given the entire field the title of Psychotronics. They study all aspects of this as a science that they are learning to find ways to research scientifically. It is real to them, and not a mere belief, although they may be using new titles by now.

However, many theories about lucid dreaming and out-of-body experiences or near-death experiences, come from the studies and experiences of those who have researched this in children and adults or have a lifetime of experiencing these things themselves. Robert Bruce is one of the definitive astral projection or out-of-body traveling experts who writes about this topic. He is affiliated with Robert Monroe's, Monroe Institute, another place that studies astral travel and meditation techniques among other things. Monroe was the pioneering astral traveler along with the founder of Eckankar, Paul Twitchell. Both men wrote about their astral traveling experiences, chronicling their experiences for the first time for the general public in the United States. Monroe wrote several books about his experiences and founded a slightly more scientific institute to study this. Twitchell related to his experiences on a more spiritual or religious level and founded Eckankar which has members all over the world now. Bruce used his experiences to inform others through his many books and works more in a healer-therapist mode.

Robert Bruce proposes that lucid dreaming is a genuine type of out-of-body travel, but of a different type and level than astral projection. He says that lucid dreams can be converted into an out-of-body experience and vice versa. In a lucid dream, at some point in the dream we gain conscious control of the dream and wake up inside the dream environment. It is then that we can take control of the dream. We can experience physical sensations in the dream such as gravity, smells and textures, etc. "Lucid dreaming, real-time OBE, and astral projections share a lot of common ground. The dreamer's center of consciousness often flicks back and forth between these states during a single experience. Often, more than one type of experience is perceived or remembered as happening simultaneously. This is caused by different aspects of the mind-split intruding on each other during the eventual shadow memory download at the end of the experience. This causes a confusing set of mixed memories, being part dream, part lucid dream, part real time, part real-time OBE, and part astral projection." (*Astral Dynamics by Robert Bruce, revised edition, Hampton Road Publishing, 2009, p.218*).

Bruce also proposes that lucid dreams are projections of the thinking mind in the mental dimension. And that OBE's are more dependent on the physical body and this is confirmed by the many bodily sensations one has while entering and exiting an OBE, such as vibrations, sounds, heart palpitations, etc. Therefore OBE's are coming from a physical dimension where as he says, half the mind and half the memory abilities have been left out. Astral projections at the lower levels do involve physical sensations and emotions such as anger and love, and moral boundaries are less well defined. The higher levels of astral travel are closer to the mind dimension and so one can have an overlapping of the physical and mind dimensions. Lucid dreams, OBE's and astral traveling can all overlap both dimensionally and experientially. Remember this when you are reading about astral travel in the next chapter, that lucid dreams and out-of-body can all still happen in the astral projections as well. While this is a complicated idea even for adults, think how a child will feel experiencing things that no one has prepared him for, or said to him, that this could happen or is happening!

Dream Recall

Remembering a dream or an astral "trip" is something new in brain or sleep research. Some of the suggestions for remembering your dreams from a sleeping state include: keeping a dream journal to write down the dream the moment that you wake up, keeping your eyes closed while recalling the details of the dream, and recording the dream in the present tense. Staying still after waking up or remembering the way you were laying while dreaming, can help you remember a dream. Repeating a mantra like "I will remember my dream" over and over again, can also be helpful as you fall asleep. Re-writing a nightmare is very helpful to rid yourself of all of those terrible feelings you wake up with from such a frightening dream. And when you have actually learned to initiate a dream from a waking state, the following can be helpful: meditation, yoga and other techniques for inducing a waking dream can keep you disciplined enough to be fully aware of what you are dreaming. One needs to keep oneself on the border between being awake and being asleep. But one other thing that can help with this type of WILD, is to take a 3 to 7 hour nap in the afternoon, so that one can stay in that in-between state longer. However, the waking dream can also cause the person to panic because they will soon or later experience sleep paralysis fully awake. Think of the child who might have gotten little sleep the night before, then has a nightmare and wakes up paralyzed, having had a lucid dream that is so real to him, that he is absolutely terrified.

There is one more suggestion for both types of dreams that happen while sleeping or awake, and that is to do some reality tests to know whether you are dreaming or not. These actually have names, such as the Pain Test or the Focus or Marker Test. Pain tests are such things as pre-arranging to pinch oneself or walk into a wall, etc. while dreaming. Focus tests can include such things as pre-arranging to flip a light switch on, look in a mirror, look at one's feet or hands, or look at a text or a watch and see if this is normal in every detail. And last, there are two ways to prolong a dream to keep from waking up too early: rub one's hands together or spin one's dream body around. Both of these sensations engage parts of the brain into producing the sensation so that lying in bed does not creep into one's awareness and the person wakes up suddenly. One can also have a "false awakening" which fools the person into thinking they have woken up when actually they are still in the dream. This is when the person really has to check for the details as they will think they are in the room in which they fell asleep, but really are not. Children can be taught this technique of reality checking for their own empowerment and protection.

Robert Bruce gives a few other ideas for Reality Testing to find out if you are in a lucid dream, an out-of-body or an astral projection, or all three combined. Keep noticing your hands and what you are doing with them in the dream. Every time you have a drink, notice the name of it and if everything that surrounds it seems normal. If you go to the bathroom in the dream, is everything normal there? Every time you check the time in a dream, is it always the same, always different, etc. Notice the food that you or others are eating in detail each time you do ingest something in the dream. Ask yourself the following questions as you dream or travel: Is this situation normal? Do my surroundings look normal? Does my body look normal? Can I float, levitate or fly? Can I pass my hand through solid matter? In other words, keep checking things that repeat themselves and see if the differences always seem normal. (*Ibid., Astral Dynamics, new edition, pp.220-221*).

Variations on Remembering Dreams

We have various lucid dreams in which the dreamer is aware that they are dreaming and know that they have not woken up. We can remember how beautiful our dreams are and remember being in more than one place at a time. More than one dream can take place simultaneously. We have vague dream recollections and can sometimes put the pieces of the dreams together to make sense out of them. Our vivid and clear dreams can also be murky and confusing at the same time. Our dreams can start out full of cloudy forms that can then progress into archetypal images and symbols or become a single dream within a series of dreams. And last, dreams, Taylor says: "In this all important sense, all dreams, particularly the dreams of sincere seekers of spiritual experience, will guide them directly to the 'roadblocks' – to their histories of childhood injury, their current self-deceptions, and their repressed 'secret' and opinions – in short, to all the things that 'block the way' and separate them from the felt-sense of transcendent meaning in their lives." (*Ibid., Taylor, p. 43*).

What Causes Dreams Psychologically?

Why we dream and why we normally don't know whether we dreamed or not, are questions still to be answered. But there are many theories out there on this psychologically, such as the developmental theory that children are being trained to learn physical and social laws while asleep. Or that adults and children are being taught while dreaming to discriminate and differentiate between what is real and what is illusion. Some believe that the waking state and the sleeping state are a way of attaining pure awareness of one's true self or the "Source," and also that the physical world is an illusion, and that meditation can help one achieve both states equally. Others believe that we not only have a waking state and a sleeping state, but also a traveling state, where we journey to other realms, parallel universes, other planets, go forward in time or back in time, and journey to other parts of the globe in our astral body.

As for me, having had all of these various experiences in one way or another, I know as a psychic that besides all of these types of dreams, I also have visions in the day time when I read for people. These visions, are they visions? Or are they dreams? Or am I walking inside the waking dreams or visions of others? And because I do this, do I then experience all that the other person is experiencing both physically and mentally? My own questions are endless and I do not presume to have answers, as so many "channelers" seem to have, or at least think they have. I like the card "Mystery" in Lynn Andrews's power deck: "A shaman can teach you about power. A magician can train you to become strong in spirit and competent in your endeavors in life. But to describe how a miracle happens or how you come to be a powerful magician is to try to explain the mystery. You can talk around the secrets of power, but if you describe them directly you lose that power and destroy the mystery, so allow the miracle of existence to emerge from the darkness and transform you."(*The Power Deck or Cards of Wisdom by Lynn Andrews, Harper Collins: San Francisco, 1991*).

Theories on Why We Dream & What Makes Us Dream

Dreams, say the researchers and theorists, can be caused for several reasons. They strengthen our memories and help the brain process these memories more effectively. Dreams may be removing sensory impressions that were not fully completed or an idea that was not fully developed. In other words, dreams are the method by which we literally "take out the junk" that is not needed. Perhaps dreams are merely the brain working on improving signals for its self or making emotional preparations for solving problems or reinforcing ideas "dreamed up." Dreams are products of being disassociated from our consciousness and getting sensory feedback or affecting mind-body interaction. In other words, dreams are a way of healing our bodies while we sleep, repairing nerve endings and expanding blood vessels, etc. Some evolutionists believe that dreams are serving an adaptive function for our own survival. Are dreams our way of separating ourselves from our own imagination? And do dreams allow the repressed parts of the mind to be satisfied with fantasy, while keeping the mind from awakening in shock?

Some of the experts such as Freud said that dreams are a way of gaining control over our emotions, especially bad ones. Jung said that dreams are a way of compensating for one-sided attitudes held in waking consciousness. Ferenczi said that dreams are a way of communicating something that we cannot say outright. Hartmann said that dreams function like psychotherapy by giving us a safe place to express our emotions and feelings. Joe Griffith says that dreams are metaphors for our lives, lower stress levels and complete emotional patterns for us in our nervous systems. That dreams regulate our moods. Robert Bruce says that dreams are our only connection with the greater reality and our spiritual roots. People all around the world seem to dream about the same things and the most common emotion experienced in dreams is anxiety, which supports the idea that dreams keep us from doing what we might do in a waking state, that they are a release for emotions, and a way for our bodies to rest and heal each night while we are sleeping.

Dream Interpretation

In the old days, dreams were used either for healing, to tell the future, or to receive divine guidance and inspiration. It is well known that famous men and women in every field of endeavor were able to dream solutions to inventions they needed to finish, or compositions they wanted to write, or problems they needed to solve, etc. Many ancient peoples induced dreams as part of a vision quest or meditation, to complete a rite or ritual of some kind or receive divine guidance. Modern theorists say that dreams are an opportunity for the conscious and the unconscious to interact. Certain medical conditions can induce dreaming and there is always the possibility that someone is dealing with either mental illness or for our purposes, the intuitive worlds. So now we have come full circle to intuitive children and dreaming and how one interprets dreams for both children and adults. We can go to a therapist, a dream interpreter or a psychic, which are all great ways to solve the problem too, but this usually costs us more money and time. The cheaper way to interpret our dreams is to either join a dream interpretation group or just get a few of the dream interpretation books and put the pieces of the puzzle together ourselves.

There are a lot of resources out there to interpret our own dreams and I will list the very best reference books that I know of right here, as well as in the bibliography. Ted Andrews's reference books Animal-Speak, Nature-Speak and Animal-Wise can give you the best starting place for symbolism for plants and animals. The best worldwide cultural or universal symbols for dreams comes from J.C. Cooper's An Illustrated Encyclopedia of Traditional Symbols. Gusavus Hindman Miller's The Dictionary of Dreams, 10,000 Dreams Interpreted is an excellent resource. Mary Summer Rain's In Your Dreams: The Ultimate Dream Dictionary and Zother's Encyclopedia and Dictionary of Dreams are updated, expanded versions and they give a quicker answer to various objects or themes. Zother's (R. Donald Papon) book even includes several different circumstances in which the same object can be interpreted in different ways. The Complete Idiot's Guide: Dream Dictionary and The Complete Idiot's Guide to Interpreting Your Dreams are both good resources as well.

An excellent resource for colors is The Rainbow Book by Shambalah Publishing and put out by the Fine Arts Museums of San Francisco, 1975. This one could be out-of-print but it is still the best one around on everything about colors. And if you want to get into the deeper and much more metaphysical theories on dream interpretation for adults you can try plowing your way through Alice Anne Parker and Ann Ree Colton's books. Understand Your Dreams by Alice Anne Parker and Watch Your Dreams by Ann Lee Colton which are both starting places. These two particular dream books are not for beginners, not from scientific research, they are channeled information that is quite fascinating and also prophetic. A good dictionary of angels and angelic beings is called The Watkins Dictionary of Angels by Julia Cresswell which might be helpful for identifying guides along the way. And while not as specific there is a large book entitled The Illustrated Encyclopedia of Symbols, Signs & Dream Interpretation by Mark O'Connell, Raje Airey and Richard Craze, which provides comprehensive and yet general universal themes concerning our dreams as well as a section on dream symbols used in everyday life around the world in the media, etc. And finally there are the waking dreams that happen in the daytime which are messages and channels to the synchronicities in our lives. Michael Avery's The Secret Language of Waking Dreams is an excellent starting place to begin to understand how to become more in touch with your own individual dream vocabulary, or the signs and symbols in you and your child's lives that indicate the synchronicities offered to use every day. This is another way to help your intuitive children understand the physical world and prepare them for the unseen ones as well.

Group Interpretations of Dreams

"Working on one's dreams in solitude is difficult and heroic. It can be done, but overcoming our inherent tendency towards selective blindness and self-deception requires tremendous effort." Taylor's suggestions for running a dream interpretation group are the following: start on time and do a centering exercise first. Decide on whose dream you will work on and have the dreamer tell their dream in the present tense. Everyone can ask questions to clarify the details of the dream. Begin your interpretations with the phrase, "If it were my dream, I would...." After everyone gives their thoughts on the dream then the dreamer can choose to respond or not to various comments. Then use a couple of questions: "Does anyone have anything to add to this dream?" or "Does the dreamer have anything to ask the group or a specific individual in the group?" And last, the group should have a group prayer circle or centering activity again to express their gratitude for having been privileged to hear the person's dream, to thank the person for sharing it, and to close the session on a positive note. Another way of interpreting dreams is of course using the various dream interpretation books or cards and piecing these parts together to define the dream for an individual person, or in pairs. (*Ibid., Taylor, p.295*).

Concerning children, it is mainly a matter of looking up each object, color, animal, or type of person, etc. and putting this information all together for you and the child to interpret. You can "play" with the various dream card decks when children are young and with you at the helm, but these will not be enough for the serious, empathic and intuitive child a ways down the road. Often in interpreting your own dreams you have some idea in the first place about what the dream means. And then of course there are lots of books with generic dream types in them, like a falling dream, a flying dream, a "I am lost" dream, or a climbing dream, etc. The shared intuition added onto the generic ideas and two or three different interpretations of a particular object is enough to figure the whole dream out. Plus, how fun would it be to sit down with your child, talk about the dream and then look up the symbols together and draw them in a dream map or write them in a journal? Doing all this with dreams or nightmares could be a much more serious business, but even more dynamic and life altering when you with your child, get to the bottom of the more serious recurring dreams.

Sylvia Browne says in her Psychic Children book that participating in your child's dreams is important. Parents have all sorts of reactions from ignoring their child's dreams to insisting on hearing every detail when the child cannot really remember all those details. She says to teach your children to make friends with their dreams. Children can learn to release their dreams when they are not real, and to analyze their night travels when they might be real. The invaluable empowering of your child comes when they feel comfortable in sharing their waking dreams and their night dreams, when you say, "Tell me about your dreams." This means they will not feel pressured to produce a dream, nor feel uncomfortable telling you that right at that moment, they have none. And journaling their dreams makes it possible for them to look back on some of these dreams and check on what came true and even what did not. (Refer to 212-213 for more information on how to draw a concept map which is called a story or dream map for children. You can do this type of thing if your child likes to draw or cannot write yet.)

"It is only when we awaken that we realize we have been dreaming. How, then, do we wake up from life's waking dreams?…Life brings us many such waking dreams to help us wend our way through the uncertain years…As we begin to see the uncanny relationship between the world around us and our thoughts, feelings and actions, our attitude about life can change considerably."

--Michael Avery, Secret Language of Waking Dreams, pp. ix ,11, 50-51.

"…every dream comes in the service of the individual dreamer's health and wholeness while speaking in a universal language of archetypal symbol and metaphor…dreams expand the very domain of health and wholeness itself by fostering and reflecting the evolution of human consciousness collectively."

--The Wisdom of Your Dreams by Jeremy Taylor, p.231

"The road to understanding the mind – his mind, all minds – lay in the analysis of dreams…All dreams contained some kind of wish or fantasy. The dream was the disguised fulfillment of a repressed wish: a psychic means of carrying on some kind of a prior determination, concern, or desire. At times, as in the case of young children, the wish was apparent or undisguised – for a sweet or for a triumph over someone who had behaved in a mean way; with adults, the wishes were usually more complex and more likely to be disguised."

--Sigmund Freud, Creating Minds by Howard Gardner, pp.69-70

"Children under the age of three or four never include themselves in their dreams. Perhaps this is because they still have some memory of the life before their present one, or because they are still in communion with elements of nature and otherworldly beings that they lose touch with by age seven. Children also arrange visits to the other side in their dreams five or six times a week, as compared to adults who only visit those they have lost on the other side, two or three times a week in their dreams and then slowly taper off. Perhaps children are not dreaming but astral traveling instead. "All sorts of magic happens when children sleep and their spirits are left to their own devices, unsupervised and unencumbered by their conscious minds."

--Psychic Children by Sylvia Browne & Lindsay Harrison, pp. 161-191

"Relaxing into sleep took the same kind of courage that jumping out of a space ship into the empty…expanse of the dark universe required."

--Nancy Thayer, American Writer, 1943

CHAPTER ELEVEN

Nightmares/Night Terrors/ Night Flying/ Astral Travel/Astral Paralysis

"The breeze at dawn has something to tell you. Don't go back to sleep. You must ask for what you really want. Don't go back to sleep. People are going back and forth across the doorsill, where two worlds touch. The door is round and open. Don't go back to sleep."

--Jala -Ud-Din Rumi

"More people are afraid of their dreams than their nightmares."

--James Grady

"A dream itself is but a shadow."

--William Shakespeare

Night Terrors & Nightmares – What Are the Differences?

A child can be consoled when having a nightmare but when having a night terror, the child can be pretty inconsolable. That is because these are two entirely different experiences caused by two entirely different brain functions. Although similar to a nightmare, a night terror is not caused by any illness or deeper medical issue. Night terrors are thought to be caused when a child awakens suddenly in transition from one sleep stage to another. This is not suppose to happen but does quite often for young children. As we age night terrors begin to lessen and disappear. Night terrors are not really dreams and nightmares which occur only in the NREM5 or REM stage of sleep, along with all kinds of dreaming. Night terrors, on the other hand, occur when we are in deep sleep before or after a REM sleep stage. However, most night terrors happen in the first three hours of sleep as the brain and body transition into more and more relaxations and deeper and deeper sleep stages.

A child may suddenly sit up and shout out in distress or even scream. Agitated and frightened by this sudden awakening, the child will be scared, thrashing, sweating, have a more rapid heartbeat and even wet the bed, unable to control his or her bodily functions. Nightmares happen in the later part of the night or early morning and the child will remember the dreams at least partially or even completely. But there are no dreams in a night terror, although in the child's mind there may be a monster that symbolizes this sudden awakening in the darkness. Night terrors most commonly occur with three to five year old children, although they can continue to occur consistently until around age 12 and even after this, in a more limited fashion, into adulthood. There are some people who suffer from them throughout their lifetime. Recent research has shown that many more adults than were originally thought, continue to suffer on a weekly basis. Doctors say that the only way to find out how or when a person experiences night terrors during the sleep cycles is to have an individual sleep study done.

Night Terror Experiences & Panic Attacks

Even though night terrors have been shown to occur only in the deep sleep stage before REM sleep and the mind is supposed to be oblivious, two things about night terrors are interesting. One can make a night terror occur in both children and adults by simply touching or awakening someone during this stage of sleep, or stop them from repeating and repeating by awakening the person before they go into NREM3 the first time in the sleep cycle. The other interesting thing is that people wake up suffering much more than is often described. They may be gasping, moaning, crying out, and then awaken with a wide eyed terror stare accompanied by a 5 to 20 minute anxiety or panic attack afterwards. A heart beat of 160 to 170 can be generated at this time. This would be enough to send one to the hospital emergency room if you had never had a panic attack before, where they will more often than not, do a couple of tests, find nothing wrong and then sarcastically say to you, "Well, just what is it that you want us to do?" as you sit there still trying to get control of your uncontrollable muscle twitching and panic. They don't know what to do in emergency rooms when they can't find anything wrong physically, you are not on any illegal drugs, and you refuse prescription drugs.

Common Experiences in Night Terrors

There are some common experiences in a night terror that seem to defy explanation, especially for those adults still experiencing them. Where do the monsters, animals, and shadow figures come from? These shadowy people seem to be someone that intends to harm them and while some people recall this experience upon waking, many others do not. Those who believe in multi-dimensions or after life visitors, especially "terrorized" adults, question whether you were hallucinating this figure or animal or not. This is a very difficult call and we really will not know the entire answer to this until we understand 100% how our brain functions, because then and only then, will we be able to delineate between imagination, hallucination, visions and real things that go bump in the night. So for an intuitive child, night terrors will continue to be a common experience, along with nightmares and dreams. And the best way to differentiate is through constant attention to detail and never ending discussion about these details and symbols.

"The only difference between nightmares and night terrors is that children can usually remember their nightmares, but they invariably remember nothing about the cause of their night terrors. It's as if their conscious minds have no intention of addressing whatever frightened them so much while they slept, so they simply block it out. While that makes night terrors very difficult to analyze and explore, I'm convinced that a major percentage of night terrors is caused by episodes of astral catalepsy (paralysis). I'm basing some of that belief on the fact that when I was a child, I often suffered from night terrors myself. I don't remember anymore about what caused them than other children do…but I can easily imagine that waking up as a child to find my spirit was just coming home from its travels might have upset me more than enough to trigger a night terror. And I'm sure that my mother, who believed that stories of bogeymen in the closet and monsters under the bed were efficient ways of keeping me from getting up during the night and disturbing her sleep, made her contributions to my night terrors as well…," So my advice is to every…night, ideally from the moment you bring your new baby home right on through their early grade-school years, make a habit of sitting beside their bed when you know they're asleep. Surround them with the white light of the Holy Spirit. And then, very quietly, so you don't wake them up, give them…" an affirmation or blessing that fits your own particular beliefs. (*Psychic Children by Sylvia Browne and Lindsay Harrison, New American Library, 2007.), p.187-188*).

Causes & Symptoms of Night Terrors

All that is known now is that night terrors are caused by an increase in brain activity that happens when the brain misfires and the only treatment is to medicate the brain out of this chemical reaction. But are we doing the right thing when we do this? At present, we do not know these answers and I have to wonder about other types of experiences that are quite real and could explain what some of these night terrors are. Common physical causes of night terrors include being overtired, stressed, fatigued sleeping in a different environment and taking a new medication. Some inherit a tendency for over arousal in sleep and it is interesting that sleepwalking, bed wetting and night terrors run in families, just as intuitive empathy also runs in families.

Symptoms include many other things besides a rapid heartbeat, panic attack and seeing shadowy figures and animals. Some of these are an inability to explain what happened, having no recall, screaming, confusion, sweating or twitching, having a difficulty in comforting the person, seeing spiders or snakes, seeing animals or people in the room, and one cannot fully awaken with absolutely no memory of these events the next day.

Night terrors last up to twenty minutes and the person is still asleep, but on interviewing those who suffer from these, there are plenty of people who remember partially or even completely, their night terror experience.

Treatments for Night Terrors

Treatment for night terrors is limited for adults, because they don't have parents any longer to comfort them, only therapists! However you may have a spouse or partner and perhaps they can do these things for you. The advice for adults is the same in many ways as it is for children. Don't eat a heavy meal at night, reduce your stress level with some form of meditation and exercise, don't be over tired – a sort of enigma I would think for night terrors and the panic afterwards, and use a medication. Agreeing with everything the person says may help as well, even if they are still not quite awake. Hugging seems to work, as I mentioned with small children, the swaddling idea can be done for the child to comfort him. Do not shout at a child or adult to wake them from a supposed dream, because the person is already terrorized and more often than not, still in a light sleep. And as always, do not tell a child or adult that nothing happened when their heart is literally beating out of their chest and may even physically hurt. Go to the methods I suggested for anxiety or panic attacks and use what works for you, even a down-filled throw may put the person to sleep quickly and thus avoid night terrors altogether.

Children will usually settle down within minutes because they have a parent there to help them through this and it is best not to try and wake the child up. It is better to just go with the flow of what is happening because if you attempt to wake them they will be disoriented and confused and it may take longer for them to go back to sleep. However, if you are trying to break the night terror cycle, waking them up about fifteen minutes before going into the first third stage deep sleep can break the cycle for the entire night. Make sure they get enough sleep, are not stressed by their earlier day by doing night time relaxation activities just before they go to bed, and make sure they are getting enough rest as well. Make the bed time routine consistent and peaceful, from story time to relaxation exercises, energy rejuvenation touch and calming affirmations, etc. There are many more ideas in the activities chapter for these night time activities before going to sleep. (*"Night Terrors" this information taken from: http://www.kidshealth.org/parent/general/sleep/terrors.html*).

Does My Child Travel at Night?

This brings up the part of this topic that few doctors or counselors would probably discuss. Yet parents all over the world have experienced this activity while dreaming and so have some of their children. Think of one woman who asked her doctor what to do because her child seemed too intense, worried too much, had anxiety and was being terrorized by his many nightmares and night terrors. Perhaps he was also gifted, a bed wetter and a sleepwalker. Could all this be something that she needed her son to see a psychiatrist for if there were no physical reasons for any of this? And of course the experts in each field either agree on her choice or don't agree, and are confusing her even more? On the other hand, would this same questioning parent accept another explanation, one that goes far beyond what is considered ordinary reasons for her son's behaviors, even by today's standards? Would she accept that perhaps her child was all these things and had all these things because he was first and foremost, grandly and beautifully, an intuitive astral traveler?

Could it be that families of intuitives, sleepwalked when they were younger but learned to astral travel later on, thus hiding the supposed problem? Could it be that some of them who were once bed wetters were now no longer afraid to walk down that hall to the bathroom because they no longer feared the real entities they were being bombarded with? No longer ruled by society's fears and their own doubts about their abilities, they didn't need to wait at the other end of the hall for hours at a time? Could it be that being empathic but not really understanding this, they worried not only about themselves and those close to them, but also about the earthquake halfway around the world and all the people involved with this disaster, because they actually knew about this disaster ahead of time? Could it be that one mother walked into her two daughter's bedroom to see what the noise was all about, and was astonished to see her two daughters on their knees facing each other, and communicating with each other in a strange language, while they were both in a full sleep state. Or that perhaps there was a little mental telepathy going on between the sisters while they journeyed to or from, who knows where, as they slept? And please note that these two sisters have grandchildren now and are living perfectly normal lives, at least for intuitives! They never had to see either doctors or counselors because their parents knew they were normal in the first place.

Famous clairvoyant and medium, George Anderson, spent his childhood in and out of mental clinics or private counseling, for what his parents were advised by the experts might be mental problems. It was not until he was an adult that his uncanny gifts as an intuitive, were discovered. He began writing his many books on the subject of grieving and eventually became the catalyst for a worldwide organization for grieving parents who had lost a child and others grieving the loss of a loved one. People sometimes comment on some of his slightly strange physical quirks like moving one hand in the air as he draws or speaks to clients in an intuitive reading. Is it possible that these physical quirks are the result of those years of being considered crazy and being exposed to "crazy" behaviors? On the other hand, is it possible that such psychics as Sylvia Browne and John Edwards who came from generations of psychics, never considered themselves odd or strange because these types of things were taken for what is granted as "normal" in their homes? Edgar Casey and Andrew Jackson Davis (a 19th century American clairvoyant) were in another category however, because they had little formal schooling in the beginning and simply accepted that others knew what they knew out of naivety. However, all of them suffered from the judgments of others in one way or another, as they became more famous. And remember there are many out there, famous or not, working quietly for our shared future as intuitives, healers and futurists.

So now we are on to the topic of astral projection, night visitors, night travels to other places, and remote viewing. A world that is still being presented as science fiction and fantasy as in the film "The Sixth Sense" or even as comedy, in the film "The Men Who Stare at Goats," even though all of what happened in the military remote viewing program was absolutely true? And we live in a world that some say is all brain function or self-created illusions which we don't understand as yet, while others believe these are spiritual awakenings and various other things. So read this part at your own risk, that risk being, that you might open up to other possibilities, other ways of seeing and feeling things, and the very ways that all the great inventors, scientists, mathematicians, composers, authors, saints and many others, gave credence too when they realized a new idea or invented something new. Your child may be among them, as may you! Let those mysteries unfold and whether you believe any of this or not, at least acknowledge it for your children, who just may be way ahead of you in their thinking and feeling, in a world that you may not be going to, but they definitely are!

What to do if You Can Acknowledge the Unseen & Unknown Around us

Discuss astral travel, out-of body experiences or "night flying," with your child if this is a part of the fears of going to sleep and you feel comfortable doing this yourself. These fears are very real for many intuitive children and whether dreaming these flights or actually experiencing them, how you respond makes all the difference. More and more people are beginning to believe and possibly prove that the majority of people do experience night flight for real and that it is a normal and natural process that goes on at night all over the world. It has been written about and told about in hundreds of stories from every country in the world, and while most scientists still say this is imagined, who really cares which it is? The fact of the matter is that it has to be addressed and dealt with in a positive and commonsensical manner. If your child is not conscious of this and has no problems with it, then you need to do nothing until, or if, it becomes a problem. If, on the other hand, it is a huge problem, don't jump to the conclusion that your child has mental problems. Psychiatrically or psychically, a child can become wounded by being dealt with too harshly in either arena. Open the package of your child's heart slowly and carefully and find out their learning style, their personality type and everything else you can about them before you decide the directions to take and the help to seek.

If you reach the conclusion after lots of careful seeking and deliberations that yes indeed, my child is a gifted intuitive or empath, a natural healer or seer, good at remote viewing or telepathic communication or perhaps has had a near-death experience, or even all of the above and more, then proceed with caution into discussions with them about astral travel. This is unknown territory in many ways and only a few pioneers can assist you at this time unless you yourself have had such experiences and this will help you a lot. Robert Bruce's and Robert Monroe's materials are two of the few which can help you in your discussions with your child on this subject so check on line and see if anyone else has written about children and astral travel. While Monroe's books are definitely for adults, they can be quite informative for those struggling with this issue and who remember bits and pieces of their night travels. But Bruce specifically addresses some of the issues for children in his books, as does Sylvia Browne in her chapter "While Children Sleep" in the book Psychic Children.

There certainly has been a lot of literature on child near-death experiences, child past life memories, childhood memories of astral travel or at least flying in dreams and lucid dream recall. These are all a kind of confirmation for astral travel. Read about remote reviewing in more depth in my chapter on "What in the world is going on for psychic children," and you will realize the depth and breadth of the research, experimentation and utterly amazing powers that are being explored in other countries concerning children. It was not until I was an adult that I understood that when doing intuitive counseling one is actually astral traveling into the memories, mind, and energy fields of the sitter, walking beside them as an astral traveling companion. Nor did I understand that remote viewing in a sense is astral travel as well. One can view the past, the future, or even into other dimensions and parallel universes and anywhere on the planet or any other planet for that matter in what physicists now say is a multi-verse. There is even the field now of psychic archaeology besides military research and private lab research into the possibilities of the human brain and psychic phenomena.

When one is doing a health scan on a person, one travels into the body and looks at the major organs, where the illnesses lay and where former injuries can be spotted, or perhaps see future ones coming. These illnesses or injuries can be seen as filmy auras, symbolic representations or felt with a healer's hands, or all three. This type of remote viewing can also be misinterpreted but is rarely "wrong." An example I can think of is when a woman came for a reading and while I was scanning her in my mind's eye for any health related problems I ran across something unusual. When I got to her face I described a slight drooping of the right side of her face, some twitching and some numbness. When she did not recognize this as a past event I then stopped and went on because I did not want to scare her about any future health problems. I was tired by then and did not look into her lower face and jaw, but just "traveled" on, not paying attention to this particular problem any longer.

A couple of days later her friend called me. It seems that the woman had a phobia about dentists and had put off going to one even though she knew she was having some pain in her lower right jaw. This information finally prompted her to make an appointment, at which point they found several abscessed teeth in a row on the lower right side of her face. She had to have oral surgery and they had to give her a mega dose of anesthetic for it. So this of course explained all the numbness, drooping and twitching afterwards, because she had so much anesthetic injected into her. I had been thinking Bells Palsy or something because I had told her not to worry about it because it would be temporary and come and go in a short period of time. Had I had even a hint of the dental phobia I would have looked deeper, seen the little thin oval of black along her teeth and sent her to the dentist right away. An intuitive reading is a two way street but most people don't realize how this energy connection is necessary, so sometimes the "reader" can misinterpret what they are seeing or jump to the wrong "channel."

One can also see the past, present and future of a person but it is up to the reader to be responsible about this information and only disseminate what is needed for the present time. One can do distance healing, distance diagnosing ,etc., but of course the reader only recommends who to see and what to do for these things. In fact, one of the leaps of faith that an intuitive has to take is first recognizing the unseen worlds, then dream them at night or actually experience them in the daytime, and finally know that time and distance do not exist when retrieving information for the person you are "reading." You only put it in a chronological form to keep from being very confused by all the information flooding in from literally everywhere. Night travel is a form of reading one's own mind, another's mind, or even intrusions from other people and things that go bump in the night. One can travel almost anywhere but with the focus in mind that you are helping someone to experience the multisensory things that will help to give them insights about their life and perhaps move them forward on a more positive path. Or help them to heal from past emotional wounds. Upon occasion one does have amazing and quite real encounters at night and then the entire view of the universe will change dramatically, as well as cause even more such encounters to happen.

Every year in my classroom of little ones who had been labeled "gifted" or in my resource classes with children who had been labeled slow, learning disabled or behaviorally challenged, from kindergarten to sixth grade, I would ask the question, "Who has ever flown in their dreams?" Without fail one-third would say I was crazy for asking such a thing, one-third would say they didn't know or didn't remember, and one-third would become quite animated and enthusiastic in stating that yes they did fly in their dreams and wasn't it nice that finally some adult had asked them about it. So in a sense, I took my own personal data on the subject and wondered if the third that said they didn't know or couldn't remember, also flew in their dreams subconsciously. I remembered my own experiences "flying" as a child and wondered if I still did but just couldn't remember. Later, when I could see myself more clearly, I knew for sure that I was still doing this and began to realize that not only did I "fly" while sleeping but I could sometimes direct where I went, what I did, and seemed to be working on remembering some of these "flights" as well, at least partially. I also realized that it was a normal natural part of my sleep pattern. I just didn't know if it was all dreaming, real out-of-body travel, or a type of mental control that powered my mind "engine!" However, as an adult I did not do a lot of it because I had better things to do with my time then. I can remember as a child thought, floating out of my bedroom window and down to the sidewalk outside, where I took a running jump down the sidewalk and then lifted off and floated over the tree tops across the city. Eventually I learned to get further and further out until I was passing the various planets in our solar system. I don't remember getting any further than this.

I also began to realize that astral travel was what an intuitive did when they did a reading. To me the difference in remote viewing and traveling is that in one instance you are simply looking through the lenses of the mind's eye and in the other, you are actually walking beside the traveler you are reading for. There is another theory as well, that besides actually being in another place in the astral body, you can also construct a world or environment that connects you to another person or persons mentally. Then speak telepathically while building whatever construct you wish to, so that in the film "The Men Who Stare At Goats," the man who stopped the goat's heart or moved the clouds around, probably did. And this is quite a scary thought in the wrong hands. But think about it in the right hands, perhaps someday we could operate on people without actually touching them to save lives, or even move a storm slightly off course to save many more lives. What was done in the remote viewing military projects in this country is being done right now using the top and very moldable child super psychics in government sponsored programs in several other countries around the world. For good or for ill, this is the wave of the future, as we learn more and more about the human brain and its many capabilities, so hopefully more good than bad will come from these discoveries.

One last thing I need to address is that of those groups who have probably for centuries, but quietly and without fanfare, taught themselves to astral project. These people became "captains" of their own astral "ship," navigating with ease and were fully conscious of where they were going and when they were returning. They didn't do this for entertainment or for self-realization, but because they had to learn to soul body travel to survive. I would imagine that they stumbled onto this from a number of factors, perhaps they came from an intuitive family, perhaps they began by disassociating from a traumatic situation, and instead of taking on different personas or more severely created multiple personalities, they chose instead to leave their physical body and travel in their astral body while they were protecting themselves from the traumatic experience. Often these happened spontaneously because of a near-death experience and then they began training themselves, or because they were a POW or political prisoner in some foreign country, who for either a brief period of time or for years, somehow learned to consciously astral project out of their situation to survive spiritually and to protect their physical body from total annihilation.

But the largest group, and probably the one that we are especially concerned about in this book are those who learn over time and terrible and continuous long term abuse, sexual, physical, verbal and psychological, to astral project in order to protect themselves from death. And often the people in this group are children. Even little children, if they are intuitive enough and open enough, can stumble on to this technique to survive any terrible and devastating attack on their person. Most psychologists would call this disassociation or going into another personality more capable of handling the situation. But it is more likely that the person astral projects out of their body to protect both the body and the soul that directs it, and also the spirit, which is the "heart" of the body and soul, and certainly the most precious part of us all.

Interestingly in one of my workshops a woman mentioned to me privately that she had learned to do this as a little girl to protect herself from the terrible abuse she endured and it was her idea when she grew up to intentionally and consciously teach her children how to do this too. Not that her children were ever abused but because her own abuse had been so terrible and so prolonged that she thought this a great technique for each of her children to have as a form of protection. Sort of like taking your children to karate classes which could probably protect them from living people and physical dangers in the physical world, but could not necessarily protect them from an attack on their soul or spirit, or an accident of some kind from which they have to survive. Or say you do have a sudden accident or illness and in order to recover, astral travel would help provide not only a respite for recovery but also further your spiritual development while you are on the mend, and especially if there is some physical damage from which one cannot fully recover and you want to see your friends or be with a loved one, etc. In other words, this would be a powerful tool for a little child suffering in any of these ways, even though many would advise a less stringent way of handling this.

However there are some who learn to consciously project if they are incarcerated in prison or a mental hospital and find their freedom at night, while in the day time they are still imprisoned. A last group would be people whose bodies are paralyzed and can experience the freedom of movement through their lucid dreaming and astral traveling. Although their body cannot move, they can take a vacation by using their astral body to feel movement again, rather like the giant puppets in the film "Avatar," a film which certainly had many metaphysical elements that probably went unrecognized by some who viewed the film. The main character was really paralyzed in the film and was able to feel and even sense his body's freedom once more by manipulating his brain waves to activate his alien "puppet." And last, there is the question of someone being in a coma, and certainly not a medical question, but one for serious thought, does this person astral project or not? And if they do, are they doing it consciously or unconsciously? Most psychics know that they can communicate with people in a coma, but intermittently or sporadically, they say. We have a long way to go in understanding this sort of condition still, although I would venture to guess that perhaps the body has to shut down while it repairs itself in some way? And maybe in this state, if one survives it, the consciousness can astral travel while the body rebuilds itself?

One of the questions that has not been answered, is when a person astrally projects, do they split into two visible three-dimensional people that everyone can see and touch? Or is the spirit body that leaves the physical body merely energy or a manifestation of that person, not solid or three dimensional? Can that solid body, as some claim, really interact with others physically, perhaps harm someone or interact in other ways physically? If this is true, then is this the real answer to ghosts, aliens, spirits, mythological creatures or even angels and demons? Are trickster "spirits" merely human beings who like to play on a midnight chess board with others who are not conscious of their actions? In other words, is this merely brain function that we do not as yet understand or comprehend? While one can immediately think of negative ways to use all this, I can think of many positive ways such as healing terrible diseases or visiting with loved ones even after they are gone. However, I personally believe that both situations are going on, caused by both human and dimensional beings and all the many interactions therein!

Night traveling is even more mind blowing in the sense that many still believe that they are simply dreaming and never seek explanations for why they wake up momentarily paralyzed or as if they fell from the ceiling into their beds or even out of their beds. They don't notice when they start sinking into their mattress or feel as if they are floating above their own beds, although those who have had near-death experiences are much more certain of their experiences as are trauma victims who consciously trained themselves to do this. And if they are given an explanation, they simply believe it in accordance with their own belief system and what the physical world tells them. However, things are at long last changing and some doctors and scientists, weathering ridicule from their peers, are now seeking explanations beyond this for what they still consider are strange occurrences but understand now, might be brain functions. Whatever you believe about this and whatever your own experiences concerning this topic, you may have children who are experiencing night flying whether dreamed or real, being awed or terrified by these experiences, and needing help understanding what is happening to them.

What To Know About Astral Projection

Types of Flying

a) Three types of speeds: Same pace as on earth, standing still while the environment moves around you, and flying so fast that you can't remember getting somewhere or getting home.

b) Three types of heights while "flying:" A few inches above the ground, over tree tops or high buildings, out into space for great distances.

c) Mode of leaving and returning: Does the body settle into the mattress, does the body lift up off the mattress, is there a sudden and abrupt return like falling into one's bed, or does one complete a "flight" in which the child gently returns, slowly and carefully, and does this "flight" or near-death change that child's view of the world permanently and irrevocably? However this "mode of transporting or travel" happens or is perceived and dealt with, this type of activity can really frighten a child.

d) Know the reason or reasons for projecting: abuse, imprisonment, a form of sleep walking, near-death, transcendence or a physical handicap, etc.

e) Does the person think they are dreaming, lucid dreaming, or actually physically or energetically night traveling?

f) Children flying without an external means in their dreams is one way to confirm that they are astral projecting.

g) Astral experiences follow a logical sequence while regular dreams do not.

h) Sylvia Browne says that "If there's a doubt in your mind that your children are taking real astral trips while they sleep, and bringing back information they'd have no other way of knowing, leave no stone unturned trying to come up with a viable, legitimate alternative. You won't find a more enthusiastic believer in validation than me...." But if you can't find one then "Listen to your child, ask the right questions, and take their word for it instead." (*Ibid., Psychic Children, pp. 168-169*).

Sleep Paralysis or Astral Paralysis

Astral paralysis or "feeling frozen" is a normal natural part of sleep, travel and dreams. Since there have been folktales and stories of these night time experiences told in every country of the world for centuries, this supports the idea that such experiences are much more common than people probably want to believe. The child can have the following experiences when going to sleep or when waking up related to "night flying": paralysis sensations, feeling pinned down, cannot cry out, being touched, internal vibrating, flashes of light, knocking or tapping noises, roaring sounds or electrical static wind sometimes called Astral Wind. Parents often perceive this as having to do with mere nightmares and dreams on one end of the scale, and on the other end, children are told that they are being visited by ghosts or evil presences wishing to possess them. Neither reason is exactly right. And it is really all in the interpretation of this experience for each individual person or child.

According to the person's background, belief systems and experiences that the person has, they can think it is a possession, a temporary transfiguration, a UFO abduction or visitation, a channeling spirit, a frightening ghost, a demon, an otherworldly visitor, an elemental or nature spirit, one of the many folklore creatures from around the world, a psychological disorder, a mental illness, a delusion, an illusion, being exposed to some smell or drug that has altered the brain chemistry, electrodes stimulating a certain part of the brain, even convincing yourself that you had a real experience when you didn't, these can be blamed on a UFO visitation, a transcendent religious experience or even a vivid imagination – the list is endless. And then, it is according to these things that one deals with the experience in like manner, either driving this force off or medicating it out of existence or performing some sort of ritual that the person believes will work. Belief is a powerful force itself, as is what we cannot see. For me, I gave up on such things and just accept what is happening no matter where it comes from, and then deal with it.

Discuss these experiences in whatever way you feel comfortable, just be sure you do discuss them with your child if he or she is being terrorized by these events. Don't show your own fear if you have any, as this will transmit the wrong message to an already terrorized child. Teach the child to breathe deeply when this happens and to remain calm, so he or she can learn to analyze the situation and solve the problem. And realize that in the physical world, consistently ignoring bad behavior and not feeding into its negative energy, is your best defense, just as it is in the non-physical world. I have assisted two families long distance who either moved into a "haunted" home or created a haunted home because of what they brought with them. In both cases they were sensitives but did not know this and had to wake up to their own empathic abilities as adults, in order to deal with what was going on. In both cases, nothing really scary or threatening was going on anyway. It was their own fears and beliefs that they had to confront in order to come to peace with what they were experiencing. Once they made peace with this, they made peace with their homes. One family stayed and declared their borders, and the other family moved and discovered that their next home was perfectly peaceful. However, they also discovered that they would now have other intuitive experiences from now on and no longer feared these events. Not much different than the phrase, "To thine own self be true," once they found peace internally and accepted their gifts, externally they could deal with whatever came down the pike.

In very extreme cases, there is even research on children and adults who can produce, usually unknowingly, raised scratch marks on their skin simply from their mental intent or mind control. The rest in a so-called "possession" is usually really good acting, a particular belief system filled with heavy duty good and evil battling and the marvelous attention the person can receive from others. It becomes the ultimate acting forte and a play worth watching, for those prone to a good negative and frightening "show" and those wanting the attention. Not to say that in a smaller group, evil and negative forces don't play a major part or that mental illness can too, but ignoring such stuff will tell you the difference over a little time. If you believe in exorcisms then by all means have one if the negative forces seem to be attacking you. Whether real or believed to be real, this will probably work, at least for a while or maybe even longer than that. If you believe in counseling then get a therapist. If you need religious blessings then do that. Whatever it takes to bring back confidence, calm and peace into your life to "de possess" yourself, because then you just might be able to assess the situation in a better way. It has been my experience that traveling trickster spirits will leave a building or home when the energy is cleared. But spirits attached to a place from long ago, more often hide out for a while and then manifest again in the same location. The only way to really clear out all of the attachments to a building, is to completely clear out anything from the foundations up, that could hold old energy for such a spirit who may have once lived in the building or even the area nearby. Even the land itself can be a conduit for negative energies and using dowsing tools can not only locate elements, it can also become a spiritual tool. For more on this, read Patricia C. and Richard D. Wright's book, The Divining Heart.

One story told to me about a two-year-old, is that he woke up in the middle of the night screaming to his mother that he was frozen to his bed and could not move. His mother went in to comfort him and calmed him down, but still, he could not move. Not knowing exactly what to do she finally asked him what was holding him down and he said that big pieces of tape were holding him down all over his body. His mother then quite carefully freed one hand of the "invisible" tape and then let her boy point to where all the other pieces of tape were one-by-one. She slowly removed each piece of "invisible" tape until they were all gone and then the boy was able to move again and go back to sleep. Did it matter whether his mother believed there was tape there or not? No! She simply empowered her child through example and at the same time, acknowledged his fear calmly and step-by-step, showed him how to do this himself, if it ever happened again, and relieved his fears about this. And if there really was something there, she, probably without knowing it remained neutral not fearful, and sent whatever it was on its way, protecting her boy from whatever was terrorizing him and giving him the message not to fear or doubt what had happened, real or imagined. This same two-year-old had announced at a huge family reunion that his grandmother would die the next day. His mother handled this by saying to her son, "That's fine dear now go and give your grandma a big hug and a kiss and tell her you love her." The next day when the grandmother did die, the child was told to tell his surviving grandpa that he loved him and then give him a big hug and a kiss. And while the parents handled this beautifully for their child, this was the definitive moment for his parents in understanding that yes, they did indeed have a very intuitive child to raise.

This temporary physiological and also emotional reaction can include all kinds of symptoms to frighten little children. The child can struggle to breathe, feel a weight on their chest, and be unable to move or cry out. They will have an internal and uncontrollable vibration coming from deep within the body, hear buzzing noises and hums, and even experience a strange wind lightly buffeting their body. They will see flashes of light or glaring lights or they may even see little blue lights out of the corners of their eyes. And because they are children, they may feel that something terrifying is sitting at the end of the bed or next to them on the bed or even more frightening, sitting on them. They may also feel that something is touching them either playfully as in light wisps of cobwebs across their face, or feel a slight breath on the back of their neck, hands or arms. Or worse, they may think that an unseen presence is holding them down or touching them maliciously or inappropriately. So giving the child a way to cope with this, whether imagined or real, can really empower small children to take control of these sorts of events that may be happening to them at night.

Robert Bruce says that sleep paralysis, astral paralysis, lucid dreaming, out-of-body and astral projections are all related to each other. That they overlap each other and are just different dimensions of night flying. Some are more mental and some are more physical in nature. Some are dreams and some are waking states or OBE's. To learn more on his thoughts about this, read about sleep paralysis and dreaming in the last chapter or go to the source and read his chapter on lucid dreaming in the revised 2009 version of his Astral Dynamics book. But I really like the original book that was bigger, more in depth, while not as commercial as the newer one. It is an adult book and difficult to plow through, but on the other hand it is absolutely fascinating. If you are dealing with a really severe and complex set of characteristics with your intuitive child, you may need this one. Bruce himself has gone to working with the most difficult child cases because he finds children so much more open to change than adults often are. And by the way, for both adults and children, he says the best way to break out of astral or sleep paralysis is to start with your big toe and when you have it moving, go to all the toes, then the other foot, then the fingers of one hand and then the other and this will wake up the entire body in a few minutes. Whatever you do, don't freak out or panic because then it will take longer to "unfreeze."

Experts in the field of sleep research who also recognize the possibility of the existence of astral travel or out-of-body or OBEs, agree on one thing and that is when these sorts of experiences happen. Say we fell asleep while in REM sleep but were startled awake, which would be rare during REM sleep, we would then be conscious of being temporarily paralyzed and would have to work at waking up our bodies. Or say we went off to astral travel in N3 while our bodies could move or at least we would be conscious of our bodies, but we got back too late for the N3 we had left in, or too early for the next cycle when we could consciously move again. Or suppose we landed in a REM of one of the cycles after being gone in our astral body through several sleep stages? So then, wide awake, we are suddenly paralyzed, how terrifying would that be if you had never had this happen before or had no information about this? And add to all this a little child having this happen, how horrifying would that be without more information and comfort from their parents?

General Suggestions for the Night Terrorized Child

For those of you who are much more aware of your intuition and do believe that your child is having real events at night, please use all of the previous suggestions to get to the heart of the matter with your child, empowering that child to not only have confirmation for these events, but also develop ways of dealing with them while young enough to not become emotionally damaged as an adult. Bed wetting is only one of several things that the child may be dealing with each night as he or she tries to go to sleep. Most parents would hope for a pleasant night's sleep for all their children every night and do not want their children to suffer from terrors during their sleep cycle. It is only in the interpretation where adults beg to differ in the causes of these nightmarish evenings, how you deal with them is much the same. So whether you believe that when the child dreams he is suffering from delusions, a vivid imagination, hidden psychological traumas, simple nightmares that occur for no reason at all, or real encounters from other dimensions, times or parallel universes, etc., strategies for coping with this are the same. And the type of help you get for the child must be based on a lot of preparation work on the part of the parents. Even belief itself is a powerful tool for steering your children in the right direction. But whatever you do, do not ignore or dismiss these night events; this is the worst thing you can do for your child's well-being in the future.

(*The following material comes from Sylvia Browne and Lindsay Harrison's book Psychic Children, Robert Bruce's Astral Dynamics and Practical Psychic Self Defense for more extreme situations, dozens of internet articles on all the many topics about the mysteries of dreaming or being terrified at night and my own personal experiences or from workshop participants.)

For those on the less severe end of nightmare experiences

a) Read a positive, non scary bedtime story

b) Drink a warm drink or even a cool one

c) Do an energy rejuvenation exercise together

d) Do a brief guided imagery activity, meditation or prayer.

e) Put a nightlight on; leave the door open or shut and the same with the closet, according to the child's preferences.

f) Do a brief meditation and affirmation together

g) Visualize what you are feeling and what is interfering in your life and then visualize these feelings growing smaller and smaller, and imagine these feelings floating away in a balloon or mist.

h) Imagine a solid wall or large heavy metal door and then remove the wall piece by piece by either melting it or breaking it apart. If it is a door take it off its hinges and push it over.

i) In the Sylvia Browne/Lindsay Harrison book Psychic Children, they list some ideas under "Tools of Protection" pp. 254 to 263 which include: "The Bubble of White Light," "The Circle of Mirrors," "The Golden Sword," "Gold and Silver Nets," and "The Dome of Light."

j) Do a "clear the heart" exercise, with both hands over your heart, then say a prayer or affirmation together and ask for a peaceful heart and assistance from your guides, angels or God.

k) Blow up a balloon slowly with a breath exercise and then pop it, either literally or using your imagination, whichever works best.

l) Do not show any fear yourself for the child, remain calm and consistent as the child prepares to go to sleep.

m) Hold the child wrapped in your arms or wrap the child in a blanket so that they can feel safe and secure while falling asleep again. Teach them to do this if this proves to be comforting for them. Tuck the blanket all around them like a soft, warm shield of protection. Use a down-filled throw, as these blankets warm you to the bone and will put anyone to sleep, especially those in an anxiety or panic attack.

n) Check the internet for more ideas under the title "intuitive parenting" and other such titles on line. There are quite a few of them loaded with other ideas and I list the few I thought especially helpful in the adult books section.

o) Have the child visualize the things that were bothering him in the dream or nightmare and help him to interpret these details in a positive way. Or draw them in a dream book and he can change them into something more positive while redrawing them.

p) He can draw the things he saw and then throw them away.

q) Use toys to reenact the dream and change it into something positive by changing the ending of it. Or make clay figures the next day and change the dream then as the child shows you his dream. There are many more suggestions in Chapters 15 and 16.

<u>For the more severe night terror problems - alter these factors if you can</u>:

a) Look for stressors that can disrupt a child's sleep pattern such as a sudden change in routine that has been made for the child, eating two hours before bedtime, family upsets that day that need to be discussed, and just plain lack of sleep.

b) "Clear" the room of any negative or disruptive energy where the child sleeps, with any of the above mentioned activities or techniques. Even if you don't believe any bad energy is being cleared out of the room, the child will. And seeing you use a technique to do this will empower your child to believe he or she can do this too. You can use sage, sweet grass, incense, scented candles, essential oils, chimes, toning, gongs or prayer and affirmations, or even just a commanding voice to shoo anything away. Or use several of these things because children are impressionable and will follow your lead in whatever way you choose to do this. It is the belief that empowers them anyway! Remove items you suspect may be carrying disruptive or even negative energy attached to them, both old and new, and check for items in the entire house that may be suspect. Sometimes these items have been there so long that one might forget to check them, especially those left by previous owners. Also remove objects that are scaring your child at night, do not discount the child's complaints about these objects.

c) Keep a good sense of humor to try and "lighten" the atmosphere in the room and alter the feelings the child is expressing.

d) If they feel "ghosts or "spirits" in their room acknowledge and honor the child's feelings about this, whether this is correct or not and whether you personally believe this or not. Confirmation of these "presences" will empower your child to find his or her own way to a peaceful sleep.

e) What to do: Do the various "go to sleep" activities suggested, use positive language and thinking when discussing these issues, honor and discuss every detail of the dreams or night time experiences and ask lots of questions while interpreting these dreams. If you need to research a past or current event in some other part of the world to confirm what the child dreamed, please do this. In one case the parents were still trying to determine if they just had a precocious child, a child with a very creative imagination, or she was indeed a gifted intuitive. The specific details their daughter was giving helped them research who the little girl ghost was visiting their daughter nightly. All the dates and names fit, the incident had happened in the next town from where they lived over a hundred years ago, the ghost was identified and they even found descendants who identified the portrait of the ghost girl that the little girl had drawn. Or in another case, an adolescent boy kept telling his father that there was a truck at the bottom of the pond near them with a young man in it. He knew the make and model, the license plate number, the color of the truck, etc. After his son kept bothering him about it over and over again, the father finally went to the police and asked them to drag the lake. Sure enough the truck was found with all information correct and the dead man had been missing for seven years. (These and other interesting stories about "Psychic Kids: Children of the Paranormal" can be found on the A&E Channel. There are several seasons and every one of them is worthwhile for parents to view and screen for the ones that may apply to their children. You can also purchase these DVDs from the Arts & Entertainment channel.)

f) Remind the child over and over that they have the power to re-write their dreams and especially if they wake up in the middle of one, it is important to finish the dream with a positive, "happy" ending.

g) Talk about signs and symbols in their dreams that are unique to them and showing up consistently in their dreams.

h) If all else fails – however keep doing the "all else's" anyway because eventually some of them will work – research shows that children with night terrors go into this particular brain wave pattern about one and a half hours after they fall asleep. So wake them up about fifteen minutes before this and let them go to sleep again. This will alter the existing brain wave pattern that often induces the terror cycle and you can give them a more pleasant night's sleep. (Encourage them to go to the bathroom at this time too, to avoid bed wetting if this is a problem for them).

i) Of course there is always the possibility of early manifestations of mental illness developing in the child, or already present in the child. But as I said when talking about spiritual crisis, you need to have all the tests for a mental or medical problem done before assuming something else.

j) Physical, mental or sexual abuse can produce or add to already existing night terrors as well as other lesser family upsets such as dealing with an alcoholic or ill parent, etc. Please make sure none of these things are present first, but do this carefully and tactfully with the experts who can identify such things, before you ever determine that these are intuitive.

k) Real physical world experiences can be terrorizing a child. In this case the dreams are manifestations of real life terrors which can be explored by the therapist to help the child heal from such terrors.

l) Children will often learn to disassociate from negative experiences and intuitive children can learn to literally separate their soul from their body and astral project right out of the situation. Using this as a way to escape horrible experiences can help them as children but as adults they may continue to use this method of night travel to escape getting close to anyone or block out negative experiences as adults, rather than facing them in the real physical world.

m) For really extreme astral experiences in children, as well as what appear to be possession states, please refer to the chapter in Robert Bruce's Practical Psychic Self-Defense entitled "Countermeasures for Children."

Dream or Story Mapping

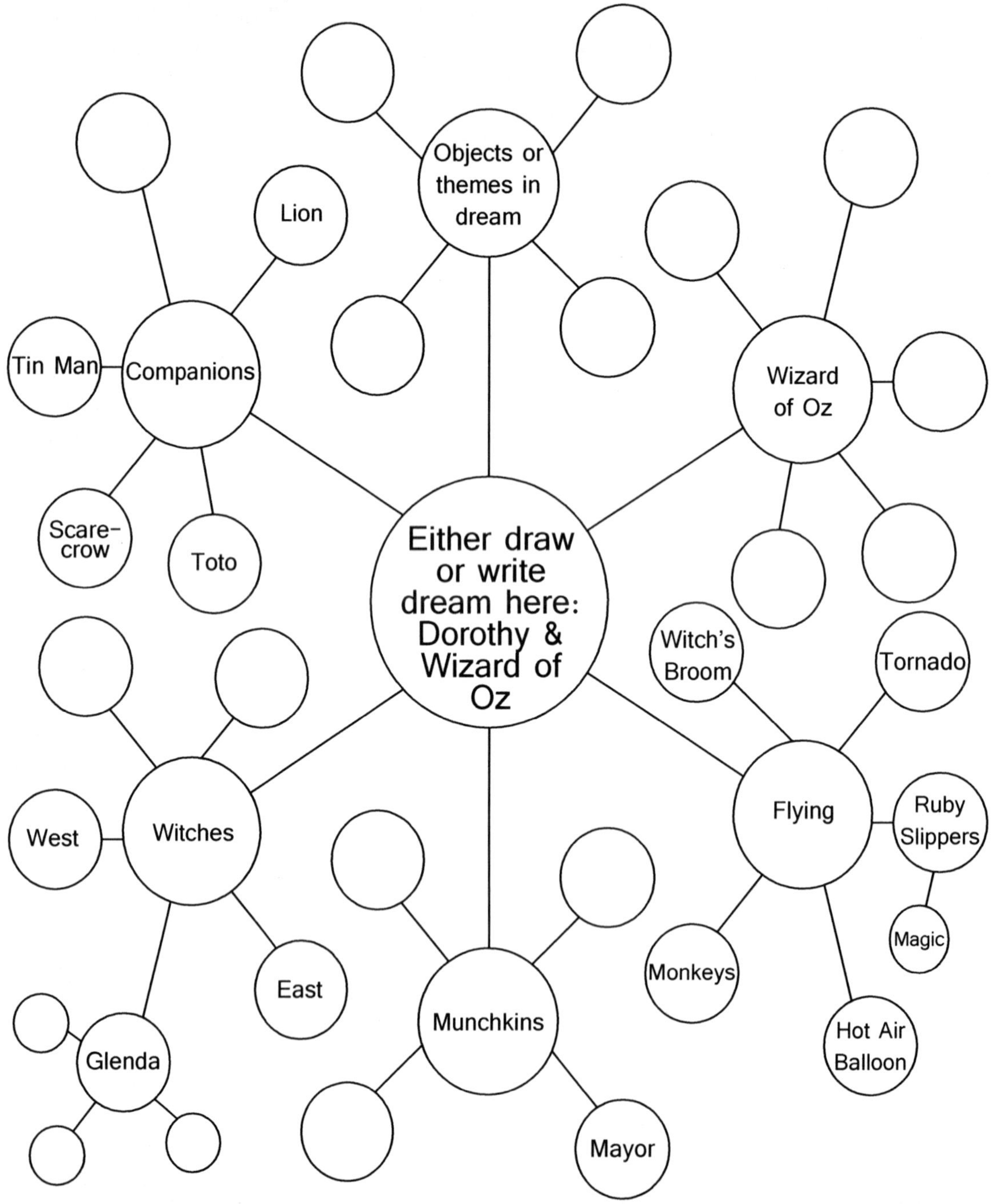

The Wizard of Oz Story Map

n) Or, if you are one of the lucky ones to have developed your ability to astral project out of your body when danger approaches, then teach your children how to do this as a precaution. The groups I know about who have been able to direct their astral or spiritual body out of their physical body and return safely are trauma victims such as terrible abuse when young, near-death experiencers who have been there – done that, POWs and other around the world political or criminal prisoners, who taught themselves to project while being held captive and people whose bodies are paralyzed. Many of them can remember where they went or were, on their "travels," in detail. It is your choice whether you choose this method or not, as the controversies are endless.

o) Make a dream or story map together and change how the nightmare ends. This consists of a circle in the middle of the paper where the dream is named and then lines come out in all directions to smaller circles where elements or categories about the dream are named in these circles. Then lines come off of each of these circles all around each one to even smaller circles and inside of each of these circles one places words which describe each element or category, etc., etc. Until the whole large piece of paper is filled with all of the descriptions, categories and elements of just one dream. The child can draw inside the circles or write words or do both, thus creating a dream map or mural of his or her dreams. These concept maps are used everywhere in the adult world, but in the child's world the power is in sitting down with your child and drawing this personal life story or dream map together. You need to have at least an 18" by 20" or even poster sized piece of paper, and then as you build this map together spend a lot of time discussing each theme or topic in detail with your child, making sure that they fully understand their analysis of this dream, and that you thoroughly understand your child's dream or story. Also make sure that you relay to your children, by repeating what they say to you back to them, a strong bonding of trust and understanding which will put out the message to them that you honor their opinions and ideas. (Check the chart.)

p) The 7 seasons of "Medium" did something no other television show had done before, it brought intuition into American living rooms. The combination of family interaction between a <u>Thinking Intuitive</u> or an analytical, logical father and an <u>Emotional Intuitive</u> or a totally emotionally driven psychic mother and a variety of intuitively gifted children, was sheer genius. Each week the show presented the feeling of what it is like to live in such an intuitive world on a daily basis. Most intuitives live with this left and right brain mix, inside their own heads. Imagine the confusion in interpreting the bits and pieces that come to us out of order and don't really come together until after the event. In other words, many of our interpretations are long in their resolution or are never solved at all. As a parent of highly intuitive children, owning this series and studying the family problems brought up, could be very helpful. However this series does contain many episodes of graphic crime material that is not for children.

q) Two other series can be helpful in understanding dreams and night travel: "Paranormal State" and "Psychic Kids." Watch them first and then determine whether your teens can watch particular episodes which show how children and teens deal with this issue of dreams and night travel, as on "Psychic Kids." Or they address, on Paranormal State," how gifted college kids handle dealing with these and other subjects, holistically.

r) Remember to instill in your children the fact that night time should not be a scary time, but a time for great adventures, great dreams and wonderful imaginings. The story of Peter Pan is a great way to reinforce all this because Peter, Wendy and all of the Lost Boys always win in the end, overcoming every night travel fear and always finding their way home. So reassure your child, whether he or she is astral traveling or simply dreaming, they can always find their way home, finish their dreams and adventures with a happy ending when they wake up, and you will be there to not only catch them when they "fall," but also to comfort them when they awaken.

"One day you will remember the Great Dream, and the way will become known to you. You entered into life through the veil of the Dream, because your reason for being here must be kept secret from you until you find your way home. You don't know who you are, but one fine day you will remember. It is like creation looking for itself. You are in oneness with all life, though you are not aware of it. You will awaken from the Dream. Let the Great Mother rest within your spirit. She is the universe. She is the womb of all life. She is the light that shines from your eyes, illuminating your daily dreams. The possibilities you dream of will become your reality."

--"Dream" The Power Deck
by Lynn Andrews

"Your personal dream is unfolding. You are the dreamer revealing the dream…the dream offers you the opportunity to merge all that you have been and/or may become. Time and space are folding. Stop and feel the interweaving of threads in the new dream. Be aware of potent dreams, chance meetings, catalytic books, and unusual encounters. As you recognize these threads from the larger dream, an exciting tapestry of meaning and purpose emerges…In the collective dreamfield, all things are possible and are constantly being created… Bring the mystic expression of yourself into the dream of your daily life." You are a skywalker into the realms of night.

--"Dreamer & Dreamed," The Mayan Oracle by Ariel Spilsbury & Michael Bryner

CHAPTER TWELVE

Other Gifts:Psychic, Kinetic Gifts & Old Souls – Past Life Memories

"The intuitive mind is a sacred gift and the rational mind is a faithful servant. We have created a society that honors the servant and has forgotten the gift."
--Albert Einstein

"Einstein stood out among natural scientists in his abiding curiosity about children's minds. He once declared that we know all the physics that we will ever need to know by the age of three."
--Creating Minds by Howard Gardner, p.89

Before I talk about the types of intuitives, there are two other areas of concern that I need to address. The fact is that all intuitives are empathic it is just a matter of the degree of this empathy and emotional intelligence, and how deeply it effects the mental, emotional, physical, spiritual and etheric bodies as intuitives go about their daily lives. However, within these types of intuitive gifts, there is a smaller group of super empathic people who are so sensitive that daily life can overwhelm them at every turn. Secondly, most intuitives have both an interest in, and an ability with, either the past, the present or the future. They actually have a forte for one of the three that can spill over into all their other interests as well. For example, I am a history buff because of my ability, interest, and fascination with the past. I would have a lot in common with the psychic archaeologists. Did I develop this interest or was it something I came in with intuitively? Whichever came first, I base what I do on this perspective as does a psychic focused on the present and one focused on the future. And since the focus is on one of the three, the intuitive becomes especially "talented" within their focus area. Just as a psychic who specializes in criminal investigation, learns to shut down their other "channels" and intuit only the hard evidence that criminal investigators would be looking for.

All Psychics & Intuitives are Empathic, it's a Matter of "Degrees"

While all sensitives are empathic, those in this smaller group of "super empaths" deal with not only a daily input of multiple channels, they also deal with chronic ailments and sometimes ridicule from others for being too sensitive, or even being lazy or weak. The best film concerning this topic depicted this type of sensitive in the Tom Cruise movie "Minority Report," where this company has risen to power by intuiting crimes before they happen and then sending a SWAT-type team to stop the crime before it happens by arresting or even killing the criminal way before the crime was suppose to take place. Three "super psychics" are kept in an isolation tank of water, in a deprivation environment. All of their bodily functions are monitored and they are simply asked to intuit 24 hours a day for information on crimes that have not happened yet and relay this information into the organic computers which then send SWAT type teams who go out to collect the criminal. The problem is that the future could be changed by the criminal's decisions, or even the circumstances around each crime, so people were often being falsely arrested or even killed for future events that didn't happen.

These three super psychics or super empaths were made to experience in every dimension of their being, crimes that eventually happened or never happened, therefore, literally being sucked dry of their energies and emotions, and even given their freedom to make their own choices concerning others. Their muscles have atrophied, they are fed intravenously and they only have each other to telepathically communicate with. At the end of the film, while they were eventually rescued and the whole program was shut down, these three intuitives were so damaged that they had to let them live out their lives out in the middle of nowhere in a little log cabin, where no modern technology, modern manmade "channels," or natural "channels" could reach them. While this science fiction film is a bit extreme, it certainly depicted a "super empaths " need for protection and even greater need to sort out the details of anything they are dealing with at any given moment of time in the day, every day. While all psychics have some of this emotional turmoil, the super empathic person is actually in danger of total collapse. They must have many other skills and stabilities to make it from day to day, and some do, while others do not. They may anesthetize themselves with various addictions or even end up leaving the planet for good.

While I experience some of this and am probably closer to the empathic extreme end of the scale, I have learned how to live with this and found enough coping mechanisms, to know myself well enough that I would not choose crime solving or missing person investigations because what surrounds such cases is way too overwhelming for me. On the other hand I am definitely not a "super empathic" but have enough of this to understand those who are often drowning in this energy maze. Those who dealt with traumatic things growing up within their individual families have even more to overcome if they are in this small category of super empathics. And while most sensitives would love, ego-wise, to be one of these people, the reality is that these people's lives are terrifically difficult and horrendously overwhelming. So if you are reading this and think that you may be one, I doubt it. This small group probably wouldn't even be reading this, because they are just trying to survive from day to day.

An example from my own life involves sitting at a lunch table in a gigantic auditorium with hundreds of attendees for a statewide conference for gifted and talented teachers. There was a surprise guest speaker, a well-known poet from Wales whom I happen to know about and had purchased and read some of his poetry books. He was one of my favorites, so I was pleasantly surprised to get to hear him read, switching over to my visual-spatial side immediately, while not expecting my intuitive side to emerge. As he began reading, the entire room disappeared except for me and him. I heard his voice, his musings about old age and fall leaves and about a group of young men going off to war from his little mining town in Wales. Then an even younger group of boys being taken from the misery of their mill and mining town out into the nearby forests by their schoolmaster and asked to hug a tree for the first time and really "feel" that tree and then write about their feelings. The decades collided from every direction and I became quite lost.

As he spoke people began to appear on either side of him on the stage. To the left were two older men, one sitting and one standing, and an older woman. To the right was a row of five equal in height young men in brown leather jackets with what looked like sheep wool linings, standing next to each other. I was at the same time feeling all of the emotions of each of these poems and all the chaotic emotions of the people in the crowd, from impatience and obliviousness, to sadness and empathy. Had I not by then had the knowledge to sort this all out, I would have either been frightened or overwhelmed, or both. And I knew that if I carried even a little bit of what I had been rushed at me, or had stayed there a little longer and allowed any of it to attach itself to me, I would have to spend days releasing this other man's memories. There had been too many "channels" from both the present and the past washing over me. I later wrote the poet to rid myself of these emotions from the past. He was gentlemanly, kind and a believer; because he wrote back confirming all that I had seen and felt. His two fathers, one dead and one living in a wheelchair, his mother, and his RAF schoolmates who had grown up, gone off to war, and having all died, left him to live on alone into his old age. He thought it was wonderful that people who cared about him had decided to drop in on one of his poetry readings, especially his old RAF mates.

Healers have this problem too when working with even a single individual. One of my friends, sharing a similar past with a client, jumped in, opened this core issue and as it flooded into her hands, she was knocked to the floor, because in connecting with this client, it became a mutual healing or releasing for both of them. That's why I always tell energy workers to do their before and after work with each client. Sit down and talk to your client and find out why they came, and know ahead of time what you share with them. After the energy work, sit down again and talk about every aspect of what was done, no matter how crazy it sounds to the client, and make sure they are in a good place before they leave. If you set yourself up to heal or release any kind of emotions in another, then you are ethically and morally responsible to have some training in a therapy work, no matter how you achieve this goal. Take a few classes, attend holistic workshops, read, or actually go to school in a related field, or, don't open such a gigantic wound in the first place and be aware that you will be affected by all the emotions around you, just as the client has. Teaching was a good training ground for me, and especially the years spent in special education, where one-to-one counseling went on all the time with parents and students.

Are You Interested in the Past, the Present or the Future?

As well as having certain fortes, most psychics have a special interest or ability with the future, past or present. In choosing to go to a psychic, consider this interest too. Perhaps you only want to know about the present and don't really care to delve into the past. Perhaps you want a quick perspective on your life only from the present. Or you want to delve deeper than this through several generations from the past, into past-lives, dramatic losses and maybe even a spiritual crisis that may be affecting your present actions. Some people just want to know what the future might bring, even though we are all masters of our own destinies and have to make our own choices anyway. Obviously I am a "past" person with my fascination of people from the past, historical sites, ghosts and these unanswered mysteries from the past. So my readings will be influenced by these things, especially when it comes to looking at one's own past or a client's. One reviewer of my ghost books said that she fell asleep in her bathtub and nearly drown from boredom, having to read all those dates and names and places that meant nothing to her. I had a great chuckle at this because obviously history was not of interest to her, it was probably the present's mysteries, that excited her, or imagining possible futures that could intrigue or even frighten her. To me history holds great unsolved mysteries, and even answers to the mistakes we make in the present, that would not be made if we had really delved into the past and unlocked its secrets. Ghosts are everywhere and even under the place where we are standing or sitting right now. Ghosts of the past are dates and places and names and experiences that we can be intrigued by, learn from, and either be frightened by or awakened by. "Not to know what happened before you were born is to remain a child forever." It is pretty obvious that our spiritual inheritance is very vital now. (*Anonymous author*)

Children Who Hear Things, Smell Things, Sense & Feel Things - Empaths

I have spent a lot of time already talking about empathic children. It seems that while this is the beginning stage of any intuitive gift, sensing things or feeling things in a certain atmosphere or in a room or from a particular person or group of people, it is also the stage where people begin to realize that they are empathic. This doesn't just mean that the person picks up on the feelings of others or has empathy and compassion for others it also means that these people "soak in" all of these feelings or emotions left in a place or taken from a person or persons. Most importantly, it is vital to understand that all intuitive or psychic people are usually extremely empathic. They developed their other gifts from this empathic foundation and have to deal with these types of sensitivities every day of their lives. They actually take on the emotions of others or the emotions left in a place or building, and they can even project into the future what feelings and emotions are coming into a certain person or place. They are likely to pick up on national or international disasters through the feelings produced both by the people in the disaster but also from animals, plants and the earth itself.

This is why most of this book is directed towards empathic people, which all true intuitives are. This is because they need so much help in channeling, sorting, controlling, managing, and deciphering all of this sensate information that bombards them especially if they don't have ways to protect themselves. And since most intuitives have to deal with these tremendous amounts of incoming sensations and feelings, they really do need to become adept at not only protecting themselves, but also interpreting the information that they are receiving. Empathic people suffer from so many sensitivities when they cannot do this. They are likely to have loads of anxiety, depression, panic attacks, and various other maladies or chronic ailments, if they don't learn to use their talents effectively and even if they do. If they have other gifts, which are stronger and more accurate, empathic people cannot reach their potential in these other areas when all these feelings and emotions are flooding in. If they learn to control and manage their empathic senses, they can then use all of their other gifts more accurately and with less painful interference from the many "radio" stations which can bombard them all at once. These channels need to be either turned down low or turned off, so that only one or two are coming through at a time. So many frequencies can really disturb the physical, mental, emotional, energy body and even the spiritual body to the point that the empathic person can collapse from exhaustion, pull inward for protection, choose to anesthetize themselves with one or more addictive "blockers" or consistently express their frustrations loudly and chaotically. Instead, they need to find healthy ways to shut down their heart and third eye openings, so that they can focus on only one or two things at a time. Electrical storms and sometimes other more extreme weather conditions can especially lay them low for a while.

Children Who Use Psychometry & Have A Sense of Touch - Energy Workers

Jim Gilkeson in his great book entitled Energy Healing: a Pathway to Inner Growth, tells of an incident when he was a young man while visiting with some friends in Italy. About twenty friends were staying with the mother of one of these friends. She herself was a mystic and poet and the whole group had danced and then sang way past midnight on New Year's Eve. He was helping to wash the dishes and was entrusted with drying off a family heirloom, an intricately designed glass fruit bowl. He picked up the bowl to dry it and it simply shattered in his hands for absolutely no reason. He was terribly mortified and felt awful about this incident. A few weeks later he received a poem from his friend's mother that was an ode to this family heirloom. The end of the poem stated "…and hands, which should be busy healing, broke it." This one incident began Gilkeson's forty year journey as an energy healer. Jim Gilkeson is a licensed massage therapist with training in meditation work and body work. For those doing body and energy work, his life story is quite interesting and will inspire you to keep getting more and more varied and interesting trainings! (*Ibid., pp.7-8*).

Psychometrics

Psychometrics is the ability to hold an inanimate object and "read" the object. All objects have a slightly different energy field, and a slightly different vibration. Objects will absorb a person's particular vibration as well as the vibrations of things around the object. But they also have their own particular frequency too. The person who is able to read this energy cannot only help find missing objects, give clues to the police who are trying to solve a crime through feeling objects associated with the crime, but also use particular kinds of objects in healing work, such as crystals, etc. You can actually do a psychic reading using objects from the person, and for the people the objects might be involved with. Tips on "reading" an object include directing your thoughts into the object, paying attention to the information and sensation that you receive from the object, and interpreting the information that you receive. The most accurate information will be received within the first 24 to 48 hours, after working with the object. However, very strong emotions will stay with the object's vibrations for many years. How much you can tell about past owners depends on the object's history and checking objects left behind or brought into the home that might be suspected of holding negative energy or at least active energy would be a wise thing to do. Getting rid of them is best!

I can remember two examples of this from my own experiences. In the first experience I was asked to hold part of an old- fashioned pipe, it came from the artifacts, where Johnson's Army camped in Utah to keep tabs on the Mormons. So in this case, I knew that this particular pipe had probably belonged to a soldier. However, I described what the soldier looked like, his plumed and ornate high top hat, unusual for a Civil War era soldier, how he cut his hair and what his sideburns, beard and mustache looked like, as well as his unusual uniform. The woman who had handed it to me, just happen to know who had owned this particular pipe because he had been a member of the camp band and did wear an unusual uniform with a higher top hat and a giant plume on it. In the other instance, a woman had brought a box of rocks, just to see if I would get anything off any of the items in the box. There were a few things, but one rock stood out in particular. After I felt it for awhile, I told her that I could see an underground apartment with a mother and her two little children in it. It was very dark, because the windows were closed off with a sort of black fog. A man in some kind of uniform broke in the front door and grabbed one of the children and ran out carrying this child. He came back for the other two but he was too late. I didn't know where the man was, nor did I know just what was happening, except that it was some sort of disaster. The woman who had brought the box of objects told me that this was a rock she had picked up from the Oklahoma bombing site when they stopped there on their way home from a trip. To this day, I don't know whether I picked up on particular people, or the famous photo of the fireman, carrying the little child out of the rubble.

Energy Work

Energy workers or body workers have training in a particular method, but most often add on many other methods that they learn along the way. The most popular currently, are the many types of Reiki. These people might be acupuncture or acupressure specialists, massage therapists, Reiki Masters, Touch for Health or EFT facilitators, Chi-Gong Masters, Therapeutic Touch nurses, or Breama Balance practitioners, etc., but they all work with the energies along hundreds of meridian points located on and through the body, which is also called the energetic or auric field that extends outside the body and encircles it with different layers of energy. Even Mother Theresa developed a energetic rubbing form of therapeutic touch for her nursing students to work on children in India. They brought about a few "miracles" for these suffering children too. I have already mentioned some excellent books for learning to use your own healing hands at home with loved ones. The best one is Quantum Touch by Richard Gordon, if you want to learn a simple method for doing this on your own. Another of his books, Your Healing Hands: The Polarity Experience would also be an invaluable resource for self-healing techniques. The best one concerning using various types of energy healing, for various types of problems is the one called Healing Hands put out by Prevention Magazine. There are many types of energy work and many books or workshops on this subject, and there are many complex energy healing techniques.

So if you are interested in healing and want to go this route, there are just so many types and so many different kinds of training, from a few classes to years of intensive and deep energy work that you would have to simply choose what appeals to you and what you can afford. Most energy workers begin with a certain type of training, and then learn many other types of training, and create their own style of healing work. But one can use simple energy healing methods at home for loved ones that will help prevent physical difficulties, or contribute to one feeling better or more comfortable while being treated by a medical doctor or an alternative health care professional, although this should never replace necessary treatments. For those on the extremely sensitive side and you are the only ones who know who you are, Japanese Shiatsu which is a gentle and light touch therapy, is the best way to go when having your body actually touched, especially because the therapists who learn this particular technique would probably have an understanding of how therapeutic touch interacts with the energy body, as well as those requiring this sort of less invasive therapy in the first place!

My favorite story about natural born healers was on one of the "Psychic Kids" episodes on A&E. There are so many types of energy work and so many types of cultures and individuals doing this work that it is best to pick what one resonates too and go from there. But the world does have natural born healers, who, whether they train in energy work or not, can simply heal, or at least, soothe the aches and pains for many people. In one of the episodes on the program, a little seven-year-old girl was asked to diagnose one of the other little girl's chronic condition or disease without knowing anything about it. The little girl lay down on a table, and the other little girl, without any training at all, ran her hands about 2 to 4 inches above the other girl's body. This little "healer" did have an adult energy worker with her, to help her find a way to diagnose the problem by drawing it. The little girl, after telling the adult where she felt the problems were located in the body, began to draw. She drew a tangled maze of black crayon lines, and on these lines were scattered red blotches or drops. It turned out that the other little girl had a rare blood disease, and with a little more training, the other little girl could have located where the difficult areas were in this mass of black lines called the blood system. And the reason this is my favorite story, is because the natural born healer, when trained, or even without training, simply has this ability.

Many people in this field have to work hard to gain the same ability and accuracy as the natural born healers. Of course there are many con artists, but those sincere enough understand all the other factors necessary in performing a cooperative healing and know that their role in the healing is simply to be a channel for all the rest. Intent, belief, determination, other holistic therapies and nutritional remedies, medical exams and some procedures, hours of prayer and meditation, intuitive communication between healer and client, the right time in someone's life and even the right place where many others have brought their healing energies with them, and much more, contributes to an actual healing. There is no mystery to all this, except that none of it has been studied thoroughly yet. And just a note for taking workshops and other trainings for energy work certifications, it is my own opinion that if the therapy costs thousands of dollars or even hundreds, be aware that you may not learn as much as you would with a middle of the road dollar figure. A training that costs too little may also be suspect. In the middle ground you are more likely to find those sincere people who want you to really learn things that will help your clients rather than take your money and valuable time.

Some of the things psychic healers must go through before setting themselves up to heal others are: assessing their own healing powers, healing themselves first, discovering which tools will work best for them in their healing work, and continuously exploring all the many healing modalities and techniques. Along with their hands, they may end up using essential oils, crystals, sound, color, Aroma Therapy, Spinal Touch, massage therapy, Touch for Health, Polarity Therapy, Reflexology, Craniosacral Therapy, Therapeutic Touch, Shiatsu, and a host of other touch therapies. The biggest problem I see in energy or body-work is that many people get caught up in the rules, regulations, details, and methods, and they end up disagreeing on how this is to be done. They end up missing the point, the point being, that all energy comes from the same source and healing is performed in similar ways, regardless of the technique. Healing work is an agreement between the patient and the healer, and involves belief, openness, and channeling help from the waves and frequencies being used in this work among many other things including guides and mentors. Hopefully in the future rather than bickering with each other over techniques and procedures, all energy workers will form communities to share their various techniques and emotional, mental, and spiritual "map," for a person's life challenges. While there are many centers who do work harmoniously, we still have a long way to go. This energy field reveals patterns of thought, as well as the flow of physical and emotional energy, and will show any areas that need healing or energizing. Some healers can see the energy field to diagnose, while others sense the fields of energy with their hands. But all touch and energy healing therapists work very hard at their profession whether they lean towards sports medicine which focuses on the physical body, or closer to the spiritual side of the spectrum, where the focus is not only on the body mechanics but also on the emotional releases and spiritual issues as the body is being worked on.

Visualizers in the Mind's Eye, Moving Pictures, Remote Viewing – The Seers

For this category I will tell my own journey or the stages I went through to visualize pathways concerning each person I "read." But it was interesting to read about the four types of imaging that Atwater talked about in her near-death experiences research, which correlated to what a clairvoyant psychic would see in developing their own private vocabulary of pictures. Atwater named them, you might recall, as: Personal Imagery or taken from one's own life, Mass Mind Imagery or taken from collective humankind images, Memory Field Imagery or cultural and universal symbols or imagery and Truth Imagery which is transcendent and spiritual. These are right on for psychics too, only I had to find my own way as an adult and this makes it easier to tell you what those stages were. I am sure now, however, that I had these abilities as a child but left them behind me and had to rediscover them later. I am also sure the first stage is feeling the atmosphere in a room and the second is beginning to recognize signs and symbols or your own "waking dream" vocabulary, whether visual or three dimensional, and then putting these patterns of symbols together and interpreting them as accurately as possible in the physical world.

After my initial few readings that happened by accident and were simplistic but in bright colors, rather like how a kindergartener would see things, I realized that in every case there was heavy cloud cover over them before I somehow in my mind began to clear them away and break them up to get to the pictures. My very first reading was very short and simplistic and happened after a Spiral Path study group class late at night when one lady stayed afterwards and asked me to do a real reading for her. I had been doing some just for fun because a few of the people stayed behind and wanted me to do this so they would not have to pay the fifty dollars to our guest speaker and they thought I could do it. It was all a joke to me until this one woman, quite seriously requested me to "read" for her. During the reading I flew into the sky and saw lots of clouds, as they cleared away I saw a commercial airplane headed for Hawaii, beautiful islands, girls in grass skirts giving out leis and quite a beautiful, serene picture. The plane landed safely and everyone was having a party. It all seemed quite silly until the woman thanked me. She said that she had been worried about her son's state of mind and I had put her at peace. I was mystified, until she explained that he was an airline pilot and flew a route between the various South Pacific islands and the United States. He had been very depressed because of recently losing his girlfriend and his mother was concerned about him. My reading had put her mind at ease because it seemed his future was bright ahead and he was headed for much fun and happiness through his work and new relationships. I can remember I sat there until one o'clock in the morning after she left and kept going over the vision in my mind, wondering what on earth had just happened. And that was the start of deciding to "practice" on all my friends who would let me.

In another early reading, which were all short and child-like before I began to practice seriously, a friend of mine had asked me to look in on her brother and see how he was doing. She didn't tell me that she didn't know where he was or what he was doing and had not seen him for several years nor that he struggled with various addictions. I saw her brother constructing a huge Lego land of buildings and bridges, all in the bright colors of these children's toys. He was also using erector sets with the huge Lego building set. I had to break through a Lego wall to get to where he was and saw that he had a girlfriend with him who looked like the earth mother type or what they call today, a "greenie" or environmentalist. And at first I thought her brother was in California because of the Lego Land place located there, until I saw the girl he was with which led me to Oregon instead. How I really got there is still a mystery to me. Anyway, before I left the place where I had known this woman, she told me that she heard from her brother. He was living with a girl in Oregon and he was actually an architect. While he probably wasn't working at his profession, I felt as though I had seen into his dreams, perhaps as a little boy or even in a fantasy land where he was constructing things. My friend at that time was very happy because she wasn't worried now about her brother, he was with someone and he apparently still had his "dreams."

After this, when I really began to try and work on seeing these objects more clearly, I went inward and tried squinting my eyes, in my mind's eye, to try and see beyond or through all the cloud cover or fog or whatever to see the individual objects more clearly. As I cleared the clouds off and they grew more opaque and more thinly veiled, I could then see misty geometric shapes in grays and blacks and whites. I saw squares and triangles and circles, which eventually began to form into something more recognizable as objects or colors or even human, animal or plant forms. Eventually I got more detail and the colors began to appear and this made it easier to discern and helped me to recognize what object or shape I was looking at. I then began to see all the details of each thing I was looking at but I could only see them in still pictures or as if they were moving over each other in different directions. Sort of like giant unseen hands were moving them about like a person putting a puzzle together and shuffling through the puzzle pieces. Then finally I began to see silent moving pictures before me or even type written words and phrases because I rarely to this day hear these words, only see them or just have a "knowing."

I finally arrived at the ability to move myself inside these movies or scenarios, walking beside the person's images coming from their own minds or auric fields or somewhere? I would view them from a distance, walk right beside the person I was reading as they experienced their memories and futures, or even moved about on my own to gather information like a remote viewer or astral traveler would. I could go anywhere, see anything, but then in many cases not know what I was seeing. You make those leaps of faith or belief or "knowings" that tell you there is no time or distance anywhere in the multiverse and that you can see anywhere in the multi-verse or on this planet, etc. You begin to build a huge vocabulary of repeating images that tell you very quickly what this person might be hearing or seeing or feeling. You open "rusty metal doors" of defenses or feel yourself inside their mother's womb and what kind of birth it was and how even this affects the outcomes in each person's life. You are using every sense to empower this person to move forward and change the patterns in their life that have imprisoned them and to free them for more understanding and progression on their own path.

Examples of a consistent visual vocabulary symbol which brings back a picture from the person's own history, include a young woman who I saw standing on a football field when a lightning strike came down from the sky and sliced down through her body diagonally. This picture was totally in blacks and whites and grays and looked rather cartoonish. I wasn't sure just what I had seen until later in the reading when she told me that she had been raped at knife point in a wide open field. This action had dramatically changed her life and the person she was today, just as being struck by lightning and surviving this, would have. Or, I saw a man fall to the ground being struck by lightning and in his case he had had a heart attack which had dramatically changed his life as well. After a while I knew that the symbol or action of being struck by lightning meant a dramatic and traumatic incident that actually created a new consciousness in the body, an actual "new "person out of the old one. And when I saw a mass of metal all wound around itself, this was some sort of car accident or motorcycle accident, from which emerged a "new "person, or a near-death experiencer who had come out the other side, never to be the same again. Or often I would see from a side view, a little girl or boy begin to glide down a long slide at the park, but as they started down they grew older and older until they were an adult when they reached the bottom of the slide. But in the course of following this slow motion sliding, we have taken a journey together in the process, leaping from place to place where events happened to dramatically change their decisions and choices as they grew older.

But this is only how I got to where I am now. Along the way came a new journey which was going into the physical body, an internal visit rather than an external one to help the person deal with illness and physical pain. My healing hands came last and this was very new and difficult to incorporate into the rest of it. But every clairvoyant is somewhat of a medium too, because sooner or later there are a few spirit visitors coming in who either guide you or are related to or guide your sitter. Sometimes you only get what I call a slide projector or power point presentation of pictures and then you have to interpret them. I often feel these beings with their hands on my shoulders as they stand behind me but I never see them. Instead they usually speak to me by showing me pictures to interpret or just giving me a "knowing." I am sometimes shown visions to relate to the sitter and then of course I have to interpret these visions for or with the sitter, depending on how in tune they are themselves. But even rarer still are the actual visitations where one sees and feels the energy or frequency of the person who has passed on or is from some other place, and they literally use your energy to visit the client. I feel or see pictures, or hear a voice speaking inside my own head and usually in these cases the person who has come to see me is in a terrible crisis. But I am sure every "reader" experiences these things in different ways. Multi-dimensional visits are still considered too bizarre to share with anyone, and if you do, it's "Never, Neverland" for you!

But you do begin to get future events, past events, and present ones as the immensity of the world around you opens up and the unseen worlds start to become a bit more visible. They say that many of the new children coming in have some of these abilities already in them and that they will not lay them on a shelf, like many of us older intuitives did. They will instead, demand to be heard and seen and understood. Some will find our planet just too painful to stay on, while others will thrive silently and in a hidden way. Still others though, will stand up and want to be counted, so the so-called "shift" is quite real at least in terms of our spiritual and brain function evolutions are concerned. But remember, this is only how it happened to me and your journey will probably be quite different. Many psychics use tools of one kind or another, but I only did this in the early days when I wasn't sure of what I was sensing. Once I began to "see" clearly I did not need tools except for myself when trying to make decisions of one kind or another or gathering confirmations about my work. I also like to contemplate how to read auric fields, understand cellular memories, or find better ways to travel into my own mind and heart or into the heart of another. Scientists have found that psychics' brain waves and heart rhythms begin to match their clients at the beginning of the reading and remain that way until the reading ends. Then the brain waves separate and each person's heart beat goes back to its own individual rhythm.

You can begin developing your clairvoyant skills by staring at a smooth shiny surface, like you are looking into a doorway of time and space. Going into a trance you can begin to see images in a mirror, crystal ball, a dark pool of water, ink, polished metal or a mirror in a darkened room, etc. Information arrives "...in the form of pictures, symbols, letters, impressions, and sensations, which appear in answer to a question that you or another puts forward." I started by closing my eyes to shut out all external information but eventually did not need to do this when just giving information, but I still do this, when I am receiving a vision or moving picture information, so that I will not lose any of the details. These scrying tools are a way to begin to clarify and clear those "clouds" away and much faster in getting to the root of the matter rather than wasting time on cards, pendulums, etc. These "crutches" can eventually get in your way, although they are also a great way to get started and a lot of people who continue to use a tool have moved on anyway to true readings because they often say that they use the tool to make the sitter feel more comfortable when they can actually see something tangible in front of them. On the other hand, there are systems or techniques which work well without using any intuition at all, such as astrology, numerology, handwriting analysis or palmistry; even tea leaves and interpreting body language have a system to them that seem to really work just as well as a direct line. This only reinforces my belief that there are simply different channels to get to the same information, information available to not only the blindfolded but those who already "see." Tools are great to keep a focus point for both the reader and the client. It helps to keep the reader focused on only one channel while adding in their intuitive information as they go along. For me, keeping it chronological works, but I can see that various tools can add to the reading immensely in terms of provided information as well as the intuited material. (*How Psychic Are You? By Julie Soskin, Penguin Books, p.90-91*).

Children Who See Auras, Colors & Do Internal Diagnostics – The "Medics"

"Recent studies using blindfold tests have shown that people can "sense" when someone is staring at them intently, even if they can't see the person doing it. Researchers believe that this information is picked up within the aura." It is the opinion of many psychics who do readings for others that they are reading the auric field of the person sitting in front of them. That we all carry, right down to the cellular level, not only specific information about all areas of our lives, both past and future, but that this information can easily be read by an intuitive or sensitive. An interesting comment on this, is that ghost investigation teams using thermal imaging cameras have upon occasion accidentally caught an exchange between two people, in which there was a dance of color energies or heat images between them, that when joined together, created a communication channel for the psychic reader to read the sitter. One must first feel the aura as an energy worker would, before being able to see the auras around our bodies. And as I have said before, while many claim to see bright colors, I see more of a thin, filmy, waif of steam like substance coming off of the body in very subtle and barely discernable colors. Occasionally I do get bright rings of color inside objects and around them with my eyes completely shut and asking to see what is inside the object helps. Traveling down into the object is the same as looking inside the body but I have to have my eyes shut when I do this and ask the other side for help. (*Ibid., p.42*).

In diagnosing illness, healers can feel the energies, while being a clairvoyant myself I see the illness in either a symbolic form or as an actual diseased organ. My interpretation of this started out as snakes and nests, the nests being the organs and the snakes being the foreign or diseased substance or growth. Later I actually began to see the organs but I am not always sure of my anatomy and so keep a big book of anatomy about, to check before I send the person on to a doctor or healer. Is it any wonder that Andrew Jackson Davis, the famous American 19th century psychic, with no formal schooling, eventually went to medical school because it must have been frustrating to not be absolutely sure just what is being seen inside the person's body and then not to be able to follow through as a doctor would be able to. It is also possible to diagnose long distance but one cannot be quite as accurate as when you have the person right in front of you. While many healers, including myself, can make a person feel more comfortable, few of us can actually heal others. So I stick to diagnosing and let the experts, be they doctors or holistic healers, do their work, although I might opt on occasion to do a brief energizing of the body with my hands a few inches away from the skin.

Recently I have found that I can reduce the pain level and that my hands heat up to activate and cool down when I am to stop. And it seems to be that my hands heat up for physical problems, but tingle in a loving energy for relieving emotional stresses. But each person practicing this has to find their own ways to "read" energy, as it is very, very individual. The places to be worked on for me have no feeling at all to them, while everywhere else I feel either a pulsation, tingling or a just a knowing. I have also learned that the comfort level reached for the client is more powerful if one is under absolutely no pressure to perform or accomplish anything. The healer and the client must have a mutual intention and belief, and I do my healings for no pay which solves every one of these problems, although I realize that many others cannot do this. An intuitive counseling session is advice and time given, so this is a different issue. And just lately I find that when I do place my whole palms on a place, my hands get red hot and then cool off when it is time to stop. But only my close friends and those who ask me to keep someone comfortable while dying, get this sort of treatment because I feel I can trust them. My training in Touch For Health, Educational Kinesiology or Edu-K, Chi-Gong and Breama Balance combined with my awakening natural healing abilities have helped me to help my friend's aches and pains and this is a very private path for me, between the person that I care for and my own communications with them or whoever they lead me to.

Healing for those of us who can do a little of this seems to be a hit and miss proposition at present, although sometimes healing does take place or at least offers some comfort to the person. There seem to be several things involved in successful healing: intent and belief on the part of the healer and the patient, trust, relaxation and little doubt, a certain amount of self-healing that has been completed, hours of meditation and frequency ascension due to spiritual work done by both parties. Endless hours in a hospital bed or a strong connection between friends or relatives can often induce healing without needing assistance at all. Then there is group healing where the amount of energy generated can cause some to instantly heal, such as at Lourdes or Medjugorje and other famous places where people go on pilgrimages in hopes of healing. There are also transitional healings when a person is dying, or folk remedies and herbals used throughout the ages to help a person heal. There are many charlatans, but there are also rare, true healers who seem to have a direct line to "the Source." Someday, the connection between healer and patient will have a natural flow that has at long last become an "exact science," based on scientific principles, identifying the correct invading pathogens or bacteria and on the computer using the specific frequencies to wipe them out. And perhaps one day in the far future, we will be able to be this exact, using only our own minds and hands.

For myself I am content with scanning inside the body in my mind's eye, locating the approximate area and type of thing, seeing an image or aura color for the problem, and then sending the person on to a doctor for a more thorough and precise examination. I have seen crohn's disease as a bunch of grapes hanging about inside certain areas of the body or a tumor as a black almond shape. And I know if the illness is progressing because I see an aura from a light green and gradations of this to a brown and finally to black, which tells me that it is in a very dangerous and life threatening stage. Because scanning the body internally is just like remote viewing, you can get confused when viewing both past and future injuries and illnesses. So you have to be very careful not to plant the wrong "seed of thought" in the person's head about future events and do a bit of generalizing unless it is something that is urgent and should be checked right away. But I am sure that each person's experience is entirely different and how you develop your vocabulary of auras and pictures can be very different. Or you may tune into Atwater's four types of imagery in a different way. Diagnosing is either empathic and sensory or visual pictures in the mind's eye or both. One can develop this skill as can children, and then one simply needs to refine it to be more accurate. What is done after this is up to the individual whether energy healer, body worker, chiropractor or doctor, etc. It is best to traverse both worlds thoroughly for now. Someday it will all be one world and that will certainly be more convenient for the patient.

Another way of recognizing a health problem as a clairvoyant is to get a vision concerning the person's primary obstacles health wise and really a major theme or pattern in their life. An example of a vision as opposed to a remote viewing into the body itself was when a young woman came for a reading and while not concentrating on her health at all, I suddenly received the following vision early in the reading. She was a little approximately eight year-old girl standing to the right of a huge tree which loomed over her like a tree of life would. All of the tree's branches brushed on the ground; it was very dark and glistened all over. Like a willow tree, it had long strings of leaves or more like globules or little solid rain drops, glowing and glistening in the darkness because the sun had just gone down. As I looked at this vision I was puzzled, until suddenly, and of its own accord, the tree began to slowly rotate in a circle, while inverting itself, and finally was turned upside down. Its trunk and roots hung way up in the air over the little girl and the long strings or network of leaves became what they really were, a literal shower of very long branches on which thousands of tiny leaves brushed down like delicate strings of tiny and glistening black beads. Their glistening shadowy auras, made me realize that I was looking at thousands of little air sacks attached to the lung's many "branches." I realized then that these were her lungs which loomed over her tiny frame in the darkness.

I asked her if she had anything wrong with her lungs and her whole life came tumbling out. She had been diagnosed with a very long named and quite rare lung disease when she was a child. She had had several operations when young and several near-death experiences. When she was just eight years old, in her most dramatic near-death experience, she had had a rather long operation in which her right lung had collapsed. She died for several minutes during the surgery, and had gone quite a distance into the other side before being pulled back. She had floated above her body, had gone through the tunnel and towards the light, but had been given the choice of returning. When she began to return, she was suddenly yanked back into life. When I first saw her, she was a young woman with this disease looming over her. I have known this woman for years now and she is still healthy and with us.

In another case, the woman was going to the doctor for a pain she had in her side. She had been for a reading before and so she asked me to look at the area and tell her if I saw anything. So when I saw the baseball sized but black almond shaped tumor where she had pointed to the pain, I simply told her to have the doctor do an ultrasound and an x-ray and insist on this if he wasn't planning to do both of them. I was very adamant that he check this area thoroughly, but I did not tell her about what I had seen, nor did I tell her the size of it. I wasn't sure if it was a tumor or a cyst, but the black color meant it was in a very dangerous state. I heard from her some weeks later. She had had an operation and was fully recovered. It had been a tumor after all and the doctor had successfully removed it. It wasn't malignant and she was going to be fine and she had called me to let me know.

Children Who Hear Noises, Frequencies, Telepathy – Listeners & Channelers

The difference between seeing visions and hearing them, is that those who have the strongest intuitive abilities in the auditory mode, have a finely tuned listening skill that picks up on tones and sounds and frequencies that the rest of us cannot hear. They may hear voices, although if they talk about this, this will often get them in trouble with therapists and loved ones who do not understand the difference between intuiting voices and imagining them, or even deluding them. These people can pick up on sounds from other dimensions or universes, other planets, other countries on the globe, and even tune in to what their next door neighbors are saying. These children can have various difficulties sorting all this information out with their many auditory "channels." They are also more likely to think that they are going crazy, because there is a much bigger stigma for hearing things than there is for seeing things. Helping each child to sort out what is real, and not real, varies with these particular children. One might also guess that most of our child prodigy composers and musicians were quite clairaudient channelers. They could hear the sounds, then put them together and often channel these sounds, into new compositions using other frequencies or rays, literally interpreting the "music of the spheres," Like I am sure other composers have from the past.

These children are also the ones who are probably the best at telepathic communication and listening to others and really being able to repeat back what they have heard in detail. They may also be our best musicians, composers, singers, and sound technicians, etc. They can also be very sensitive to sounds out of the range of tones and pitches that most of us can hear. This is both a good and bad thing, because on the one hand, hearing these various sounds, voices and phrases, etc. can give them special capabilities in many fields of endeavors. On the other hand, it makes them very sensitive to all of these external and internal sounds, even within the body, so that they may be dealing with more sensitivities, chronic ailments, and more severe illnesses than the rest of us. One might say that having this as your primary gift, is a much harder road than being clairvoyant, clairsentient or clairkinetic. People with this super ability, can really suffer when surrounded by electrical lines, power stations, construction equipment or road work, and many other noise pollutants in our society today, including large, noisy crowds of people. Even my crystal bowls are hard on these particular "hearing" intuitives, as are changes in the weather and all the environmental sounds that modern man has infused into our world.

Channeling

Channeling is done either in "automatic writing" or in hearing someone dispense information through the auditory channel. This particular type of intuition can often either contain a dramatic play acting performance or a trickster spirit pretending to be a guru or master teacher. They might decide to piggyback or form a parasitic relationship with the live person for many years. However, they are also real "masters" or "avatars" who really do channel their information to a fortunate person who has reached a certain high frequency or spiritual level, or simply a person who is naturally intuitive and gifted in many psychic ways. So it is hard to determine just what is happening in channeling cases. There are very famous channelers who are religious leaders, great mystics or saints with a direct channel to God. But there are also many intuitives out there that are being duped in various ways by the "unseen," or are tricking others themselves. A few great channelers write and speak for years dispensing spiritual information to their followers. Again, determining what is real and what is imagined, negative, or faked, is very difficult to do in this particular area of psychic work, although thorough dissecting of this channeled information may reveal a conglomeration of thoughts that have already been presented by previous live 'masters.' I would speculate that consistent positive information with good intent combined with newly channeled information gained over a long period of time, is the best way that one can tell the difference.

Channelers are receiving information from another dimension, another realm, and another time in the future or past, and or perhaps even from another species. Many famous writers, composers, inventors and in many other kinds of professions, could be considered "channelers" because they received information in their dreams or even daydreams which led them to invent something, compose something, finish a theorem or write a great masterpiece, etc. So the idea of channeling information is pretty acceptable, even when perhaps a famous composer seems to mimic the work of another famous composer long since dead. This universal life stream, or universal consciousness or as some call it the Akashic Record, is the idea that all of the history of the universe and the earth and its inhabitants is contained in this huge repository from which all of us can "channel" information. So therefore, we all have the capability of channeling either new or used information which we can then take and put together in a new way to present something seemingly new to mankind. So channeling itself is a viable idea, but channelers who transfigure into their great master or guru still make me suspect. But that is only me. However, I know that for myself I have certainly channeled information into my stories or writings from other dimensions or frequency levels or perhaps even past lives without even knowing it. So anything is possible!

In the Russian research, rather than calling this channeling from the universal Akashic Records, they took a different view of this and named it Artificial Reincarnation. Because they saw this ability to either reproduce these creative or inventive works from the great masters, or add on to what they had done, or even rearrange it as the student's own master work, as a technique which could be taught to anyone under the guise of what they thought was a person able to "reincarnate" the great master through his or her works. And how they did this was to place the subject in a deep trance and then implant the idea that the person was the reincarnation of a great master. The people who did this were able to do things they normally could not do in their waking state at first, such as read and write music or oil paint without any training, dance like a ballerina, sing like an opera star, etc. Eventually, after several sessions, the person was able to do these tasks in a waking state and with great accuracy. The theory is that the person is drawing from the collective unconscious and their own cellular memories, while using more of their brain power than we at present know how to do. This explains why many modern day geniuses are able to do this very thing, draw from geniuses from the past, to create and combine entirely new inventions or ideas and even explore creative endeavors from multiple perspectives. They are, in a sense, literally inhabiting the consciousness of those who have passed before us and drawing from multiple sources, to create something more refined from the past or even the future. They can literally become a particular person from the past enough to produce exact copies of that person's works or inventions; when they were not familiar with them before this. Channeling is like the internet, make sure who you are talking to is really who they say they are!

Kinetic Kids: Moving & Rearranging Matter, Poltergeist Myth – The Movers

The theory about young children or teenagers affecting movement of objects is that this is simply a walking energy field that can be sent out from a person. That people who have this particular ability can be taught to control and use this energy like a human remote control, i.e. remote viewing, psycho-kinesis or telekinesis, teleportation, bi-location, etc. The child or teen has not yet learned to focus or control this ability and many do this on their own without training of any kind. However, for our purposes, let us look at how various spiritual practices view this phenomenon. One theory is that our spiritual life force or "chi" is at a certain level or frequency of vibration, as all living and inanimate things in the world have their own vibrational frequency. These outbursts of energy are simply at a higher frequency level than people are, so this is how spiritual energy meets solid matter sometimes quite dramatically or even explosively!

Most kinetic kids are simply experiencing one of their intuitive gifts that sometimes are blamed on other phenomena when it manifests. Objects fly or lights dim or go on and off, there are knockings on the wall, doors and drawers open or shut on their own, and technical equipment breaks down. It is proposed that such things as table tipping and Ouija boards are simply manifestations of this phenomenon by someone in the room who either does not know they are doing this or they are perfectly aware that they are. While many American scientists insist that most of these abilities have proven to be unreal as yet, scientists in other countries take these things quite seriously. Scientists in Australia teleported a laser beam encoded with data, broke it up and then reconstructed an exact replica nearby. They teleported light by destroying the light beam and created their copy from light particles known as photons. Someday this technology will be used for teleporting matter and someday, we will be able to do this with our minds alone! Children totally blind from birth have proven to be quite capable of identifying colors through touch alone and people off the street can be trained to remote view anywhere in the world, or skin read text and colors, as well as use psychometry to read objects and histories or even futures, with a bit of training, although there is a smaller group of genetically produced intuitives who trained themselves and are better at it.

What can you do as a parent? Tell them what you know about this phenomenon and what current research acknowledges. Discuss your child's fears about this and help them to understand that there is nothing wrong with them. This is something that simply happens to many people. Those who do readings or are energy workers and all who are in touch with their own intuitive gifts, joke about effecting electrical equipment all the time. However, there is a theory about this too, that when a psychic or healer has this happen in a very pronounced way, their "polarity" is off. This means that the negative and positive balance in the body is not in balance just like the negative/positive ends of a battery grow weak and slow things down or cause them to work erratically. The polarity has to be fixed or re-balanced to stop these brief bursts of energy from being thrown off and causing objects to move or electronic equipment to malfunction. This is accomplished through a re-balancing of the energy body by an energy worker. And last, the very best of this type of energy should be held in the hands of the healers as there is nothing more powerful than God's or the universe's energy, even if it's in our own brain power.

Astral or Out-of-Body or OBEs, Remote Viewing, Bi-Location - The Travelers

When one makes the leap that there is no time or distance and that one can effect things anywhere in the world or for that matter, the universe and multi-verses, and then learns to direct and navigate one's OBEs or remote view a place while sitting at home in your easy chair, then you are a Traveler. This is an old world word for gypsies, which is what these particular intuitives would be. As adults they might go into a field like the CIA, or FBI, or military or industrial spying, and this is where the term PSI spies came from. And like the gypsies as they were in the old days, they would always be on the move and nearly always "invisible" to the rest of the world. The cloak and dagger aspect of these Travelers makes them very intriguing to many people, although the dangerous aspects are also apparent. However, there are many positive uses for these gifts or even "trained in" gifts, and as I said earlier, going into the body for medical diagnosis is even a form of remote viewing and astral travel, as well as in other fields such as counseling, historical investigation and psychic archaeology etc. The history of remote viewing in the United States which I will go into more detail about later, includes these researchers discovering that when you start out in just one field of paranormal abilities, you then end up, no matter what, investigating all the fields and all the types of abilities, because the researchers just naturally evolve, often becoming more spiritual or more rarely, manipulative and power hungry. However, there are also many positive ways that these abilities can be used.

But as for children, they may very well astral travel and remote view without any training, not understanding what they are doing and take these particular abilities for granted, thinking that everybody can do these things because of their great fantasy worlds when very young. As children get a little older they both developmentally and intuitively set aside such abilities if they are not fostered or recognized as "special." If they are fostered, then they will probably reach their maximum potential around 12 or 13, the researchers in other countries say of child psychics. They also say that these children will continue to expand their gifts on whatever level they settle into. What these children need to be taught is responsibility, honor, integrity, honesty and compassion for their fellow man, animals and their planet. If all of this is instilled at the same time then we have a world which is community-oriented, with many kinds of people and species, working together cooperatively and not seeking to harm others or control others or have power over others. A tall order in this day and age, as these Travelers begin to multiply in numbers, both through training and evolution, we need to have these other things in place in our children's hearts, minds and souls, or we will be headed for disaster. Because it is my opinion that these particular children, who may have other gifts and talents, but bi-location, remote viewing and astral traveling are their fortes, are the most powerful ones and can either wreak havoc or bring about amazing miracles. And If not "the Federation," then what will we do?

Near-Death Kids All Over the World Who Develop Extraordinary Abilities

In the group of children who develop extraordinary paranormal abilities as the result of a near-death experience, these children have been known to emit a great force that can move or rearrange matter, or have an incredible ability to heal themselves and others, or simply have a super intelligence when it comes to intuitive talents. Some come back with extrasensory abilities and can channel information and become psychics or clairvoyants. Data indicates that 64% of the people who have had paranormal or mystical experiences had a near death experience before the age of 12. These near-death experiencers found that they affected anything electrical, they were unable to wear watches or would confuse microchips, had an effect on electromagnetic equipment, and they were actually able to 'hear' electricity as well. They were very good at guessing games and had a hypersensitivity to light, colors, and sound. In other words, they had a myriad of intuitive abilities that appeared quite suddenly.

They also seemed to have a high degree of telepathic and precognitive abilities. They were able to practice and control their telepathy to an astounding degree. They were both "senders" and "receivers" when it came to mental telepathy, while most people with this ability tend to be stronger in one particular area or the other. Some of them reported having headaches before major catastrophes, both local and worldwide. I know for myself that when I have an extremely uneasy feeling or an un-interpretable dream just before a disaster strikes, I cannot choose which disaster I am not going to feel and which ones I'm going to feel or dream about. Apparently, some adults, who have had near death experiences as children, have learned to recognize and control these sorts of warnings. Others found that they could astral project or night travel at will, most people who experience astral travel, cannot control or direct them. On the other hand, soul travel can be taught to people and also the ability to control and direct these travels can be taught through meditation techniques. However, many who experienced a near death could spontaneously do these things when they returned from their experience. Yet the data shows that over half of these child near-death experiencers do not end up using their newly found psychic abilities to contribute in some way to the advancement of mankind. Instead they tend to stay married, settle down into a quiet life and find simple peace in this quiet life, although there is a smaller group who become addicted to various things as a way to anesthetize themselves from the unpleasantness of life in the physical world. It makes one wonder why?

Children Who Have Reincarnated Lives – Old Souls

India of course is the primary leader of the idea of a child coming back with the memory of someone else's life immediately or at least quite soon after the other person passed away because of the strong beliefs in reincarnation in east Indian culture and religions. This would also be true for many in China as well. And recently in Japan and Burma, there are now children claiming to be reincarnated from World War II soldiers. Some see these amazing details that these Japanese and Burmese children produced about these soldiers as being a real phenomena, while others see it as a national yet spiritual post traumatic stress crisis from the war that the entire country has not dealt with still. In America this is a rarer phenomenon, or perhaps is only rare because parents are so embarrassed or frightened by their child's behavior that they do not address it outside the family unit. But more likely in our country it is an obliviousness to such phenomenon because what the child says is dismissed or not believed, or is attributed to the child's vivid imagination. Sometimes, however, the child is so insistent that it forces the parents into attending to this, frightened that their child is perhaps crazy or "terrifyingly" intuitive. One thing is certain they obviously in most cases, have a very intelligent, creative and imaginative child, in the first place. But when the details of another life are added on to this in what appears to be an obsessive but overwhelmingly accurate manner, this can especially be disturbing to those parents who believe in and practice a religion in which their theology does not include reincarnation.

Types of Soul Memory

There are several types of, or theories of Soul Memory. The first theory is that the children do indeed remember their previous life in the first early years of their new life, usually between the ages of 2 and 5, and then begin to forget these details between the ages of 5 and 8. So in America especially, parents tend to dismiss this as imagination until the child begins school. It is only when the child is persistent and so detailed that the parents become alarmed or intrigued. On even rarer occasions, some children retain the details of this other soul or life into their adult lives, especially if they live in a culture where belief in reincarnation fosters their "soul memories." Some consistent characteristics are the children manifesting similar birth marks or even birth defects as the other person, or similar skills, aptitudes and mannerisms. If the other person died violently, the children may manifest phobias related to how the person died.

Second, there are adults who have some sort of accident or often head trauma happen to them that then causes them to open a channel or avenue by which they remember someone's life from some other decade or century. There are many famous books that have been written about this sort of thing, even down to the person seeking out any relations or descendants or even becoming an actual part of the previous family in rare cases. But there is a third theory and that is that the child is simply highly intuitive and is pulling information from the Akashic Records or universal library of information available to all of us about a particular individual and obsessing on this. This "library" may also be considered the cellular memories that each of us contain in our own bodies. Or there is a fourth theory, and an even more interesting one, that the child makes a connection with a ghost or spirit who wants to use the child to communicate with their loved ones on some unfinished business or just as an entertainment or experiment of one kind or another for the spirit or human astral or bi-locating, shape shifting traveler.

A fifth theory is that of artificial reincarnation that the Russians talk about, where a person can be put into a light trance and given the suggestion that they are another person, usually a famous person. Very non-specific information about the other person's life is given to the subject over several sessions, which then produces amazing details that seem to be coming from the patient's own mind. Over time, this person can then not only produce amazing details about the other person's life, but also reproduce copies of the person's talents such as paintings or compositions, etc. without any prompting from the trance guide. The Russian research suggests that this is an amazing function of our own minds, to be able to reach into our own cellular memories that is housed in the planet's memories and the histories of its peoples, even down to the individual level! But there is still the mystery of why a very young child would pick a totally unrelated life from his or her own and then have hundreds of details about this other life that are absolutely accurate. Some religious people speculate that the answer to this is simple too. That we are all related by DNA down to the beginning of the very first people on the earth and therefore house these detailed memories about others, seemingly not related to us, when they actually are, although scientifically, this is a "stretch." Young children "trance out" all the time and this may have something to do with them picking up on otherworldly information as they are so much more in touch with their intuition at a very young age.

Types of Difficulties Parents, Adults & Children With Soul Memory Experience

I am spending just a little time on this because more often than not, it is very young children who seem to come in with these often startlingly accurate memories of another person's life. And in many of the cases the actual person can be traced and identified through historical records and family members. And because parents of these children are so frightened by their children's knowledge and behavior that they are put into a crisis mode upon realizing the scope of their child's abilities and knowledge about another person who has passed on. In many cultures and countries, including the United States, these memories begin to interfere with the health of the family and the well-being of the child because reincarnation is not an acceptable option. But like most things, including intuitive abilities, the parents simply acknowledging and discussing in detail what the child brings to the table, will take care of this.

Once again, it is in the details and confirmations that parents of such a child will find their answers and comfort. It is also common with young children that once they have that confirmation with historical documents and photos, or even in meeting the families of the individual they know so much about, the so-called therapy completes itself. It is quite common that within months of these confirmations, young children begin to forget all this stuff and begin to live the child's life that they deserve to have. However, if the family and others keep these memories alive for these children, of course they will retain them both for the two families and for the notoriety they might gain as they grow up, if reincarnation is honored within the family and culture or country. But researchers in this field find that the very best "therapy" for the child is to have them meet the other family and realize that time has moved on, i.e., the house is no longer there or the siblings aren't little children anymore, etc.

The mystery of this phenomenon lies in the amazing detail that a small child can relate about the other person, especially if the other person's life can be researched. There are many books on such cases concerning young children and the evidence is presented thoroughly, yet as to why this happens is still a mystery. With an adult one can suspect the person of having a detailed memory of a past life or that the person is so intuitive, they are simply retrieving information from another person's mind whose consciousness has survived them. Past life memory information is so convincing in some cases that the adult has traveled to the home country of the other person who they think they are and having met with relatives or ancestors of the deceased person, convinced them that they are visiting with their relations again. There are plenty of materials out there on this subject from all the many sides of this question, from reincarnation to brain function, but most of them are on the believer's side of this issue, which are tied to religious views within the countries where these reincarnations from past lives are observed in children.

The Researchers of Child Past Life Memories

Ian Stevenson from the University of Virginia Health Science Center's Division of Personality Studies, is the guru of these types of studies of children all over the world. He has published volumes on this topic and says that boys are more likely to have this happen than girls and that often previous lives end only one or two years before the child is born who remembers his or her past life. If the deaths were violent then the space between the person's death and the child's birth is very small, where the space of time is greater with natural deaths. "In a few cases, however, strong identification with the previous person in childhood may interfere with personality development, and occasionally more severe problems occur." This statement was made many years ago by Stevenson and just like everything else concerning children of the "Now," this particular phenomenon is on the rise as well. (*"Children's Memories of Previous Lives," by James G. Matlock, in Parapsychological Research With Children: An Annotated Bibliography by Athena A. Drewes and Sally Ann Drucker, The Scarecrow Press, 1991, p. 33*).

A good but short skeptical article which explores all the physical world reasons for these claims is in the book entitled Parapsychological Research With Children. This is an explosive issue for many people, and really opens a can of worms if it someday proves to be true. It would rock the Christian religious world to the core. Another book that is written by a skeptical journalist entitled Old Souls by Tom Shroder, has the author following Ian Peterson around Asia as he chases down his various case studies. On the other side are Dr. Helen Wambach, Dr. Brian L. Weiss, Dr. Jim B. Tucker, Dr. Raymond Moody, Dr. Tineke Noordegraaf and author and mom, Carol Bowman, who all write about the healing powers of exploring past life memories in children both in the United States and Holland. They all offer hundreds of case studies and in Bowman's case, her own children; but few advise the parents on what to do with these events, except for three: Americans, Carol Bowman and Dr. Jim Tucker and Dr. Noordegraaf, who publishes in Holland.

How Children Cope With Their Soul Life Memories

Children who are experiencing this phenomenon can begin to display ADHD behaviors or in more severe cases become literally lost in the other person's life, not very different than an intuitive child's distractions when experiencing transfiguration or "silent movie" visuals. In one case mentioned, the three year old was convinced that he had once been a policeman. His mother forbade him from talking about it and so he did until a researcher of this phenomenon came to call and then he began to talk freely about it again. When he was allowed to talk about it he calmed down considerably, but had also become more absorbed in his past life memories. It finally got to the point where it was dangerous for him, when he was found out in the middle of the street trying to direct traffic. Another child, in a documentary I saw, at five years of age had parents who checked out the lists of details he had related, had a researcher locate the twenties Hollywood hopeful and his still living daughter, took their boy to see her and this brought closure for the boy. Upon seeing that what he remembered was all changed and that people had grown up and moved on, over the next few months the memories faded for good and he returned to being a little boy again. However, his parents may have not even yet realized the intuitive potential of their little boy and the on-going adjustments that this will bring as he grows up. Out of dozens of items about the previous person's life, the five year-old boy had around a ninety percent accuracy rate that could be confirmed concerning a man who had lived clear across the country from where the little boy lived. The man had been a Hollywood dancer and had bit parts in the movies in the twenties and thirties and once a researcher located photos of the man, this little boy picked his former life's portrait out of several photos of him standing with many other people, accurately and without missing one of them. The five-year-old also named or identified some of the man's relations and friends, plus identifying the man's home in Los Angeles, etc.

But since we are mainly concerned about children dealing with the aftermath of such experiences, be they imagination, intuitive experiences, near-deaths or reincarnated lives, let us leave this issue to those who want to explore it further. There are several books on children with reincarnated or soul memory lives. Jim B. Tucker has an excellent one called Life Before Life: A Scientific Investigation of Children's Memories of Former Lives. He really explores all these various issues that I paraphrased here and has gone out to help parents of such children himself. So he explores all the sides and perspectives to this issue as well as the things to do to help families out who are really in crisis because of their young child's seemingly obsession on a past life. His suggestions are the best and he may be available to help you or can suggest someone if he is not, especially in extreme cases where the family is at its wits end! But it is also important to sort out what is giftedness, intuitive talents and abilities, and if real, tuning into or out of, the soul memories of another. These children probably possess all three of these abilities and all three need to be addressed individually.

Dr. Tucker, a psychiatrist, has carried on Stevenson's research at the University of Virginia due to the generosity of a large inheritance from a man who funded Stevenson's work even after his death by leaving a large sum of money specifically to the afterlife research program. But Tucker is much more interested in researching childhood cases in America mainly because of the lack of this research in our own country. He states that these are the following types or characteristics of memories of previous lives: predictions of a re-birth before it happens, an announcing dream of a re-birth, intermittent memories of the parent's wedding or the conception or even of being born, memories of the previous death that is often violent or sudden and rarely of natural causes, detailed statements by the subject, birthmarks or birth defects related to the previous person. The children have recognitions of persons or objects or locations related to the deceased person, exhibit unusual behaviors on the part of the subjects, display mannerisms of the previous person and might even be speaking another language without any training in that language beforehand. A fact of great interest is that in most cases, the children only talk about the last years of the previous person's life and don't know much about the deceased person's earlier life. The median range of the new birth from the death of the previous life is around 15 to 16 months. Same-family cases are rarer but do cover a substantial portion of the reincarnations related by children.

Investigating the Ways of Either Proving or Disproving Reincarnation

Dr. Tucker offers clarifications and reasons why other explanations for this phenomenon cannot be supported through having discussions on fantasy versus reality with the parents and children. He states that knowledge acquired through normal means can be ruled out in most cases and that faulty memory can be checked and re-checked to rule this one out. Genetics can also be researched and ruled out, although cellular memory is an unknown at this point due to our own inability to understand this possibility. Just knowing anything there is possible to know through a universal library is still a theory and cannot be proved at this point. Tucker does cover the idea of transfiguration and possession either by another human or a spirit and makes a pretty good argument to rule this one out for re-incarnated children as well. And while he cannot prove reincarnation, he can quite nicely disprove most of the other theories for past life memory which leaves the idea of reincarnation wide open to be proved. Although types of paranormal phenomena such as reading someone else's mind telepathically especially in same-family cases, or gaining knowledge through a paranormal way, such as trancing out or being hypnotized to receive information from the universal "stream of consciousness" or Akashic Records. These are things we don't know enough about at present to rule out.

Tucker also covers the issue of the population explosion which most people believe is the main reason for the impossibility of reincarnation. He states that reincarnation seems to not happen to everyone and if it does most people have no memory of other lives. So only some people would have this experience of remembering a past life while most of us do not. That it makes sense that those remembered ones have unfinished business because so many of them are the result of violent or sudden death. Apparently mathematically, population growth is predicted to max out around ten billion people later in this century, which is still a number that would allow for reincarnation as long as the time between each life is shortened to include the population increase to less than 15 months. "...we may all have previous lives even though most of us do not remember them. If this is true, then the usual process may get disrupted either by a factor in the previous life or by some factor in the next life. This may lead some memories to be present in the next life, and therefore, even though everyone may reincarnate, our cases are unusual because of the presence of the memories." (*Ibid, Life Before Life, p. 214*).

All this allows Tucker to make the supposition or propose the theory that some sort of consciousness survives after we die or that we have a consciousness that involves memories, emotions and even physical injuries, ailments and physical marks, to carry over from one life to the next. He also states that many physicists now consider that consciousness is an entity separate from our brain and with connections and important functions with the universe. He suggests that parents not ask leading questions of the child but just let the unfolding of the past life memories happen naturally and matter-of-factly. Prompting the child can lead to the child making things up or not focusing on his or her present life. That it is better to just write every detail down and constantly reassure the child that he or she is in a present life and is safe from painful memories. For children these are merely experiences of their everyday life, while often parents are either over reacting or under reacting because of their own belief systems and cultures.

I found Stevenson's and Tucker's discussions and proofs to eliminate other reasons for past life memories other than reincarnation logical and very compelling. Yet one thing did occur to me in terms of knowing the intuitive life as I do, which a scientist or psychiatrist might not have experienced and therefore would not think exists. There is a metaphysical argument that suggests such a thing as a child or even an adult astral traveling at night and being targeted by a fellow traveler, spirit or human being or otherwise, who can then "piggy-back" this other soul and "spoon fed" the information to this soul from another previous life in full detail. Or there is the idea that DNA research can someday prove that we have the memory of all of our ancestors since the beginning of time imprinted in our bodies. This argument comes up a lot within the Christian communities since they believe that we all come from the same beginnings then this would mean that we are all related in one way or another and could have cell or brain memories which we can access subconsciously. And here is another idea, that energy and frequencies connect every living thing on the planet, or perhaps even to some extent inanimate objects and even the earth itself. And can it be that we all have an all-knowing memory of everything that has happened historically on the earth within that untapped ninety percent of our brain power? Knowing how intuition works from my own experiences, I would guess that we haven't even gotten to "the tip of the iceberg" in this field as far as the idea of reincarnation or brain ability is concerned. Scientists, but especially physicists, might scoff at the first two ideas, but they really can't scoff at the last one of an energetic resonance throughout our universe affecting us, because they are just now proving the existence of such things. Not only that, but they are now realizing that the basic principles of science are now totally under question as "truths" today.

Same-Family Cases of Reincarnation

In some cases a strong desire on the part of one family member to return as another family member in a later life is expressed before the first relative's death, or even expressed in a dream or vision given to another family member after the person has passed on. It is often said that this child or that child has characteristics, mannerisms, looks, or even the same talents as that of a favorite aunt or uncle, etc. Or that a part of or piece of this particular relative has come back in a niece or nephew or grandchild, etc. The characteristics that consistently appear in same-family reincarnation cases are similarly placed birthmarks or birth defects related to the deceased person's own chronic conditions or ailments. Even the exact same chronic ailments can manifest in the past life memory child. These are things which are both predicted by the deceased relative before they die and then carried through from the previous ancestor to the current descendant. A lot can be proven in a same-family reincarnation that cannot be proven when it is a total stranger from another area of the country or even a different country. However, Dr. Tucker states that if the child has the intuitive skills to garner detailed information about a total stranger from another area or even distant country, who passed away before him, there is still something that does not make logical sense. And that is that children more often than not, have these physical marks that came in with them from day one. They also begin to manifest emotional traumas related to the past life long before they begin to express their past life memories of another person or even identify them.

How Past Life Memories Can Affect Your Child

In Carol Bowman's first book Children's Past lives: How Past life Memories Affect Your Child, she does give data from the other people's research on commonalities with childhood reincarnation and she talks about how children can be more vulnerable to this phenomenon and not just because they are so close in age to the previous life. She states that it is easier for a little child to accomplish a trance-like state on his or her own without any adult guidance. And in fact younger children go in and out of a trance state all the time, but no one really knows what they are experiencing when they are in this state. The brighter and more creative the child, the more this happens, an interesting thought concerning both child reincarnation memories and intuition in general. This also corresponds to the Russian research on artificial reincarnation and trance induced states. Sometimes two children will have the same reincarnation memories together, each child will remember who they were in relation to the other. At least a third of those studied had a phobia that corresponded to the way they remembered dying. They also remembered how they died and often died violently. And nearly always these memories are a natural phenomena, meaning that they are spontaneous, there is no prompting on the part of others, and they verbalize these memories with a matter-of-factness, calmness and logic all their own.

Bowman gives four signs of past life memory in children: the child uses a matter-of-fact tone in relating the details, these details are consistent over time, the child displays knowledge beyond his or her own experiences, and there are corresponding behaviors and traits to the past life experience. One of the things that will stand out is the display of knowledge that is way beyond the child's experiences and sometimes the ability to speak another language that the child could not have learned by any other means. Another is that many of the children display the mature emotions of an adult in remembering details of this past life that are way beyond the comprehension of a pre-schooler. They may even remember what happened to them immediately after their death in the previous life. And with the fourth characteristic of behaviors and traits, the children often show emotional ties to the previous person's world, as well as actual physical mannerisms. For example they may have phobias directly related to previous life experiences which may include memories that are related to the manner of death. They may also display talents and abilities of the other person that a person of their age couldn't possibly have yet, or they may have birthmarks in the same shape or place that the previous person had or have physical marks related to how the previous person died. They may even have physical mannerisms specific to the person whose life they are remembering or they may have similar chronic illnesses or even birth defects that are near or exact copies of the deceased person's birth defects.

Anything the child runs into or any one of the five senses may be activated to help the child to gain even more memory of a past life. They may see a location or place that jars more of their memory details and conversely, upon seeing a location and how it has changed over time, this may stop some of the memories overnight! Seeing a person from the other person's life or even a photograph, may activate more memories or help them to fade over time. Bowman has one theory that perhaps her own past life memories could have triggered her two children to have more memories of their own through a sort of telepathy, since she had not spoken to them about her own memories. However, the parent's belief system about reincarnation could influence the children to be looking for such things too. Either way, real memories or not, they can still be used to help heal the child.

Helping Parents to Cope with a Young Child With Soul Memory

Bowman feels that parents should never blame themselves for what is happening, because it just is occurring! She also feels that past life memories can bring benefits with them and asks parents to do the following to keep these memories as much a normal natural part of the child's life as possible, whether they fade or are retained. She says, that as a parent, one should stay calm, acknowledge the truth of the children's stories and details, discern facts from feelings with the child, understand what your child is trying to express and understand the meaning behind what the child is saying, but allow their emotions to emerge naturally, and clarify with the child what is past and what is present. "Resolving a memory may not happen all at once. In most cases the process of remembering and venting emotions unfolds gradually. The memories may come up repeatedly over a period of days, weeks, months, or even years. Your child may talk of her past life, once, then again, a year later, and never again after that. Or you may have one of those loquacious children who frequently drop casual references to their past life into their chatter seemingly at random, tickling you with surprise each time." (*Ibid, Children's Past Lives, p. 281*).

Past life memories can also emerge in a very young child's dreams or nightmares. So that once again, here is yet another cause for sleep disturbances discussed in the sleep section of this book. However the cause doesn't matter as long as the same things are done to stop the nightmares or sleep disturbances. But following this line of thought, Bowman says: "A dream of a traumatic past life death or trauma, alarms you into noticing it. It causes your child to wake up screaming, run into your room, and jump into your bed, whimpering for protection. For children with recurring nightmares, this scene appears night after night, devastating the midnight peace of the whole family." So while this could be the cause of a recurring nightmare specifically, how you handle it is the same, with detailed discussion about the dream, acknowledging the dream, telling it or writing it down or drawing it as you rewrite a safe or "happy" ending while awake. Most often, recurring nightmares when told to another and explored, will dissipate over time, but in the case of trauma from a past life, this can carry on for a while and really terrify a pre-schooler or at least distract the child from having a normal early childhood experience. (*Ibid., p. 292.*)

The most important issue here however, is how the parents handle their own beliefs when it comes to reincarnation. I see this issue as no different from my previous advice on simply acknowledging the truth of the experiences whether they are from intuition, vivid imagination, real night or day time experiences that seem out of the ordinary or reincarnated lives, etc. Parents can deal with all of these various issues, beliefs or realities, in much the same way as I have already stated several times, by honoring what their children tell them, seeking the details and expressions, recording them, checking out the evidence and confirmations, and moving on with consistent confirmations of love and empowerment so that their children can become grounded and perceptive adults who can make their own good decisions in life when they are adults, whether they retain these past life memories or more often, do not.

What Are All The Gifts An Intuitive Child Can Have?

The list of occupations and gifts in the intuitive world is rather endless, but I will start by listing those we are most familiar with: Astrologer, Dream Interpreter, Palm Reader, Psychic, Intuitive Therapist, Energy Worker, Healer, Medicine Man or Woman, Shaman, Psychometric, Psychic Crime Investigator, Psychic Police Sketch Artist, Prophet, Mind Reader, Psychic Magician, Archaeological or Military Remote Viewer, Horse or Animal Whisperer, Holistic Healer or Reiki Master, Pet Psychic, Seer, Astral Traveler, Mediums, Rebirthing Instructor, Breath Work Facilitator, Yoga, Tai Chi or Chi-Gong Instructor, Martial Arts Instructor, Meditation Guide, and on and on and on. On the more practical side and a much more acceptable pathway at present are such things as a Transpersonal Therapist, Transformational Therapist, Massage Therapist or Rolfing Instructor, Chiropractor, Homoeopathist, Naturopath, Herbalist, Acupuncturist or Acupressure Specialist, etc. But of course these are choices that adults make. For children we simply need to let them explore the various gifts that they seem to have, practice them a little bit, and send them out to choose what they will use intuitively in their physical world life, and while some of them will actually choose one of these ways of making money in the world, most will integrate these gifts into their everyday life.

If you are in a family or community or religion or culture that does not accept your gifts and after trying all the ways you can think of to make this world work for you; then you will have to wait until you are an adult and find your own community - and hopefully a spiritual one rather than a dark one. In Julie Soskin's book she lists the ways to discover your abilities, gives an explanation of each gift and then a few starter activities. Her table of contents speaks for itself: Discover Your Psychic Potential, Extra-Sensory

Perception, Psychic Tools, Psychic Healing, Encountering Spirits, Psychic Protection and Higher Consciousness. And under each of these headings she has all the basic questions that teens would ask about each one of these and what activities that would be most appropriate to do together with your child. She also provides checklists to help you determine whether you have some intuitive abilities in several of these areas or not. I highly recommend this book for those ready and willing to work with their children in a responsible and careful way. (*How Psychic Are You? by Julie Soskin, Penguin Books, 2002*).

But you can also find books and computer articles on various topics with many activities for teens that can be done with supervision, and adapt these for younger children. Topics include: astrology, palmistry, numerology, face and body reading, aura reading, handwriting analysis, card reading, color interpretation, and many other activities that are done just for fun. None of these sorts of things introduce any of the darker arts, and in fact you can help your children avoid searching through these not so good worlds as teens because they have already been taught that these things are not to be dabbled in unless guided by responsible adults. Learning about your own intuitive gifts can enhance one's life and using drugs that put you in an altered state of consciousness can more likely reduce one's intuitive powers rather than enhance or expand them. This is an innovative way to have that "don't use drugs" talk, which will engage your teen in a more positive way. However, others will tell you that certain drugs, used only as an adult and under the guidance of a shamanic mentor might enhance a shamanistic experience. My own experience from my youth in the sixties, while limited, certainly showed me that all these types of blockers interfered with my ability to intuit and enjoy all of the aspects of my gifts in many different dimensions. They also blocked receiving the entire message being sent to me. These interferences destroyed not only the depth of the experience, but especially the joy in having it. Shamans would probably beg to differ with me, but that was my experience, and that is what I tell young people who do this. I tell them to stop blocking their intuitive experiences with what they think will help enhance them. And to realize that these otherworldly experiences are much more enriching and more powerful just as they are, because you can remain totally focused on them "soul-wise."

> The most wonderful part of having such gifts and the understandings that go with them is having the skills to assist others through the difficulties of daily life and also to recognize the joys in life when they come along. Going to bed at night is an adventure these days, with dreams, lucid dreams, astral travels only vaguely remembered, and even night visitors that one has to figure out and either welcome as a teacher, friend or ignore as an unwelcomed guest or nuisance. The daylight hours, with daily meditation, becomes all sorts of waking dreams to interpret and understand, in nature, with animals, and even just in daily signs and symbols all around you. Along with this is noticing the beautiful colors and other sensory things in nature, as well as the many synchronistic experiences

that you would not have without daily spiritual and meditation practices. The intuitive life can be pretty spectacular if you take care of yourself and others as best you can, in body, mind and spirit.

"Taken out of the context of eternity, psychic children can seem like an eerie, haphazard, inexplicable quirk of nature… Out of context, babies are blank slates when they are born,…and they're shaped by some combination of genetics and their environment. The debate rages on about how that combination works exactly, and why so many children seem to be reflections of neither genetics nor their environment."

--Sylvia Browne, Psychic Children, p.3

"What is feeling? It is a scientific fact that our bodies are surrounded by energy fields. I suspect that when a child is remembering a past life and enters a state of consciousness, something shifts within the energy field around the child's body. Perhaps when we tune into what the child is saying, we are doing more than just listening – we are reacting to this change in energy. We can actually feel the change as it registers in our own energy fields as well as in our brains…Whatever the explanation for this feeling, it can be quite unnerving. Some parents are shocked by both what the child is saying and by their own bodily reaction. They feel disoriented, unbalanced, as if they were in free fall, slipping through a crack in reality. Don't worry. This is normal. It cannot hurt you or your child."

--Carol Bowman, Children's Past Lives, p.205

"On the other hand, reincarnation may normally occur but without memories continuing from the previous life. In that case, we may all have previous lives even though most of us do not remember them. If this is true, then the usual process may get disrupted either by a factor in the previous life like an unexpected death or by some factor in the next life. This may lead some memories to be present in the next life, and therefore, even though everyone may reincarnate, our cases are unusual because of the presence of the memories."

--Dr. Jim B. Tucker, Life Before Life, p. 21

"If we are all spiritual beings, we should aspire to treat others with all the respect that implies, and treating children with such respect must include listening to them. Just as children in this book may have important knowledge to impart to us, so may others if we are ready to listen to these small fellow travelers on this most remarkable road of life."

--Ibid., Life Before Life, p.234

“Because consciousness is an unbroken continuum that stretches from death to birth, children may remember and describe events that happened anywhere along the continuum.”

--Ibid., Children’s Past Lives,” p. 214

“What you learn on the outside of yourself isn’t what’s important. It is what you learn from the inside that tells you the truth.”

--Katie, a Crystalline child, age 6,
Children of the Now, p.81

CHAPTER THIRTEEN
What In The World Is Going On for Psychic Kids?

"What is beginning to emerge is a new picture of the human being, not as an alienated creature, but a being enmeshed in the ebb and flow with everyone and everything around him. The pulsing magnetic fields of machines, earth, moon, and sun, the thoughts and emotions of ourselves and other people – all affect the force fields of our bodies, and in turn,...our psychic powers."

--Psychic Discoveries Behind the Iron Curtain, p.77

"Hearts communicate instantly by touching the spirit link."

--a line from classical Chinese poetry

Researching, Studying & Training Children Outside the United States

In countries like China, Japan, Russia, Holland, and Mexico they are way ahead of the game because they have at one time or another, identified these particular children, who are "loaded" with this talent, sometimes put them in special schools and trained them to reach their maximum potential, unfortunately for both good and not so good uses. America is behind these other countries in this field, unless of course they have continued their secret projects that were begun during the Vietnam War to remote view the enemy's locations from coordinates alone, and see how far one could go with this and also explore forms of mind control. There are some civilian research projects doing this but not to the united degree and beliefs of the previously mentioned countries. And children have definitely not been studied to the extent that they were in these other countries, but I can also understand the temptation to use these abilities or even fake them for the attention children would receive from their various governments.

The most severe and dramatic phenomenon is often blamed on such things as alien abduction and possession, according to people's belief systems. The drama and attention a child can gain from all this is pretty phenomenal too, whether faked or real. Not to say that there are not really people who totally believe having had these experiences and often "serial" experiences as well. They are sane, sincere and more often than not keep quiet about these things because of the stigma of being thought "crazy." But obviously these true experiences that a minority of people have, find themselves not putting on "public performances" because it is bad enough to have had an inadmissible experience in the first place. And then to not be believed is even worse. If I admit to having seen "ghosts" then I cannot discount those who have seen or had experiences with "aliens." Even such things as transfiguration can be mistaken for a very good performance by a very good amateur actor or actress, or just as developing mental illness where multiple personalities can exist, can be mistaken for psychic phenomena. Deciphering and sorting this all out, has not even begun in many, many countries. And, maybe someday, the word "belief" will become the word "fact" instead. For myself, I now believe all phenomena are simply parts of the multi-verse, from angels to aliens, and that when we can use all our brain functions, we will also understand and interact with all of these various paranormal capabilities, whether they are considered outlandish or used for the betterment of mankind every day.

United States

The United States began their various secret military programs right after the Cold War when the U.S. realized the Russians were doing psychic research and the U.S. was not doing anything in the government, although there were plenty of private programs even in the fifties. After World War II and during the Cold War of the fifties, the United States began to realize that other countries, Russia and China in particular were experimenting with paranormal or psychic abilities with animals, children and adults. They were also developing scientific research methods far superior to our own in which to research such things in adults, as well as in the military and political arenas, etc. By the 1960s the U.S. could see that this type of research might be a threat to our national security. Private facilities were researching such things but they were few and far between. By the seventies, the U.S. felt that they were behind the Russians and Chinese in this field and they had better start finding out something about all this stuff that they still considered "woo-woo." Thus it was that it was the military that first paid attention to and got the funding for these things monetarily, rather than the scientists and therapists who, while still researching, struggled for funding. About this time we had the UFO files from the fifties closing down and the remote viewing programs were started up in our country in the late sixties and early seventies.

I won't go in to great detail about these remote viewing programs because you can read many books on the subject but I think Jim Marrs's book PSI SPIES gives the best and most concise history of these programs when they were "outed" in the late eighties and early nineties. Quite a few books came out on the pioneering work of the seventies and eighties, and these went way underground after this and were not talked about, but I would assume some form of these original programs are still going on to keep up with other super powers. And of course there are those who claim that none of this was true and simply propaganda on the part of the Russians, who only claimed to be researching these esoteric subjects. People said it was all just fabricated to keep the Americans guessing and never really happened. Others said such rumors were perpetrated on both sides just to fool the American public. However, conspiracy theorists strongly believe that all sorts of paranormal research has been going on in all three governments (Russia, China and the United States) to this very day.

You can also read Stephen Schwartz's The Secret Vaults of Time, which is quite scholarly and is about psychic archaeology. It also contains some great biographies of who Schwartz considers the psychic "fathers and mothers" of this field from history. The people involved with the military remote viewing program shared many of the same civilian psychic trainers with the psychic archaeologists when they broke off from the military remote viewers because they had more scientific and peaceful interests. Many of the other books on these remote viewing programs are a sort of wallowing in one's own ego books and don't really tell you what the history of the program was. A quick way to learn about these programs but in a lot less detail is to rent the movie "Men Who Stare at Goats" – billed as a comedy and actually a pretty good one – it is really true and the characters in this film represent sections or groups of people who were involved in these remote viewing programs. And when I say everything in it was true, that includes stopping the heart of a goat and walking through a wall.

The best book on how to learn to remote view, which they said anyone can learn, is an older one by Ingo Swann who was the head of the psychics in the military remote viewing program when it originally started, entitled erroneously Everybody's Guide to Natural ESP. And it is actually the best book on learning how to remote view and teach yourself to do it. This book really does not talk about any other kind of ESP in depth and Swann is the best to teach remote viewing to you. The participants in these programs claimed they could take anyone off the street and teach them to remote view in the space of three months. And for the most part this is absolutely true, but like any skill there were those who learned to do it better than others, and then there were natural inborn talents which produced the best remote viewers in the program. In a military setting this must have produced a highly competitive atmosphere. Swann basically designed the whole program although several others claim this honor, and when the programs were "outed" in the early eighties, Swann definitely liked to talk about his brain child once it was no longer "top secret."

Suffice to say, that while these various military and eventual civilian Remote Viewing programs surfaced after the silence was broken on these top secret programs, much more than simple remote viewing was going on. The term Remote Viewing means seeing through distance and time and most people start out thinking that they can only see a short distance. In training the men to see long distances away, they were also asked to look at coordinates on a map, which were then used in war time to either locate individuals, send in assassination squads or to locate bombing sites, etc. Interestingly, as these military men began to expand on this capability such as viewing certain people in foreign countries or finding locations anywhere in the world either drawing details they got on paper or using coordinates to do this, they also discovered that they could "see" particular locations in the future or past, as well as under the ground, and into the oceans and outer space. In other words, they could take anyone off the street and teach them these skills, although some had natural talents for this sort of thing way above others, and far surpassed those who had to "train." The possibilities became rather endless and the competitive atmosphere was of course pretty steep with many political implications internationally.

Discovering that they could move objects, rearrange matter, view absolutely anywhere, and even affect people's decisions and health with mind control, they began to feel themselves somewhat invincible and naturally, what people will do, is either choose to be responsible citizens or try to gain power over others in these particular arenas. But there was a factor that they were not expecting to happen. As they gained knowledge and skill and power in these various arenas, they were also becoming more and more spiritual. It seemed that most people when confronted with this type of power also became responsible for it and much more aware of their stewardship on this planet. Most of them began to realize that everything was connected with everything else and that harming one thing anywhere would harm everything else everywhere. But there was always that small portion of people who were trying to still make a place for themselves in the annals of evil and wrong doing. Nearly all of the people who left these supposedly defunct programs, went into some sort of spiritual practice either for themselves or for others. Those who remained and are probably still "top secret," are very likely still working on weapons of destruction much more powerful than any manmade stuff could be. Psychically, this type of thinking is extremely scary and extremely powerful. So let's hope that what we don't know about the link between developing one's psychic abilities and one's spirituality, is also just as powerful a link or even more powerful than this.

Since the United States never really focused on the training and teaching of the super psychic children of their country as a national treasure for the future, there are only many individuals and groups who are doing this sort of thing, but even they are working mainly with adults and not children. There is a lot now about children in the United States or raising such children or honoring such children coming in now, as the intuitives of tomorrow. Many people have studied areas of this such as soul memories, giftedness or near-death experiences among children, but few, if any, have studied the entire range of intuitive abilities in children until just recently. And even now it is scattered and not a national "trust" to do this. The closest we have come in our country to studying intuitive children would be in the near-death experiencers arena and the gifted area, although in a more limited fashion. In the metaphysical world there has been a lot of attention paid to intuitive children, but just now books are coming out on this subject and researchers for children in many fields are now interconnecting with each other after years of separations, because this, after all, is what America is all about, diversity, freedom and lawsuits!

There are some great centers or institutes that have continued to research psychic phenomenon and skills however, such as the oldest national one, ASPR or American Society for Psychical Research, the Rhine Research Center, the Edgar Cayce foundation or ARE (Association for Research and Enlightenment), the Monroe Institute, the Easalen Institute, and many, many other smaller such research centers across the nation in various states and at many universities, including a more well known research institute at the University of Arizona, the Center for Consciousness Studies where one can get a degree in parapsychology. However, I did run across an article by Athena A. Drewes entitled "Testing Children for Paranormal Abilities." She quotes Louise Rhine stating, way back in 1968, that children too can have psychic abilities although on a simpler level, but still similar in form to adult experiences and abilities. This author explains why America is so reluctant to test and work with children on psychic research. She says that American researchers assume that children are not intellectually ready and don't have the attention span and willingness to fit research designs. She also states that researchers may not know how to change their adult expectations or how to interact with children to achieve the best results. And last, she mentions that researchers cannot grasp the developmental levels of children and design their research accordingly for child subjects.

The other major reason is that the legal issues would be endless and further complicate designing a research program for children. Even the ethical issues surrounding such research would be overwhelming, involving parents and teachers and everyone else they would need, to work with children. The author then gives various ways to overcome all of these issues and makes a plea for how very important it is for the U.S. to do research in the parapsychology field with children. She talks about guarding against fraud which would be a big problem in the U.S., and gives the best developmental stage of children to develop the maximum life-long intuitive potential for children. She says the years between approximately 2 to 9 are the best stage in which to study children's intuitive abilities because they are in the early stages of pre-cognitive skills at 2 to 6 years of age and it is the easiest time to be taught.

One of the obstacles in the United States is the fact that intuitive skills seem to entirely disappear when American children enter public school, which is not true culturally in many other countries. And part of this in the United States is parents' reluctance to acknowledge the realness of such experiences. Children, especially children under the age of five, are told to ignore such memories of other souls or spirits or whatever they are experiencing. Experiences that defy explanation are directed towards imaginary play or excused as vivid imagination, as long as they do not interfere with the child's ability to function. And then when they do, it is often assumed that the child has psychological problems or a chemical childhood syndrome of some kind, such as ADHD. So that by seven years of age, most children in America begin to fit in, which both wounds and confuses highly intuitive children until they can reawaken to who they really are later on. However, developmentally it is also known that 7 to 12 is when most children set aside their magical thinking for more down to earth skills. She also reinforces what the Chinese found out, that outside factors can influence the success of the studies including lack of belief on the part of researchers, the moods of the children, the weather, the stress and pressure placed on them to perform and the children being given immediate feedback. It seems that fear of and doubts of, these gifts, is reinforced in American schools to the point where students lay them aside until they are adults, way beyond the natural developmental stage.

However, things are changing a bit, even in America, and the damage done to children who are our own "super psychics" is lessening for the first time in years. But Drewe's best quote is what she says at the end of the article: "Both types of parents – advocates and skeptics – would do well to encourage children to discuss their unusual experiences, to listen patiently, and rather than dismissively retorting 'That was only a dream,' present an explanation, or perhaps alternate explanations that would satisfy the child's curiosity and facilitate his or her critical thinking capacities and cognitive development." However, as positive as this statement is, it was indeed disturbing to look through this book for a right brained visual spatial intuitive learner who would simply crumple under this type of cold, uninspiring and excruciatingly detailed questioning and intimidation. And because it is parapsychology research which should be a little better than the rigorous scientific research standards set in America, it was very disheartening to feel the separation between the heart and the mind, being held onto so rigidly. On the other hand, this 1991 book is a tour de force in terms of compiling a bibliography of published research materials from America on the subject of child psychics, as well as naming the various research centers, etc. (*"Testing Children for Paranormal Abilities" by Athena A. Drewes, was taken from Parapsychological Research, McFarland & Co., 1991, pp.211-220*).

An interesting look at the stages in American history of the types of intuitive generations of children since World War II is what Atwater calls a process of "generational spread" or "generational energy imprinting." Rather than dwelling on Indigos or Crystals, etc., she uses certain periods of time in U.S. history: 1) The intuitive G.I. Joe Builders were operating within 6 % of the population from 1901 to 1924. 2) The intuitive Silent Caregivers were operating within 11% of the population from 1925 to 1942. 3) The intuitive Baby Boomer Rebels were operating within 27 % of the population from 1943 to 1960. 4) The intuitive Generation X Survivors were operating within 29% of the population from 1961 to 1981. 5) The intuitive Millennial Fixers were operating within 29% of the population from 1982 to 2001. 6) The Generation Adapters have an unknown as yet operating percentage for the intuitives but have a range from 2002 to 2024. Atwater also predicts the next generation as being the Aquarians who will arrive around 2025 and continue until around 2043. As a generation, they will be the greatest humanitarians in the entire history of mankind and the intuitive/spiritual generations we have ever had. As noted by the various percentages deemed "intuitives," these percentages have been on the rise with each successive generation.

She says that the Greatest Generation having gone through two world wars and the Great Depression developed practical discipline, uncommon valor, commitment, persistence, and upheld the power of authority and tradition by having a strong faith; while intuitively they stabilized energy all over America. Between the world wars were the Silent Caregivers who remained silent through caring for others, remaining alone in a crowd, they withdrew and challenged little, and yet were socially concerned and produced a long list of famous helping professional leaders, civic leaders, civil rights leaders and advocacy movements. Intuitively they helped to expand a world view and kept an open heart towards others. The Boomers or Rebels were somewhat self-centered, broke all the rules, received massive amounts of entitlements after the war and became visionary idealists who fostered a sort of spiritual euphoria from their arrogance and creative independence. Intuitively they brought in new churches, new media, new entertainments, new communications, new spiritual awareness, but in the aftermath they also brought in many ills such as drugs, AIDS, financial disasters, etc.

Generation X Survivors were considered the lost generation who turned tribal and primitive in nature. Through forming tight clans such as gangs, having high divorce rates, fostering the idea that greed was good, and seeking instant gratification with a dark, brooding cynicism, they seemed to have "lost" their way. Intuitively, they brought in a strong instinct for survival, entrepreneurship, dug for the truth in all things and found relationships more important than wealth. The generation of Millennial Fixers brought in with them new traditions, innovative thinking, intuitive knowing, spatial reasoning and old soul understanding, along with single parent households and a myriad of small advocacy groups. Intuitively they brought in a return to ethics, commitment, and causes. But most important they brought in a happy confidence and enthusiasm to pair with their abilities to get at the truth in all things and commit themselves to progress. Children and young adults are now in the age of the Generational Adapters who Atwater predicts will have focuses on security, responsibility and restructuring their social world. They will keep the world under their watch, make changes behind the scenes, and deal intuitively with the predictions of a major shift in consciousness during their lifetimes. Through their hands a new America will be reborn with new thinking and new strength and enthusiasm. The energies coming in with this present group are providing us with many quite young mystics and seers, wise beyond their years, way ahead spiritually and intuitively than their predecessors. Better equipped both brain-wise and spiritually, this generation will overturn the chaos of the times and herald in a much more positive futuristic outlook. America is finally in a "New Age" of spirituality that will lead to the most spiritual, intuitive and humanitarian generations of them all. (*"The March of the Generations," Chapter Five, Beyond the Indigo Children by P.M.H. Atwater, Bear & Co., 2005, pp.38-50*).

China

In China in the 1980s, they trained their young "super psychics" until they were 12 or 13 and then waited for when their scientists, health professionals, militaries, or governments, etc. would need to call them up again. They were put in special schools designed to develop their abilities with teachers who were highly trained professionals and intuitives themselves. They went back to their homes after elementary school where they continued to hone their skills but did not have to worry about losing their families or miss out on their family time and social skills, etc. China had learned through scientific research that these traits are never lost and that those children identified can reach their maximum potential while young, retaining their gifts for a lifetime. Those among the "super psychic" category, people with more girls than boys and about 50 such children, continued to contribute to the research going on at the time, demonstrated their gifts for foreigners, and forged ahead in various fields to help others or further other research in many different fields of study. Based on the belief in "chi" or an energy field, their highly educated researchers were working to bridge the gap between investigating psychic phenomena that these children produce and the scientific model of research which does not at present provide a way to research this phenomenon. In other words, it was not a matter of belief for most Chinese, but a matter of gaining an understanding of what they already knew exists, although there were still those in the government that balked at doing such research.

The book on this is entitled China's Super Psychics by Paul Dong and Thomas E. Raffill. In the book they talk about their famous adult psychics and what they can do, the stages of their research from a rise to prominence in the country, controversies and conflicts, experiments and documentation, Japan and China's psychic war, Chi Gong and the paranormal, the children of China, skeptics and the psychics of Taiwan. But we are mainly interested in how China identified and researched their children for their various abilities and what they found these children could do. It is also interesting that each culture and country government would have a slightly different view or even a dramatically different take on these types of children and their abilities. Considered a national treasure in China they were mentored, specially trained, honored for their gifts and abilities and especially protected from foreign visitors who sometimes came to discredit them. All children in the eighties were trained in their regular elementary schools, but the top students were identified and sent to special schools for "super psychics" for the elementary years.

In China it is believed that there are five types of EHF or psychic abilities believers, those who will never believe in it, those who are inclined to believe, those who have mixed feelings, those who believe seeing is believing and those who stubbornly even upon actually seeing it, will still not believe. It is also said by many scholars and especially one in particular, Ms. Fen Chung, a well known scholar in China, that "Let a hundred flowers bloom, let a hundred schools of thought contend." She says that in trying to stop research in this field, or not allowing ways of finding those techniques that will facilitate such research in the EHF field "...there is a great danger of suppressing new science. Maybe the one who is putting the 'anti-science' label on others will one day have the label of 'step-mother' put on his own head." (*Ibid, p.68-69*).

Doing this nationwide research could give rise to things like competition and cheating, because these children and even some adults would want to not only please their parents, but those who honor them as well. On the other hand, "cheating" in China is a very dishonorable thing to do and something, if caught, can ruin one's entire life. So I am of a mind, unlike many American skeptics, to think that this does not happen very often. Although there have been many famous psychics from various countries who found themselves in a bind and did cheat, but got caught doing it, I think for the most part they were truly psychic but just wanted to add onto this to seem more accurate than they really were. And there is another reason not to cheat in China, because there is a huge population in the country who are believers in "chi" or the energy body that surrounds and goes through each one of us.

The practice of Chi-Gong or Qui-Gong is an honored and deeply held centuries old practice in China. Inborn intuitive traits are believed in but also there are inductions, faiths, illnesses, and accidents which can bring out one's intuitive powers. But in China there are three other ways specific to what they believe: practicing the art of Chi Gong, having psychic ability spread through the energy field or chi through practice or spontaneously, and an interesting one specific to China, Japan, and India, which is hunger. These three countries have the highest proportion of psychics and spiritual masters historically and having very large populations they have had widespread periods of starvation in these three countries. When one is in a starvation mode it is believed that one enters a state of "bi gu" or fasting and through this state one begins to feel and understand "chi" on a deeper level, thus developing third eye capabilities much more easily. With "hearts spirit link," part of an everyday expression in China, many Chinese believe they are describing the connections between people's minds and hearts. While there are many skeptics too, traditions and beliefs in China go way back when talking about "chi" and how to use it intuitively. However, it is the Russians, another "hungry" nation, that have proven that both brain waves and heart rhythms become exactly the same when people link telepathically. Therefore hunger and fasting promotes the development of psychic abilities.

The philosophy behind Chi Gong is that one seeks to describe what is, and not why it is. It is a practice of using healing powers on oneself and on others. Showing that Chi Gong really works will lead to proving the various psychic powers, say the Chinese believers. They hope to use what they call 'systems science' on Chi Gong to observe actual effects, compile data on this, gather materials on techniques and publish all this. They also want to compile publishable materials on ancient practices of Chi Gong from Buddhists, Taoists and Confucians and find out if ancient practices conflict or are compatible to modern day practices. And then to find out if the ancient practices and the modern day practices can be studied under modern principals of science. Then, they believe, they will be able to classify all the techniques and study and divide them into various types. They also say that not only does the body and mind develop intuitive and physical health but intellectual health through the study of Chi Gong. A number of elementary teachers in China have trained their students in the art of Chi Gong. The results were that all of their academic scores went up, but interestingly, they were most dramatic in mathematics.

Chi Gong or Qui-Gong, which many still believe in China, can raise the consciousness of the entire nation and promote national well-being for all. With approximately 20 million people in China practicing Chi Gong, it was thought that this would raise the energy level of all China's citizens, making them a world super power. This practice of Chi Gong nationwide had increased the ranks of psychics "...to slightly less than the total for the rest of the world combined." In China and anywhere else where this technique is practiced, Chi Gong is thought to maintain the stability of one's psychic powers, raise psychic abilities to their highest state and introduce a resonance with the universe and every energetic thing on earth. The practice of Chi Gong can maintain a healthy body and mind through meditation, breathing and other techniques that will keep the psychic person at his or her highest state and therefore, their highest intuitive state. Chi energy can keep the body's immune system up, keep circulation going, warm the body, and control the effects on bodily fluids and balance the yin and yang or male and female energies. Being aware of the earth's energies and the seasons of the year can all contribute to a higher psychic vibrational health as well. So while millions still practice Chi Gong, China's new regimen frowns on its use. (*Ibid., China's Super Psychics, p. 129-140*).

The super psychic children of China have been studied for the following abilities: reading or knowing color perception by ear, foot, stomach, palms, tongue, scalp, fingertips or armpits; moving, transporting, relocating or starting up mechanical objects; seeing through human bodies or into them as well as wrapped boxes and describing the contents; performing mental arithmetic faster than a calculator; magnifying objects by sight or mind; mental telepathy; clairvoyant vision of past or future events; seeing through walls and performing psychic writing; opening locks or breaking small objects; remote viewing; having telescopic and X-ray vision; and sensing atmospheres and what is in another person's mind. Breaking twigs with the mind was a common practice in these tests as was telepathic block arranging, but the best one that was definitely a cultural or traditional metaphor for these super psychic Chinese children was the opening of a flower with your mind or moving a flower from a garden into the classroom. Because in China opening a flower is thought to bring good fortune and during the Chinese New Year people are greeted with either the phrase "Happy New Year" or "A flower opens to prosperity."

The national training program was implemented in 1981 in all of China's elementary schools using all kinds of intuitive techniques to raise not only the abilities of all of China's children but to also identify the super psychics who would need additional training in their own special schools. Within a year three thousand Chinese children had been identified with extraordinary psychic powers. And surprisingly one of the things they learned over time was that children when trained so young, will manifest their maximum potential as a psychic whenever they choose too as an adult. Out of every hundred children they trained, thirty children displayed psychic talent.

They also learned three important things from this ongoing program in the schools and the first was that parents came to realize or felt that naturally born psychics had greater powers than trained ones. That psychic power was not always stabilized in children and according to their moods they could come and go erratically. But the researchers also learned that many more children trained in EHF techniques appeared than natural born psychics through this training. They felt that rather than dividing between inborn naturals and trained ones, it was much more important to divide by the children's abilities. And China felt nationally that they had an obligation to not only see children as their future wealth, but they also had an obligation to protect their children.

Later the Chinese designed a shorter program to train children aged between fifteen and twenty. Ten days of intensive small group training took place when the national interest was not so opposed and it had been proven that children really were not only improving in their intuitive abilities but also academically. However, in training these older children they found that younger children had less cluttered minds and could concentrate better, as well as being more moldable or receptive to the training. Younger children seemed to be more adaptable to the stresses that these trainings caused them and the two side effects of this training, headaches and anxieties were less prevalent among the younger children. Teens had all those other stressors and interests that could interfere with their training sessions and make it hard to attend to their intuitive talents.

The Chinese on one occasion invited a group of American and Canadian scientists and skeptics to watch demonstrations of their child psychics. The Chinese found out rather quickly that this group had come in looking for fraudulent practices and that the children, when put under pressure to perform under these circumstances, could not show their abilities in front of these experts which then led the experts to see "fraud." It turned out also, that many of the famous Chinese psychics who were going to come mainly to watch, had been warned ahead of time that the Americans and Canadians would "... disrupt the demonstrations in all kinds of ways, such as unfriendly remarks, nasty faces, rough movements, and many requirements and restrictions...which would affect the mood of the demonstrators. If the demonstrator is not in a calm and cheerful state of mind, the EHF powers will not come easily. This is well known among psychic researchers." So the famous adult psychics did not show up. The hosts from China felt that these experts that they had invited were insulting and humiliating to the psychics they had invited to participate in these demonstrations. (*Ibid., p.217*).

The authors of China's Super Psychics felt that incidents like these perpetuated the separations between American and Canadian researchers and Asian researchers when it came to psychic phenomenon. Because China has invited many such groups from Japan, Taiwan, Hong Kong and India without incident and all of these groups felt that they had witnessed nearly all successes and some of these countries, before going to China had not been favorable to them in their media there. And even though the people of Taiwan in particular looked down on psychic research, after their visits they began their own research in their homeland and with their own children. One of the key factors involved in this failed meeting with Westerners was because in Chinese culture one's greatest fear is to lose face to foreigners and the more you fear, the more likely you are to fail. The more times you are asked to explain something, the more you will mix things up and make matters even worse. This could make someone think that you are trying to cover some things up for the children's failures to perform their gifts. "And scientific experiments are generally black and white, giving either positive or negative results, and there can be no excuses for failure." (*Ibid., p.224*).

Since the eighties and the publication of this book, China has undergone some significant changes that have affected their advanced studies on psychic children. A new government cut back on this research because once again, this type of research might not be the best way to spend a government's money, and ended the nationwide psychic training in all elementary schools. However, individual studies continued just like in the United States in areas of interest in the country of China. In 1992 a six month study at Hangzhou University, conducted by seven scientists, investigated training 1,222 elementary school children in skin or body part reading. There were 623 boys in the study and 599 girls. They started with training the children to read with their ears after testing to find those who could already do this. They found that around 12% of the children between ages 7 to 13 could already do this. But in the age range of 14 to 18 only one 17 year-old girl could read with different body parts already. The best age for training children was found to be at age 9 and after the training program was over they had had a 20% success rate among the remaining children.

At China's Banghu Medical Institute, 1,388 teenagers were tested and among them the researchers found 180 students who could read without using their eyes. Another study found that in training young adults from 18 to 20, the trainers had better success with less educated people than university students. The researchers felt that this was because university students were much busier and with all their multi-tasking they could not concentrate on the task at hand. However, most psychics know that the more you remain child-like, the more accurate you will be psychically, because you do not block yourself with judgments and doubts. Another university study at Shaghai's Fudan University in the engineering department, they tested for some gifted intuitives and came up with 46 children, 18 male and 28 female, who they trained from 1986 to 1993 in all sorts of extra-sensory and psychokinetic abilities. The children developed great abilities but under the pressure of the study also developed headaches, dizziness and fatigue.

There were several studies in the 1990s on see-through or X-Ray vision with children. At Xinjiang People's Liberation Army Hospital 117 tests were performed with children making medical diagnoses. Twenty two cases were diseases of the head and 17 cases were diagnosed correctly by the children. 53 cases involved the liver and the children got 43 of these diagnoses right, with another 5 partly correct. In 19 trials of recognizing the fetal positions in the womb, the children were correct in 16 of the cases. A paper was also published by a professor Tang Jianmin of what he thought were the factors that contributed to a child being highly successful at see-through vision. He found that women could do this much more often than men, there were more children than adults who could do this, more children in rural areas than in cities could do this and that more American children than Chinese children were able to be successful at medical diagnosis with see-through vision. However, he also found that more Chinese adults than American adults could also do medical diagnosis with X-Ray vision. He also felt that the higher success rate among both children and adults involved spending less time on practices involving vision such as reading, TV watching, driving and fine vision work. Children in China spent more time reading and studying than did American children and thus American children could be more successful at see-through vision.

At the end of the 1990s was when the controversy began because the government did not like how many Chi Gong masters were promoting these psychic studies as well as their own practices as mysterious spiritual powers. By 1999 the Chinese government had banned one very famous Chi Gong group called Falun Gong and arrested their leader for fraud. The Chinese government also did not like the idea that so many groups were promoting a rejection of conventional medicine. The media began attacking such practices while the government continued to support scientific research at the universities, institutes and hospitals, etc. But while in the 1980s many high ranking government officials supported psychic research, today a new generation of leaders don't remember the old research or don't believe in it. So that China today is just like the United States with many smaller and divided groups researching on their own without a cohesive coalition of nationally linked researchers in the paranormal field. (*"China's Super Psychics Revisited" by Thomas E. Rafill at www.spiritofmaat.com*).

Until we get more information on what the Chinese are doing now, because in a sense they have gone underground too, there is one last piece of information from 1997 which states that to date 100,000 super psychic children had been recognized. No one knows exactly where this statistic came from or if it is even accurate, however if it is, this means that there is still ongoing research on the psychic children of China that is still way ahead of the U.S. All Chinese research on psychic individuals is being done at Universities and in hospitals today. And if you want to read the skeptic's side of this one, read the article by Raymond Lee entitled "The Exceptional Human Functions Research in China" and "Observing Psychic Wonderkids: Pitfalls and Precautions" by Stanley Krippner in the book Parapsychological Research With Children by Athena A. Drewes and Sally Ann Drucker. Quite interesting for "auditory processors," they are a bit disheartening for "visual-spatials"! "Whole brainers" will enjoy both sides of this topic!

Russia

While Russia is not specifically working with children, their research has been ongoing for years and they are definitely way ahead of the United States in this area. When Psychic Discoveries Behind the Iron Curtain by Shelia Ostrander and Lynn Schroder from Prentice-Hall, first came out in 1971, it was the first book of its kind, and actually is still one of a kind in the new century because now, Russia too, has gone somewhat underground while amassing a huge body of research way ahead of anything the United States could possibly have done in all the previous years. So think of all that I paraphrase here as ongoing research, still quite important in Russia in general. This book also provides a general outline for most areas of paranormal research and is the foundation or basis for material being researched all over the world. So by introducing this material and following those strands that I can to the present, we will have explored many of the areas of psychic phenomena being researched today.

In this book there are several nationally famous and historic psychics' life stories from Russia, Bulgaria and Czechoslovakia. Time is spent on the mystic history of Russia and witches and shamans from Russia's "soul" past. They discuss the mind to body links in their research and explain the differences culturally between how Americans look at psi research and people in the Baltic countries look at the same thing. What Russians called their scientific research at the time was Psychotronics rather than a "woo-woo" name here in America, like parapsychology, paranormal or even metaphysical investigation. Something here that is to be looked at as instantly suspect and a belief, in Russia is seen not only as something deeply woven into their past and culture, but also scientific brain research that is all real and just not understood and fully proven as yet. There is no "belief" about it! However, Russia like any other country has its skeptics and critics.

The following subjects are a brief recap of some of the material in the book, but I have tried to update the various sections as well. Interestingly, this book is still controversial today. Some see the entire book as fraudulent and made up material, while others, who attended many of the sessions at the time, say this is fact. You make up your own mind as you read about each subject, because with over forty years having passed by, many of these topics have been altered, renamed and confirmed, while others have been discredited, or so some believe! It is however, still interesting to me, having actually experienced some of these things, that the strongest skepticism reigns supreme in America to this day. And that would be quite alright, if not for the viciousness of this skepticism in terms of personal attacks and generic statements that true skeptics, being true to their own principles, would never make.

To me a skeptic is a person who is open to the unknown, while trying to disprove something that is known but has no solid evidence to back it up. I consider myself one, for all my own experiences, and even though experiencing things from the unknown confirm things for me on the feeling level, I still try to analyze and explore each issue that comes up for me as a skeptic. These are many phenomena still being explored by universities, hospitals and private facilities all over the world. This early book about Russian research was one of the first ones to give us a general outline of most of these unexplained mysteries as they were perceived then, described, often renamed and altered in their appearance and scope, and yet are still being researched today. The book provides a great way to explore psychic phenomenon categorically and will give the reader early histories and wonderful insights about different areas of the paranormal that children may be experiencing. By comparison, American research on these subjects is very compartmentalized and the paranormal research on children only offers three topics having been thoroughly researched: near-death experiences in children, gifted children who are intuitive, and just recently, children who have experienced past live recall. And only recently in the United States, at least in the metaphysical world, has it been okay to discuss intuition in children via such labels as Indigo and Crystal children which reflects at least a portion of the population's interest in these topics. I have provided several book references on these topics in the bibliography if you want to know more about these theories on the "new" children.

The main phenomenon explored at the time and which the soviets consider as brain research were named and studied over the last decades in terms of the following topics: 1) What makes a person psychic? 2) What is mind over matter and mental telepathy in outer space or between family and close friends? 3) Kirlian photography of auras, the energy body, eyeless sight, x-ray diagnosis and healing with thought. 4) Time travel, seers or futuristic predictors. 5) Artificial reincarnation and trance-like states. 6) Suggestology educational learning and astrological birth control. 7) Pyramid power & dowsing. 8) Psi spying and creating a psychotronic generator which can amp the brain power of the person or even work on its own to induce psychic powers for many uses. There are some interesting highlights about these various areas of research that are not well known in America. While Russia and her surrounding countries have not worked with children that much, they have worked with plants and animals and adult humans, and often not in a humane way, but in the Russian way, those who have lived there tell me. With passion, "the mystic soul of Russia," and "the dance of the supernatural" integrated with major scientific research, all in one.

What Makes a Person Psychic?

Russian scientists found that there is a force field around and running through everything on the earth. This force field is influenced by our brain waves and the energy waves or frequencies that are everywhere and anywhere at all times. Russia's top psychics often had headaches, fatigue and lost weight when trying to move objects or influence someone telepathically. Other things that affect, influence or block, all human's psychic abilities, trained or with natural talents, to influence matter or even the human brain, were force fields around machines, natural energy fields emitting from the sun, moon, and planets, and last, human emotions. In other words if skeptics watch these demonstrations and voice their opinions, then the psychics or trained telepaths cannot perform successfully. But most important they discovered that the force field around humans, plants and animals and even inanimate objects carry wave frequencies just like our brains do, that interact with each other all over the planet. Knowing how to vibrate at a certain frequency is what causes one to be termed "psychic" and successful at moving matter and energy around. Enmeshed in the web and flow that surrounds it, it is easy to understand what makes our universe tick, our planet continue operating, and our human bodies and brains continue to run. In other words, the force fields in and around our bodies' effect us, everyone else, and especially our psychic powers. And many of their researchers feel as we do that they hope that all of this knowledge does not fall into the hands of those who would use these discoveries as weapons.

"We suspect that a psychic, naturally, probably unconsciously, attunes his brain waves to the rhythm of another person's brain,' one of the younger physicists told us. 'This rapport helps him get the other man's thought, or, as in the case of psychic healers, to affect the other person in some way. We think that many people can learn to tune to each other in about three months,' He didn't say how." The Soviets found "…proof of physical harmony between sender and receiver – hearts beating in rhythm, brains in pattern – at the time of telepathic communion… there was synchronization in the cycle of heart activity in sender and receiver. This showed up clearly on the electrocardiograph attached to each of the distant psychics. There was a simultaneous increase in arrhythmia, a quicker heartbeat, and greater cardiac noises. The scientists also spoke of simultaneous changes in the frequency spectral structure of the tremor registration curve during the moment of 'biological contact' in telepathy." And this research has since been proven to be absolutely valid. (*Ibid., Iron Curtain, p. 124- 125*).

This was Russia's greatest discovery in showing man as a pulsating field of energy, dynamically interacting with all other fields like a note swirling in a symphony. They also discovered that good receivers were born when the sun is quiet and good senders in mental telepathy were born when there was sunspot activity in our solar system. They interpret this as a sort of cosmic biology which is only the tip of the iceberg in this field of research. Another thing they discovered in their research was that the force of the human gaze can transform an angry person or animal to stop their attack by transfixing them momentarily. No wonder, I thought, that getting my pupil's attention through eye contact in the midst of a conflict with someone else, could not only stop but dissipate this escalating conflict! I always thought it was my commanding presence, but then, maybe it takes a little of both to soothe the savage beast! The Soviets take this a little further however, and state that our eyes really do send out rays of energy to the pineal gland in the body of the other person, the very gland that is associated with the mystic third eye or chakra in Eastern mystical practices, in charge of our psychic powers. This spot between our two physical eyes emits magnetic waves like the ordinary visions in our physical eyes, and can temporarily, at least, stop a person or animal in their tracks. They were also studying animal telepathy and its link to human telepathy and vice versa. All teachers, of course, know what "the stare" is all about!

Mind Over Matter & Telepathic Links

The twenty-third letter of the Greek alphabet is pronounced "psi" which has become a general term for the whole field of the paranormal. And the Russians in researching mind over matter reached the conclusion that brain waves could eventually be decoded to create a sort of psychic wave length Morse code. So that not only could people learn to speak telepathically to each other but also influence another's thoughts and health through this method, as well as spy on others. The implications of this are enormous and overwhelming for both good and bad effects. It also means that one can move objects over either short or long distances, transport them to other places far away or pick up objects from far away and make them appear where the person is, or even more far out, bi-locate to a targeted location or be found in another place or two places at the same time even in OBE's, or even make matter melt so that one can walk through walls. And that anyone can be trained through a meditative state to have telepathic successes. And because China, Japan and India have many masters who can do these sorts of things, the Russian government even arranged for yogis from India to come to Russia and be studied in their labs in the 1960s.

They also studied the link between mothers and their children using animals at first, and quite, in American's view, brutally. Taking mother rabbits' babies away from them, transporting them far away and killing them one by one to see what the mother rabbits' physiological reactions would be in the lab. They also tested human mothers who were separated from their babies, for example the child is in the hospital having tests done while the mother is out in the waiting room. Communication was 65% successful in all their research, of course mothers everywhere know this is absolutely true, but it took the Russian research to prove this. In America one man did research over 500 cases of parent-child communication between parents and their children who were ill, and found a high incidence of telepathic linking. Interestingly, the Russians also experimented with this with their cosmonauts in outer space and discovered that they could have a telepathic link with each other which they trained them to do, as well as with their loved ones and coworkers on earth while they were in outer space. They discovered that they could use a form of hypnosis to help increase telepathic abilities as well. These abilities to move things about were influenced by the person's health, mood and the weather. They also found that telepathic influence was better with rotating objects rather than static ones.

Unfortunately intricate telepathic codes are already being used around the globe or information is passed in an undetected way, perhaps not as accurate yet but still better than the internet! Scientists in Czech labs have discovered that there is a change in the blood volume within the person's body when they are communicating telepathically with another with whom they have an emotional tie. Other minute changes in the body take place as well. And Russians scientists have also discovered that one can put people to sleep telepathically at a distance, not just one person but a group of them! However, not everyone is susceptible to hypnotic trance or holding strong visual images of a person or persons, and not everyone will respond to this suggestion. Telepathic sleep does do something good however, it opens one up to a clearer communication channel than when awake. While the Russian scientists state that control of a person's attitudes towards another person's race or nation is not a viable option, there are many who like the idea of using this sort of hypnotic trance technique or telepathic suggestions while sleeping as propaganda in their own country to influence its citizens.

The main thrust of this particular research is to increase the "circumference" of each person to include increased brain power awareness and capabilities in all humans, to turn the lights on so to speak in people's brains and their vision, and to set more life in motion. Also to increase the range and power of all these psi abilities in all adults and children and step everyone up to the knowledge that the whole universe and our planet specifically, is constantly in motion, as is everything on it. In America, we still see this as a New Age concept of the evolving shift around us within and without. In Russia, they have already recognized the interwoven "rug" of our planet, researched many aspects of this, and used the heart of their history and roots as a foundation. America has to step up to the plate, not just as an aware nation psychically, but also as a nation of compassionate "good" to forestall evil in the world. Not well known in America is the fact that Hitler, the last most powerful evil we have encountered so far in our entire world over two decades and two world wars, was a skilled psychic himself, studied the black arts and occult from childhood and used these things in planning his various campaigns and training his men and fellow leaders. Whether schizophrenic or possessed, Hitler could be seen displaying other voices and faces by those who worked closely with him on a personal level.

Eyeless Sight, Medical Diagnosis, Healing & Kirlian Photography

Eyeless Sight or Skin Reading

Eyeless sight is the one area where Russia and China overlap each other. In China it is called skin reading or tongue, armpit, feet, hand, and finger "reading," where the person reads a book or individual words or identifies colors, etc. Both in America and Russia, researchers have found that this particular intuitive ability will completely blank out when the person is in emotional turmoil or very ill. However, Russians did more research with blind people and found that adult vision impaired people did not take to eyeless reading like their younger counterparts. They think this is because adults were so use to using their sense of touch that this blocked out their ability to read or see with other body parts or their skin.

A Russian researcher found that when he put colored paper in insulated trays, the blind adults did just as well as seeing people or blind children. Scientists speculated that the reason for this was that skin readers had special cells with rods and cones that used infrared rays that bounced off isotopes in the body sending the rays to the hands or body part that was doing the reading. Light and electricity have something to do with eyeless sight; readers cannot perform in dim or night light. The color of the light in the room and how bright the light is, can affect any blind person's ability to use eyeless sight or even to just function in their home. Certain colors could be sensed from a greater distance when these factors were included in the tests. Researchers also discovered that skin readers could read at a greater distance from the text when the texts were placed on a plate of weak current positive electricity. Hands and faces were found to be the most sensitive and the Soviets renamed this science Bio-Introscopy.

Medical Diagnosis/X-Ray Vision & Internal Remote Viewing

"For centuries, mediums have been describing a phenomenon they call the aura. They diagnosed illnesses, and states of mind from the cloud of energy they saw around people. Probably the aura seen by a psychic is made up of numerous elements of the human force-field, including perhaps heat radiation, electromagnetic fields, and many other things still unknown to us." The energies have something to do with frequency waves, say the mediums. But other psychics describe diagnosing the locations and types of illnesses through an internal remote viewing in which one looks down inside the body as in X-Ray vision and sees the organs and the diseases. For myself I use both, but can only describe how I learned to do it on my own. I at first saw snakes and nests, the snakes were the disease and the nests were the healthy organs. But then as I looked I could see that the areas of the body that were ill had a darker aura. A light faint green was a healthy area and gradations to a muddy brown were areas growing ill and gradations to black were illnesses already there and dangerously advanced if solid black. Later, along with the auras, I began to see the organs themselves, the shapes of the diseases and if it was a system such as lymphatic or blood or nervous system, I would see nothing and the type of system would come to me in a printed word or a simple 'knowing." I can also feel the illness as I run my hands over the body, but I am not always as accurate or more often right with my hands, like I am with the inner sight. Because this skill is new to me in just the last few years and one has to practice for many years to become more and more adept with this ability, I am at the beginning of just testing my natural abilities as I go. (Ibid, p.205 – 206.)

Healing & Kirlian Photography

Since Russia has always had a number of well-known psychic healers who use laying-on-of-hands to heal people, it is only natural that they would also study this area. These healers say that pain brings these colors to the surface, as well as strong emotions, and that the lights are brighter emanating from the body where the places to be healed reside. The Russian researchers also found out that stimulating particular acupressure points in the body would increase not only general psychic abilities but most specifically healers diagnosing illness would become more accurate in doing this. When Kirlian researchers mapped out the Chinese meridian points and matched them to the then craze of Kirlian photography, they saw minute color flares emanating from plants and then from the body. They then found exact matches for all of the over seven hundred acupressure points to these little flares of misty colors that they had photographed. So while what they really photographed became suspect later, not all of what they observed was by any means incorrect.

"The mind does not work directly on the brain. There is an etheric body which is the link between mind and the cells of the brain…Far more minute corpuscular particles than scientists are yet aware of travel along these threads from the etheric body, or double, to certain regions of the body and to the brain. I might call them life units…This invisible body…is the only channel through which mind and life may communicate with the physical shape. Should a thread snap between the two, there is immediately a failure in control…Each animal and human has a unifying invisible body made out of modified ether. It should be possible to devise in time an instrument where by this body can be perceived." (*Ibid., Iron Curtain, p. 211, quote from English medium Geraldine Cummins in the 1930's*).

Semyon Davidovich Kirlian was the best electrician in Krasnodor in Russia near the Black Sea. He saw a demonstration of a high-frequency instrument for electrotherapy in 1939. As the patient was treated Kirlian saw a little flash of light between the electrodes and the patient's skin. He decided that if he put a photography plate between the patient's skin and the electrode that he could take a photograph of this tiny light that he was seeing. But he also realized that the photo plate would immediately be ruined when it was exposed to the light from the electrode. So he used a metal plate on himself but it was dangerous and he did get burned when he placed his hand on the plate. However, he also came back with an amazing photograph of an aura of light around his hand or luminescence. He became intrigued and eventually invented an entirely new type of safe photography to photograph these lights and he said that he realized he had opened a window on the unknown when he did. He and his wife Valentina kept working on better and better and more accurate equipment to photograph these auras around our bodies and plants as well. And from this came diagnosis of plant diseases and eventually people using this auric field photography, which will probably go down in history as the single most important psychotronic discovery in Russia.

"Kirlian photography has lately come under fire as scientists argue over the source of the aura. Many scientists today believe that Kirlian photography auras are actually pictures of the item's humidity or temperature. However, whether the image surrounding items in Kirlian photography are actually moisture, heat, or light is not the issue. The fact is that these photographic studies show marked changes in response to emotions. They also show that matter absorbs and reflects emotions of its holder or owner." Items strengthen and increase the amount of information a psychic reader can detect about their client's emotions, thoughts and lives. And the energy that is being detected or scrutinized is encoded with all sorts of sensory, mental, and spiritual information. It is contained in everything including our very atmosphere. (*The Lightworker's Way by Doreen Virtue, Hay House: Carlsbad, California, 1997, p.265*).

Orgone Energy

Other scientists as early as the 1940s, including German scientist Dr. Wilhelm Reich, found an orgone energy in organic matter even in water, wood, wool and the atmosphere. "Reich eventually developed a pistol-like apparatus which could influence orgone energy, and in several monitored studies. Reich effected weather changes with this tool. Reich believed that the blue sky was actually visible orgone energy, since he surmised that the energy was blue-colored. Satellite photographs of earth verify that a blue electrical covering does surround the planet." The idea being that we can work on healing our earth just as we can on healing a person's body. So the thought that we can affect the weather, earth energies and even move the clouds around with our minds is not becoming such a far-fetched notion as it once was. If the mind or a machine can move matter of any kind, then we just have to discover how it is done and what amount of energy it takes to do it. Scientific research of today is finally beginning to catch up with the powers discovered and used by ancient man, but at a higher level on the "spiral" of knowledge. Dr. Nikolai Kozyrev became the second researcher on orgone energy and became as famous as Dr. Reich with his continuing investigations into the uses of orgone energy. Both men were credited with this discovery and its ongoing research.(*Ibid, p. 266*).

Today, Orgone Energy is marketed all over the world as a holistic healing agent, through various forms such as Zappers. You can also make your own Orgone bars from various recipes that are claimed to capture this orgone energy and transmit it to the body for healing. There are even thousands of groups who manufacture these bars and go out and bury them around powerful digital cellular communication towers because they think that these towers have created a thick blanket of DOR/negative energy which promotes drought, fear, and significantly hinders Chembusters operations. This worldwide grass roots movement is called the Orgonite Gifting Movement and chunks of orgonite are constantly being buried around these towers. Even Reich's Cloudbuster machine, which was said to remove negative energy in the atmosphere and in the process disintegrate clouds or even change the weather, has been improved upon by the Chembuster which is made of six-foot copper pipes embedded in an orgonite base with quartz crystals added which is claimed to do the same thing as Reich's machine, suck the negative energy from the sky.

If you want to know more about this subject look up www.orgonite.com info or www.world without parasites.com. I can only say that I have some, they do work, and why they work, I haven't a clue! Wherever I have pain, I place them while I meditate, and then I am pain free for a while. Whether it is belief or a real energy, or both, I don't really care. Since there seem to be no side effects and it doesn't go through my stomach, I am happy with this. They were made for me, so they didn't cost much! Reich originally had what he called Accumulator Boxes or Oracs Boxes which were much more powerful. And he claimed to heal various ailments with these accumulators in 1930s and 40s by placing them next to the patient. By the sixties, the Russians were researching this German scientist's work and by the eighties, scientists all over the world were researching both Dr. Reich and Russian Dr. Nikolai Kozyrev's work with orgonite and this has continued to this day.

Tachyon Energy is also something to study and research on the net. The Japanese were the first to investigate this energy ray and how to harness it as a planetary power source. It also eventually worked its way into the holistic health field just like orgonite. And while not as powerful to me as the orgone, I do have my tachyon triangular chakra cells to use as part of my self-healing process. I would put them in this order – but perhaps it is my own belief that "powers" this: crystals, tachyons and then orgones – orgones being the most powerful of these three amplifications of healing. You can download plenty of articles on this and there are many companies out there selling tachyon products, which have become quite sophisticated in the last thirty years. I think their best feature is the claim that they will not only boost your immune system but keep you younger, longer. If this is true, it is certainly better than layers and layers of beauty products or plastic surgeries trying to do the same thing. With all these types of things, the golden rule is to keep using them. People are notorious for purchasing such products and then dropping them either because they take too much effort, or they cannot see results right away! The best website for information on these is www.tachyonsolutions.com.

Time, Seers , Prophets & Artificial Reincarnation

Some of the Russian discoveries concerning time include the idea that the density of time has something to do with telepathy. That time would be thinner near the sender and denser around the receiver in telepathic communication. They also believe that eventually time will develop into a physical reality that we can study and measure and that stars in the night sky get some of their energy from time. That when we have a new understanding of time we will also understand ESP and all the other pieces of the puzzle will fall into place. There are several theories on travel through outer space as well as time travel itself such as jumping from or punching through a black hole into another black hole, to travel through space and time faster than light travels. There is a lot we don't know but the Russians think we will get to these understandings much more quickly through psychic research or Psychotronics as they called it then.

The people who can predict the future are a reality to the Russians and they listen to their predictions seriously and with much contemplation in ways to research this. One of the interesting things they had discovered was something called Artificial Reincarnation. The person is placed in a deep trance and made to believe that they are the reincarnation of a famous artist or composer, etc. After several sessions of this, the subject, if reincarnated from a famous artist, begins to draw better and if reincarnated from a famous composer, begins to read and write musical notes without any previous knowledge of this. Eventually the artist is painting amazing portraits and the composer is composing music, they might even eventually copy the style of art or music of the person they have supposedly reincarnated from. But the question is, is this mind suggestion or a real reincarnation memory? On the other hand, does the person need to know the answer to this if they are learning a new process in any field that they could not have possibly learned before? But more importantly, will they retain the new skill and knowledge forever? And can they retain details from that deceased person's life as well? There are so many questions yet to be answered.

Researchers say that putting a person into a state in which they are then submitting to new laws, opens up the unexplored side of man's psyche. The person is thinking, forming relationships and judgments, acquiring their own experience through this process that consequently produces new creative potential and then this new ability becomes the person's own. In other words, people who went through this process, the Russians claimed, did retain it. The main discoverer of this was Dr. Vladmir L. Raikov who in studying this phenomenon also found that there was a connection between this artificially caused reincarnation and the use of brain power. He thought that when he took a person through this process there was evidence that they were using a great deal more of their brain functions. That his subjects were drawing on the collective unconscious to develop these skills, or as psychics would say, they were "channeling" from the "universal life stream" from which all knowledge flows, with "storage" in each individual person's body as a cellular memory.

Educational Suggestology or Modern Day Learning Techniques

Suggestology was a whole new kind of mind extension that came from Bulgaria. It is the scientific study of suggestion and a method of reaching and making use of the unknown reserves, powers, and abilities of the human mind. The laws of suggestion apply to many fields and this method is not to be confused with hypnosis. You are always in a waking state with Suggestology and aware of everything around you. Yogis in India use the suggested state in their specific Yoga exercises, but they do not call it Suggestology. Doctor Lozanov was the person in charge of this research at the time, and called it healing with thought. What happens when you use this method is that one can eliminate attachments to things, fear of the unknown, and other psychological problems that keep people from accomplishing new learning. The person goes into a deep state of relaxation, and you can not only learn subjects, but you can also heal faster and more efficiently from illness. In other words, Suggestology researchers speculated that this methodology could someday work like an anesthesia to anesthetize the body during surgery and during the healing process.

But they also thought it could revolutionize education, by using a teaching method that Dr. Lozanov created. This method sped up learning, increased retention, required virtually no effort on the part of the student, and could teach both the most challenged and the most brilliant at any age, requiring no specialized equipment. Hundreds of people from all levels of society were able to learn an entire two-year language course in as little as 20 days. It was considered a very practical method, basically teaching the mind to make contact with the teacher, based on Yoga techniques. Twelve people sat in reclining chairs in a comfortable room with subdued lighting and listened to soothing classical music. The instructor spoke in a calm voice, and then, unexpectedly, in a hard commanding voice. She continued this rhythm, on a special scale of intonation. The students were told not to pay attention and to let their conscious mind be totally occupied with the music. The students were surprised to discover that while they thought they hadn't learned anything, they could remember to read, write, and say many words in the new language after each day. In only a two-hour session, they had learned, about 150 words, and within a month they had learned and retained 2,000 to 3,000 vocabulary words and had a good grasp of the grammar.

The Russian researchers said that Suggestology worked because it helped the student to learn 5 to 50 times faster using a Yoga technique called Savasanna. This involved using suggestion, muscle relaxation and creating a brain, which was free of the usual anxieties and stresses. This meditative state helped fatigue vanish, and left the brain unhampered to learn and absorb new material rapidly. "The secret of the technique is that material doesn't reach the memory in the ordinary way, because the student doesn't participate consciously in the process. Instead, the student has a calm, intuitive perception of the material presented. During the time the teacher intones words against a musical background, there seems to be distinct physiological changes in the body and changes in the brain waves. The alpha rhythm of the brain predominates. Memory and intelligence show improvement for some time after a Suggestopedia session…Man's brain remembers a colossal quantity of information – even how many steps it took you to walk to the bus stop. These unknown perceptions show his subconscious has startling powers. There's nothing supernatural about expanding memory or receiving telepathic information," said Dr. Lozanov. (*Ibid., Iron Curtain, p. 292-293*).

Since the seventies, educators from all over the world have gone to Bulgaria to study the claims of Suggestology and the countries of India, Germany, and Russia have founded their own institutes to study and use Suggestopedia, although under different titles. Forms of this type of learning have been used in many parts of the world over the years, using a variety of names both commercial such as the Rosetta Stone language programs and in the educational field which sprang from information based on Dr. Loznov's research. But before his research this method of learning was not perfected, so what was mainly established was that people could use a distinct method to learn foreign languages. For adults, this method is fabulous, and probably could be used on the high school and college levels, as well as in all other walks of life and fields, where adults need to learn specific materials. And now that we are in the computer age these methods are offered through computer programs that include all of the components including subliminal phrases and music, etc. The computer programs use the intonations, varying sound levels and rhythms to teach certain kinds of materials. Nowadays, one can see this type of learning program being sold everywhere, but it is still not perfected enough to work well en mass, and especially with young children, although the language programs like the "Rosetta Stone" are being used everywhere. With the computer age however, one can see how this type of learning has been created online, voice and all, with a computerized "teacher."

Astrological Birth Control

Besides finding ways to help ensure safe reliable birth control without pills, contraceptives, or operations; help many sterile women become fertile; help women who have had had several miscarriages have full term babies; help ensure a healthy baby; eliminate many birth defects and mental retardation problems and allow parents to choose whether they have a girl or boy; the Astra Research Center for Planned Parenthood of Czechoslovakia, claimed that they had discovered many things, because of using what they called astrological birth control. And while these are amazing claims, researchers had found since that birth control via astrology seemed to work. At the time, this research team was led by Dr. Eugene Jonas. And they were dispensing prescriptions based on the position of the moon, the sun, and the planets. For example, a woman's fertility period, they found, simply followed the phases of the moon. They also found that highly sensitive women seemed to experience a recurring cycle of heightened sexual desire, on certain days, but always within 30 days. Parents, in choosing the gender of their child, were simply asked to work their astrology chart backwards and tell the researchers the date then of intercourse and then they could tell them what the sex of their child would be. And according to their research this method became 98% accurate at the time. Like all data from Russia, discoveries either disappeared or went underground after the 1970s, so hopefully, Dr. Eugene Jonas's discoveries will continue to be researched and some are already available internationally. But it is interesting that astrology and birth control, having been around throughout the ages, had been rediscovered only because these researchers took it seriously at the time.

Pyramid Power & Dowsing

Pyramid Power became a craze in the eighties and most of us are familiar with what this power is supposed to do, keep us younger, fitter and stronger by being submitted to time under or inside a pyramid shape. The Egyptians knew this, but for some reason this was considered a "new" discovery when the Russians began to research this energy again. Soon there were even life size pyramids that one could purchase and sit in, in the privacy of one's own home. But for all the various modern materials and theories about what the pyramids should be constructed of, it is really the shape that people think infuses a person or an object with these qualities. One can build up one's immune system, cure chronic illness, remain younger, etc., etc. These are all claims that have yet to be really proven and yet the Russians did prove that even inanimate objects made of metal could in a sense, keep regenerating. For example, they used razor blades in some of their experiments and these razor blades were kept sharp for weeks by placing them under the pyramid shape. I used to have my students do an experiment by placing a tiny piece of bread under a simple cardstock pyramid that we made. These pyramids stayed in the classroom for several weeks. They also placed another piece of bread in a tiny covered box made of any material they wanted. In every case, the control being that these were in my classroom where they could be watched, the bread in the box turned entirely dry and moldy and the bread under the pyramid stayed fresh and moist. Although I suppose skeptics would say that some of my little gifted kids could have found a way to replace the bits of bread without my knowing.

Dowsing is another one that has been around probably since the beginning of man. Ancient Egyptians and Chinese healers used dowsing equipment. Even the world's military has used dowsing rods to locate underground tunnels and booby traps, etc. But dowsing was also used extensively in Russia for centuries and their folklore passed down through the centuries, also says that murderers and thieves could be located by using dowsing rods. Researchers where interested in researching other practical uses for dowsing rods and pendulums. They found out that dowsing could be quite accurate, especially with some improvements being made. Dowsing rods are used essentially to find underground water sources, minerals, and even buried treasures, etc. However, the Russians decided to try to create a way to test dowsing capabilities, which the Western world said was impossible. And maybe one of the reasons they were not as skeptical as Western scientists, is that many Russian scientists themselves could use dowsing rods with a very high percentage of accuracy. And this is some of the information the Russian researchers found: These radiation waves were even sensitive right through the bodies of humans, because no matter what they shielded their subjects with, their dowsing rods still worked. A forked branch dowsing rod cut from a shade tree worked longer than those cut from others, and, if the dowsing rod was repaired in any way it stopped working. Women were more accurate dowsers than men. They also found that the rod could be used to solve many technical problems such as locating underground broken electrical cables or water pipes, etc.

They then gave this science a new name called the Biophysical Effects Method or BPE, which began to be used to uncover the vast natural resources all over Russia. They examined questions that Western researchers did with machinery, such as the question can one use this sort of thing when flying over terrain rather than being so close to the ground? They discovered that this natural wave or force was everywhere they explored and they then discovered particular aspects of this force such as the fact that a vast amount of water and the speed of its flow determined how well the dowsing rods worked. They seemed to be accurate on either side of a river's shore but would not work within the stream itself. They asked themselves if mineral deposits deep in the earth emitted an energy ray that the dowsers could pick up accurately, and found this to be true. And they found that this force fluctuates, especially during lightning storms and other weather anomalies. They also found, for example, that gold deposits can be found more easily at sunrise rather than at sunset, because at sunrise the dowser will lay directly over the deposit but as the sun moves across the sky, the force field from the gold will deflect to spots further and further away from the actual vein. And they related these findings to the force fields that surround and go through all objects animate and inanimate on the earth.

In the book The Divining Heart the authors talk about the Seven Spiral Steps in learning dowsing. I had never thought about muscle testing, kinesiology, remote viewing, energy healing and dowsing as being a spiritual journey, but these authors do. The stages chronologically are: finding locations by sight, targets located up-to-the-horizon, locating targets beyond your sight, training one's hands and fingers to dowse without tools, on the ground, under the ground and on maps. The fourth stage is to achieve a complementary spiritual awareness in cooperation with nature to dowse through time and distance and the fifth stage is to discover and identify disharmonious energy fields and bring them into harmony with earth energies. The sixth stage is to be able to rearrange forces in the natural world, and only the great mystics, saints and spiritual masters achieve this level of dowsing. And of course they are talking about rearranging matter itself, transporting objects, healing illnesses, and bringing harmony to the world in general through earth energies. Science is getting there too, so there are lots of moral questions coming up in the future!

Questions like what happens when one change is created? Can this one change affect many other energy fields and what happens when it does? This interconnection of all things can either wreak havoc or bring about miraculous changes on the earth. The authors also talk about teaching those who wish to pursue this field of study, that they are custodians of the land and that everything around us can teach us something. But who will teach these concepts to the scientists, politicians and military leaders? On the other hand, when a remote viewer psi spy working for the military was sent to bi-locate and spy on another country's secret weapon research, he accidentally stepped inside of the energy beam the weapon was emitting, while seeking to understand how the weapon was being tested. He was unable to get out of the beam's flow of energy for quite a while and was literally entranced by what he was experiencing even though he also realized that he might be dying. While in the energy stream he was caught up in the beautiful colors and lights even though he knew that if his other body was dying, his entire consciousness might die too. Yet by experiencing this overwhelming surge of energetic powers, when he did eventually wake up and manage to pull himself out of the stream, he was never spiritually the same again. The experience was like an amazing near-death experience and he was unable to return to his previous consciousness or even to how he viewed his previous life.

And the last topics they discuss are very relevant too, like dowsing for positive energies, ley lines and the best places to build. They say these energies are a reflection of each single creative impulse on our planet and where these energies meet or cross each other is a powerful grid of ley lines which encompass the entire earth and provides energy spots on which to build our meeting places or houses of worship, etc. The American Society of Dowsers sees all forms of dowsing, remote viewing, and energy healing through time and distances, as a way to manipulate energies for positive change and healing, for planetary stewardship, and exploring the multi-verses. They call this a heightening of sensory intuitions and the exploring of Supersensory Worlds, which is the seventh level of spiritual dowsing. Within the seventh level they name four ways of thinking about psychic realms: understanding and working with invisible fields or auras, exploring the invisible kingdom parallel to us in nature such as in elementals and animals, learning to attune to higher frequency planes, and last, developing an understanding of interactions with "worlds" not familiar to us. In other words, it is learning to break through our limited views of the worlds that we cannot see around us or near us. They say that creative imagination is true intuition and that our present limited view of our world is different from what our scientists now tell us. (*The Divining World by Patricia C. and Richard D. Wright, Destiny Books, 1994*).

Psychotronic Generators

It was in Bulgaria that scientists first thought about creating a machine that would work with and measure the energy fields around all things on the earth. Since scientists in Russia and her surrounding countries had now identified the existence of this energy field and confirmed it for themselves they were now willing to try and replicate it in the laboratory. "This bio- energy, which we called Psychotronic Energy, seems to be behind PK, it may be the basis of dowsing. It may prove to be involved in all psychic happenings. The psychotronic generators draw this bio-energy from a person, accumulate it, and use it. Once charged with your energy, the generators can do some of the things a psychic can do." This generator was called at the time, the Pavlita generator and Robert Pavlita was an inventor and designer for a Czech textile plant. He designed the experiments that the scientists conducted. He will in the future be considered the father of such technology, now being worked on across the world. Russians thought it was fraud proof but that proved to not be so later. (*Ibid., Iron Curtain, pp.366 – 388*).

However, it was the first machine of its kind and scientists did have much success with it. The idea that this force could be harnessed and directed at will, has now been proven to be true, but we still have a long way to go to actualize and prove this. We can only hope that its many uses will be for wonderful technological advances and not for mass destruction and mind control, etc. Unfortunately, PSI spying is covering equal ground and one can just imagine the many uses that people will come up with concerning money and power and control over others. This first of its kind machine, proved to be able to detect and record this energy that they said the human organism produces. And these scientists were pioneers in this field that continues today, in both private and government sponsored programs all around the globe, including the United States. Our psychic children can be viewed as a commodity for evil or a wonderful wave of the future, and if their psychic gifts can be reproduced in the laboratory through brain research, what wonders will we see in the future, or what horrors we will witness if put in the wrong hands, for all the claims of fraudulent practices now.

One of the things never addressed but proven to be true in much of the psychic research in Russia was that they found many of their psychics to exhibit an ability they could not understand. These people seemed to be several people at once, like a subliminal flicker, they could be seen to be using many different voices and other faces appeared as they "intuited." Perhaps this is why people often tell me my living room is full of people that I cannot see when I read? Is there a spiritual component to psychic ability as well, that a machine cannot reproduce? Whatever the answers will be in the future, some conclusions were drawn in this book that may be startling to Americans. That Russians are aiming at the uses of PSI abilities, rather than just proving they exist. Russians consider PSI research as a vast scientific field, rather than something yet to be proven by American scientists, many of whom still mock these discoveries as hoaxes or frauds. Russians are focusing on many different fields of research and gathering information from a wide range of expertise. Soviets are well informed about research in the United States, while the American government and private research facilities know less about Soviet research. Soviets see PSI as physiological and not statistical, psychological or philosophical. Many of them have a national enthusiasm for this type of research. They look at their scientists in these fields, who talk more freely about their own personal psychic abilities, as great men and women, just like their composers, Russian ballet instructors, inventors, mathematicians, etc. In other words, their attitudes towards these types of things, encourage their young people, rather than discourage and shut them down when it comes to psychics producing paranormal phenomenon and becoming involved in this type of research. But like all countries, Russia has its many skeptics too!

Early PSI Research in the Baltic Countries, Mexico, Japan, Holland & All of Europe

In Europe when Uri Geller was so popular, he broadcast his spoon, fork, knife bending and wristwatch starting activities in various countries with amazing results. You were asked to place these objects in front of the television; I even remember doing this in America. But in the European countries they received many phone calls after his shows with an interesting phenomenon going on. Many children, after only seeing one demonstration of this were able to reproduce this phenomenon over and over again on their own. In one country alone, they received calls saying that over 1,500 children had done the same thing, bending silverware or restarting wristwatches on their own. Nowadays, one can develop ESP abilities by taking a class on this subject. Many people can bend a spoon with a high success rate. Yet many people are still astounded by what they think is "magic" rather than a brain wave technique. Whether real or imagined – does it really matter in the scheme of things, which it is?

Too bad Uri Geller became tempted to add onto his amazing abilities with magic tricks. Skeptics say that children or adults "convince" themselves that they have bent the spoon with mind power, even while they are exerting just enough pressure on the spoon to bend it, unbeknownst to themselves. I have yet to hear the explanation for the watches, as I remember that this was what I did, concentrated on the watch with a dead battery, coming to life again or ticking again. And the watch did begin to tick again, I did not imagine it. It kept ticking all afternoon, but the next day when I took it out of the box, it was dead again. At the time I believed that Geller was sending some sort of power through the television because I was around twelve or thirteen years old. Now I know that he was simply saying to all of us children that we could do this on our own. But I was certain I did not imagine it, as I did nothing to force the hands on the clock to change. Perhaps the power to imagine something is an energetic force of its own!

In Mexico City they found over one thousand children who could see with various parts of their body, called skin reading in Russia and called eyeless sight in China. Some people call this the "Hundredth Monkey" phenomenon, while others see this as a world on the brink of discovering the abilities of their own individual brains and the connections we have with each other everywhere in the energy fields that surround and integrate us all. And if you have never heard of "The Hundredth Monkey" theory, read Ken Kesey's book. The idea is that when one person makes a discovery that moves mankind forward, this can affect a hundred other people and so on, until the idea jumps across oceans, moves like a wave across continents, and finally awakens every human being on the planet to a new idea or new way of doing something. And it is this ripple effect that will awaken our brain powers, our hearts and our spiritual links. However, one set of people see this as advances in technology and brain research, while another group see this as a spiritual energetic force generated from within each of us. We shall see. I have no problem combining it all into evolution with energy fields and with God as an energy force, so powerful that the creation of the universe and other universes happened over time and from some distance away.

In Romania, Poland, Bulgaria, Hungary and East Germany, parapsychology is being researched as a true science in many forms. In Japan, China, Mexico and Russia now, psychic children as well as adults are being studied as a science in many fields. Even in America, many private research facilities are researching much of this phenomena and one would expect that our government is researching secretly to keep up with the Russians and the Chinese, but more likely for political and military reasons, although research concerning children is probably not going on very much at this point. While in the private sector, I have already mentioned the difficulty one faces when trying to include children in such research projects. However, experts like Linda Kreger Silverman and P.M.H. Atwater, have spent their lives researching children and they are now coming to similar conclusions.

A brief mention of Holland here is absolutely necessary because it seems that some pretty innovative ideas and programs have come out of several Scandinavian countries but especially from Holland. Van Dyke's "way before their time" programs for deaf/blind autistic-like children were in place about the same time as Jean Ayres came along with integrative developmental ways to teach all children, and way before Dr. Greenspan's considered current programs for Autistic-like children and children with Aspergers. It was Holland which led the way in taking Royal Rife's energy healing techniques into the computer age with programs like I Health, which created an integrative energy wave, light and sound healing computer program based on Rife's massive classifications and identifications of the many invading pathogens. And it is in Holland where Dr. Tineke Noordegraaf and Dr. Rob Bontenbal have been using past life therapy so successfully with children in the last decade that this type of therapy has become accepted all over Europe. Parents from all over this continent are traveling to Holland with their child for help and many therapists from other European countries are now training in their methods. These therapies have helped children with such difficulties as diabetes, palsy, phobias and sleep disorders.

What in the World is Going on Culturally for Psychic Children?

There are many ancient cultural traditions and techniques that still exist today in some sort of compilation of the old and the new, where intuitive practices are still encouraged for children and adults as well as rites of passage such as the vision quests among various Native American cultures, the dream walkers in Australian Aboriginal practices or the Huna tribal ways in Hawaii, etc. Some children are still groomed for these sorts of practices even in our modern world, part shamanic master, part medicine man, part prophet and part the heyokied "backward walkers" who while a bit crazy or challenged in some other way, were revered within the tribes of plains Indians for their unique talents.

Indigenous people can teach us a lot about what sorts of things we are missing in our modern world, especially for the coming of age in children and teens in acknowledging and exploring their psychic abilities.

Crawford gives one example of this mentoring in her book on the ancient practice in the Huna community in Hawaii, where an adult or Hanai adoption takes place. Each child has a mentoring adult to train them in spiritual practices while developing their own special skills as an intuitive. And in the ancient times the child was literally removed from their natural parents for a time and went to live with their Hanai parents for mentoring. Whatever gifts the child was born with were considered of equal value in their culture, intuitive or not. This Huna system encouraged inclusion and minimized differences and no intuitive child felt all alone. However, even the Huna culture has a dark history of shamanic practices that might still continue today in some form. Max Freedom Long went to Hawaii in 1917 as a teacher and ended up staying for years. He wrote several books about his experiences there, so if you want to know about all of the parts of this culture you can read The Secret Science of Miracles, his first book in which he explores both the dark and light sides of Huna cultural magic, instant healing and promotion of psychic abilities of their young people, etc.

"The Huna tradition values intuitive gifts in children and conveys messages to their children of valuing these gifts. They don't elevate or denigrate the gift, but rather, meet it in a respectful and purposeful manner. Children can know that their gifts are valued when the adults around them appreciate the perspectives and insights they bring. Since the Hawaiian culture took these gifts seriously, it was poised to offer specific kinds of parenting and training for children exhibiting these gifts." The elders made sure that their grandchildren knew that these gifts had certain social and cultural expectations tied to them. These children are taught that "reading" someone without their permission, or simply walking up to someone and announcing their intuitive findings was extremely impolite and that there are many rules and social mores that they needed to learn, to be a responsible intuitive. Much like what Native American children were taught and mentored in, in early America with a respect for the natural world. (*Ibid., the highly intuitive child, pp. 158-159*).

In collecting general information about what sort of psychic research is going on in foreign countries and even in the United States, especially concerning children, it is a scary proposition to say the least. Will we go to a "good" world, a "bad" world, or one like we have now in which chaos reigns supreme? I can only hope that we are indeed "shifting and evolving" and are being given a choice to move forward in the right direction together. And that the new generations of intuitive children will lead the way. These "children of the paranormal" are beginning to voice their opinions much more loudly now. In conceiving a new paradigm of worldwide communities, they are testing the limits of this "old world," in order to create a new and better one. They are warriors in this new world coming and however much they may seem selfish and oblivious to outside observers, they really are <u>Builders and Adaptors</u> in disguise, making their way forward for the <u>Humanitarian Aquarians</u> of the future.

> "...everything you seek and everything you experience – everything – is inside you. If you want to change anything, you do it inside. The whole idea is total responsibility. There's no one to blame. It's all you."
>
> --"Ancient Hawaiian Teachings of Ho'oponoponop," <u>Zero Limits</u>, p. 41.

> "When this 'inner family' is in alignment, a person is in rhythm with Divinity. With this balance, life begins to flow. Thus, Ho'oponopono helps restore balance in the individual first, and then all of creation."
>
> --Ibid., <u>Zero Limits</u>, p. 44

CHAPTER FOURTEEN

Guiding Psychic Kids Through Physical & Intuitive Worlds – Activities

"...mysterious areas of research postulate...the belief, the knowledge, and even the experience that our physical world of the senses is a mere illusion, a world of shadows, and that the three-dimensional tool we call our body serves only as a container or dwelling place for something infinitely greater and more comprehensive than that body and which constitutes the matrix of real life."

--Holger Kalweit, Dreamtime & Inner Space

"The power of intuitive understanding will protect you from harm until the end of your days."

--Lao Tzu, 600 BC

Sensitivities & Health:

1) Tell them the Flower in the Woods story and then have the "there is nothing wrong with having a sensitive body" discussion with them. Once you get the idea, you can gear this story to any type of children's group or even adults by changing the subject matter and location.

   To gage just how sensitive you are, pretend that you are walking through the woods and you see a flower by the side of the path. Do you never even see the flower, or just never even observe it? Do you stomp on the flower as you walk by? Do you tear some flowers out of the ground and let them wilt in your hands as you head for home? Do you continue walking although you noticed all the flowers in the field? Do you stop and admire the flowers and all of the other lovely scenery and then walk on? Do you notice that one of the flowers has a petal missing or that it seems just a little ragged and dry and then walk on? Do you notice several other things about the flower and as you walk on you think about that poor little flower for a few minutes? Do you stop and examine the flower, noticing all the details concerning it, get some water from a nearby stream to pour onto it and then walk on? Do you sit down and contemplate what to do for this one poor flower? Do you begin weeping for the flower uncontrollably and the people hiking with you think you are crazy or "too sensitive?"Do you never do anything about it but spend the rest of the day thinking about that poor little flower? Do you spend the rest of the day by the flower trying to help it to continue to grow? Do you get others on the path involved in saving this flower? Do you begin to think about all the poor flowers that are suffering in those particular woods? Do you begin to realize that there are poor suffering flowers all over the forest and try to get expert help to save them? Do you find yourself unable to sleep or work because there are so many suffering flowers all over the neighborhood you live in, in all the forests of your state, country and eventually all over the world? Do you have to stay home and become a hermit because you can hear all these flowers screaming as they are ripped from the ground all around you? Flourish this with your own ideas or use something less silly, depending on what your child will respond to. You will be surprised about the kind of information you can gain from this one little story. I used it or a variation that my students could respond to, every year in my classroom, to quickly identify my super empathic, emotionally intelligent students who would need additional emotional support now and then. I had them raise their hands when I got to the one that they thought that they would do for or with the flower. A few kept their hands up through the whole story, and there they were!

2) Help empathic children to trust their intuitive "Yes" and "No" answers:

   "Yes" feels lighter, tingles, sparkles, vibrates, opens, loves, has a happy heart, feels like a shower, a warm rain on the skin, the room actually "lightens," or feels comforting, etc. "No" feels heavy, sad, tight, flat, dim, dark, blank, you can't breathe, there is a heaviness on the chest, the throat constricts or sometimes there is a slight headache, stomachache or some body aches, etc.

3) There is a tendency for more sensitivities to sounds, smells, light, and other environmental pollutants, which calls for even more attention to diet and a need for a high PH content of at least 7.0 in your drinking water. Also have your child eat a 60% alkaline food to 40% acidic food diet to maintain the child's health.

4) Introduce and play with, various kinds of exercise or disciplines such as Tai Chi, Yoga, and a type of Karate, Chi-Gong practices, gymnastics or running, all the many individualized sports available. Team sports are also good but can be added in as an addition to an individualized one.

5) Do Daily Maintenance Skills:

   a) Do Energy Field repair and rejuvenation exercises:

Number One: A quick brushing down the body as you are standing or sitting, three times, is an old Chinese Meridian wash technique for clearing energy. Just spread your palms out and brush a few inches away from the body to the floor over and over until you have brushed the whole body thoroughly.

Number Two: In this one you shut your eyes and imagine two very wide invisible paint brushes and begin, in your mind's eye, to brush all around your feet until you feel a tingling, warmth or coolness and then continue on to your lower legs and knees, upper legs and hips, hands, wrists and lower arms, elbows and upper arms and shoulders, neck and face, around the top of the head in a clockwise motion. Then let a shower of light violet light pour from these paint brushes from the crown of the head downward until you are completely incased in this curtain of violet light. You can also use this method for a chakra cleansing by imaging that you are brushing around each chakra internally along with the whole body Meridian Wash, using the imagined paint brushes.

Number Three: A third one is to stand with your legs slightly apart and your arms at your sides slowly turn your palms face up and put your arms straight out from either side of your body. Begin to feel a small ball of energy in each palm and then slowly, very slowly bring your palms together until you reach a point where the energy joins together into one ball of energy and then roll this ball of energy back and forth in your hands, top palm and lower palm, back and forth, as you "play" with this ball of energy. After a minute of this slowly extend your arms upward to the sky and wait until you feel energy or tingling begin to cascade over your whole body. Enjoy this energy shower and in your mind say an affirmation of thanks for all that you are grateful for.

b) Chakra Balance Exercises, there are some good CDs for this, such as "Chakra Balancing" by Stacy Dean and Gerald Jay Markoe or "Journey Through the Chakras" by Jackie Haverty, that will teach not only affirmations for the seven main chakras but also the most commonly matching colors and how to visualize them as well as basic breathing exercises which you and your child can learn together. The basic chakras are 1) Root/Red or tail bone; 2) Sacral/Orange or two inches below your navel; 3) Solar Plexus/Yellow or stomach; 4) Heart/Emerald Green; 5) Throat/Light Blue; 6) Third Eye/Indigo or deep purple-blue located in the middle of forehead between eyebrows; and 7) Crown/Light Violet or top of the head. Balancing or cleansing the chakras can be done once a week at the most or at least once a month at the least. Add this in as needed after your relaxation exercise and before beginning your self-healing techniques and meditation. Some people like to check if their chakras are out of balance by using a pendulum held over the chakra or a special pendulum of colored beads that are in the order of the chakras. One can hold each bead and place one's intent on that chakra and then let the pendulum swing for a "yes" or "no" answer. Or simply ask in your mind and trust the answer that you get for each chakra.

Cleansing the Chakras can be done in several ways. A foot above the head is the anchoring light of pearl or metallic white and a foot below the feet is another pearl or anchoring silver light in the earth. One, you can brush around each chakra with an invisible paint brush, but always do them in order from the Sacral to the Crown of the head and then anchor in your feet and your head with the 8th and 9th Chakras. Two, or you can spin a small ball of light through each chakra until once again you feel a tingling sensation and then move on to the next chakra. Three, some people visualize each one as a pendulum swinging ball of light that swings back and forth through the whole etheric body which is thought to be about a foot in front and a foot behind you or even a little larger than this as you cleanse each chakra. Four, you can add in an affirmation for the qualities of each chakra which you can learn from the various guided CD chakra balances. Five, or you can use a mantra, chant or sound for each chakra as it is being cleansed, the same or a different one for each separate chakra. All of these variations clear the auric field of any negative or polarized energy. Six, then "ground" yourself by putting a ball of white light bouncing above your head and one going down into the earth under your feet about a foot in both directions to finish the exercise, securing you to the ground or planet, as well as to the higher chakras above your head.

You can add in a general meaning of each chakra although there are so many variations, I just tried to combine a few of them into one set of thoughts. The Root Chakra represents vitality, courage, self-confidence, physical power, working on the physical plane and being grounded. The Sacral Chakra represents happiness, confidence, resourcefulness, desire, sexuality, procreation, creativity and devotion. The Solar Plexus Chakra represents wisdom, clarity, self-esteem, digestion, assimilation, and working towards one's highest purpose to manifest one's goals. The Heart Chakra represents expressing love in thought, word and deed and the love of self and others. It also represents the soul/heart consciousness, the releasing of emotional traumas, balance and self-control. This chakra is also the base or foundation for the higher levels of consciousness, or higher chakras. Some people like to add in an additional chakra located in the thymus which is teal in color and represents the maintenance of your body, good health and physical well-being. I have never heard a name for this chakra except Thymus/Teal. The Throat Chakra represents an authentic expression of one's own truth, the ability to verbalize and use the power of the spoken word. It also can mean self-expression, knowledge, and decisiveness.

The Twelve Chakras

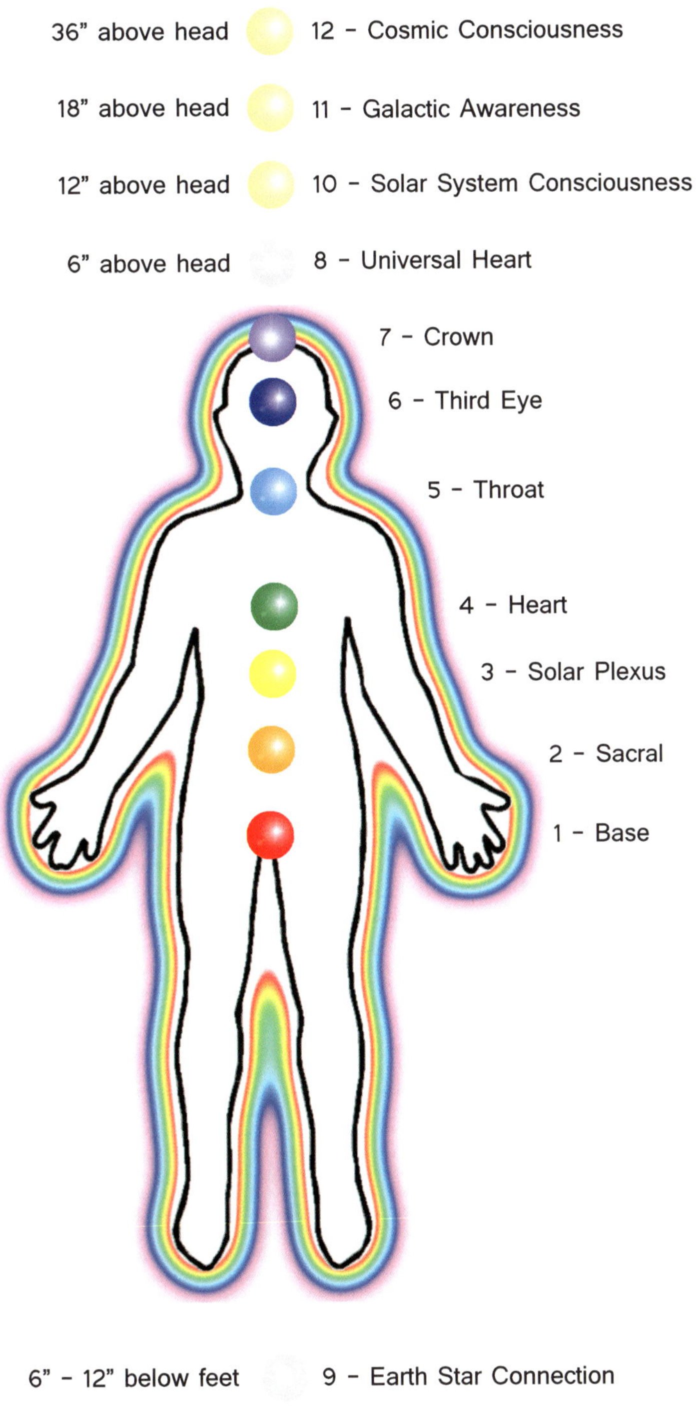
36" above head
12 - Cosmic Consciousness
18" above head
11 - Galactic Awareness
12" above head
10 - Solar System Consciousness
6" above head
8 - Universal Heart
7 - Crown
6 - Third Eye
5 - Throat
4 - Heart
3 - Solar Plexus
2 - Sacral
1 - Base
6" - 12" below feet
9 - Earth Star Connection

The Third Eye Chakra represents inner wisdom, spiritual awareness, channeling intuition, developing mysticism and understanding, and perceiving divine perfection in all things. The Crown Chakra is the Gateway the higher level chakras and represents gaining self-knowledge, understanding beauty, creativity and inspiration. It also represents gaining and perceiving oneness with the infinite in terms of peace, wisdom and the God force.

While many people believe there are 12 Chakras and many others believe there are many more than this, I will just briefly mention the other five chakras. While the colors are either all white or vary according to different belief systems this is one interpretation of the other five: just above the crown is the 8th Chakra/Pearl or Silver-White which is located a few inches above our heads and is called the Universal Heart which connects us to the Heavens. Just below our feet about a hand's length is the 9th Chakra called the Earth Star/ Pearl or Silver-White which connects us to our planet and roots us to the earth beneath our feet. The 10th Chakra is located about a hand's length above our heads and is called the Solar System/Yellow-White Light to which it is connected. The 11th Chakra/Yellow-White Light is located about 18 inches above our heads and is called the Galactic Awareness which connects us to the galaxy. And the last or 12th Chakra is located about 36 inches above our heads and is connected to the Cosmos Consciousness/Bright Yellow- White Light or the entire Universe. These five chakras represent the holographic octave that one wants to achieve for "transpersonal consciousness," or to be connected with every realm and being. (*The 8th Chakra, Jude Currivan, Hay House, 2006*).

The 8th chakra or Universal Love is the Bridge to other dimensions and worlds, learning to travel through time and distance, and gaining perceptions and understanding of these worlds. The 9th chakra is the Earth Star and Grounds us to our home planet to help us understanding our physical world and the many earth energies and wisdoms. The 10th chakra is the "Soular" System, a clever way to introduce that while this is about understanding our own solar system, it is also about soul travel and learning to heal the soul so that we can be prepared to travel anywhere in the cosmos. The 11th chakra is the Galaxy Gateway that provides us with the wisdom and guidance to navigate through multi-dimensional realms. And the 12th chakra is the Cosmic Consciousness which is all about becoming one with the source, remembering who we really are, and understanding transcendence and transformation as well as the deeper working of the cosmos.

c) Shower a white/gold light Most Powerful Shield of Protection or pyramid over the body. You can do this at the end of any of the previous exercises by imagining a shield of protection pouring over your body in a violet light from the top of your head and then the "thicker" gold/white light coming down over this one from above your head. As you continue to do this once a day, you will begin to feel a tingling all over your body which feels as if you just took a warm shower.

d) Let go of other people's energy by shaking or brushing or washing it off, taking a shower or scrubbing hands and arms with water, self-healing "draw" or guided CD, heart cleanse, visualize the energy leaving your body. Do the deep breathing exercise: inhale through the nose, hold for four counts, exhale through the mouth. Do three of these to get the air deep into the bottom of your lungs. Take the oxygen in slowly because your body may react to taking in more oxygen and it might feel strange at first. Few of us know how to breathe properly except for perhaps singers and athletes or yoga and meditation practitioners, etc. You can also use a healer's technique for clearing energy after a session with someone, and there are many of these. The one I know involves holding your arms straight above your head with your hands in fists. You then put your thumbs over your fists and then behind your fists going back and forth several times to release any energy that you may have picked up from the client. Variations on this is to flick your fingers or hands, rub your hands and arms or brush them off, or wash your hands and arms with soap and water.

6) Keep yourself "grounded": push down gently on your head with your hands and gradually sink into your chair, place your feet on the earth, walk on the grass barefoot, garden, get out in nature, take a walk, play with mud or clay, use your pottery wheel, do a nature treasure hunt, hug or climb a tree and stay there a while, do some movement or exercise, rub feet and arms and legs, play a musical instrument, etc.

7) Meditation – Why does one meditate every day? "Meditation has two purposes. First, it centers your mind upon spirit within. In that way meditation helps you stay calm, creative and loving during the day. You are more apt to see the true perfection in all situations, instead of reacting to the illusion of problems. Meditation is a method that helps you exist in the eye of the hurricane during your daily affairs. Second, meditation gives you access to the infinite universal wisdom so you'll receive whatever information or guidance you seek. We are often so busy that we don't hear the answers to our prayers. Third, meditation is a quiet period in which you have a private tutoring session with Spirit. You get to ask anything you want, with full assurance of receiving an answer." (*The Lighworker's Way by Doreen Virtue, Hay House: Carlsbad, California, 1997, p.185*).

Meditating for at least ten minutes in the morning before you begin your day and ten minutes before you go to sleep at night is all you need to completely change your perspective on life and how you see nature and others in all their positive aspects. I like to spend at least half an hour to 45 minutes each morning and then do a brief meditation and prayer for those in need at bedtime. But try out whatever will do for your schedule. On the days that I cannot meditate because I am too caught up in the world, I throw on a CD guided meditation and just let it seep into my subconscious while I sit there contemplating all those irritating little issues that will not go away. You do not have to be a great master to do this. You do not have to try so hard that you feel that you have "failed" at meditation. Just let the time flow, whether with the clutter in your mind or without it. Every time you meditate you lift others in your life up just a little, as well as yourself. This is your time and for your own healing and your own insights. Yet others will benefit from this. If all else fails, slap on some soft music and just lay there, the power is in the intent and not in the amount of time you spend or how well you do it. Always send the excess positive energy created to loved ones who need it after your meditation by shutting your eyes, visualizing the person or place and then sending this energy like a ribbon, rippling cloth or gentle ocean wave.

Children can learn to do this with you or on their own, after a few "lessons" with you. The younger they are, the more quickly they will see the power in this for their own spirit's renewal. If you take it seriously, then they will. After only one or two sessions with my students at school and never using the world "meditation" because of their rather silly preconceived notions, they had the idea and we did it as needed, unbeknownst to the powers that be. In an ideal world, we would have done it every morning, and we did, but in many other ways, especially after the chaotic world of their weekends. This calming down quiet time can be done simply with music or reading to them or drawing about themselves, etc. People always wondered why I could manage my classroom so well. Discipline was short and sweet and to the point, followed by a "meditation" of one kind or another. Once children feel empowered, they can then begin to work and to learn, to love themselves and others as much as one can expect in our present school situations. We had our small group noisy times too, but I always tried to have quiet, "safe" times when the atmosphere of the day required it.

Another important thought is that meditation brings us synchronicity in our lives. Most of us do not believe this, even when it is right in front of our faces, and yet it is quite true. One has to meditate for a while before this synchronicity begins to show up, and of course, you have to look for it and realize that there is a connection between being closer to your own inner being as well as closer to our planet and all of its other creatures. After a while, if you are consistent and do it every day as much as possible, you will first notice how clearer and brighter everything is, and your focus begins to change from the stresses and miseries of the world to its beauties. This does not mean that you quit noticing and or helping those in need, but rather you begin to make the right choices instead of the wrong ones and this leads you to knowing yourself much more clearly as well.

Once this happens then the saying "let the river flow by itself" begins to be relevant. A touch of joy enters one's life, a deeper awareness of everything around you begins, and if you are in a "hungry" environment or country, you begin to understand your own state of affairs even more readily. Soon, those things you thought coincidences become an everyday occurrence and you actually look for them and recognize them for what they are. You see the symbols in nature, with animals, and with people. Somehow, no matter your belief system or religion or lack of such a thing, whatever beliefs you have will become more important to you as well, and if you continue for a very long time, you will begin to understand the true meaning of community. Understanding your fellow man is the most difficult, but it will come too. So spend this time with yourself as much as you can. You really don't need a teacher except at the beginning, and even then, meditation is a personal thing, done for yourself and for those whom you love. Meditation is also the most powerful tool for developing your intuitive talents and also spreading positive energy to others. If you meditate every day and then take a walk down a mall, every person you brush pass will become somewhat "energized" and a little bit more awake to their own spiritual purposes on earth. This is the real "key" to the shift that so many seem to dread. Group Meditation has a power all its own and can move an individual into a group consciousness that can send out healing energy into a worldwide consciousness for peace and community. (I have plenty of CD guided meditation suggestions just a little later.)

8) Edu-K Exercises, perhaps one set daily for each day of the week: Whole Body Coordination, Personal Ecology, Self-Awareness, and Positive Points for you and your child to do together. I always did in my classroom "Five Wishes" as one child held the forehead points on their partner sitting down in front of them, they gave each other five wishes with the added bonus of getting to know one and other. Get your own materials from the bibliography, or even seek out a facilitator for Edu-K in your community if your child appears to be one that will need deeper work. (These activities are covered in depth in Chapter Nine under Educational Kinesiology but all their activity books are super to use with your child at www.braingym.com.)

But briefly here, one always starts out with four things called the PACE, which is a big drink of water (activating the water system), rubbing the

Edu-K PACE

Exercises:

Cross Crawl

Brain Buttons

Glass of Water

Cook's Hook-Up

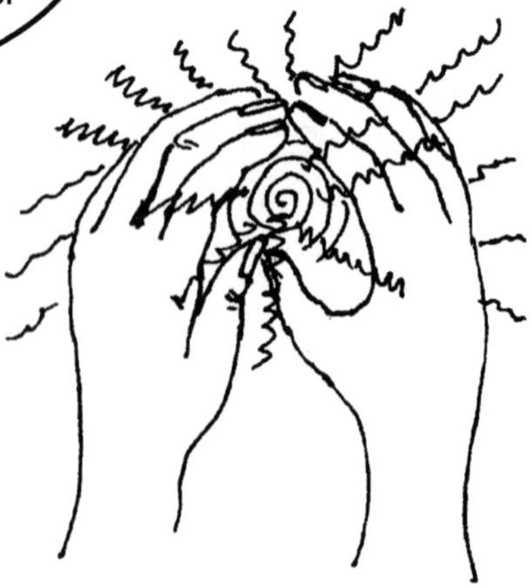

Energy Cages

Bring the two halves of "energy cages" of light in each palm slowly together until you feel a "ball" of energy. Then roll the energy ball around in your hands as you bring the left and right brains together in your imagination. Blend and mix the energy.

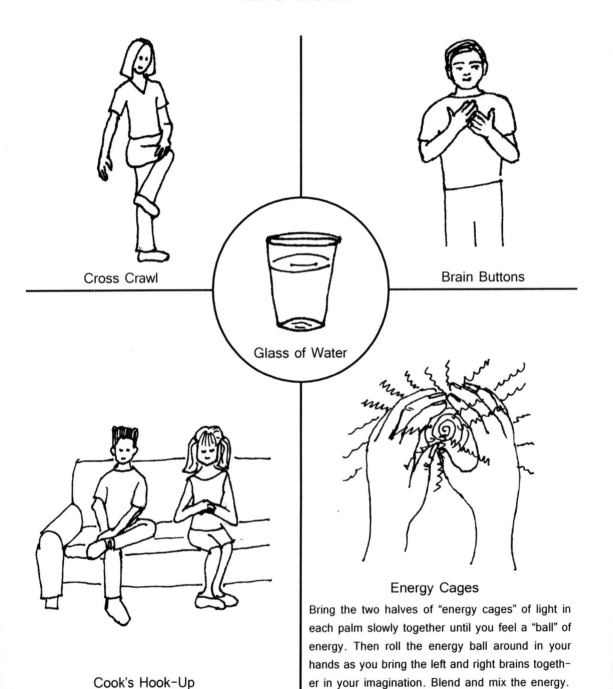

sores spots just below your collar bone on either side called "Brain Buttons" to wake up your lymphatic system, do the "Cross Crawl" which is marching in place slowly, alternating the left palm to the right knee and the right palm to the left knee, over and over until you have done twenty of these sets. This activates both sides of the brain to work together. And last you do the "Cook's Hook-Up" where you are sitting down with the left ankle over the right knee and your hands grasping the ball of your foot and your left ankle and vice versa for one minute each, and then still sitting form a cage with your fingers and hands and put your tongue on the roof of your mouth and count to 30 in your mind. This activates the nervous system and integrative brain functions. Even if you only do this set of exercises with your child, you are doing a great deal to build up the immune system and to get the body ready to function as an integrative unit. The Brain Gym Handbook is the best one to have for learning all the other specific exercises. I always added in an energy awareness exercise to the PACE to help the children become a little aware of their energy body. For example you can stretch your arms straight out to either side of you and slowly bring your hands together at midline. Somewhere in there you can feel a ball of energy and hold it and play with, turning it left and right with your palms or rolling it back and forth, children absolutely adore the magic of this!

9) Use the six minute Healing Code exercise before doing your EFT Tapping procedure. They fit together like a glove because you do your affirmations, your memory releases and focusing at the beginning and then do the four realignment code points, focusing on the same issue or painful area in the body using the same scale of one to ten. Only you do the Healing Code, repeating the sequence three times in a row, check your scale again and start on your Tapping. The tapping you do as many times as needed at each sitting until you are down to a one or a two on your "scale." Do them together three times a day. Check the Healing Code book for clearer drawings of the positions. These are powerful centers and you should feel this right away or in a couple of weeks.

10) You may add in a Self-Healing Draw if you would like the session to be even more powerful and healing for you. Tap lightly seven times around your crown or the top of the head in a clockwise motion. Use two fingers from each hand and rub behind each ear several times. Then pinch your fingers together and hold one hand and then the other. Then take your hands and hold your toes for a few seconds. Then either lay back down or sit in a comfortable chair and begin to imagine or visualize energy as a color or as a feeling being drawn up through your feet, legs, pelvis, trunk, hands, arms, shoulders, neck and into your head. As the energy draws upwards imagine those things that do not serve the body falling away from you like pieces of a body cast or crusts, peeling away from the body. About ten

The Healing "Draw"

1) Tap seven times around the top of the head clockwise. Use two fingers.

2) Using two fingers, rub behind both ears.

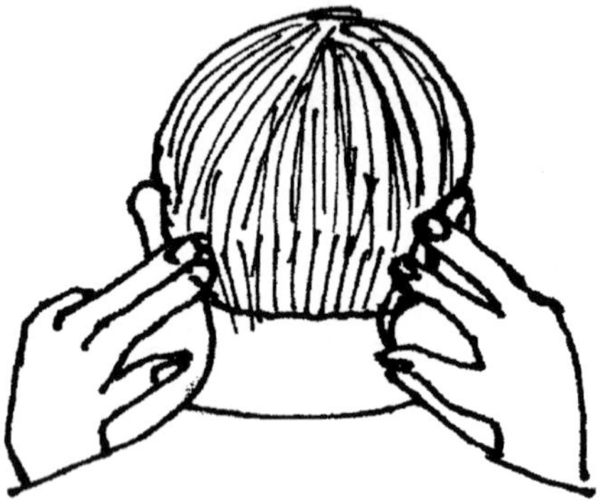

3) Squeeze fingers together using left hand.

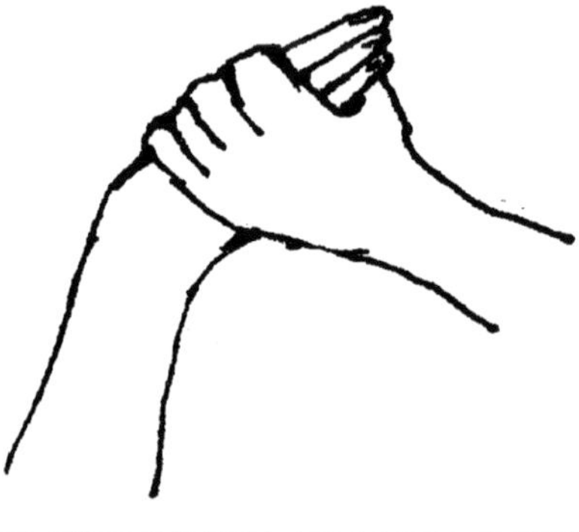

4) Squeeze fingers together using right hand.

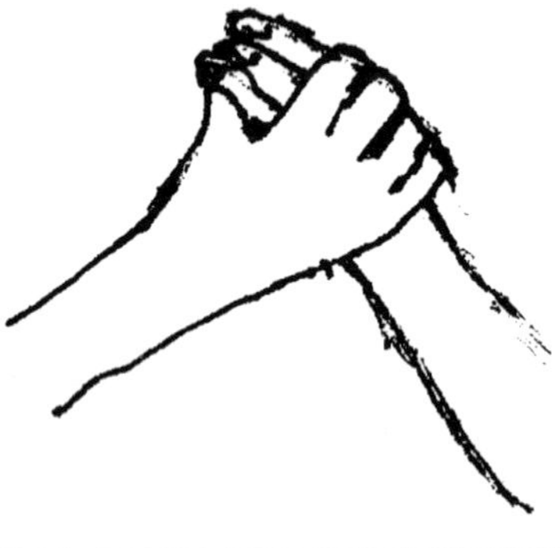

5) Squeeze toes together with hands.

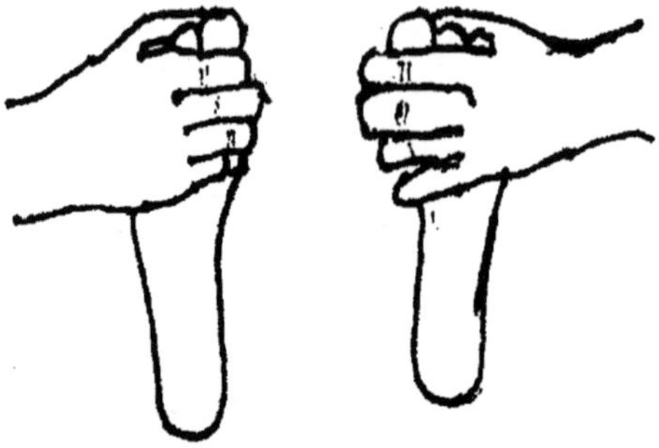

6) Begin draw by imagining pulling energy up through the feet and on up through the body.

Courtesy of Barbara Williams

minutes of this is enough to clear the body of emotional and hopefully physical toxins. (This idea courtesy energy healer, Barbara Williams and please check the chart on the following page to see how to do this properly on yourself.)

11) Since disease comes from inflammation and inflammation comes from stress, and stress comes from anxiety, poor diet, lack of exercise, and unresolved emotional issues, then Reverse Chain this! Remove all outside toxins that you can from your neighborhood and home, or at least be aware of them in your environment. Do what you can with this. Then remove as many internal toxins as you can from your body. Balance the alkaline/acidic foods in your diet, drink plenty of 7.0 range PH water, eliminate artificial sweetners and soft drinks entirely and you will naturally lose weight, keep your trigger points to below "crashing" over and over again, and eat a much healthier diet that can foster and maintain your health for you and your children. Many processed foods with poisonous food dyes will also naturally be eliminated from a 60% alkaline/40% acidic diet. And many allergy food triggers will also disappear. Next, use a method for realigning the body and empowering it, such as the Healing Code. Also use a method to give your body a daily tune-up, such as the Tapping exercise or a healing Draw or Paint Brush exercise. And Meditate daily to pull all of this together. There are many other methods or techniques for doing these three things: realigning, tuning-up and reducing stress so choose what you would like. Do not forget to do a Chakra Cleansing Exercise once a week using either a guided CD or one of your own. The ones I am giving you are the best I have found so far that don't cost a cent. You can also do all this by running to doctors or holistic health professionals but that will cost you a lot more. If you maintain your body, mind and spirit in these ways, then visits to professionals will lessen but not lessen your pocketbook. And finally a form of physical exercise is also needed whether walking a bit, doing a form of self-exercise, doing a sport, or even dancing.

Maintaining Intuitive Balances and Boundaries:

1) Model Conflict Resolution techniques for your child. My favorite among the ones out there that I always used with my students and works for any age, although often older students are just too angry and have to be calmed down first before you begin the process. This same procedure can be done at home as well.

Step One: Have the two students stand on either side of you apart from each other and if a larger group is involved, have the whole group pick a leader to stand in for each side and send the rest to sit down and observe. No one is allowed to talk except who I indicate; calmly and repetitively tell any one this that begins to speak until they are all quiet.

Step Two: If there are witnesses then you can have the best two witnesses stand next to the two leaders, one on each side that the group votes for.

Step Three: Indicate who is going to speak and make it clear that the other per son will get their equal turn, insist that they listen while the other person speaks.

Step Four: The first person gives their detailed account of what they think happened and what the problem is and everyone else is quiet and listens. If anyone speaks you calmly tell them not to and if someone observing continues to be disruptive they are asked to leave. How ever this rarely happens if you and the others have picked the leader of each group, who would be the disruptive person in the first place.

Step Five: Then the second person talks, same procedure.

Step Six: Witness number one gives their impartial account of the incident if there are any witnesses.

Step Seven: Witness number two, if there is a second one, will give their impartial account of what happened.

Step Eight: The first leader gets a rebuttal.

Step Nine: The second leader gets a rebuttal, although often you don't even get this far because one or the other leaders crumbles under the peer pressure of the witnesses who nearly always give an accurate account of what happened and the two witnesses are usually in agreement.

Step Ten: By this time and in 90 percent of the cases, the whole thing blows over and the two leaders agree to agree or disagree, but still agree to get along better, shake hands and go back outside to play, as most such conflicts happen on the playground.

By going through this procedure however, you are not only showing your concern as the supervisor but empowering the students (and every student involved) to learn how to solve their own disagreements in this role playing activity. When everyone can see that this will be the consistent and counted on reaction to any disagreement, conflicts are reduced by quite a bit. That other 10 percent might end up in the principal's office or with a more severe but fair consequence, and of course, the teacher has "The Stare" to fall back on as well! Parents can use a time out rug or a family communication game which provides consequences.

2) Help them determine if they are feeling their own emotions or someone else's. Ways to check this are: facial clues, body language awareness (there are some fun exercises for this in Face Reading Secrets by Rose Rosetree), muscle testing, asking questions about what details they notice, help them to be very aware of how they express their own feelings, and locate where the problem is coming from.

3) Teach them to balance their intuitive gifts with taking good care of themselves as well, spiritually, etherically, physically, mentally and emotionally. That these five "bodies" are separate and yet interconnected, is a hard concept to conceive of or understand. However, all five "bodies" need to be in balance with each other to have a grounded and happy life. For example, the body can have a memory of abuse long after this abuse has been worked on emotionally and mentally. So the body has to be helped along to release and heal these memory imprints.

4) Teach them when to listen to their inner voice so they know when to say something to others about their intuitive flashes and when this would be totally inappropriate to do so. They should know not to ask intuitive questions at inappropriate times. These "Hits" or "Pop Ups" can really get one in trouble in a lot of situations and using one's common sense and appropriate social skills with each situation that comes up, is your child's best bet. Showing off at first would be tempting and probably will be done, but eventually the child will see that they may be hurting or disturbing others by relaying this information too soon, or even at all. Predicting what kind of pizza will be ordered by several teens is only okay as a parlor game!

5) Deliver information to your child openly and honestly. Intuitive and gifted children and probably most children will know, if you are not doing this and will call you on this too! One year when I was teaching there was an incident where an adopted child in a born again Christian family, was stealing exorbitant amounts of items and foods rather obsessively in my classroom. I met with the parents several times to try and deal with this situation as they wished too. The child knew exactly what he was doing and was just waiting to see just how far he could go with his discussing parents whose rules were mainly that their child should just want to be a good Christian child. When finally I just couldn't stand it anymore, I turned and said to the child, "You just feel like you are starving all the time don't you?" "You just never have enough of anything and you have to hoard these things to stay safe, don't you?" The entire atmosphere changed at that moment as he relaxed and smiled and was so grateful that an adult had finally said what he couldn't say. I have always felt that the parents got it too, but did not want to admit this. But by saying this, the child became empowered and was ready to talk.

6) Respect your child's intuition and confirm its "realness." Don't dismiss their intuitive insights, but discuss them at length. Children have insights but they also have short, quick flashes and you need to help them differentiate between the two. I have always called these quick and sudden flashes, "pop ups," when something comes out of your mouth and you really don't know where it came from. They nearly always get you in trouble even as an adult, so be prepared to explain them when they come to your child. Best advice for anything like this is to wait twenty four hours and think about it before you act, unless of course it is something serious like someone getting on a plane that might crash, and even then you can only warn, but don't push it unless your feeling is that strong.

7) Explain the difference between intuitive thoughts and magical thinking or a vivid imagination. Real experiences can sometimes be confirmed and how one feels is different. Some can feel an immediate sense of danger or fear; others can feel an overwhelming pressure to pass newly intuited information along to its source. I know that I have to pass along any additional information I get about someone as quickly as I can to stop myself from carrying it around with me. Checking for immediate confirmation of the information can help relieve the child's worries and anxieties, if this is possible and can be done, and keep a record in a diary about such things for additional confirmation and the possibility of something similar coming up again in the future.

8) Help the child refine his or her intuition by gathering the feelings, all the impressions, and any other information gathered intuitively. Then sit down and sort it all out together. Some intuitives use tools to help them with this, like cards that will confirm for the child that what they are intuiting is accurate. Stay calm and focused on the issue at hand, pause to reflect after the information comes in, because this always gives one a different perspective on things, however, don't allow this reflection to enter into the arena of doubt! Take action as soon as possible and use your chosen modes of calming yourself down and removing or gaining energy for the task at hand. Going to the library or internet or gathering information through interviews, books, newspapers, can really legitimize the child's intuitive "knowings" in full detail. And again, keeping a record of these more dramatic impressions can really encourage and confirm for the child, his or her abilities and insights. Use your dream symbol books too! And make sure you confirm the history of objects in the environment, to make sure these objects are not affecting the child's energies or emotions or both. Sometimes a single object can have a negative history or have a connection to the child, but not in a positive way.

9) Use various methods to tune down the frequency overloads on your intuitive radio by empowering your child. Find out how your child has learned to turn the intuitive channels on and off, or if they don't have a technique help them explore the possibilities and choose one. Opening and shutting the eyes, using a trigger object to differentiate the two worlds, visualizing turning the faucet on at the beginning and then off at

the end – Lisa Williams uses a hat – or anything else that comes into the mind of your child. Sorting out the "channels" when you are being bombarded by several at once, can also be helpful to shut some of them down, so you can concentrate on what is important at that moment.

I will often get interfering impressions right in the middle of a reading that I find out later go along with some theme in the reading but are really connected to a natural disaster or crime somewhere else in the world. By opening my "channel" to read, other channels will come in occasionally, or even other so-called spirits who want to have their say at an inappropriate time. I remember these peculiar visions or incidents, but most often do not even mention them in the reading, and then later I write them down. And quite often, I find out about the incident later or it happens in the near future and I recognize it and understand the rather unusual connection to the reading I was doing at the time. One time I spent twenty minutes going down the path of a close sister's life instead of the person I was reading for. And since the person sitting in my living room had never had a reading before she just kept telling me that none of these events had happened in her life. Had I been a less experienced intuitive reader I would have thought that I was terribly wrong. Instead I went back and retraced my steps, asked the woman some pertinent questions and found out that everything was absolutely correct concerning her sister's life. She had asked me some questions about her sister and I had remained on her sister's "channel" for quite some time before we straightened it out. Once the woman realized what had happened she confirmed every detail about her sister's life for me and we got back on track.

Other times this interruption is connected to the reading in a rather strange way. For example, one time I was doing the ancestral guides, metaphorical guides, and other guides, for a friend and behind the line of people was an extra young woman who kept jumping up and down with a baby in her arms trying to get my attention. She had her brown hair piled on her head and wore a long dark skirt and a white blouse with long sleeves, indicating pioneer times. Finally I stopped the reading and told my friend that this young woman was trying to get my attention and seemed to want to be recognized in some way. I described the young woman and asked my friend - because I could ask my friend - to please check this out in her family ancestry if she would. I was also startled at the family resemblance between this young woman and the person I was reading for, and I knew especially that if an ancestral spirit would come to anyone, it would be my friend. One, because she would pay attention to this, and two, because she would follow through until she found out what this was all about. I just didn't know that her mother would too, or that she and her mother had a very strong intuitive connection as well.

In any case, I had a very strong feeling that this spirit wanted to be acknowledged and found, even though my friend – her descendant - knew nothing about it. My friend did follow through, and called her mother who was quite interested in her family's genealogy. Her mother researched looking for lost babies and couldn't find any lost babies unaccounted for on either side of the family. But finally she found a census in which the great great grandfather on one side of the family showed dates that were the same, while they were different for his wife. With further research through some death certificates, her mother found out that their great great grandfather had come across the plains with his young wife Mary. When they got to the Salt Lake Valley, Mary was pregnant. She had had her baby but it had died and six months later this Mary also died. The young man, John, turned around and married another woman named Mary about three years later. The first Mary had been totally forgotten in the records because she was thought to be the second wife.

But this family went even further than this. A cousin located the two graves in the Salt Lake City Cemetery but found that while the mother had a headstone, the baby did not have one and was therefore going "unrecognized." The mother, the cousin and an uncle, bought a grave marker for the baby and placed it on its grave. The census had shown that the baby was buried next to its mother and the sexton had confirmed this. They had a small ceremony for the lost Mary and her child, therefore giving her the recognition she deserved, but more importantly her infant child had now been "recognized" by some of her descendants. It was the first time that I had a real confirmation of the afterlife, because while everything else could be explained through some sort of mind reading or reading of the etheric body or even cellular memory in the body of my sitter, absolutely nothing could explain, why this young woman was begging for recognition in my vision. No one knew she or her baby existed.

10) Help your child to begin to construct an intuitive vocabulary, whether visual or auditory or tactile, or smells or tastes, etc. Keep a journal when a word or picture or object or touch or even shaking someone's hand, induces a certain reaction or gives one information about the situation or person. These will eventually become consistent and will make information arrive more quickly for your intuitive child. For example as a visual intuitive, I get universally themed pictures that I can look up in a book, I get pictures specific to the person and we have to interpret these together or I get consistently appearing pictures or objects that tell me which path to take. For example, if I see a walnut or pinecone in the abdomen, I know there is either a baby about to be conceived, a baby about to be born or has just been born, or the woman sitting in front of me wants to have a baby or lost one, etc. Sometimes these generic symbols are cartoonish and sometimes they are quite strange like the walnut/pinecone symbol. If I see a pearl in the womb, then I know that this particular child will be special in some way.

Sometimes I will immediately see something right in front of my face and know what path to take. One time when a woman walked in the door I had in my mind's eye a wedding gown hanging in front of my face until I talked to her about this and it turned out that that was what she did. She owned a dress shop and made wedding gowns. Keep those reference books around though for interpreting things, the ones I listed in the dream interpretation chapter, for plants and animals and flowers and trees and symbolic objects and cultural interpretations too. This is a great place to begin your own personal vocabulary collection for future reference, along with a good waking dreams guide book, a few other animal, plant, flower interpretation books, a kinds of dreams book, kinds of angels book interpretations, at least one international and historical dream interpretation book, or join a dream interpretation group before choosing to pay a dream interpreter, because you, yourself are the best interpreter of your own dreams with a little study and practise.

11) Help the child to expand this vocabulary to include a personal, cultural, universal and spiritual "dictionary" that can help all children to guide themselves in their lives. Becoming captain of their own "soul ship" will serve them all their lives. Sometimes called waking dreams, sometimes addressed as looking for signs and symbols in one's life, these various happenings and objects and metaphors will eventually become like sentences rather than individual words. A string of guiding images or events will explain many events in a person's life and act as warnings and guides in all that the child does, especially in making decisions and understanding experiences that they have had. In Michael Avery's book entitled The Secret Language of Waking Dreams, he provides additional information for this technique for all of us and not just for individual's more in touch with their intuition, or for our children. This is a very helpful guide if you wish to help your children get started in learning to do this. It is pretty vital for any of us and certainly a key element in "reading" for others. Avery says that we all have signs in our lives involving guidance, warning, protection, confirmation, insight and prophecy in learning to read our own intuitive signs and symbols.

12) When intuiting something always check the details and facts, leave the future out of this temporarily, and check the sequence of events that got you to the original intuitive conclusions along with your actual research and interviewing. Put everything in a consecutive order, as time and distance can be all messed up otherwise. Go step-by-step to follow the sequence of events and role model this over and over again until the child begins to do this on his or her own before they ever come to you to help them analyze their thoughts and intuitive flashes.

13) Intuitive flashes come at great speed and often the child's emotional development is not ready to receive them. This can scare or overwhelm a child. Help them to slow down the process by looking at each part or section of a "flash" in a logical or even chronological fashion. Calm their fears through discussion and relaxation exercises:

Exercise One: Always take three deep breaths before starting any relaxation exercise. Imagine placing a bean bag or brick on top of one hand and then the other, then on one foot and then the other, one on each shoulder and finally one on top of the head. This will push the entire body into the chair. For a lighter touch for more sensitive people do the following: with your eyes shut, go slowly and calmly through each body part step by step, placing a sponge, balloon or bubble on your head, shoulders, chest, arms, legs, hands and feet as you feel yourself slowly sinking into the chair.

<u>Exercise Two</u>: Take three deep breaths and then imagine a large light green or pink or blue toothpaste tube squeezing into the top of your head slowly. Make it cool or warm and tell them that you are squeezing more and more into the inside of their head and as it runs down through the body it is cleaning out all the anxiety, physical aches and pains, and emotional trials of the day. Mention each area of the body as the toothpaste moves down to the feet and toes as well as the hands and fingers. Once the person has been talked through this exercise then have them squeeze the toothpaste out their fingers and toes and keep pushing new toothpaste into the crown of the head until the whole tube is empty.

<u>Exercise Three</u>: A white or gold or some pastel color, or one that the person picks, mist, cool or warm, pours over the body from up above the ceiling or sky, if outside, and slowly descends over the outside of the body as you talk them through this. Then it begins to pour down inside the body, as you talk them through the various body parts to their feet. Describe this color like a shower of light that makes the skin tingle, circulating around and around through the body until the person is tingling all over as if they have actually taken a shower.

14) <u>Make intuitive empathy a part of their daily life</u> by establishing a safe place to be (mine was a certain apple tree where I could hide and contemplate the world) and give them the time and permission to spend in this place on their own. Also give them permission to explore their creative talents, supply the materials and time to do this, show them that play is important, that it is okay to be curious about things, that adults are comfortable being silly and they can be too. I can remember one day with my gifted second graders, I came in and threw a "giggle shark" on the floor and they all looked at me like I was crazy. The shark went around in a circle on its side and laughed and laughed. A couple of days later I came in for the start of the day and all my students were hiding under their desks. They suddenly jumped out, threw themselves on the floor in the fetal position and ran around in circles giggling. This set the tone for the day and we had a good one. There were no more "little adults" around!

15) Balance play with work and chores and activities, and never ignore children or make them feel invisible when it comes to their intuitive talents.

16) Actively advocate for your child at home, at school, and in clubs, sports or community meetings of any kind. Acknowledge his or her gifts where it is appropriate to do so.

17) Help your child to bond with an intuitive someone they can trust, no matter how easy or difficult this may be to let go of your own bonding long enough for your child to have this opportunity. But also monitor this!

18) Above all, model a positive attitude when possible and accept each child in all the dimensions of who they are! Avoid labels of any kind, including Indigo or Crystal kids, so that your children can be who they are without misdiagnoses or labels of any kind.

19) Although this last one would be an individual choice, intuitive empathic children, gifted children and just about any particular child can often come with an understanding of a spiritual gift or "mission" which can overwhelm those around them. This can have both positive and negative effects on the child. A child may feel so deeply about the world's problems that they need to do something about this or feel anxious and upset most of the time. Help the child to do something real that can help. Perhaps they are concerned about our polluted water and you can invent and build a better water filtering system together, or the natural disaster that happened across the world can be the basis for collecting extra clothing and sending it to one of the world health organizations, etc. Let your child take action in some small way, write a letter or e-mail about an issue or copy cat a relief campaign right in your hometown. Support their concerns and give them coping mechanisms for the worry and anxiety that they will probably feel concerning these new realizations about the world. (See Anxiety/Panic Attack chapter).

20) Spiritual awareness can also be in terms of a religion or an empathic child choosing to help others or even as an adult by choosing a spiritual path as a religious spiritual leader, priest, healer or shaman, etc. This issue must be dealt with within the family's own belief system, but many empathic children will bring this up themselves.

21) Be sure to journal or scrapbook for the whole intuitive family or for the individual child. Keep dreams and intuitive moments, drawings and vocabulary in this journal as well as drawing concept or story or dream maps, which are fun to do and quite informative.

22) Let the child explore the types of intuition games that are light and fun, but make sure they understand that these are only games for now, like palmistry or astrology, numerology or I Ching, Runes or cards, tea leaf or coffee grounds reading, etc. (Read Julie Soskin's book carefully).

23) Lead your child through some child meditations or creative visualizations that are not much different than the never ending tales you tell them at bed time. There are many, many ideas for this sort of thing in the activities chapter, in books and many other adaptable child meditations in the multiple intelligences materials, besides the Starbright series by Maureen Garth.

24) Sylvia Browne and Lindsay Harrison provide some great, what they call Tools of Protection in their book called Psychic Children, pages 234-257. These are not new ideas but have been around for quite a while, so I added a few of the ways I adapted these basic ideas for children to help them cope with fears in the night or even in the daytime. They list the idea of a large floating clear plastic bubble which the child can either build around them or step inside of and travel around in them. You can make it your favorite pastel color or leave it clear and combine this with affirmations of safety. I used to use this one in a creative visualization where the child can fly into outer space, or visit under the oceans or bounce on top of the waves, or even ward off things that frighten them at night. They navigated their bubble with their eyes by looking up or down or left or right, or used their whole head in the same way. I would then have them draw where they went in their "bubble" and had taught them in addition to their traveling, a way to protect themselves when they were either imagining something or experiencing something quite real. Fun house mirrors , which they call the circle of mirrors, is another one I used in creative visualizations but mainly in our Brain Gym exercises when working in partners to look at each other and then yourself and analyze what you see. This worked great for self-esteem because the children were required to only make positive comments about their partner and of course everyone just loved this idea. I also modeled or we role modeled how to be this way with others. Browne just adds in the idea of building this wall of fun house mirrors around you in a circle and then seeing this as a circle of protection, while I had them stare at their reflections and experience all their different emotions in each mirror, making them all happy and safe, wiping out any angry or sad expressions until they felt safe and protected in their house of mirrors.

We spun actual nets in the classroom to support each other or when being required to try some new exercise in gym, etc. You use a huge skein of yarn rolled in a ball and the end of the yarn skein is thrown or handed about until the class has woven a spider's web together. The more artistic or symmetrical the web when we finished, the more we had something which would protect us from outside harm. We practiced this a lot until the class had made a really good web. Or we made an imaginary net that would catch us when we fell or help the children to not be afraid. Or we would imagine an invisible parachute or blanket which the children held in their hands in a circle and pretended to bounce one child in the center, while that child pretended to bounce up and down in it. Sometimes in gym we used the real thing and made all kinds of round shapes out of the parachute because it took the whole community of students to make the shape correctly. We made mushrooms, pancakes, a tent and whatever they could think of. I just couldn't do a golden light net, although we did do this kind of thing in our creative visualizations and they hopefully learned the same thing and used it at home. The dome of light is a very common theme in meditations where the group constructs this dome like scaffolding or a smooth walled dome of light. Then the group places those they are concerned about inside this dome and the whole group concentrates on sending positive energy to those placed inside. Constructing a dome of light together can be very empowering, both for the group and for those placed inside. At school I could not use this sort of thing but I did use an imaginary playhouse or tent or parachute which we could all sit under and not only share energy but provide protection for each other in this way. Hopefully the children learned from this to build their own "cover" at night or in the day time.

And of course I could not use a sword of protection at school but there were always water guns and blowing bubbles to push someone away from you. I spent time talking to them about what kind of shield they could make for themselves that they would feel safe in as well as not being dangerous for them. What could they build in their imagination that would protect them from bullies and what sort of harmless weapons they could build for either protection or to push the danger or a dangerous person away. Even when they wrote their stories they were required to come up with a non-lethal way of getting rid of the villain. They came up with such things as bubble or popcorn machines, shooting silly putty or silly string at them or even shape shifting them temporarily into what they should really look like. It was all just to get them thinking about other ways to handle these situations, with humor being a foremost one in their minds. But at home an imaginary golden light sword or laser sword could be imagined and used at night for protection under the direction of their parents.

25) Especially use Julie Soskin's book, How Psychic Are You? It is full of adaptable activities for many of the kinds of intuitive abilities and even has questionnaires for many of them so the child can mark the checklist and see if they may be gifted in this area or that. Another fun book among many is The Medicine Wheel Earth Astrology by Sun Bear and Wabun or the Medicine Cards by Jamie Sams that tells you about more animals.

26) Catherine Crawford mentions one activity in her book called Ducks and Sponges for learning to set boundaries. I know I have already mentioned this but even the adults in my meditation group found this a much better way to understand communication styles than auditory processing and visual-spatial learners, so I want to remind you again about this way of discussing these learning styles for all those sensitive empaths out there. Afterall, repetition is the way both adults and children learn something new, it just has to not be recognized as such! Duck people just let the emotions of others roll off their back easily. They are effective communicators, can go at anything step-by-

step and have no trouble moving from one task to another. Sponge people (intuitive empaths) physically register the feelings of others and have trouble walking away from conflicts or even confronting others. They carry away with them all sorts of emotions and physical aches and pains from any conflict and often cry at the drop of a hat, especially women. So Ducks and Sponges often cannot communicate with each other, as visual-spatial learners and auditory processors can find communicating with each other difficult too. Sponges use terms like "I feel..." or "I sense...," while Ducks use terms like "I think..." or "I noticed...," and play twenty questions on only one topic. Sponges jump from subject to subject because when communicating with each other, they already know where the other person has jumped too, often intuitively, and this is very confusing for Ducks.

"Ducks think that Sponges are overly sensitive, high maintenance, and emotionally unbalanced. Sponges think that Ducks are insensitive, lacking in empathy, and oddly quick to move on after upsetting situations." But Sponges can learn to finely tune their body and minds and emotions to provide great insights into how other people feel. Their abilities can become their allies and they can learn to move on too after conflict. So rather than accusing each other, children can see that we are all generally either "ducks" or "sponges" or sometimes a little of both. (*Ibid., the highly intuitive child, p. 85*).

27) In Almine's book, How to Raise an Exceptional Child, she has several good ideas from pp. 188 to 215 specifically for intuitive children. Body Parts as Dream Symbol charts and a small dictionary of Body Parts for Dream Symbols help with building children's self-esteem.

28) Doreen Virtue offers two really good things in her Lightworker's Way book, the second section of the book offers beginning ideas on ways to be a better "lightworker" by building up your own skills step-by-step, and she also has a section in the back called "self-help resources" with the names and phone numbers for organizations who assist one with recovery options for various health, dysfunction, addiction problems that might be helpful for you and others you know, as well as lead you to the type of help you might need with your child. Virtue is both a PhD psychologist and an intuitive reader and has the best of both worlds for those just beginning to awaken. These are the qualities one should look for when choosing to go to a holistic reader or healer, both therapy and intuitive skills combined with a little common sense. After all, all of us are: "Those who have developed 'psychic' powers (and) have simply let some of the limitations they laid upon their minds be lifted." (*"A Course in Miracles" as taken from The Lightworker's Way, p. 111*).

29) Buying and watching some of the episodes of Psychic Kids or Medium or even Paranormal State as a family, or with a parent, might be worthwhile. Some of my friends don't like Psychic Kids because they are so dramatic and seemingly "forced." However,

I think you can pick and choose the episodes for the age of your child, and they might inspire your child or make them feel not so alone. Others think they are too labeling, or there is too much emphasis on "Look how special I am!" "Psychic Kids" is into its third season, although season one is the best still. I think with pre-discussion and post discussion, some of these episodes might be helpful for either young children or teens.

Medium on the other hand is no longer on but you can buy all seven seasons and pick and choose what you watch together or watch them as parents to pick up some ideas on how to handle some situations with your intuitive children. Based on a real live young mom intuitive, Allison DuBois, who dreams her solutions to crimes and other family situations, in the show, Allison has three children and a very left brained aerospace engineer for a husband. Most of us have these two "voices" in our own heads, the skeptical and logical auditory processor who helps us analyze things, and the emotional visual spatial communicator, who follows what our heart feels. When they work together well, our logical and analytical side sorts out what we dream or visualize emotionally. On the other hand, many of us spend our lives in conflict and sometimes in confusion, trying to figure out the "messages" we receive when we fall out of our "whole brain" ideal. This is a great show on the very real side of living as an intuitive in a family, although the crime scenes are way too graphic for children and need to be avoided.

Paranormal State is the best ghost hunting show but you may have to get the CDs as it seems to have disappeared. They come in and help a family after other experts have tried and failed to find a solution. They use whatever they can to help this family while trying to stay within the belief systems of that family. They combine what all other shows leave out because their intent is on helping the family and not proving or disproving anything. So if a Catholic family needs a Catholic priest exorcist or the family is living on an Indian burial ground, they may bring in a medicine man from that particular local tribe. Once they had a case that involved a haunted upright piano. The antique dealers who had bought the thing had moved it out on their front porch within a week after having it in their house. The amazing activity that it had brought with it had them quite frightened to pass it along to anyone else. The Penn State group had a piano expert and historian come in to try and identify it or any history it might have. They also brought in a piano tuner, to see if perhaps mice or some other critters were causing the disturbances, etc. None of these other experts could really explain the disturbances all over the house that had begun when that piano had been moved into the house. Even blessing the house didn't work. Finally, with the permission of the owners they dismantled it and took it out in pieces, which they then buried in an open field in an undisclosed location, which ended all of the disturbing phenomena in the house.

What makes the show so interesting is that this is a group of young people who are bright, innovative and true believers, who are also skeptical about everything they investigate. College kids from Penn State University who bring along whatever experts they need in any field, to help the family who has already been assisted by more than one other investigative group who could not find a solution to what is presumed as a paranormal problem in the family home. So watching these young people solve the cases is interesting too, as often university students would be quite skeptical and this only adds to their innovations as a team of investigators and problem solvers for families in dire need. They are at the same time expanding their own intuitive skills, but without all the drama and performance art of most such ghost shows, or the close mindedness of being too skeptical of what they experience or find. And this is because their main focus is always on helping the client within the parameters of their own belief system, as well as learning more and more from their experiences that will assist them in future investigations.

30) Use the activities provided in the next chapter to not only empower your children but also to inspire them to be who they are and to find out what they think, but also to explore all of the various gifts and talents they can have. So that what they can't do, becomes only a part of who they are and this will challenge them to work harder at those things that are more difficult for them. Many of the activities are concrete, practical ways to explore intuitive talents and bring one's family closer together.

31) Interestingly, in my case and with my particular "brain wiring," in the physical world I am terrible at math and yet in the intuitive world during my readings, the information that comes to me first is mathematical. I get all sorts of numbers first and a mathematician once explained to me that if I could have ever gotten through the so-called lower math of algebra and geometry and had achieved enough knowledge to do advanced "visualization" math, I would probably have been better at this kind of math. Some interesting thoughts for both you and your child on this. Many intuitive visual-spatial learners do deal with sensitivities and learning disabilities that seem to reverse themselves when operating intuitively.

32) If you are not the thorough type and don't want to bother reading through the next bibliographic chapter with brief critiques from me, then to find everything you need, here is a brief list of the very best activity books for all the subjects in my book:

a) Seven Ways of Knowing – David Lazear

b) A Class Act/Funny Bones/Showtime/Onstage – Norman Delue (Four separate books!)

c) Unicorns Are Real – Barbara Meister Vitale

d) Face Reading Secrets – Rose Rosetree

e) Class Building/ Teambuilding/ Community Building / Multiple Intelligences – Kagan Cooperative Learning Books, different authors

f) Social Skills/ Life Skills/ etc. – Darlene Matrix

g) Psychic Children – Sylvia Browne & Lindsay Harrison

h) The Secret Language of Waking Dreams – Michael Avery

i) Astral Dynamics/ Practical Psychic Self-Defense/ Energy Work – Robert Bruce, read the chapters on children in each one

j) 101 Games for Autism & Asperger's – Tara Delaney

k) 1001 Ideas…Autism & Asperger's – Ellen Notbohn & Veronica Zysk

l) Starbright Meditations series – Maureen Garth

m) Spritual Parenting and many others books – Hugh & Gayle Prather (For working with teens especially.)

n) Upside Down Brilliance and many other books – Linda Kreger Silverman

o) How Psychic Are You? – Julie Soskin

p) The highly intuitive child by Catherine Crawford

q) Anything labeled Higher Thinking Skills or Multiple Intelligences will probably have excellent activities inside them that can be adapted for all ages and varieties of children.

r) How to Raise Exceptional Children by Almine

s) All Multiple Intelligences activity books are great! Especially Teacher Created Materials: Multiple Intelligences Activities for k-4 and 4-6.

t) All Educational Kinesiology and Brain and Vision Gym activity books

u) All the Usborne activity books are stupendous!!!

33) And be sure you let your child pick a place or provide that hiding place for your intuitive child or children. If they pick it, then it is their private place to be guarded and protected by the rest of the family, and not to be invaded unless invited in! The same holds true if you provide such a place for the child like a tree house or an outside tent or playhouse, or even a blanket tent in their room, or like I had as a child, a cherry or apple tree which I could climb way up in and pretend to hide there. A beautiful exam-

ple of my own mother's intuitive conflict was if I hid in the tree, I was punished for not doing my daily chores with the other children at the prescribed time, and yet when my mother was in her old age she would often comment on one of her fondest memories about me, watching her daughter high in the top of this apple tree, just contemplating away! I have often wondered where my mother "intuited" when she was child, before she "forgot" and "grew up."

34) Read, read, read to your little children! Especially all the fairy tales, all the popular children's classics and the newest tales that each generation will remember for a lifetime. This not only fuels the imagination but it also fosters a connection between your own childhood memories and those your children are creating. For intuitive children, it especially confirms your permission to intuit in their own lives as they need to.

"Animals, trees, plants and flowers enter and exit our lives every day and offer us guidance and support if only we will be open to it…every aspect of nature is woven into your daily life…and this awakens you to the ancient knowledge of spirit animals, plants and trees. Learn how to determine their roles within your life. They will touch a primal part of your heart and soul – and stir long dormant embers. They will become your friends, your teachers and your companions."

--Ted Andrews, The Intercession of Spirits, p.1

"Imagine a childhood filled with the presence of spirits, faeries, animals, angels, loving ancestors and more. And yet you would be unable to speak of them, knowing it would invite scorn and ridicule from family and friends…Imagine giving up the security of a good career to follow a new path in life – guided by the spirit world – knowing it defied logic and that family and friends would make jokes and look for you to fail…Imagine that you opened fully to the reality of that world once more today. Would it change your life for the better or make it more complicated? Would you have the heart to follow?"

–Ted Andrews, The Intercession of Spirits

CHAPTER FIFTEEN

Multiple Intelligences & Energy, Academic, Stress Reducing Activities

"Only human beings have come to a point where they no longer know why they exist. They don't use their brains and they have forgotten the secret knowledge of their bodies, their senses, or their dreams. They don't use the knowledge the spirit has put into everyone of them, they are not even aware of this, and so they stumble on blindly on the road to nowhere – a paved highway which they themselves bulldoze and make smooth so that they can get faster to the big empty hole which they'll find at the end, waiting to swallow them up. It's a quick, comfortable superhighway, but I know where it leads too. I've been there in my vision and it makes me shudder to think about it."

--Lame Deer, Lakota Sioux Shaman,
Lame Deer Seeker of Visions

"In each human being dwells an infinite power, the root of the universe. That infinite power exists in two modes: one actual and the other potential. This infinite power exists in a latent condition in everyone."

--Elaine Pagels, The Gnostic Gospels

Before Reading This Chapter Please Read This:

I incorporated the bibliography into this chapter because the information after each book is vital for you and your children. The epilogue on an educational and spiritual utopia comes after this chapter in hopes that you will not skip this information, especially the Multiple Intelligences material which P.M.H. Atwater even mentions in her book Beyond the Indigo Children. So go through it carefully and glean what you can to help anyone you know who is a wounded intuitive, any teens who are dealing with overwhelming intuitive moments and with more such children coming in all the time. These little children arriving with each new generation will know a lot more than we do, but will understand life on earth even less as these many shifts take place. They are coming in to facilitate change, but the old ways will still be there, and those of us who have lived through these times will need to help them adjust. These newly "brain wired" children will teach themselves and teach us how to live here and how to begin the new world of brain wired, heart wired, spirit wired people who want to form a world of community and understanding.

Multiple Intelligences – Howard Gardner

But before you check over the topics listed here we need to talk about one more thing and that is Howard Gardener's Multiple Intelligences, a vital topic for all children and one that has remained too long in the domain of "gifted." All children would benefit from being introduced to all of these types of learning, and also from knowing which ones are their fortes, which are their challenging areas, and how to build and balance all of them within each child. In the various areas of: Verbal/Linguistic, Musical/Rhythmical, Logical/Mathematical, Spatial Body/ Kinesthetic, Interpersonal, Intrapersonal, Mechanical, Naturalist, Emotional, and Existential, are the identified types of intelligence and learning, according to Gardner. Many others have added onto his initial work and Dr. Spencer Kagan has taken Gardner's material and successfully integrated it into his Cooperative Learning empire. With workshops all over the world, valuable materials of all kinds available, the Kagan Cooperative Learning company only has one problem I know of, and that is prejudice against this philosophy of cooperative learning by established school districts who think they have to adopt the whole program in order to use it. The Waldorf schools already have developed their own ways of doing the same thing.

All children would benefit from being introduced to all of these types of learning. I used the Kagan materials and merged them into the other things I had garnered over time. They were especially wonderful for social skills and defined learning styles because the materials seemed to accommodate or facilitate styles of learning quite easily. My own philosophy for teaching children to learn their academics, socialize and feel empowered as children, was one-third drills and basics, one-third cooperative learning and learning styles, and one-third self-worth, belief in one's self, instilling confidence in one's identified talents and abilities. Knowing the developmental stages of children helped a great deal, as well as teaching conflict resolution before many incidents got out of hand. And last, providing a comfortable, safe environment filled with trust, having a respect for each other, sharing lots of humor, and adding a "pinch" of knowing you were loved. Students wanted to come to school because they never knew what was going to happen next. I accomplished this by putting everything in the morning, because that was when the "fish bowl" went on in the gifted program. No one ever came in the afternoon and if they did, it was pretty rare. The rulers and regulators, testers and overseers, were tired themselves at this point in the day or had meetings to attend elsewhere and had other things to do. Even my students knew what I was doing and relaxed as soon as lunch arrived, because they knew we would have all afternoon to really do learning and have fun exploring all sorts of subjects. And behind the scenes was a very structured and organized day.

Multiple Intelligences Wheel

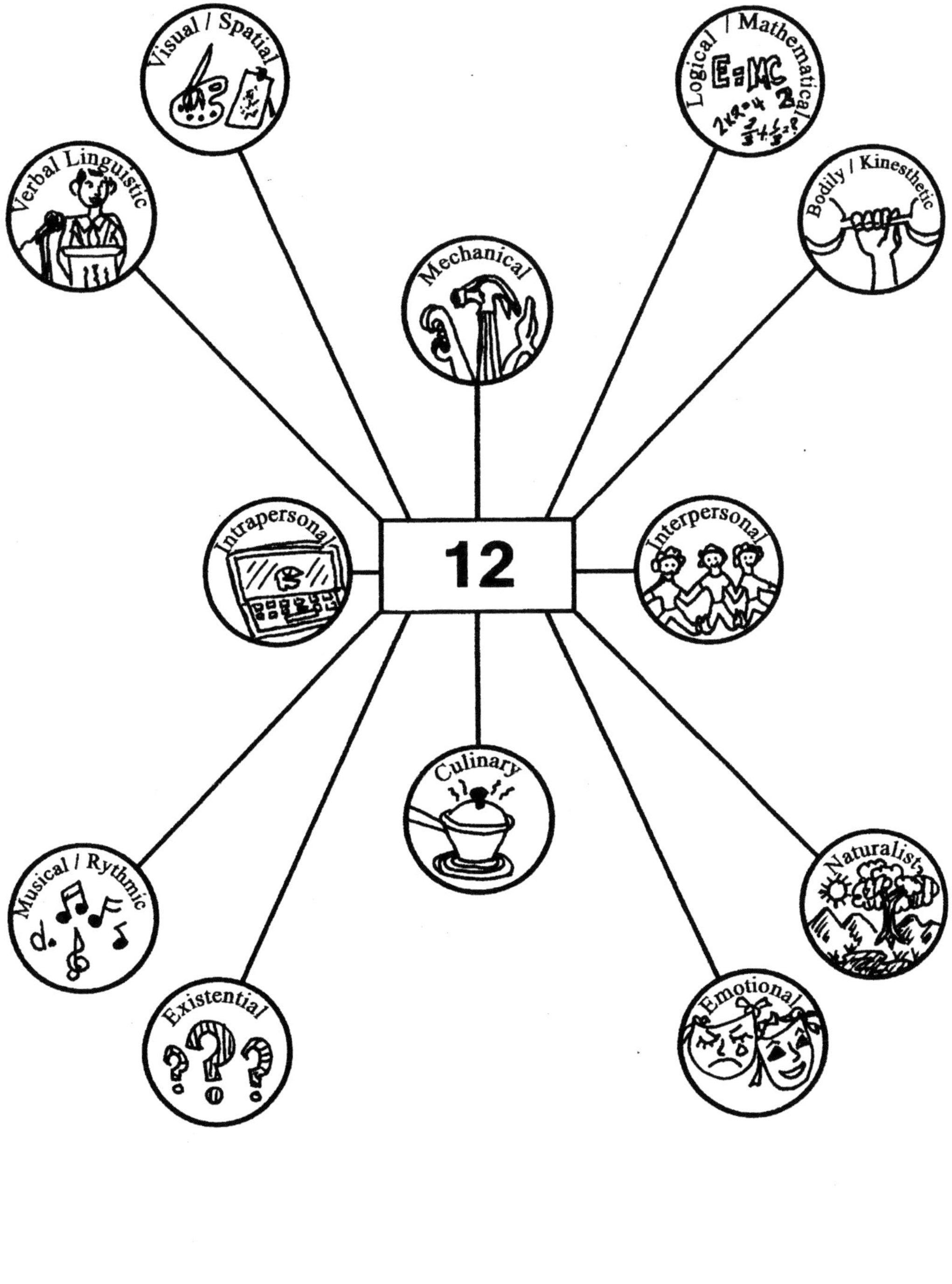

Some teachers saw the later afternoon as down time and provided busy work in order to get their paperwork done earlier. I saw this time as a way to structure something that my students could explore on their own. And it somehow worked because my students usually got high scores on their tests anyway, whether I pushed them or not. They knew they were in a secret conspiracy with me, and enjoyed this part too! This was our time together without interference, and as the year progressed, we became a cohesive community. We did all sorts of multiple intelligence activities and units in small groups, laughed a lot, and learned a lot together. The students learned what all the types of learning meant and learned what they could excel in, what they needed to work on, and that everyone of them had talents and abilities that made up for anything they struggled in. So if you want to know more about multiple intelligences, here are the best books to tell you all about it and once you know them and work with them, then more and more ideas will come to mind. The best of the activity books are listed on the next page after the main reference book on MI. They are listed again in the Social Skills section because they use the MI ideas but focus on social and community skills.

Suffice to say, educational reform is available in every classroom if you want to do the extra work, are willing to perform a few covert operations in the afternoon, but look good for the powers that be each morning. And it is extra work to really teach, and then do the paper work that so many think is actually teaching, or at least keeping track of what is being taught whether it is really applied to anything in life or not. Quite a few teachers seemed to be obsessed with competing with their student's scores on these academic tests. I guess they took this as a measure of their teaching abilities when it was required of them to give these tests, which were often changed under the guise of keeping up with the times. My guess is that these tests were given to teachers under the oppressive tact of this being a measure of "good teaching." Those who did not buy into this tactic who were brave enough to question this silliness, existed in a smaller group of visual-spatial rebels, many of whom kept in touch with each other when they found each other or otherwise kept to themselves, keeping their heads down in case of being found out and questioned. I can even remember meeting one teacher new to our school on an even rarer occasion, who looked me in the eye, and said to me "Busted!" when I mentioned something about how did she know this or that? As she said, it was even rarer to meet a fellow public school intuitive, hiding in the underground!

We definitely became islands in the storm, because when they did try to get rid of us, we were too popular with the parents and our students and our "scores" were okay. It never occurred to them to ask us why. My fellow VSL teachers had their own stories to tell of the same harassments whether they were in regular or gifted programs. When you don't fit the mold in public school teaching, you can have an in depth understanding of what most visual-spatial learners, auditory learners and kinetic learners go through at school every day. In the little ones it produces confusion, frustration and low self-esteem, and in the older ones it produces anger, numbness and depression. So, being full of hope for the future, I cannot wait for the educational reforms to come pouring in when big business gets it and uses their muscle to change things. After all, they hold the financial power and have the willingness to change things to get better workers, right? I just wish they were better informed as to what to do!

Multiple Intelligences Activities

****= Excellent ***= Very Good **= Good *= Somewhat Worthwhile

**** Kagan, Dr. Spencer and Kagan, Miguel. Multiple Intelligences: The Complete MI Book, Kagan Cooperative Learning, 1998. (This is the definitive book and has probably been updated since this printing. This is for you to read but also has many, many activities for kids of all ages in the various areas of: Verbal/Linguistic, Musical/Rythmical, Logical/Mathematical, Spatial Body/ Kinesthetic, Interpersonal, Intrapersonal, Mechanical, Naturalist, Emotional, Existential.)

**** Kagan. Miguel and Robertson, Laurie. Cooperative Learning Structures for Class building, Kagan Cooperative Learning, 1995.

*** Lazear, David. Seven Ways of Knowing, Skylight Publishing: Palatine, Illinois, 1991. (This book is for adults to read but also lists many activity ideas for the various intelligences that are above average and can be used with any age students – just pick and choose and adapt!)

**** Miguel, Laurie. Cooperative Learning Structures for Team Building, KCL, 1997.

*** Shaw, Vanston. Community Building in the Classroom, KCL, 1992.

*** Teacher Created Materials, two books put out by Teacher Created Materials, Mul tiple Intelligences Activities for K-4 and 4-6, Inc.: Huntington Beach, California, 1996. (Two separate books, activities ready to be used immediately!)

Note: The very best activity books from Kagan are listed again under the section: Social, Conflict Resolution & Group Cooperation Skills.

Bibliography for Child Activities & Adult Information Books:

Child Activity Books for Special Areas Often Not Covered in Schools:

This material was taken from the following sources and if I put it in here, it means that these are the very best sources available on the practical, down to earth ways to help your child deal with or improve his or her intuitive talents. They also contain the very best, up-to-date information and resource listings for activities and academics for all children.

All the books listed here cover areas that you cannot often get from schools like art appreciation, drama, mind stretchers, social skills, group cooperation skills and conflict resolution skills, higher level thinking skills activities, and intuitive activities such as learning about body language or the various psychic abilities, although there are a few on the academic areas, but even these are "mind stretchers." All the books can be adapted from very young to junior high and some even to high school. They supplement the technology that young children use often without understanding the underpinnings of just plain concrete fun and using nothing expensive at all. In all my years of teaching I found that children, at least in the elementary years, absolutely loved the old-fashioned games once they were taught to them because it engaged the whole person rather than selective parts of learning. In other words, these specific books address the multiple intelligences often left out in schools. (Except for music which children can learn separately in their after school lesson and through after school activities such as band, orchestra or just plain dancing and singing.)

The Activity Books for Children:

Art & Art Appreciation:

**** Anholt, Lawrence. Matisse: The King of Color, Barron's Educational Series, 2007. (Anholt has a whole series of picture books on the lives of famous artists which can be used to kick off whole discussions and attempts to draw and imitate the following artists: Degas and the Little Dancer, Leonardo and the Flying Boy, Picasso and the Girl With the Ponytail, and Camille and the Sunflowers. He cleverly relates each artist to a true story about an adventure or relationship each artist had with a child and even my most challenged and most underprivileged children were enraptured with these tales!)

** Brumbeau, Jeff and Marcken, D.E. The Quiltmaker's Gift and The Quiltmaker's Journey, Pfeifer-Hamilton Publishers and Orchard Books , 2000 and 2004. (Great picture book way to introduce making a paper squares quilt or a real quilt together, along with The Keeping Quilt by Patricia Polacco.) Bush, Heather and Silver, Bur ton. Why Cats Paint, Ten Speed Press: Berkeley, California, 1994. (This is an adult book but great for kids who love cats and other animals.)

** Compestine, Ying
Chang. The Story of Chopsticks, Holiday House: New York, 2001. (Great introduc tion to learning to eat with chopsticks, a great fine motor skill and fun unit!)

** Heller, Ruth. Designs for Coloring Books series including: Snowflakes, Birds, Butterflies, Cats, Flowers, Geometrics, More Geometrics, Optical Art, Seashells, The Hebrew Alphabet, etc. (from Grosset & Dunlap.)

**** Houston, Gloria. My Great Aunt Arizona, Harper-Collins, 1992. (A children's illustrated book for adults and every teacher who ever taught!)

**** Liao, Jimmy. The Sound of Colors: A Journey of the Imagination, (this excellent picture book and others can be found at www.Ib-kids.com and was printed in China. This book can be used in many ways from understanding the handicapped to discussing the world of our imaginations, etc.)

** Martin, Jacqueline Briggs. Snowflake Bentley, Houghton Mifflin Company: Boston, 1998. (This is a picture book with a true story about a young man who studied snowflakes by photographing them. He became the international expert on snowflakes. This can be followed with many snowflake activities.)

* Melmed, Laura Krauss. Little Ott, Lothrap, Lee 7 Shepherd: New York, 1997. (This is a story picture book about a little girl doll maker which can introduce making dolls.)

** Krull, Kathleen and Hewitt, Kathryn. Lives of Artists, Harcourt, Brace and Company, 1995. (This is a child's series of books for older elementary and junior high, written by different authors but the same in a colorful and artistic format on brief biographies of the lives of: musicians, writers, artists, athletes, presidents, etc.)

* Reid, Lori. Color Crazy: A Guide to Understanding the Colors of Your Life, Element Children's Books, 1998. (Great book for children on the various colors.)

* Rodriquez, Rachel. Through Georgia's Eyes, Henry Holt & Co.: New York, 2006. (Picture book on the life of Georgia O'Keefe.)

* Sweeney, Jan. Suzette and the Puppy: A Story About Mary Cassatt, Educational Publishers, 2000. (A picture book on the famous woman artist.)

* Visconti, Guido and Landmann, Bimba. The Genuis of Leonardo, Barefoot Books, 2000 and Journal of Inventor Leonardo De Vinci pop-up book by Jaspre Bark and David Hawcock, Silver Dolphin Books, 2008.

---Remember that pop-up books are great for kids too. You can introduce making a paper pop-up book or card after looking at a few. The best and most intricate books are made by Robert Sabuda, Matthew Reinhart, Sam Ata, and Chuck Fischer, and for the younger children, Jack Tickle and Gill Guile. Many famous children's writers now have one or two out, as well as all the fantasy, cartoon heroes and many fairy tales, even by Disney.

Drama & Playwriting:

** Authors Unknown. Reader's Theater. (Books put out by Evan-Moor Educational Publishers which offers a book for each grade from first to sixth grade.)

*** Delue, Norman and Hayward, Thomas B. Stage Write: A Playwriting Curriculum for Kids and Teachers, Good Apple, 1996.

**** Delue, Norman. A Class Act: A Creative Drama Guide for Teachers, Good Apple, 1994. (The best ever for drama, you can add to this, anyone can use the lessons and they are super movement activities which you can develop a whole curriculum around or add other activities to what you do at home.)

**** Winters, Lisa Bany. Funny Bones: Comedy Games and Activities for Kids, Show time: Music, Dance and Drama Activities for Kids and Onstage: Theater Games and Activities for Kids, all from Chicago Review Press: Chicago, Illinois. (All three of these books are huge and packed with activities that could be used from young children to high school aged kids, adapted a little! The best I could find!)

Higher Level Thinking Skills & Mind Stretchers:

** Authors Unknown. (Puzzle Island is a book put out by Discovery Toys and it is a great small group game or individual game to keep your child busy. This is a book for all kids and even the highly gifted ones.)

*** Cole, Joanna and Degen, Bruce. Mrs. Frizzle's Adventures in Imperial China, Scholastic Books, 2005. (A picture book chalk full of information and some activities, this is only one example of many other such Scholastic picture books and DVDs on many of the other Mrs. Frizzle's adventures on various subjects from the "Magic School Bus.")

**** Levy, Nathan, Burke, Amy and Fisher, Emily. Creativity Day-By-Day, NL Associates Book, Inc. Publishers, 2004. (Nathan Levy has a whole line of products for gifted kids that include dozens of higher level thinking skills ideas that stretch the brain and can be starter ideas for all kinds of units and activities at home or at school. One other book I especially like is called 100 Intriguing Questions for Kids, great for teens and adults too!)

*** Seyba, Mary E. Imaging: A Different Guide for Parents of Gifted Kids, Educational Impressions, 1984. (Super higher level thinking skills for all children who like to draw and figure out how things work.)

**** Vitale, Barbara Meister. Unicorns Are Real: A Right-Brained Approach to Learning, Pro-Ed, 1982. (Many higher level thinking skills along with drawing activities are great for developing intuitive skills too.)

**** Usborne Publishers put out all kinds of amazing activity books for kids of all ages such as Codes & Ciphers or Secret Messages. (There are at least three of these that a child can spend hours on, there are several detective and spy books, several math and science activity books, etc. Everyone of them is excellent to base a huge unit on for teachers or just to do with your children at home such as Crimebusters Investigate, Tracking & Trailing, Disguise & Make-Up, The Spy's Handbook or Detective's Handbook, etc. Once you get one or two, you will want all of them, especially if you are a homeschooler parent or trying to enhance your child's schooling at home. There are over 25 little books packed with activities and mind stretchers that even include historical activities such as Rome, Castles, Pyramids and some geographical ones too!)

Intuition Development: (Also refer to the list of dream interpretation books for more ideas.)

**** Andrews, Ted. Animal-Speak, Animal-Wise and Nature-Speak are all reference books available through Dragonhawk Publishing. (These are super books for teens, but would have to be interpreted for younger children on nature and animals and what their spiritual meanings are for us when we see or experience them.)

** Garth, Maureen. Starbright: Meditations for Children, Harpers, 1991. (Kids can read these to and try them themselves.)

** Hay, Louise. You Can Heal Your Life, Hay House, 1984. (Full of affirmation ideas for every ailment and internal organ in the body.)

***** Rosetree, Rose. Face Reading Secrets, Ottheimer Publishers, 1994. (Great for kids to try out either drawing these things or trying to read them on other people.)

*** Sams, Jamie and Carson, David. Medicine Cards, Bear & Co., 1988. (These cards and text can be used in conjunction with Ted Andrew's symbol books on trees, plants, flowers and animals. A fun one for kids too if done with your own children.)

**** Soskin, Julie. How Psychic Are You? Penguin Books, 2002. (These various activities can actually be done by teens on their own or with supervision. They can also be adapted for younger children.)

Social, Conflict Resolution & Group Cooperation Skills:

* Galbraith, Judy. The Gifted Kids Survival Guide for Ages 10 & Under, Free Spirit Publishing, 1984. (This is placed in this section again because kids can read this for themselves with a bit of interpretation from their parents, if the information applies.)

Kagan Cooperative Learning materials offer many books on learning to get along with each other. There are whole cooperative learning schools. So I used these to supplement everything else I was doing to foster social skills, conflict resolution skills and getting along in small groups, which is what most kids will be doing in their adult work world. These are the mega books and are packed with activities on how to get along with each other, which nips in the bud, needing so much conflict resolution in the schools, if you practice and use these techniques consistently with your children or students. Great for the upper grades too!

**** Kagan, Miguel and Robertson, Laurie. Cooperative Learning Structures for Class building, KCL, 1995.

**** Miguel, Laurie. Cooperative Learning Structures for Team Building, KCL, 1997.

**** Shaw, Vanston. Community Building in the Classroom, KCL, 1992.

*** Goldstein, P. Arnold, Gershaw. N. Jane, Klein, Paul, and Sprafkin, Robert P. Skill streaming the Adolescent: A Structured Learning Approach To Teaching Prosocial Skills, Research Press Company, 1980.

**** Mannix, Darlene. Social Skills Activities for Special Children K-5, Life skills Activities for Special Children K-5, Social Skills Activities for Secondary Students and Life Skills Activities for Secondary Students are all excellent resources for teaching social skills. (Although these were written for students with problems, each lesson, story and subsequent activities are starter places for an even better discussion depending on the level of the students or children you have. I used these same books from the severely handicapped to the gifted with great success.

The more involved kids really learned from these activities and lessons and the gifted students found them entertaining, intriguing and fun, when after learning these skills, they were expected to use them, especially in the cafeteria and on the playground. The secondary ones are just as useful.)

*** McElmurry, Mary Anne and Herrick, Elizabeth Tang. (A series on social skills activities in five books for younger children: Appreciating, Belonging, Communcating, Coping, and Sharing for ages 2-8 from Apple Activity Books.)

*** McGinnis, Ellen and Goldstein, Arnold P. Skillstreaming The Elementary School Child: A Guide for Teaching Prosocial Skills, Research Press Company, 1984.

* Muir, Kerry, editor. Childsplay: A Collection of Scenes and Monologues for Chil Children, Limelight Editions: New York, 1995. (These are role playing techniques for conflict resolution methods.)

Autism, Aspergers, Out-of-Sync Kids & Sensory Motor Skills:

**** Delaney, Tara, MS, OTR. 101 Games and Activities for Children with Autism, Asperger's and Sensory Processing Disorders, McGraw-Hill, 2009. (Super book actually, full of what it advertises, down-to-earth and easy to understand and do.)

**** Dennison, Paul E. and Hargrove, Gail E. E-K for Kids, (An excellent reader for young children and teens when dealing with these particular body-mind coordination issues. The book Brain Gym has all of the child exercises in it with illustrations of the various exercises and what each of them, or sets of them are for! E-K For Kids is currently out-of-print but hopefully it is included in one of the other books and used copies can be found on line. Many new materials including books on Vision Gym can be found at www.braingym.com. Vision Gym can be especially helpful for sensory challenges in this area. There are many more books on this website for all areas of the Brain Gym and Edu-K programs to build physical integration and academic skills.)

** Griffin, Simone & Sandler, Dianne. Motivate to Communicate: 300 Games & Activities for Your Child with Autism, Jessica Kingsley Publications, 2009.

**** Kranowitz, Carol. The Out-of-Sync Child Has Fun, Practical Activities, Perigee Trade, 2006. (Carol Kranowitz is the guru for Out-of-Sync kids and has several other books on the subject, some of which might be chock full of even more activity ideas, besides her definitive book and workbook listed in the adult section.)

** Myles, Brenda Smith. Simple Strategies that Work! Helpful Hints for All Educators of Students with Asperger's Syndrome, High-Functioning Autism, and Related Disabilities, Autism-Asperger Publishing Company, 2006.

*** Notbohm, Ellen & Zysk, Veronica. 1001 Great Ideas for Teaching & Raising Children with Autism & Asperger's, Future Horizons, 2010.

** Tilley, Kelly, MCIS, OTR. Active Imagination Activity: 50 Sensorimotor Activities, Sensory World, 2011. (A spiral stand-up book that is small and can be transported easily wherever you go.)

* Walton, Susan. Coloring Outside Autism's Lines: 50+ Activities, Adventures, and Celebrations for Families with Children With Autism, Sourcebooks, 2010.

Parent & Adult Information Books:

* Almine. How To Raise An Exceptional Child: Practical Wisdom for Spiritual Mastery, Spiritual Journeys LLC: Newport, Oregon, 2010. (A "channeled" book this is actually a compilation of latest research, old folk remedies and advice, all rolled into one! There are some great ideas in this book.)

**** Andrews, Ted. The Intercession of Spirits: Working with Animals, Angels & Ancestors, Dragonhawk Publishing: Jackson, Tennessee, 2008. (Excellent resource for those ready to go into the deeper realms with their child and this book includes a list of his dozens of other books and CDs which would be valuable for your in formation about intuitive children).

**** Andrews, Ted. Animal-Speak, Llewellyn Publications: St. Paul, MN, 1998 as well as Nature-Speak and Animal-Wise, Dragonhawk Publishing: Jackson, Tennessee, 2004, 1999, respectively. (These are "must have" reference books to look up spiritual meanings for signs and symbols in one's life. Animal-Speak – North & South American domestic and wild animals; Animal-Wise – exotic and world wide animals; Nature-Speak – trees, flowers & plants. Andrews was a teacher for ten years and an animal expert who intuited this information after studying each animal's habits and "life maps." While he was also a prolific writer and psychic medium, he spent his life involved with his concerns for children, animals and nature.)

*** Atwater, P.M.H. Beyond the Indigo Children, Bear & Company: Rochester, Vermont, 2005. (This book is a great read, as all of Atwater's books are. It does not give suggestions for what to do, but as always, it is fascinating material and this one is mostly on the new world coming and the choices our children will have to make. Do read it, it will help you feel better about a lot of things concerning your children and students, but it will also make you think about the miscommunication going on now just about everywhere and on many topics about children.)

**** Atwater, P.M.H. Children of the New Millennium: Children Near- Death Experiences, Three Rivers Press: New York, 1999.

**** Atwater, P.M.H. The New Children & Near-Death Experiences, Bear & Co.: Rochester, Vermont, 2003. (These are the same book but the updated version has new and important information in these two definitive books about near-death experiences in children.)

*** Balch, Phyllis A. Prescription for Nutritional Healing and Prescription for Herbal Healing, Avery/Penguin Group: New York, 2006. (These are the definitive alternative health reference books for nutritional healing. Each book is close to a thousand pages and lists all the common minor ailments and many of the big ones and what to do using foods, vitamins, herbs, and other supplements. They are less than 30 dollars so you definitely get your money's worth from a nutritional counselor who has been through all this along with her children!)

*** Bowman, Carol. Children's Past Lives: How Past Life Memories Affect Your Child, Bantam Books, 1998. (Bowman is a mom herself and her first book spends a lot of time on the past lives of her own two children. She describes her journey to understanding what was happening to her children, then to her. She also discusses what the experts on the subject have to say and gives some practical advice on what to do in the second half of the book. There were only two books on this subject concerning American children, that can really help you and this is one of them!)

** Browne, Sylvia & Harrison, Lindsay. Psychic Children, New American Library, 2007. (Best book concerning night terrors, nightmares, dreaming and kinetic children. Browne's book also lists some great "Tools of Protection" to use with children before going out the door in the morning or going to bed at night.)

**** Bruce, Robert. Astral Dynamics and Practical Psychic Self-Defense from Hampton Books Publishing Company: Charlottesville VA, 1999 & 2002 respectively. (These two books were meant to be just one huge reference book which would have been close to a thousand pages, according to Robert Bruce. So you really need both of them if you are dealing with extremely difficult and "beyond our comprehension at this time" problems, intuitively. This is a huge encyclopedia of the paranormal with hundreds of practical ways to deal with difficult situations that no one seems to be able to identify. As the psychic self-defense book states on its front cover, these techniques are for: "Understanding and surviving unseen influences" in our lives. Robert Bruce is from Australia and works with the Monroe Institute founded by Robert Monroe, the original guru on astral travel. After many years of working with adults Bruce has turned to working with intuitive children because he finds that he can help them much more easily than adults. He continues to give workshops and for those of you way out there on the cutting edge so don't miss an opportunity to attend one of his workshops if it comes along. I got to go to a three day one and it changed my life! But many found it just too overwhelming and "far-out," so get on the internet and check him out first. He has forty years experience being an extremely intuitive child and adult who night traveled everywhere and has remembered a lot of it. Many experts in the metaphysical world have asked Robert Bruce, "Where were you years ago when we needed a "translator" for our work?" He offers lots of practical advice for adult intuitives and tells the truth about his many "travels." Parents ready for this will love the information it provides, and however difficult it is to get through the information, you will be fascinated! Robert Bruce is now working mainly with very difficult child cases, as well as presenting workshops and writing.)

**** Buchholz, David, M.D. Heal Your Headache: The 123 Program, Workman Publishing: New York, 2002. (Actually this book should be called heal your bodily inflammations which is 90 percent of all illness. This inflammation is what is behind the manifestations of most illnesses before they get out of control and become progressively deadly. Empathic sensitives suffer even more with our growing toxic environmental pollutants. A must read for any one aware of what is really going on!)

** Carroll, Lee & Tober, Jan. The Indigo Children, Hay House, Inc.: Carlsbad, California, 1999. (A rather nebulous book for parents of smaller children, this book lists all Starseed, Indigo, Crystal, Star Kids, Angel Children, Old Soul children – and all the other titles I've missed – it basically gives good information on the raising of all children, but does make one aware of just what empathic and thinking intuitives are all about. Perhaps there are more aware children arriving, and perhaps it is more likely that the rest of the world is finally catching up to what was already here – you decide!)

* Colton, Ann Ree. Watch Your Dreams, Ann Ree Colton Foundation of Niscience, Inc.: P.O. Box 2057, Glendale, California, 1973. (While an old book, it has been re printed and is available. This book is for those who really want to explore the very esoteric side of dreams both intellectually and metaphysically.)

**** Crawford, Catherine. the highly intuitive child, Hunter House Publishers, Alameda, California, 2009. (Best reference on this entire list for overall information and practical application exercises and activities for intuitive children, from an art therapist and marriage and family counselor.)

** Crook, William G, M.D. and Crook, Cynthia P. Tracking Down Hidden Food Allergy, Professional Books: Jackson, Tennessee, 1985. (Best book for tracking down childhood allergies without having to pay professionals to help you! I am sure there have been more printings of this book since this one.)

*** Currivan, Jude. The 8th Chakra, Hay house, Inc., 2006. (Everything basic you want to know about the 12 chakras.)_

Day, Peggy & Gale, Susan. Psychic Children, A.R.E. Press (Edgar Casey Foundation press) Virginia Beach, VA, 2004. (Best book on the places across the nation where people are helping intuitive children in programs, day camps and all the various things they are trying to do.)

**** Dennison, Paul E. and Hargrove, Gail E. E-K for Kids and Brain Gym; Personlized Whole Brain Integration. (The website www.braingym.com offers many newer books as well, including several on Vision Gym. Hopefully they have incorporated the E-K For Kids book into these materials as it was the most successful book for explaining to kids the theory behind Edu-K and why they are doing the exercises. However you can find invaluable exercises for sensory integration, increasing success academically and socially at school, and also for self-worth and self-esteem for any child, but especially for empathic children who need to learn focusing and body awareness. Look under the title sensory integration on Amazon and you can find both older books, E-K for Kids and Brain Gym.)

** DeSalvo, John, PhD. Andrew Jackson Davis: The First American Prophet and Clairvoyant, Delaney Books, 2007.

** De Salvo, John, PhD. The Seeress of Prevorst: Her Secret Language and Prophecies from the Spirit World, Destiny Books, 2008.

Dillard, Sherrie. Discover your Psychic Type , Llewellyn Publications, 2010. (This book gives you several psychic types of people and describes their characteristics, great for high school kids.)

**** Dong, Paul & Raffill, Thomas E. China's Super Psychics, Marlowe & Company: New York, 1977. (This book bases its research mainly on child psychics and explains why. Following the Chinese belief in "chi" or energetic fields which is called the practice of "Chi-Gong," these top scientists are trying to bridge the gap between the psychic fields and the scientific methods of research.)

** Drewes, Athena A. & Drucker, Sally Ann. Parapsychological Research With Children, The Scarecrow Press, Inc.: Metuchen, New Jersey & London, 1991. (A huge bibliography of American parapsychological research papers completed on intuitive children.)

* Eason, Cassandra. Psychic Families, foulsham: London & New York, 1995. (The only good part in this book is at the very last where Eason lists "Fifteen Ways of Encouraging Positive Psychic Bonds.")

**** Eide, Brock & Eide, Fernette. The Mislabeled Child, Hyperion: New York, 2006. (Two doctors who run a neurolearning clinic and are looking at the "whole" child rather than various parts that rarely fit together well for any child. A great reference to lead one away from labeling).

* Galbraith, Judy. The Gifted Kids Survival Guide for Ages 10 & Under, Free Spirit Publishing: Minneapolis, MN, 1984. (This is for kids 10 or under to read or have someone read and interpret for them.)

Galinsky, Ellen. Mind in the Making: The Essential Life Skills Every Child Needs, Family & Work Institute, Harper studio, 2010. (Teen developmental and brain functions.)

** Gach, Michael Reed. Acupressure's Potent Points: A Guide to Self-care for Common Ailments, Bantam Books, 1990.

** Gardner, Howard. Creating Minds: Anatomy of Creativity Seen Through the Lives of Freud, Einstein, Picasso, Stravinsky Eliot, Graham and Ghandi, Basic Books, 1993.

*** Gilkeson, Jim. Energy Healing: A Pathway to Inner Growth, Marlowe & Company: New York, 2000. (This book is not for children but has many really good advanced exercises for energy healing. So why have I mentioned it in this bibliography? Because the first chapters write eloquently and poignantly about the path of an empathic intuitive and healer, in words and phrases that we all can relate to. And that you as the adult can convey to your children or pupils to comfort them on their own journey.)

** Goleman, Daniel. Emotional Intelligence & Why It Can Matter More Than IQ, Bantam Books: New York, 1997. (Want to know about all your children, students and any others? This is mainly theory and information to have more awareness on this vital subject.)

**** Goode, Caron B. & Patterson, Tara. Raising Intuitive Children, New Page Books: Franklin Lakes, NJ, 2009. (Shares many stories from children of all ages and discusses various important topics concerning intuitive children.)

**** Gordon, Richard. Quantum Touch: The Power to Heal, North Atlantic Books: Berkeley, California, 2006. (There are many, many books out there on the art of energy and touch healing, but few are for lay people who just want to learn the basic techniques for use on their own family or children. This book comes from the premise that we are all "healers" and "energy workers" and can learn simple techniques to help our families and friends that is "love directed" towards those we care about. Not only can anyone do these simple techniques but what a wonderful way to share with your child, positive talks and exercises, while teaching them about their own natural talents as "healers.")

**** Grandin, Temple, PhD, & Margaret M. Scariano. Emergence: Labeled Autistic, Vintage Books: New York, 1994

*** Grandin, Temple, PhD. The Way I See It: A Personal Look at Autism and Asperger's, Future Horizons Inc.: Arlington, Texas, 2011.

*** Grandin, Temple, PhD. Thinking in Pictures: My Life with Autism, Vintage Books: New York, 1995. 2006.

**** Greenspan, Stanley J. MD & Weider, Serena PhD. Engaging Autism: Using the Floortime Approach To Help Children Relate, Communicate and Think, Da Capo Lifelong Books, 2006. (The definitive and best practical guide for parents in raising and not labeling an autistic child.)

** Harrington, Michael. Touched by the Dragon's Breath, Susan Creek Books: Wilsonville, Oregon, 2009. (A great adult explanation about the positive aspects of "the shift" and all its many ramifications!)

** Hay, Louise L. You Can Heal Your Life, Hay House: Santa Monica, California, 1984. (This book has been published and republished many, many times. It is a popular book for every generation which includes dozens of affirmations for positive thinking and specific ones associated with various ailments and organs of the body to promote good health.

You can incorporate these affirmations in many of the activities that you do with your children.)

**** Kagan Dr. Spencer and Kagan, Miguel. Multiple Intelligences: The Complete Book, Kagan Cooperative Learning: San Clemente, California, 1998. (This is a huge definitive book about the various intelligences explaining them in depth and giving teachers and parents many ideas for activities. It is the basic book and then there are many others which are listed just before the children's book section.)

* Keyes, Jr., Ken. The hundredth monkey, Vision Books: Coos Bay, Oregon, 1985.
Keynes, Randal. Annie's Box: Charles Darwin, His Daughter, and Human Evolution, Fourth Estates: London, 2001. (Or see the film "Creation" with Paul Bettany and Jennifer Connelly, 2009, a much better representation of the mystical life of Darwin.)

**** Kranowitz, Carol Stock. The Out-Of-Sync Child, A Skylight Press Book: New York, 1998. (An absolute must and the best book on the subject of sensory integration in children. All of us have a bit of difficulty with these coordination and tactile issues, but some of us have these things interfering with our ability to function in life. Kranowitz will tell you what all of these eight difficulties can be and if you resonate to this information yourself or see it in one of your children, one of your grandchildren, a student or friend, etc., then this will be a "miracle" answer to many things and give you the right directions to go without labeling children. Not everyone is dealing with this one, but those who are will be amazed! Also buy her workbook for teachers written with several others, because this is more detailed and specific information on assessing and working with your child: Answers & Questions Teachers Ask About Sensory Integration from Sensory Resources, Las Vegas, Nevada, on the web as well. Any of Kranowitz's books are great, whether they are activities for children or information for adults.)

*** Lazear, David. Seven Ways of Knowing: Teaching Multiple Intelligences, Skylight Publishing: Palatine, Illinois, 1991. (This book is listed in both bibliography sections because it is an adult book but lists many activities for teens and many that can be adapted for younger children.)

* Lewis, Stephen & Slawson, Evan. Sanctuary: The Path to Consciousness, a Novel, 2008. (These people are a bit controversial. They use energy frequencies for healing people via the computer and to avoid the law they operate from another country. Their ideas however, are solid and the book is very interesting to read. On the other hand, their healings are quite expensive, but then, aren't the fees in the medical world just as expensive if not more so? And do either avenues have a high success rate? Worth your time to read this, this is just one other pioneering

frequency and wave technique that can really work or might be suspect too. Until we get a handle on this energy healing, it is all hit and miss for now.)

* Long, Max Freedom. The Secret Science Behind Miracles: Huna Magic, and Ho'Opono, Ho'Oponopono Instant Healing, Copyright Max Freedom Long, 2009.

** Losey, Meg Blackburn. The Children of the Now, New Page Books: Franklin Lakes, NJ, 2007. (This does provide interesting and thought provoking checklists and general information on the theories behind all sorts of kids supposedly coming in but there are few practical applications for assisting these types of children. It lists Crystalline, Indigos, Star Kids, Angels on Earth, etc.)

**** Loyd, Alexander & Johnson, Ben. The Healing Code, Grand Central Lifestyle: New York & Boston, 2010. (The simplified Healing Code technique combined with the simplified Tapping technique, affirmations, belief, visualizations, meditation, diet and a physical exercise of some kind, is the ultimate package for self-healing of any kind, either emotional or physical. Being in charge of your own health and healing is the "wave" of the future and being in charge of those you choose to help you along the way either in the medical or holistic worlds, is also – excuse my pun – another "wave" soon to come! This simple four-part "code" for the body can be used for both physical ailments and emotional core issues.)

*** Lundgren, Paul. The Book of Shiatsu: A Complete Guide, Touchstone, 2003.

*** Martinez, Susan B., Phd. The Psychic Life of Abraham Lincoln, Career Press, 2009.

**** Marrs, Jim. PSI Spies, New Page Book: Franklin Lakes, New Jersey, 2007. (A great book on the history of psychic research in the U.S. military, it mainly focuses on remote viewing which then broadens into many other areas of psychic research. The Edgar Cayce Foundation and the Monroe Institute are two other foundations which have books on their histories of psychic research in the United States on the civilian side. There are many other such institutes across the nation that are private or sponsored by universities who do brain research or offer parapsychology degrees, etc.)

* Milner, Murray Jr. Freaks, Geeks And Cool Kids – American Teenagers, Schools, and the Culture of Consumption (A book on the caste system in the high schools of today.)

**** Morse, Melvin and Perry, Paul. Closer to the Light: Learning from the Near- Death Experiences of Children, Ivy Books: New York, 1990. (The other definitive exploration of this subject, this was the first of its kind by a medical doctor.)

**** Ostrander, Sheila and Schroder, Lynn. Psychic Discoveries Behind the Iron Curtain, Prentice-Hall, Inc.: Englewood Cliffs, New Jersey, 1971. (One of the classics of psychic history, this book has been reprinted and updated many times since the seventies and still contains excellent information about the history of psychic research in Russia, which is ongoing to this day.)

* Parker, Alice Anne. Understand Your Dreams, I.J. Kramer, New World Library, Novato, California, 2001. (Louise Hay recommends this one for dream interpretation, but it is on the deeper channeling level.)

* Pliskin, Marci and Just, Shari L. The Complete Idiot's Guide to Interpreting Your Dreams, Alpha, 2003.

Pluke, Rob. Parenting the Sensitive Child, self-published, 2008. (What I like about this book is it doesn't get into any metaphysical stuff and it was written by a man who is a "counseling psychologist." He really gives some good advice, insights, and encouragement to parents of sensitive children.)

**** Prather, Hugh and Gayle. Spiritual Parenting: A Guide to Understanding and Nurturing the Heart of Your Child, Three Rivers Press: New York, 1996. (This is one very powerful book for all the kinds of parents out there who are helping to raise a child. They explain very clearly, just how off course we have become in our culture in understanding and raising children. And they take a great deal of time explaining how to get back on course, especially with adolescents and the false labeling that they have today in our society.)

Preuss, Harry and Bill Gottlieb. The Natural Fat-Loss Pharmacy, Broadway Books, 2007. (Just trying to save you time by looking through dozens of natural weight loss and wellness books out there. Childhood obesity is a big problem now and many of us struggle with our weight anyway!)

**** Rosetree, Rose. Face Reading Secrets, Ottenheimer Publishers, 1994. (Body Language and face reading guide book.)

** Schwartz, Stephen A. The Secret Vaults of Time: Psychic Archaeology and the Quest for Man's Beginnings, Hampton Roads Publishing: Charlottesville, Virginia, 2001. (This is the only one of this scholar's books that you would want to tackle! It includes a brief history of this group's involvement with the secret military psychic spy programs in America, brief biographies of famous psychics whose specialty was historical remote viewing, and some of Schwartz's excavations. He is so brilliant that he has a bit of difficulty translating his thoughts to lay people, but offers an excellent self-healing CD through the Monroe Institute.)

Sinetar, Marsha. Spiritual Intelligence, Orbis Books: New York, 2000. (Calling them "early awakening" children this author gives some good advice about incorporating spirituality into a child's life and also understanding when a child chooses spirituality at a very early age and makes it his or her own.)

**** Silverman, Linda Kreger. Upside Down Brilliance: The Visual-Spatial Learner, DeLeon Publishing :Denver, Colorado, 2002. (An absolute must for all children and their parents, this was originally written about and for gifted children and their parents. However, this is true about all learning styles on a scale from Auditory Processors (Left brained) to Whole Brain Learners (in the middle) to Visual-Spatial Learners (Right Brain). We are all there somewhere, with a balance of skills from either side! They have many other books on the subject, just get on www.gifteddevelopment.com or go to the publisher's website. And don't forget Crawford's explanation of the AP's and the VSL's for children, "Ducks" and "Sponges! Learning styles, communication styles, and intuitive styles superimposed.)

* Snyder, Debra J. Intuitive Parenting, Atria Paperback/Beyond Words: New York and Hilsboro, Oregon, 2010. (This book has some additional metaphysical and energy work exercises for you and your child to do together.)

**** Soskin, Julie. How Psychic Are You? 76 Techniques to Boost Your Innate Power, Penquin Books, 2002. (The very best book for introducing the types of intuitive abilities to younger children – adapted - and teens can do them on their own. They are beginning exercises to discover your fortes, and activities and checklists for various age groups. These activities can even be used in the classroom under the title of "creative arts".)

** Steiger, Brad & Steiger, Sherry Hansen. Children of the Light: Children's Near-Death Experiences, Signet Books: New York, 1995.

**** Steiner, Rudolph and the Waldorf schools. (You can go at this one from his many books or from many of his shorter writings. He founded the Theosophical Society in the late eighteen hundreds in Germany, took a lot of attacks and ridicule from many, many groups and then broke from his own Esoteric School of the Theosophical Society to found the Anthroposophical Society and the School of Spiritual Science in 1923, although he died just a year later in 1924. His first Waldorf school for children was founded in 1919 and he had four of these schools during his lifetime, two in Germany and two in England. There are now over one thousand Waldorf schools worldwide and another 160 schools just in America. They have training schools for their teachers, like the Sunbridge Institute in New York and each teacher moves up through the grades to eighth grade with their same class. The lower grades focus on the arts and basic academics and the upper grades focus on scientific observations and investigations required to become a confident, independent thinker in the world they are going too. These schools started out as non-profit schools but now, just like everyone else they are moving to charter school status or depending on school vouchers.)

**** Sulloway, Frank J. Born to Rebel: Birth Order, Family Dynamics, and Creative Lives, Vintage Books, 1997. (Fascinating but huge book on birth order in families with lots of famous people mentioned from history on subjects like temperament, gender, family niches, people who were exceptions to the rule, social and scientific data on this subject and why some people change spontaneously with the times while others cling to the prevailing dogmas. A left brained look at "the shift" before it was even being discussed!)

*** Swann, Ingo. Everybody's Guide to ESP, Jeremy P. Tarcher, Inc: Los Angeles,1991. (Old but one of the best on how to remote view and what psychic research is all about.)

* Taylor, Jeremy, In the Wisdom of Your Dreams, Jeremy R. Tarcher/Penguin, 2009.

* Taylor, Troy. The Haunted President, Whitechapel Press, 2009.

**** Tucker, Dr. Jim B. Life After Life: A Scientific Investigation of Children's Memories of Previous Lives, Piatkus Books, Britain and St. Martin's Press, New York, 2005. (This and Bowman's books are the best available on how to help parents and children through this often devastating experience, depending on how obsessive and verbal the child is about a previous life.)

* Turner, Kristina. The Self-Healing Cookbook, Earthtones Press, 1987. (This is not just a macrobiotic cookbook, but a way of looking at food, body healing, mind healing and mood leveling using whole natural foods. She lists signs of imbalance and balancing the food to the body as well as seasonal and color of foods eating to put your body into rhythm with earth energies, foods and even your moods.)

** Underwood, Paula. (An Iroquois oral historian who was interested in reawakening the sort of teaching that her people had done for centuries with the young Native American children of today. She wrote several articles on this including: "Learning Your Way Through Chaos" and "The Great Hoop of Life." There are several websites devoted to her teachings on spiritual learning, in particular http://www.learningpeople.org/value_approach.html and http://en.wikipedia.org/wiki/Paula_Underwood. Information to really know about and follow if you are interested in spiritual learning at all!)

** Unknown author. "Inside Your Teen's Head," Parade Magazine, November 28, 2010, pp. 4-6.

* Virtue, Doreen. The Crystal Children, Hay House, Inc.: Carlsbad, California, 2003. (A little book literally, but really worth reading!)

** Virtue, Doreen. The Lightworker's Way, Hay House, Inc.: Carlsbad, California, 1997. (A beginning book but the second part "A Guide to Psychic Communication and Spiritual Healing" is really worth reading if you do intuitive readings or want to have one.)

* Walker, Sally Yahne. The Survival Guide for Parents of Gifted Kids, Free Spirit Publications: Minneapolis, MN, 1991. (This is the same as the other one but it is for teens rather than young children and they can read it themselves. Make sure you tell them beforehand that we are all "gifted" in one way or another!)

** Wilcox, David. The Source Field Investigations, Dutton, 2011. (Very interesting material on historical and present day proofs of the shift in consciousness and updates on the latest Russian research.)

*** Wright, Patricia C. & Richard D. Wright. The Divining Heart: Dowsing and Spriritual Unfoldment, Destiny Books: Rochester, Vermont, 1994.

Zwet, Johanna van. A Parent's Toolbox for Spiritual Growth, A.R.E Press: Virginia Beach, Virginia, 2000.

Dream Interpretation Books:

*** Adamson, Eve & Williamson, Gayle. The Complete Idiot's Guide Dream Dictionary, Alpha Books, 2007. (Very good dictionary of dream interpretations.)

**** Andrews, Ted. Animal-Speak: The Spiritual & Magical Powers of Creatures Great & Small, Llewellyn Publications, 1998. (Excellent physical properties and intuited spiritual meanings of the animals in a dictionary of birds, animals, reptiles along with bird mysteries and reading signs and omens in nature, etc.)

**** Andrews, Ted. Animal-Wise: The Spirit Language & Signs of Nature, Dragonhawk Publishing, 1999. (Excellent dictionary of exotic birds, mammals, insects and sea life from all over the world with physical properties and intuited spiritual meanings.)

**** Andrews, Ted. Nature-Speak: Signs, Omens & Messages in Nature, Dragonhawk Publishing, 2004. (Excellent dictionary of the physical properties and spiritual meanings of land forms, trees plants and flowers, as well as the rhythms of the seasons, weather and astrological cycles.)

**** Avery, Michael. The Secret Language of Waking Dreams, Eckankar, 1992. (Excellent foundation book for recognizing and interpreting day visions and dreams

*** Bear, Sun & Wabun. The Medicine Wheel Earth Astrology, Prentice Hall Press, 1980. (While this is a unique Native American based astrology, it also contains lots of information about various animals that could be helpful in dream interpretation.)

**** Carr-Gomm, Philip & Stephanie. The Druid Animal Oracle: Working With the Sacred Animals of the Druid Tradition, A Fireside Book/Simon & Schuster, 1994. (Especially for those with a background from the British Isles, these are cards but the book that accompanies them is fascinating and filled with the Celtic meaning of each animal, beautiful illustrations and most interesting, traditions and folk tales concerning each animal or bird or sea life from Wales, Scotland or Ireland. They even include four mystical dragons of earth, sea, fire and air.)

**** Cooper, J.C. An Illustrated Encyclopedia of Traditional Symbols, Thames & Hudson, 1978. (A must have, if you can find it with international interpretations from all over the world

**** Cresswell, Julia. The Watkins Dictionary of Angels, Julia Cresswell Copyright, 2006. (Excellent reference for angel meanings from all over the world.)

** Dee, Nerys. The Dreamer's Workbook: A Complete Guide to Interpreting and Understanding Dreams, Sterling Publishing Company, 1989. (This is a beginner's guide for interpreting dreams.)

** Fontana, David. The Secret Language of Dreams, Chronicle Books, 1994. (This one talks about the general themes of dreams, the history and perspectives on dreams, has a small dictionary of dreams and is beautifully illustrated.)

** Guiley Rosemary Ellen. Encyclopedia of Angels, Facts on file, Inc., 1996. (A lot of text on the biographies of famous saints and angels.)

**** Guiley, Rosemary Ellen, Encyclopedia of Mystical & Paranormal Experience, 1991. (Wow! You'll want this as a basic guide to the paranormal!)

**** Miller, Gustavus Hindman. The Dictionary of Dreams: 10,000 Dreams Interpreted, Prentice Hall Press, 1984. (Brief definitions but huge and an excellent resource for dream interpreting.)

*** O'Connell, Mark, Airey, Raje & Craze, Richard. The Illustrated Encyclopedia of Symbols, Signs & Dream Interpretation. (A fascinating look at the world, history and themes behind dreams, beautifully illustrated!)

**** R. Donald Oapon (Zother). Zother's Encyclopedia and Dictionary of Dreams, A Fireside Book/Simon & Schuster, 2004. (This one gives several ways to interpret a symbol or objects in a dream, giving the different circumstances in which the symbol or object appears.)

** Pliskin, Marci & Just, Shari L. The Idiot's Guide to Interpreting Your Dreams, Alpha Books, 2003. (Great basic reference for all the many sides of dreaming and dream interpretation.)

**** Rain, Mary Summer. In Your Dreams: The Ultimate Dream Dictionary, Mary Summer Rain Copyright, 2004. (Excellent but brief interpretations of objects and symbols, but the power in Mary Summer Rain's interpretations are her intuitive interpretations!)

Reid, Lori. The Complete Book of Chinese Horoscopes, Barnes & Noble Books, 1997. (Great book for teens and even younger ones if interpreted a little, but also really helpful in dream interpretation.)

**** Sams, Jamie & Carson, David. Medicine Cards, Bear & Company, 1988. (Although these are cards, the book that comes with them is a wealth of information about various animals and their intuited meanings in relation to the Native Americans and how they look at nature, with beautifully illustrated book and card drawings.)

** Taylor, Jeremy. The Wisdom of Your Dreams, Penguin, 2009. (This is a book about group dream interpretation and how to do this!)

A Short List of Titles of Biographies of Super Psychics:

Intuitive adults and teens can sometimes be inspired by reading about others and how they coped with their psychic abilities growing up. I purposely put down both historical autobiographies and biographies and more modern day books, which are well written. There are also books written about extremely gifted psychics who I feel were the most true to their calling and had extraordinary talents. There is a huge collection of such books which are literally "endless," but these are the ones that I am aware of and have read. Each of these books contain something special for young men and women to relate too in a world that still to this day keeps so many of us "invisible." While these are the stories of more famous intuitives and mostly American ones, remember that there are hundreds of us who are doing our work quietly and without fanfare. And don't forget the clergy, great teachers, creative artists of all kinds, and every genius in every field of endeavor, saints and avatars, most of whom were also highly intuitive healers!

Allison, Dorothy, A Psychic Story, Mass Market Paperbacks, 1980. (Reader and psychic detective, featured on various TV shows like "Unsolved Mysteries" before she passed away.)

Anderson, George, We Don't Die: Conversations from the Other Side, Berkley Books, 1989. (Went into grief work, has several books, charges a lot for individual readings, website, very intriguing upbringing.)

Brinkley, Dannion, A Peace in the Light, Harper Paperbacks, 1995. (Works mainly for older citizens, quietly and with great talent, has a made-for-TV movie about his life.)

Browne, Sylvia & May, Antoinette, Adventures of a Psychic, Hay House, Inc., 1990. (Practically has an empire and charges a lot for individual readings.)

Browning, Norma Lee. The Psychic World of Peter Hurkos, toExcel/iUniverse, 2000. (One of most famous psychics of the past century.)

Buckland, Raymond, The Spirit Book: Encyclopedia of Clairvoyance, Channeling and Spirit Communication, Visible Ink Press, 2006. (Wow! This is a must have book with brief descriptions of types of paranormal abilities interlaced with brief biographies of famous psychics from all over the world, as well as historically famous intuitives!)

Caudill, Maureen, Suddenly Psychic: A Skeptic's Journey, Hampton Roads Press, 2006. (A physics major who worked as a senior scientist, Caudill one day realized she was a psychic!)

Cooper, Paulette & Noble, Paul, The 100 Top Psychics in America, Pocket Books, 1996. (Very brief biographies of the lesser known psychics, just under the likes of Edwards, Anderson, Browne, Van Praagh, Holland, Williams, etc.)

DeSalvo, John, PhD, Andrew Jackson Davis: The First American Prophet and Clairvoyant, Destiny Books, 2007. (A 19th Century Spiritualist who became a medical doctor and occasionally advised Abraham Lincoln.)

DeSalvo, John, PhD, The Seeress of Prevorst: Her Secret Language and Prophecies From the Spirit World, Destiny Books, 2008. (Amazing story about a centuries ago woman, who spent the last half of her life in bed while people from all over the world came to have her read for them or to foretell the future. She channeled a mathematical language from the universe that no one can explain even today.)

Edward, John, One Last Time, Berkley Books, 1999. (Famous today, has his own show on TV, psychic medium, has a few books out.)

Eiseley, Loren, The Immense Journey, Vintage Books, 1957. (Anthropologist, naturalist, fabulous writer about the natural world, way intuitive and way spiritual!)

Garrett, Eileen. My Life as a Search for the Meaning of Mediumship, Oquaga Press, 1939. (Most famous psychic of her time.)

Goldsmith, Barbara. Other Powers: The Age of Suffrage, Spiritualism, and the Scandalous Victoria Woodhull, Alfred A. Knopf, 1998. (Read about some of the other Spiritualists of the times as well. Woodhull became so famous advising the captains of industry, she even attempted to run for president.)

Holland, John & Pearlman, Cindy, Born Knowing, Hay House, Inc., 2003.(A favorite of mine because he specializes in recognition of past or historical events among other things, plus as a young man he went to England and knocked on the most prestigious mystery school in England that is very hard to get into. They tested him and admitted him right away.)

Home ("Yume"), Daniel D. Incidents in My Life: The Autobiography of the Most Sensational Psychic of All Time, University Books, Inc., originally published in 1862. (One of the greatest psychics historically, and the only man never to be de bunked even when levitating!)

Lord, Bob & Penny, Visionaries, Mystics and Stigmatists, Copyright, Bob & Penny Lord, 1995. (All the famous saints and mystics from history, their life stories and miracles they performed.)

Marrs, Jim, PSI Spies: The True Story of America's Psychic Warfare Program, Career Press/New Page, 2007. (Besides the history, Marrs mentions several of the military psychics and their stories and abilities.)

Martinez, Susan B., PhD, The Psychic Life of Abraham Lincoln, Career Press/New Page, 2009. (Finally, the truth is being told about our most psychic and mystic American President.)

McMoneagle, Joesph, Memoirs of a Psychic Spy, Hampton Roads Press, 2006. (The best of the life stories of military psychics is McMoneagle's and he has written several books and works with the Monroe Institute today.)

Meade, Marion, Madame Blavatsky: The Woman Behind the Myth, Author's Guild Back In Print, 2001. (How real was she? How much was magic and how much was true clairvoyance? A fascinating and very famous psychic from history.)

Monroe, Robert A., Journeys Out of Body; Far Journeys & Ultimate Journey, Doubleday 1971, Broadway Books, 1990 & 1994. (All of Monroe's books are great and they all tell bits and pieces of his own life journey as well as his many journeys into the unknown night. However, the most he talks about his own life is in Journeys Out of Body.)

Montgomery, Ruth & Garland, Joanne, Herald of the New Age: The Spiritual Odyssey of the World's Leading Psychic Authority, Fawcett Books, 1986. (Author of many books, many appearances, quite a fascinating life. You may also want to read about Arthur Ford and Jeanne Dixon, who were two famous psychics through the last decades along with Montgomery.)

Myer, Nancy & Czetli, Steve, Silent Witness: The True Story of a Psychic Detective, St. Martin's Press, 1993. (Myer started out doing readings then began working with a police department and eventually began giving workshops to police departments all over the country to teach them how to get in touch with their intuitions and use them effectively in their police work and on detective cases. She has become quite an effective "cop" herself and is now known as Nancy Weber.)

Nickell, Joe, Psychic Sleuths: ESP and Sensational Cases, Prometheus Books, 1994. (The following psychics are in this book: Peter Hurkos, Gerard Croiset, Greta Alexander, Bill War, Rosemary Kerr, and Phil Jordan.)

Orloff, Judith, M.D., Second Sight, Warner Books, 1996. (A doctor's journey into an intuitive life.)

Over, Raymond Van, ESP and The Clairvoyants, Award Books, 1970. (Brief biographies of more psychics.)

Pollack, Jack Harrison & Bama, James. Croiset: The Clairvoyant, Bantam Books, 1965.

Praagh, James Van, Talking To Heaven: A Medium's Message of Life After Death, Dutton Books, 1997. (Van Praagh's life story is quite fascinating, has several books, charges a lot, lots of appearances, and had a four hour mini-series on TV about his most famous case, entitled "Talking to Heaven.")

Reiner, Noreen, A Mind for Murder: The Real Life Files of a Psychic Detective, Hampton Roads Boos, 2008.(Best at finding missing persons, dead or alive, and using psychometrics.)

Russell, Robert. The Journey of Robert Monroe: From Out of Body Explorer to Consciousness Pioneer, Hampton Roads Publishing, 2007. (First to chronicle OBE's in the 1950s, Robert Monroe founded the prestigious Monroe Institute.)

Scallion, Gordon-Michael, Notes From the Cosmos, Gordon-Michael Scallion, Copyright 1997. (Considered a futurist or modern day Nostradamus, Scallion specializes in the prediction of natural disasters, tells his life story and amazingly found a way to turn his nightmares around into positive warnings for others through a newsletter and website, etc. Now, his spiritual awakenings had broadened to other areas after the sudden onset and demise of his channeled information on natural disasters.)

Schwartz, Stephan A. The Secret Vaults of Time, Hampton Roads Publishing, 2001. (An anthropologist, all his other books are quite technical, but this one is full of the life stories of all the people from around the world that he considers to be fathers of psychic archaeology, Chapters 1-5.)

Smith, Eleanor Touhey, Psychic People, Bantam Books, 1969. (Many ancient seers and a few modern ones, up through the sixties and their brief life stories.)

Smith, A. Robert, The Lost Memoirs of Edgar Cayce: Life As a Seer, A.R.E. Press, 1997.

Stockton, Bayard, The Biography of Robert Monroe, The Donning Company, 1990.

Stone, Joshua David PhD, The Ascended Masters Light the Way: Beacons of Ascension, Volume Five, Light Technology Publishing, 1995. (Life stories of many of the famous avatars, religious founders, saints, and ascended masters from both history and all over the world, etc.)

Sugrue, Thomas, The Story of Edgar Casey: There is a River, A.R.E. Press, 1973. (The classic biography of Edgar Cayce.)

Symonds, John, Madame Blavatsky, Medium, Magician, Thomas Yoseloff, 1959.

Taylor, Troy. The Haunted President,White Chapel Press, 2009.

Wangler, Chris, Famous People of the Paranormal: Psychic, Clairvoyants and Charlatans, Ghost House Books, Canada, 2005. (Life stories of twenty eight of the most famous psychics of all time, including Rasputin, Mesmer and Wolf Messing.)

Wicker, Christine, Lily Dale: The True Story of the Town That Talks to the Dead, Harpers, 1995.(The history of a 150 year old town founded in New York state by Spiritualists which still houses today, a whole community of psychics, and written by a journalist skeptic who spent the summer there.)

Williams, Lisa, Life Among the Dead, Simon Spotlight, Entertainment, 2008. (Delightful and interesting biography of a younger psychic's adventures!)

A Few Websites That Might Be Helpful:

Intuitive Parenting for Intuitive Kids-

www.empoweredparent.com
www.gifteddevelopment.com
www.heartglowparenting.com
psykids.org.(Camps & Classes for Kids)
www.intuitivechildren.net (Workshops)
www.braingym.com

Here Are Some Suggestions for Meditation CDs:

Asian Meditations & Music:

"Golden Spa Tones: Tibetan Bowls" by Dean Evenson & Walter Makichen
"Singing Bowls of Shangri-La" by Thea Surasu
"Tao of Healing: Soundings of the Planet" by Dean Evenson & Li Xiangting

<u>Chakra Cleansing Guided Meditations & Music</u>:

"Chakra Balancing" by Stacy Dean & Gerald Jay Markoe
"Chakra Suite" by Steven Halpern
"Crystal Bowl Chakra Chants" by Jonathan Goldman & Crystal Tones
"From Heart to Crown" by Rob Whitesides-Woo
"Journey Through the Chakras" by Jackie Haverty

<u>Guided Meditations</u>:

<u>Self-Healing Meditations:</u>

"Freedom from Stress," "Effortless Weight Loss," "Freedom From Back Pain," But the two best are "Freedom From TMJ" and "Accelerated Healing" all by Denise Lynch from her <u>Power Dreaming</u> series.

"Healing" by Stephen A. Schwartz (Excellent)

"Infinite Healing, Body, Mind & Spirit," "Journey to the Fifth Dimension," and "Journey to the Crystal Palace," by Jackie Haverty/ Paul Armitage.

"Music for Sound Healing" (music only) by Steven Halpern

"Morning & Evening Meditations" by Louise L. Hay

<u>High Frequency Soothing Meditations & Tonal Sounds</u>:

"Expand the Light: Photon Light Breath Meditation" The Omnipure Series by Kirkland & Laura Ross (Extremely powerful guided meditation, I hope they produce more guided ones plus music ones soon!)

"Crystal Bowl Healing" by Steven Halpern (Soothing & powerful with chanting included in some sets)

"Musical Medicine: Music to Energize the Soul" by Kirkland & Laura Ross (Omipure: Expand the Light Series – soothing but powerful music)

"Sonic Bliss" Omnipure Guided Meditations by Kirkland & Laura Ross (music)

"Sounds of Light: Crystal Voices" by Deborah Van Dyke & Valerie Farnsworth (soothing

with some chanting)
"Tonal Alchemy" by Steven Halpern (soothing)

"Tone of God: The Perfect Resonance" by Denise Lynch (Not music, only frequencies and tones, and not for everyone!)

Meditation Music – Fantasy:

"A Promise of Angels" by Midori
"A Promise of Fairies" by Midori
"A Promise of Serenity" by Midori
"Fairy Heart Magic" by Gary Stadler
"Fairy Ring" by Mike Rowland
"Gifts of the Angels" by Steven Halpern
"Inner Peace" by Steven Halpern
"Reflections of Fairies" by Gary Stadler
"Silver Wings" by Mike Rowland

Meditation Music – Native American:

"Earth Spirit: Native American Flute Music" by Carlos Nakai
"Inside Monument Valley" by Paul Horn & Carlos Nakai
"Journeys" by Carlos Nakai
"Songs of the Indian Flute" Volumes by I & II by John Rainer, Jr.
"Tear of the Moon: Incan Pan Pipes & Native American Flute" by Coyote Oldman

Meditation Music - Ocean & Sea:

"Guardians of Atlantis" by Dan Gibson's Solitudes Series
"Ocean Surf: Timeless & Sublime" Dan Gibson's Solitudes Series
"Waterscapes" by Dan Gibson's Solitudes Series
"Songs and Sounds of Orcinus Orca: The Killer Whale" by Paul Spong
"Whales Alive" by Paul Winter & Paul Hailey

Meditation Music – South American:

"Medicine Woman I, The Gift II, The Rising III, Prophecy IV," (This Medicine Woman series is all South American meditation music with an upbeat sound)

Meditation Music – Universe & Outer Space:

"And the Stars Go With You" by John Serrie

"Hearts of Space: Universe Sampler" by various artists
"Music From The Pleiades" by Gerald Jay Markoe
"Return of the Comet" by David Lange
"Structures of Silence" by Steve Roach
"The Sky of Mind" by Ray Lynch

"When we lose our ability to dream, we lose our commitment to life. We lose our connection to our soul. Life becomes a drudgery without any hope of change...Human beings are dreamers, that is the way our Creator made us. Anything else is an unnatural way of life."

--Ibid.,Last Cry, p. 233

"We are about to undergo a radical change in the way we think, feel, perceive, as well as expressing our living of life as a species. Consciousness is about to make a hollow leap, what science calls the jump. We are about to become a new life form expressing ourselves in a new fifth dimensional reality."

Last Cry: Native American Prophecies: Tales of the End Times
by Dr. Robert Ghost Wolf, p.141

EPILOGUE

How Can We Reach the Children of Our Future?

"In our experience, all 'problem children' are scared children. Eliminate fear and, unless there is genetic damage or some other highly unusual condition, any child, including teenagers, will begin to settle into a gentler attitude and approach to life... To simply remember God turns your mind towards your source of peace. Remembering is a gentle act that requires no expertise or noticeable effort... With every emotion whether it is manifested in the form of discontent, anger, depression, sadness, loneliness, or great fear, you can still remember to love."

--Ibid, Spiritual Parenting, p.208

"The moral test of government is how that government treats those who are at the dawn of life, children; those who are in the twilight of life, the elderly; and those who are in the shadows of life – the sick, the needy, and the handicapped."

--Hubert Humphrey

"There is always a door that opens in childhood to let the future in."

--Barton Gregorian

Throughout my teaching career with children, I have always said that a third of every classroom in the world is not being reached at all, and now, those more experienced in their research of children say that the amount has changed considerably in the last fifty years when the newly "wired" intuitive children began appearing. They say, and both Atwater and Silverman seem to now agree on, this with the people who take polls state that it is more like 80 or 90 percent. "Here's what the pollsters tell us: 40 percent of the students in attendance at American schools are predominately visual, 40 percent are predominately kinesthetic (feelers and movers), and 20 percent are predominately auditory. Yet the average educational system is based entirely on auditory learning, which bypasses 80 percent of the students." *(Beyond the Indigo Children by P.M.H. Atwater, Bear & Co.: Rochester, Vermont, 2005, p.132).*

And while many agree with Atwater's statement about how the new schools should be, these ideas are still a way off future dream. "Educational systems now and in the future must include in their basic curriculum classes on intuitive or psychic perception (beginning with kindergarten), the body-mind connection (how belief as well as life choices affect health and healing), environmental and economic sustainability, and the keys to success – creativity, spirituality, meditation and yoga." She includes eight intuitive principles from Dr. Jeffrey Mishlove, PhD, had another unique book in the seventies called The Roots of Consciousness. A classic now, and way ahead of its time then, Mishlove says now that these principles of a new kind of education will one day form the "roots" of an educational system in the future. These are: 1) Inner Essence or intuitive guidance and self-esteem, 2) Complex Wholeness or achieving higher and higher levels of refinement and integration, 3) Unique Integrity or each person can come to represent a unique integration of human possibilities, 4) Autonomous Purpose or being guided by our own unique purpose and honoring the rights of others, 5) Paradoxical Authenticity or seeking inner peace and serenity while being able to not wall ourselves off from other's pain, 6) Conscious Evolution or refining and healing both our inner self and the world, 7) Living Community or supporting and nurturing communion with all beings, and 8) Conscious Value or valuing that which refines and enhances consciousness for all.

Paula Underwood, an Iroquois oral traditions educator, says on her website learningpeople.org that spiritual learning is the intersecting of three pathways: the community in which we live, those who leave their community to search for other possibilities of learning and return to share, and those who leave for the greater worldwide community and never return. She says that learning is a choice to move through life in the direction of wisdom and then sharing that wisdom upon our return at a higher level on the spiral of learning. She advocated mind, body and spirit learning and honored the enablers of learning who had returned after a life time with "Old Eyes Wisdom" to help their people. She also said that "you become what you do" and must learn to find at least six plausible solutions for any problem to be solved. That personal experience can teach you to 1) always state your opinion on something in three different ways: once to 2) listen, once from the heart and once to check for understanding. On the Third step path you first center yourself, and then second, you look around and assess things. Fourth, you always remember to be true to yourself and understand just where you stand on things. Fifth, you decide what to do and then take action. Sixth, you evaluate later. Her teachings are an excellent set of lessons for cultural understanding between individuals, communities and nations, especially for teens and young adults.

While all these thoughts on educating our young contribute to a utopian world and one that we may one day have, the reality is that right now we have everyone and his brother telling us how to fix our educational system, and we even have foreign countries telling us that they have a better way. Actually no one has a better way financially and countries in which their children's scores are higher in schools have higher cultural expectations that contribute to the academic ones. So these sorts of comparisons are much more complex than that children in another country are doing better academically than American children just because of the teachers or teaching methods. There are many private schools out there that have a better way to teach and even touch a little on the intuitive worlds, but even these schools are struggling for money. Most people, who cannot afford anything else or can't move, or can't transport their kids, or maybe don't know how to advocate for their kids, or simply can't advocate; are simply watching others who know very little about the front lines, trying to put a band-aid on a huge gaping wound.

From politicians trying to keep their constituents off their backs to parents stressed out and wanting more hours of school for their children so they can lessen their child-care bills - and who can blame them in the present economy? From homeschoolers who may or may not be qualified to teach, to businessmen and women disappointed in the level of abilities in their workers, or to private or alternative schools which are myriad and have no common basis unless they are a national chain of schools. These alternative schools do rake in the money, in some cases, but on the other hand, most of them struggle creatively to find alternate funding. Some private elite schools do offer a lot of consistency, but only for those able to afford such things. Older students think they have the answer by dropping out or educating themselves through the ever growing technological smorgasbord being laid before them, and educators continue to remain so compartmentalized that they fight among themselves most of the time, often functioning in survival mode. Right down the line from college to high school to junior high to elementary and even pre-schools, the children's "dumbing down" is blamed on the school level that they attended before their present one. Administrators have their hands full fulfilling federal guidelines, trying to keep the local or state unrealistic "fixers of education" happy, and handing off as much as they can to the teachers. I am not being negative, just honest, having been there myself as I held my hands against what was outside my classroom door to maintain a positive atmosphere for my students.

Just about everyone has a criticism of one kind or another about public education and the few that try to find a solution are so far off base that those of us who are or once were in the trenches for many years, wonder why everyone thinks that we did or do not know, what we are doing. Or that teachers have not changed with the times, and that they still put their students first above all else, even in the face of all these insurmountable odds piled up against them with the constant barrage of changes that really do not work. Most of it is just extra work to look good and even that isn't working. As educators, most of us continued or are now continuing to make things work even with the insurmountable odds stacked against us in ever growing heights and depths. And most of teachers are perfectly aware of the changes in the students of today and how little they are able to meet their new ways of learning because of antiquated materials, un-air conditioned buildings and large class sizes. But teachers do all this anyway, hopeful that the students understand what they are teaching them. Teachers run Waldorf schools in public school classrooms every day, but with a great deal more stress, less money, and a lot more student bullying and outside interference from those who seem to think they know better than those actually doing the teaching. The students want to learn, want to get ahead, and even think they know what needs to be changed in how they are doing things. And they probably do know, with a little help from their teachers and others involved in the process of educating our children.

Perhaps, and I say, just perhaps, those doing this job do have a few very good suggestions, the major one being that those in and around the teachers and their students, open their eyes, listen more carefully and open their hearts to what they are observing, sensing and feeling when they walk into a classroom. And even before this, please do walk in to a few! Most teachers continue "teaching" regardless of all the"hullabaloo." And most teachers know how different students and their modes of learning are, or even how different the world is today, than it was, when they started. Inside each classroom are the internal workings that do succeed, but there is no one to measure this success because everyone outside this classroom hasn't a clue that teachers and their students have already "moved on" even though the materials available are limited and they are not given the technology that the children have in many of their homes. Those who make the decisions for teachers on how to really see and measure what success is, don't seem to have a clue about what they are doing in this arena either. Most of the time the tests we were given to give, were either invalid or time wasting, and even changed so often that if you asked questions about this, people were absolutely astonished that you would!

So here are my six keys to success, that continued to work no matter who or what was handed to me each year. The six keys to a successful classroom are simply these: have consistent expectations, build a community, do your best to unwrap each package carefully, celebrate each child's abilities, empower your students and foster a joy of learning through humor and trust. Along with this is giving each student space and time for their learning style, helping each small community in the cooperative learning style learn to communicate so that the larger classroom community can have peace and structure. Following through on everything that comes up for each child is also important. Knowing that you have their back is what counts, especially if this is not happening consistently at home. Fostering respect for each other and letting them know that you care deeply about each one of them and really do know them intuitively, emotionally, socially and mentally. The spirituality is a given, if all these other things are taking place. A teacher has "failed" if she or he has not opened every package by the end of the year and made the student aware of these understandings about themselves. A teacher has also failed is she or he has not achieved a cohesive classroom community by Christmas or even earlier. You cannot teach in an unstructured atmosphere, nor can you really expect students to learn and retain that learning, if you run your classroom like a dictatorship. Learning has to be shared, given and received, through cooperation, being inspired to learn, and caring about those around you. All the rest, from academics to silly tests that never seem to really assess anything and are constantly changing on the whim of some new idea, are just the added headaches that good teachers have to do to satisfy someone else's idea of what "education" should be.

I sometimes wonder if anyone ever thought of going in and asking each teacher from a particular teaching style, what they do? And then from this, creating several assessments of these various identified styles based on these findings? Perhaps the person being assessed happens to know best, what needs to be assessed. However, having your hands and mind and heart free, to explore such things as spirituality, creativity and intuition in the classroom would be a great thing to have. When you have to do these things covertly, you are always in danger of being discovered and punished for having allowed "these unbelievable things" into your classroom. I can remember on more than one occasion being accused of either messing with a child's brain structure or "fortune telling" at school. And sadly, anything new, because of the nature of the fourth world thinking, sooner or later evolved right back into an auditory processing style of learning. And what is the fourth world thinking? It comes from Hopi Elders who say that our present world where each person stands at the center of their circle of consciousness slowly turning in a tiny circle to defend themselves against anyone entering their circle, will be replaced with the fifth world coming. In this world, each person will welcome as many as they can into their own circle of consciousness until it is full and then each circle or community of people will join more communities to share and honor and interact with each other. This is not literal, but a way of thinking that will be new to many.

The theorists and educational gurus come up with the new ideas to fix things and by the time they get translated into the schools, not much of what they came up with exists and we were and are, right back where we started. Just like "recycled conversations" or the post office, public education has become a series of underfunded and "recycled programs" and curriculums. However, lots and lots of teachers just ignore all this and keep changing with the times and keep struggling to move forward themselves, but with added workloads and not enough of the best technology in their rooms. They also have to face a public who blames them for the ills of the system but supports and praises them as teachers. The "bad apples" in teaching are often the product of these wrong ways of thinking that they taught themselves or had someone else teach them. I can remember many an administrator who tried to "teach" me and failed. Probably because what I was doing, seemed to always work. Intuition was a non-measurable factor in the classroom. It just existed.

The new children are demanding more and learning much faster than the educational system is; both by the technology available and by their intuition and community oriented thinking. And though they seem selfish and demanding, they are simply saying "No more!" and asking for different ways of seeing, working and believing. Not as much damage as people think, is really going on in individual classrooms, unless the "captain of the ship" or teacher is a "bad apple." Where I see the real damage, is on the playground and in the lunch room, where children are bullied and left on their own to manage things. They need to be directed every minute, and with their teacher every minute, and the teacher needs to give them as well as be given, "breathing time" for herself and her students within the constraints of the day, but within the community of caring that has been built within that classroom. But remember I am only addressing the elementary school years and not the secondary years because the issues are quite a bit different.

On the secondary level we have a beautiful example in the film "The Emperor's Club," which was an excellent teacher movie along with "Goodbye Mr. Chips," "Mr. Holland's Opus" and an old Jane Wyman film from the forties that seems to have disappeared altogether, even the title. The other films were all the same, but these four shared something that the others did not, the interior life of a true teacher's heart. Why they did what they did and what they did when they felt they were failing their students. And how they taught by example, to remain true to one's self through all adversity and hardship. The sleepless nights worrying about this student or that one, the caring too much but never stopping to care, and the self-questioning of every move they made. Beyond all types of classrooms, the secondary teacher especially, must teach by example. When Kevin Kline's character goes to visit the father of a troubled student he is told by this boy's Senator father that he is there to teach his son, but not to mold him. That molding his son was his father's job. Years later Kline comes face to face with this highly successful student who has failed to succeed as a human being, molded carefully by his father. The student has everything but his soul, and through this experience, Kline realizes why he teaches, and returns to the classroom for a few more years of trying to "mold" as many of his students as he can. Because as Hugh and Gayle Prather state in their book called Spiritual Parenting, we are all parents and role models, every one of us.

The idea of one teacher following her students from kindergarten to eighth grade is a good one because whatever the teacher lacks in his or her abilities could probably be made up in the community formed learning that the students themselves bring into this. And teachers choosing and applying their community-oriented curriculum is a good idea too, since they would all decide together from their various different learning styles what academic and cultural curriculums were needed for the area the school is located in. Using individual talents and abilities that they could share with each other, they could also teach something they are good at and can get excited about which would inspire their students. An integrative curriculum from year to year would also keep the various teachers and their teaching styles uniform for smooth transitions from year to year. This along with a smaller class size, the ideal being no more than 12 kids and some supplies and room to explore - really not much when you think about it – would probably be less expensive than the waste of money going on now.

Recess should be under the direction of the individual teacher's style and in a small manageable group. Children could eat their lunches in their rooms, so that the whole day can run peacefully, quite structured and supervised. Teachers who balk at this idea have to remember that they have twice as much stress and work when taking care of the problems on the playgrounds and the angry parents who are at the schools because of these problems. Recesses will therefore be staggered, in very small groups, and supervised by someone who reports every day back to the two or three teachers whose students are on the playground with grades closer to their own age. Sixth grade could have their own recess alone. Lunch could be served to students in their classroom or they bring their own from home, and a healthy lunch is presented to them even if they do not partake of it. After eating, they can play quietly in the room because gym time is every day and because they share gym with another class, at least in the good weather months. Then the students would have a sufficient exercise program whether in the gym or outside. There needs to be consistency at all times, because so many of the students come from environments in a world where consistency has been forgotten.

But of course the real issue is that a school should be small and in its own community. Administrations should be very small and teachers should be able to run their own schools without a principal, cooperatively, making democratic decisions together and being empowered as teachers. The school secretary can take care of all the management issues, and really does now. Administrators should be required to visit their schools as an acting principal, although they are really facilitating managers who can offer suggestions and check for compliance of federal and state guidelines, but they do not run the school, the teachers do. Schools should be in the communities where the children live requiring no busing or fewer car pick-ups since they can walk home with their parents or friends. Teachers will have a curriculum but they will also have the freedom to infuse this curriculum with their own interests and ideas because this inspires them to inspire their children. Throughout their elementary school years students will be exposed to different teachers with different interests or have the same one throughout, but these teachers will have to be people who communicate well, understand learning styles and foster them in their classrooms. Each room will run as a small community full of even smaller foursomes learning to get along, being taught conflict resolution skills in detail, also organization skills, social and emotional intelligence skills, planning skills and communication skills as well as academic and physical education skills.

Discovering their own unique talents will be the frosting on the cake, and they will feel free to discover not only their academic talents, but their social, intuitive, emotional, physical, mental, spiritual and metaphysical talents as well as learning how to work in small groups and then in one bigger "small" group which is the entire classroom. A lot of the academic learning will be done in the morning, in a quiet environment on the computer for older students and with the teacher for the younger students. This learning will be done in the Russian Suggestology style, or in a more modern example, the Rosetta Stone style, so that retention will be a success story for all of them as they learn at their own level. In this way every student will have successes. The other two thirds of their learning day will be in interactive ways with other children and the teacher, learning both cooperatively and individually at the same time. But this morning quiet time will allow them to relax and discover that they can all learn without the stresses of feeling less able or having their self-esteem lowered by the competitive atmosphere they now face every day in school. When learning is equalized, many of the problems of getting along disappear, and those with a learning challenge get to have their own style addressed, whether it is "show me, "tell me," "let me try it" or "let me move to understand."

Though I tried to manage all this anyway, it was exhausting with all of the other interruptions that others considered important silliness. No young beginning teachers would quit such a program as this, if teaching is really what they want to do, even with the low pay. And on top of this, if community volunteers came in for small groups and then had an organized and consistent program and taught something in their expertise field such as physical education or art or music, etc., teachers could spend time with individual students who need additional help, rather than on stuff all those consultants, advisors and administrators now gone from their rooms, "cooked" up for them to do. Apparently the statistic now is only five years tops in the classroom before the incoming younger teachers quit and choose some other profession or go to a private school which often offers more support for their teachers. The smaller and less expensive private schools are always struggling and offer very little in the way of anything beyond "sitting and doing your work" all day and probably with some retention but perhaps not a lasting retention. Most of the slightly larger ones have good programs, and the really large ones are usually excellent but very expensive.

Yes, there are outstanding Waldorf schools, Montessori schools, Challenger schools, Parochial schools, Mead schools, Reed schools, Waterford Schools, and lots of other schools with their own philosophies that are one of a kind, and every country has their versions of these sorts of things. But the reality is that only the few can go to these schools and often in the middle group of parents who are struggling to pay for these types of schools, they end up having to put their children back in public schools after a year or two because they cannot afford them. The lower economic students are stuck with what is available, although there has been progress with particular schools in this arena too. If all elementary schools ran the way I have described, education would be equalized and children would learn from each other, educationally, ethnically, culturally and socially. And frankly, if middle schools ran the same way, by the time students reached high school they could decide their own ways of learning or not learning, either by computer, in small groups, or out in the world working. They could begin college or a trade as juniors and seniors and the whole concept of high schools might disappear, sophomores might be the last year of a traditional school day because at 16 now, the world is opening up. And if this strikes fear in the bones of law enforcement officers, remember these children have already had a lot of training to get along and find a place in the world for themselves. They can do all their high school stuff as young adults instead of in a school that does not serve them well anymore. They'll still have those high school memories, but not in a confined space.

But then these are my own wistful musings, and I only taught 36 years so I probably don't know much, except for what I tried to put in this book. Everything I state here also applies to parents and their intuitive children and everything in this book can be done at home or in addition to whatever school your child or children go too. No matter what one proposes for education in these chaotic times of change from the fourth to the fifth world, it immediately becomes controversial. There will always be those, used to the old ways of an auditory processing world that will balk at what is coming in our community oriented future. But our children will not. They are already saying among themselves that there must be a better way, although it looks as if they are just refusing to grow up and go out into what *is* already there. The technological world is moving so fast that the older generations who did not grow up with computers can't keep up. And the younger generations who did, often don't have the money to keep up with all those newly inspired "toys" becoming available monthly.

But the surprise is coming and has been coming for quite some time now. The Spirit-Brain connections are coming from within our children's evolutionary mind and heart, as well as in what we see in the outer world around us. Rather than a doomsday prophecy, we are all evolving at different rates or frequency levels, and the synchronicities of this energy is like a tsunami that will come flooding back over us from the ripple effects of what we have already done or are doing both positively and negatively right now. It is how we will manage all this that will decide our fate and that of the earth. Our children have a pretty good handle on this already, and they will help the rest to adjust, but there is a lot of hard work ahead, as well as the power of letting this river of energy flow by itself. And this is something new for many of us, going out of our "try brain" and into our "flow" one, although some of us are already on our way. The difficulties and the joys that are coming, are going to be very overwhelming!

As for my own "teacher accountability" I will take a few lines from the letters on my "teacher wall" in my study where I write. These letters were something I kept and framed, to read on the worst school days, so I could remind myself of why I did what I did and why I chose what I chose. From private school to state institutions, to pre-schools and handicapped schools, from low income schools to middle of the road schools, to even kids being driven to schools for gifted programs, I've seen it all. And while it was often the most difficult route but also a much more interesting and challenging one, I got there anyway, and I honor what I learned with every class and year I taught. My hope is that I was able to inspire and guide each one of my students to move to a better place than where they had been:

"Not only has her math SAT score improved to 97, but her self-confidence has skyrocketed. I know that you have encouraged her to express herself – that has made all the difference in the world." Apparently, infusing self confidence was more important than how I taught math!

"She has enjoyed being in your class and being part of the community you have created. It was the perfect environment for her – the perfect mix of structure, freedom, respect and humor." Whoops! Was I doing the right thing when we "played?"

"The skills you have taught her will serve her all through her life." Oh boy, was she only suppose to learn academics to be a good worker cog in the wheel?

"It has been wonderful to see him exposed to a wide variety of topics and to see his interest get sparked in so many different ways." I'm not sure, but I think visual-spatials have to be inspired to learn and so do creative types and intuitive ones and probably most, if not all children, on the planet?

"The minor accommodations you made for our son in your room made a significant and positive difference. Your ability to observe his needs and subtly intervene was wonderful and appreciated." Perhaps I was not supposed to individualize? Maybe he should have been "labeled" and compartmentalized and sent "out" for help? But then of course, with my special education background, I could be the help?

"On the way to school each morning, he always asks with great anticipation, 'I wonder what we will do today?' Your class is an adventure to him. I don't know of any subject he dislikes." Fun and humor are great companions for true learning.

"In a year when the world itself has not had much to laugh about, you provided a safe, comforting, nurturing environment for the class." And hopefully one that prepared these kids for the future they are going to.

As for parents and all of us who see ourselves as parents, I agree with the following golden rules for parenting of any kind, whether parent or teacher or coach, that Hugh and Gayle Prather put at the end of their book, paraphrased here: Advocate, befriend and listen to your children. Use both your physical world and your intuitive or higher guidance, and when the physical world guidance fails you, then look to a higher source. Remember and keep promises to your children. Never shame, mislead or hurt a child. Pay attention to, and respect your child's needs and desires, discount nothing. Keep your children safe by being firm, consistent and intervene only when necessary. Give them the freedom to use their own minds, to choose and decide, making the mistakes that they must to learn. Never forget their innocence or your own understanding of childhood imagination. I only have to add one more golden rule of my own: Honor each child's cultural differences and foster their various intuitive and creative knowings and talents. In these ways you can love and cherish those you raise, counsel, coach and teach. If these things were done for every child, to the best of all our abilities, the new world coming would be magnificently childlike too. (*Ibid, Spiritual Parenting, p.288*).

The spiritual desert is on its way out now and I am happy for this. I probably won't get to see all this, except from the other side, when I visit. But someday, children all over the world will not suffer any longer, nor will any of them have to die young of disease or self-deprecations. They will have plenty to eat they will have love, shelter, comfort, guidance and safety. They will all be able to have a childhood, use their imagination and intuition in all that they learn and create or invent. They will know they are loved and cared for, and most of all, they will have the skills to get along with each other. Not a one of them will be spiritually above or below the other. And there will be no more divisions between spirituality, creativity and intuition on the one hand, and academics, science and technology on the other. All of this will merge into an integrative whole for the children of the future. And I will visit in "spirit" after I'm gone, because I have the heart of a teacher and cannot help myself.

> "Our task must be to free ourselves by widening our circle of compassion to embrace all living creatures and the whole of nature in its beauty....We shall require a substantially new kind of thinking if mankind is to survive."
>
> --Albert Einstein

> "We realize that what we are accomplishing is a drop in the ocean. But if this drop were not in the ocean, it would be missed." "Every person for me is the only person in the world at that moment."
>
> --Mother Theresa

> "It is only with the heart that one can see rightly; what is essential is invisible to the eye."
>
> --<u>The Little Prince</u>
> by Antoin De Saint Exupery

ABOUT THE AUTHOR

Age 5

Linda Dunning taught children for 36 years in Colorado and Utah. She taught pre-school and elementary aged deaf-blind multi-handicapped and severely multi-handicapped children as well as autistic and behaviorally challenged children. She then taught underprivileged children in resource K-6 and ended her career teaching gifted-talented second and third grade students in a regular elementary classroom full day program. She has her B.A. in Elementary Education and her Master's Degree in Special Education with additional certifications in Visually Impaired and Gifted and Talented. She presented workshops throughout the mountain west on the multi-handicapped and is currently doing small group workshops for parents on those subjects often left out of the classroom, especially learning styles, communication styles and becoming better informed about psychic and intuitive children. She is especially interested in helping all those who will be working with these unique, creative and gifted intuitive children of the future.

She has studied Edu-K, Touch for Health, Breama Balance (Tibetan energy work), Tai-Chi and Chi-Gong and has been doing spiritual intuitive counseling sessions for the last 25 years. As a clairvoyant she has a special interest in leading creative visualization and meditation groups, as well as doing individual emotional release and energy work sessions now that she is retired. As a writer, she has published three Utah real ghost story books so far in her six part series on the history and hauntings of Utah. She has also written several other unpublished manuscripts on various eclectic subjects as well as publishing several of her poems in anthologies. She has won several awards in the Utah Original Arts Council Writing Competition: First Place Short Story in 1980, Second Place Non-Fiction in 1992 and First Place Non-Fiction in 1995, as well as in other lesser competitions. She is still looking for a publisher for her book on stage and movie star's biographies who came from Utah or were strongly connected to the state, entitled Away From The Fold.

Dunning was born and raised in Utah and has a strong interest in preserving the stories and tales that come from her home state. She comes from generations of artists and actresses, architects and builders, musicians and singers, and intuitives and healers. She finds her own path both rewarding and challenging, but remaining true to yourself is what is most important in living a service-oriented life she says. Nurturing Unique Children, is as much her own story as it is for many other walking wounded intuitives of her generation and all the others that have come after this or before it. More of these children are coming in all the time and those of us pioneering in this field are being called upon to help them learn to live wonderful and fruitful lives on an earth that needs a lot of help right now. Dunning lives with all of her animals and a husband who accepts what she does to help others.